THE SEER'S DEVOTIONAL

DESTINY IMAGE BOOKS BY JENNIFER LECLAIRE

The Seer's Devotional

The Seer Dimentions

I Decree Breakthrough

Victory Decrees

Tongues of Fire

Exposing Prophetic Witchcraft

Cleansing Your Home from Evil

The Making of a Watchman

Discerning Prophetic Witchcraft

Your End Times Prayer Secret

The Prophet's Devotional

Deliverance from Prophetic Witchcraft

Decoding the Mysteries of Heaven's War Room

The Spiritual Warrior's Guide to Defeating Water Spirits

THE SEER'S DEVOTIONAL

365 DAILY DEVOTIONS
THAT ACTIVATE AND ENGAGE
YOUR SPIRITUAL SENSES

JENNIFER LECLAIRE

DESTINY IMAGE® PUBLISHERS, INC.
P.O. Box 310, Shippensburg, PA 17257-0310
"Publishing cutting-edge prophetic resources to supernaturally empower the body of Christ"

This book and all other Destiny Image and Destiny Image Fiction books are available at Christian bookstores and distributors worldwide.

For more information on foreign distributors, call 717-532-3040.
Reach us on the Internet: www.destinyimage.com.

ISBN 13 HC: 979-8-8815-0651-3
ISBN 13 eBook: 979-8-8815-0652-0

For Worldwide Distribution, Printed in the U.S.A.
1 2 3 4 5 6 7 8 / 30 29 28 27 26

DEDICATION

This book is dedicated to you. Yes you. The one God wakes up in the night with a revelation and a prayer burden. The one who sees things in the spirit you can't always explain. The one who has always known there was more. There is more. And God is about to show you how to walk in it.

ACKNOWLEDGMENTS

This book did not come without a fight. I want to thank Vanessa Angelini, whose faithfulness behind the scenes makes everything I do possible. To my Awakening House of Prayer family in Fort Lauderdale and beyond. You are not just an assembly, you are a community of warriors. And to my intercessors who stood in the gap when the attacks came and the delays mounted. This book exists in part because you would not let go. I am grateful.

CONTENTS

INTRODUCTION

After speaking on the final day of the first-ever Global Prophetic Summit in 2017, hosted by Cindy Jacobs and Generals International, I went back to my hotel room to pick up my bags before heading out to the airport.

I had about an hour to kill and felt led to share about the seer's anointing. I went live on Facebook and started a simple lesson from my hotel room in Dallas. I did not expect what happened next. The Holy Spirit's presence was suddenly overwhelming. I actually bowed my head live on camera and momentarily could not continue because of the weight of the anointing.

I felt a mantle fall upon my shoulders. At first, I didn't know what exactly was happening. I just knew it was both heavy and energizing at the same time. I ended the broadcast and the anointing remained. It was a profound experience, similar to how the Lord has mantled me in the past.

I asked the Lord what it meant, and He explained He was giving me a new anointing, commissioning, and mandate to raise up seers and seeing people. He told me to launch a School of Seers (which is hosted at schoolofthespirit.tv) and a community for seers and prophetic people (ignitenow.org). Within two months, despite transatlantic travel assignments, the school was up and running.

We have equipped tens of thousands of students in the seer dimensions. I've discovered that the seer dimensions—with dreams, visions, trances, out-of-body experiences and the like—are inexhaustible. Scripture shares so much more than many realize and the encounters in this realm, when in line with Scripture, also open our eyes to what God is doing and what the enemy is trying to do.

As you read the pages of this book, I want you to remember the words of Jesus in Luke 8:17-18 (AMPC):

> For there is nothing hidden that shall not be disclosed, nor anything secret that shall not be known and come out into the open. Be careful therefore how you listen. For to him who has [spiritual knowledge] will more be given; and from him who does not have [spiritual knowledge], even what he thinks and guesses and supposes that he has will be taken away.

I've discovered this spiritual principle is true in the seer dimensions as well. The more I teach on the seer dimensions, the more my eyes open to these supernatural realities. I've gained and shared wisdom on this journey and, by the grace of God, continue to gain and share more.

Since I embraced the mantle, the Holy Spirit has also given me practical insights to help seers understand their gift and believers break through obstacles to seeing in the spirit. Some, but not nearly all, of those insights are found in the pages of this book. More are found in my books on the seer ministry, as well as my school.

This devotional was birthed from the truths I've dug out in Scripture, as well as the many encounters I've experienced in the seer dimensions. It's designed to help you see what's possible, grow in your seer gifting and other spiritual senses, and avoid the pitfalls along the way.

Take the time to reflect each day on what I am sharing, meditate on the Scriptures I offer, and pray the prayers I've shared. These are part of my spiritual practices that have helped me ascend in the seer dimensions. God is no respecter of persons. In other words, God shows no favoritism (Acts 10:34). If you sow to the spirit realm, you will also reap (Galatians 6:7-9). God wants you to see what He is trying to show you.

My prayer for you is that God will flood your spiritual eyes with light so that you will know the hope of His calling, your inheritance in Christ, and the power that's available to you in Him. I also pray that you will stay balanced, Word-grounded and Spirit-led, avoiding the traps of the enemy that come along the way. Stay humble, stay hungry, and you will ascend.

JANUARY

Then the secret was revealed to Daniel in a night vision.
Daniel 2:19

JANUARY 1

WHAT IS A SEER?

Are all apostles? Are all prophets? Are all teachers? Are all workers of miracles?

1 Corinthians 12:29

Seers are prophets who receive their revelation by peering through the veil of the spirit realm as God allows. Not all prophets are seers, but all seers are prophets. The seer is a type of prophet. Most prophets can see, and most seers can hear. These are two streams from the same Holy Ghost river.

Prophets, as we've come to know them in the modern-day prophetic movement, operate in the *naba* realm. *Naba* is a Hebrew word that means "to prophesy, speak as a prophet; prophecy has its focus on encouraging or restoring covenant faithfulness, the telling of future events encourages obedience or warns against disobedience."

Again, not all prophets are seers, but all seers are prophets. At first glance, some may ask, "What does it really matter if they are all prophets?" God distinguished them in His Word, so it matters.

Giving a natural analogy, when you go to the hospital, there are many kinds of doctors. They are all trained in practicing medicine, but they specialize in different areas. Some are cardiovascular specialists. Some are ear, nose, and throat specialists. Some are orthopedic specialists. I don't want to go to a foot doctor to have heart surgery or a heart doctor for an eye exam.

As I write in-depth in *The Seer Dimensions*, prophets and seers are two streams of the prophetic anointing, but they specialize in different aspects of the anointing. Even within the realm of prophet and seer there are many different distinctions and types of prophetic flows.

Seers consistently have dreams or visions, see angels or demons, see words written over people's heads. Seers see lights and colors. Seers may see Jesus or Heaven or hell. A seer perceives with spiritual eyes—the eyes of the Holy Spirit. Indeed, seers perceive, detect, experience, visualize, recognize, become aware, encounter, examine, watch, explore, judge, encounter, discern, look, investigate, inquire, receive, and apprehend—and equip, according to the Ephesians 4:11 fivefold ascension gift mandate.

PRAYER

Father, in the name of Jesus, help me discern in what stream I am swimming. I don't want to assume an anointing that's not mine based on periodic visual revelations. I want to be accurate about my calling.

JANUARY 2

ALL SEERS ARE INTERCESSORS

Now therefore, restore the man's wife; for he is a prophet, and he will pray for you and you shall live....

Genesis 20:7

All seers are prophets–and all prophets are intercessors. Let that sink in: All seers are prophets—and all prophets are intercessors. The first time you see the word *prophet* in the Bible, it's directly connected to prayer. Genesis 20:1-8 reads:

> And Abraham journeyed from there to the South, and dwelt between Kadesh and Shur, and stayed in Gerar. Now Abraham said of Sarah his wife, "She is my sister." And Abimelech king of Gerar sent and took Sarah. But God came to Abimelech in a dream by night, and said to him, "Indeed you are a dead man because of the woman whom you have taken, for she is a man's wife." But Abimelech had not come near her; and he said, "Lord, will You slay a righteous nation also? Did he not say to me, 'She is my sister'? And she, even she herself said, 'He is my brother.' In the integrity of my heart and innocence of my hands I have done this."
>
> And God said to him in a dream, "Yes, I know that you did this in the integrity of your heart. For I also withheld you from sinning against Me; therefore I did not let you touch her. Now therefore, restore the man's wife; for he is a prophet, and he will pray for you and you shall live. But if you do not restore her, know that you shall surely die, you and all who are yours." So Abimelech rose early in the morning, called all his servants, and told all these things in their hearing; and the men were very much afraid.

You know the outcome of the story. Abraham prayed for Abimelech and the results were immediately visible. Although we don't always immediately see the results of our seer intercession, we know that if we ask anything according to the will of God He hears us and answers us (1 John 5:15).

Part of your seer assignment is to pray through what you see in the spirit. As you are faithful in that assignment, God may reward you by showing you the outcome of your prayer for someone you may never meet or a city you may never visit.

PRAYER

Father, in the name of Jesus, thank You for gracing me to stand faithfully in my assigned gap. Would You let me see the impact of my intercession to encourage me to keep watching and praying when I'm weary?

JANUARY 3

TO KNOW HIM

But seek first the kingdom of God and His righteousness, and all these things shall be added to you.

Matthew 6:33

As seers and seeing people, God wants us to know Him—really know Him. Paul, the apostle, who experienced an abundance of revelatory encounters, understood the critical importance of knowing Christ. Paul had out-of-body experiences. Paul fell into trances. Paul had life-changing encounters. Paul had great discernment. And Paul's prayer was "that I may know Him..." (Philippians 3:10).

But Paul said something deeper: "Yet indeed I also count all things loss for the excellence of the knowledge of Christ Jesus my Lord, for whom I have suffered the loss of all things, and count them as rubbish, that I may gain Christ" (Philippians 3:8). That's an intense commitment to knowing the Lord.

And Peter echoes the sentiment in Paul's declaration. Peter fell into a trance on a rooftop. His shadow healed people. He raised a woman from the dead. Peter was familiar with the seer dimensions, but He sought to know the Lord more than he sought to see in the spirit. (Read that again!)

Remember, Peter was the first one to discern that Jesus was the Son of God. Jesus told Peter that flesh and blood didn't reveal that truth to him. Peter received the revelation directly from the Father.

That same Peter encouraged us to "grow in the grace and knowledge of our Lord and Savior Jesus Christ..." (2 Peter 3:18). Peter also said, "Grace and peace be multiplied to you in the knowledge of God and of Jesus our Lord" (2 Peter 1:2).

And long before Paul and Peter walked the earth, the prophet Hosea emphasized knowing the Lord in Hosea 6:3: "Let us know, let us pursue the knowledge of the Lord. His going forth is established as the morning; He will come to us like the rain, like the latter and former rain to the earth."

Before you ever seek to see the Lord in a vision, seek to know the Lord.

PRAYER

Father, in the name of Jesus, I want my chief aim to be knowing You. Please, show me what is in the way and I'll remove it. Remind me to seek You early when You can be found—and to seek You throughout my day.

JANUARY 4

RECOGNIZING THE MASTER

Then their eyes were opened and they knew Him; and He vanished from their sight.

Luke 24:31

We can know Jesus—really know Him—and still not recognize Him in the seer dimensions. We may get familiar with Him manifesting in a particular way, for example, then suddenly He appears in a completely different way. No matter how He appears or moves in the spirit realm, Jesus wants us to discern His presence. He wants us to recognize Him.

Remember when Jesus told His disciples to take the boat and travel to the other side of the lake? Suddenly, the boat was tossed by waves and fierce winds. The disciples were no stranger to seafaring and yet were struggling to command the boat, so the gusts must have been especially strong. Matthew 14:25-27 reads:

> Now in the fourth watch of the night Jesus went to them, walking on the sea. And when the disciples saw Him walking on the sea, they were troubled, saying, "It is a ghost!" And they cried out for fear. But immediately Jesus spoke to them, saying, "Be of good cheer! It is I; do not be afraid."

The disciples had walked with Jesus from city to city, but they did not recognize Him approaching on the sea. At some level you can hardly blame them. Who would expect a man to walk on water in the middle of a storm? Because they had not experienced this aspect of Jesus, they were spooked by the Savior coming to rescue them.

Similarly, on the Road to Emmaus, Jesus appeared to men and they did not recognize Him. Once their eyes were opened, they said, "Did not our heart burn within us while He talked with us on the road, and while He opened the Scriptures to us?" (Luke 24:32).

Jesus wants us to discern Him however He manifests in the spirit realm. At the same time, He wants us to recognize counterfeit Jesuses.

PRAYER

Father, in the name of Jesus, will You teach me to exercise the powers of discernment so that if You appear to me in a way that seems foreign to me, I will not be afraid? Please teach me how to recognize counterfeit Christs.

JANUARY 5

DISCERNING "ANOTHER JESUS"

*For if he who comes preaches **another Jesus** whom we have not preached, or if you receive a different spirit which you have not received, or a different gospel which you have not accepted—you may well put up with it!*

2 Corinthians 11:4

Was that really Jesus you saw in that visitation? Or was it another Jesus? Don't let that question offend you, rather let it spur you toward discernment. Jesus Himself said, "For many will come in My name, saying, 'I am the Christ,' and will deceive many" (Matthew 24:5).

While Jesus was talking about flesh-and-blood false christs, make no mistake: there are false christs appearing to people in the spirit realm today. People really can see Jesus in the spirit if He allows it. But not everyone who says they see Jesus are telling the truth. Then there are those who are seeing another Jesus. They truly think it's Jesus.

Paul spoke about "another Jesus," so how do you discern a false appearance of Jesus in the seer dimensions?

One way is by studying visions of Jesus in Scripture. People recorded visions of God several times. And in the New Testament people had visions of Jesus 11 times. In my School of the Seers, we go into each vision in-depth. Knowing the real Jesus will safeguard you from falling for "another Jesus."

"Another Jesus" is a false Jesus. "Another Jesus" may be a figment of someone's imagination.

"Another Jesus" may be a vain imagination from the enemy. "Another Jesus" may be satan in disguise. "Another Jesus" comes in a false dream or a false vision.

"Another Jesus" will give you a different spirit and share a message that's contrary to God's Word. Second Corinthians 11:4 (AMP) says, "For [you seem willing to allow it] if one comes and preaches *another Jesus* whom we have not preached, or if you receive a different spirit from the one you received, or a different gospel from the one you accepted. You tolerate all this beautifully [welcoming the deception]." (Visit www.schoolofthespirit.tv to tap into a whole series on this.)

PRAYER

Father, in the name of Jesus, help me discern true from false christs in the seer dimensions. Give me such a strong gift of hunger that I will devour the Word so that I will not walk into deception.

JANUARY 6

GOD IS IN THE DETAILS

Thus speaks the Lord God of Israel, saying: "Write in a book for yourself all the words that I have spoken to you."

Jeremiah 30:2

There are many revelations in the Bible—from Genesis to the book of Revelation itself. Have you ever noticed they all have one thing in common? They are all recorded in great detail.

The men of God who received prophetic words, prophetic visions, prophetic dreams—or got caught up in the Spirit or fell into trances—chronicled their encounters. And thank God they did, or we would have little to fall back on or learn from.

The first step in processing your prophetic revelation is to record the revelations in a journal. That's part of being a good steward of the revelation you receive, which sets you up to receive more. Remember, he who is faithful over little can be trusted with much (Luke 16:10). Recording your revelations—scribing and chronicling what you hear and see prophetically—is insurance against forgetting critical details that could change the interpretation and application.

As I wrote in my book *Decoding Your Dreams*:

> *Here are two words of advice for you in the realm of recording your dreams: Don't wait. Let me repeat those words: Don't wait. Don't wait until a week later. Don't even wait until an hour after you wake up. Write down your dreams as soon as possible after you dream the dream. The serious dreamer will keep a dream journal or a voice recorder—or at least a notepad and pen—on their nightstand so they can capture at least the outline of the dream before its buried in sleep or the business of life.*

Long before I wrote *Decoding the Mysteries of Heaven's War Room*, based on an epic vision of the war room in Heaven, I recorded the encounter in audio form. There's no way I could have remembered the intricate details of what I saw if I hadn't immediately recorded it. Yes, the Holy Spirit can bring things to our remembrance, but if we are going to be excellent stewards we need to be excellent chroniclers.

PRAYER

Father, in the name of Jesus, would You help me get into the habit of quickly chronicling what You show me in the seer dimensions? Help me write down the dreams, visions, and encounters with detailed accuracy.

JANUARY 7

PRAY LIKE MOSES

And he said, "Please, show me Your glory."

Exodus 33:18

I heard the Lord say, "My glory is not to be taken lightly. My glory is not to be mocked. My glory is to be entered into with reverence, with holy fear and trembling, with awe.... For I am indeed pouring out My glory more and more as the darkness begins to rise in the earth.

"I am determined that My people not only taste and see My glory, but walk in My glory to demonstrate to a lost world that I am a living God and a loving God. I am looking for carriers of My glory who will steward My presence and release My gifts without seeking their own glory. I am looking for those who will host My presence with kingdom understanding and look beyond a single meeting to the transformative power of My Spirit on earth.

"I am calling on you now to press into My glory, not for your sake but for the sake of the nations. My glory will indeed cover the earth like the waters cover the sea."

Ask God to show you His glory. There is precedent for this in Scripture. In Exodus 33:18, Moses asked the Lord, "Please, show me Your glory." Some translations say, "show me your glorious presence" (NLT; Common English Bible). Other versions say, "Manifest thyself to me." Still other versions (CEV; Brenton's English Septuagint) says, "I pray you will let me see in you in all your glory." And God answered him.

The Bible uses various words for *glory* more than 350 times. God's glory is one of the foundational themes in Scripture. There are many manifestations of God's glory, which I write extensively about in *The Making of a Watchman*.

Ask God to show you His glory, and don't get in your mind about how the glory will manifest. Get educated on the glory and you'll recognize it when you see it. And when you do, bask in it.

PRAYER

Father, in the name of Jesus, please, show me Your glorious presence. Help me discern Your glory in my midst in ways that I may not have recognized. Provoke my heart to be a student of Your glory.

JANUARY 8

MASTERING SEER VOCABULARY

So also you, unless you uttered by the tongue words easy to understand, how would it be known what is spoken? For you would be speaking into the air.

1 Corinthians 14:9 WEB

Do you speak seer? Every seer needs to understand and embrace the unique vocabulary of the seer dimensions. Like doctors and lawyers, seers have their own lingo. Put another way, there is a spiritual language seers need to adopt in order to accurately describe their visual revelations.

If you want to communicate what God has shown you accurately and in a way that people can understand you, it's critical that you become fluent in what I call "seer speak." It's critical that you build your seer vocabulary.

Let me unpack this for a moment. A language is a system of words or signs that people use to express thoughts and feelings to each other. A *vocabulary* is a stock of words employed by a language, group, individual, work, or field of knowledge. You need to learn seer language, which may be somewhat foreign to you at first, and then build out your vocabulary. But just like you learned your native language—or even a foreign language—you can learn to speak seer.

Your seer vocabulary may be somewhat limited now. That means you'll have a hard time articulating what you see in the spirit. Your ability to express yourself in terms of what God is saying to you in your dream, visions, and encounters may be limited and you may be frustrated—or frustrate others who can't grab hold of what you are saying.

When I was in college, I signed up for the Word of the Day from *Merriam-Webster* to expand my natural vocabulary. Much the same, being biblically literate and spiritual curious demands a seer spend time expanding his or her seer vocabulary.

In *The Seer's Dictionary*, I've purposely spent time defining words seers need to know, as well as specific concepts around false encounters, time, seasons, the names of the Father, Son, and Holy Spirit, angelic beings, and anointings because I believe understanding the seer dimensions through these lenses is part of the healthy development of a seer.

You can get a copy of *The Seer's Dictionary* on my website at www.jenniferleclaire.org. It will give you language for what you have experienced—and what you haven't experienced yet.

PRAYER

Father, in the name of Jesus, would You help me learn the language of the seer dimensions? Would You help me to build out a robust seer vocabulary so I can share my encounters accurately and relate to other seers respectfully?

JANUARY 9

FILLED WITH THE ONE WHO SEES EVERYTHING

> *And do not be drunk with wine, in which is dissipation; but be filled with the Spirit.*
>
> Ephesians 5:18

You need the Holy Spirit—and you have Him. When you were saved, the Holy Spirit came to live inside you. But there's a deeper immersion for you. There's more.

Jesus is the Baptizer, and He wants to fill you with His Spirit to overflowing. And it's not a one-time experience. Ephesians 5:18 tells us to be filled with the Holy Spirit, but that Greek word for *filled* actually translates "being filled." In the book of Acts we saw the apostles were filled several times—and I'm quite sure all the fillings were not chronicled.

The following are some Scriptures to build your faith in the promise of the Holy Spirit filling you:

> If you then, evil as you are, know how to give good gifts [gifts that are to their advantage] to your children, how much more will your heavenly Father give the Holy Spirit to those who ask and continue to ask Him! (Luke 11:13 AMPC)
>
> And they were all filled (diffused throughout their souls) with the Holy Spirit and began to speak in other (different, foreign) languages (tongues), as the Spirit kept giving them clear and loud expression [in each tongue in appropriate words] (Acts 2:4 AMPC).
>
> So too the [Holy] Spirit comes to our aid and bears us up in our weakness; for we do not know what prayer to offer nor how to offer it worthily as we ought, but the Spirit Himself goes to meet our supplication and pleads in our behalf with unspeakable yearnings and groanings too deep for utterance. And He Who searches the hearts of men knows what is in the mind of the [Holy] Spirit [what His intent is], because the Spirit intercedes and pleads [before God] in behalf of the saints according to and in harmony with God's will (Romans 8:26-27 AMPC).

Jesus is the Baptizer, and He baptizes us with the Holy Spirit when we ask and believe. If you've never been filled with Spirit and you want to be—or if you want a fresh infilling—pray the prayer below in faith and open your mouth. Speaking in tongues is one of the evidences of being filled with the Spirit.

PRAYER

Father, in the name of Jesus, I surrender full control of my life to You. I ask You even now to fill me to overflowing with Your Spirit, just as You have promised to do if I ask according to Your will.

JANUARY 10

PRACTICING THE PRESENCE OF GOD

"Am I a God near at hand," says the Lord, "And not a God afar off?"
Jeremiah 23:23

When I discovered Brother Lawrence's book, *The Practice of the Presence of God*, it changed my life. I can't tell you how many copies of this small book that I've read, marked up, dog-eared, and then ultimately gave away to someone else in my path that was as hungry for God's presence as I am. It's still a #1 Best Seller on Amazon in the mysticism category even though penned hundreds of years ago.

Practicing the presence of God brings you into a fellowship and intimacy that positions you to see as He sees. Many times God is trying to show us something but we are not sensing the stirring to look. The following are a few quotes from the book, which you can find free online, to inspire you:

> *One way to re-collect the mind easily in the time of prayer, and preserve it more in tranquility, is not to let it wander too far in other times: you should keep it strictly in the presence of God; and being accustomed to think of Him often, you will find it easy to keep your mind calm in the time of prayer, or at least to recall it from its wanderings.*
>
> *That we should establish ourselves in a sense of God's presence, by continually conversing with Him. That it was a shameful thing to quit His conversation, to think of trifles and fooleries.*
>
> *I cannot imagine how religious persons can live satisfied without the practice of the presence of God. For my part I keep myself retired with Him in the depth of centre of my soul as much as I can; and while I am so with Him I fear nothing; but the least turning from Him is insupportable.*

You practice the presence of God by acknowledging Him (Proverbs 3:6), by talking to Him, by praising and thanking Him. Don't talk about Him as if He's not in the room with you; rather, embrace the reality that He is with you all the time, everywhere.

PRAYER

Father, in the name of Jesus, please remind me to practice Your presence. Help me to remember to talk with the Holy Spirit. Teach me how to practice Your presence anywhere I am and all the time.

JANUARY 11

A WORD TO THE EMOTIONAL SEER

A heart full of joy and goodness makes a cheerful face, but when a heart is full of sadness the spirit is crushed.

Proverbs 15:13 AMP

We are emotional beings. Sometimes we feel joyful; sometimes we grieve. Sometimes we feel bold; sometimes intimidated. Sometimes we feel triumphant; sometimes completely and utterly physically and emotionally exhausted.

The problem is, unsubmitted emotions can skew what you see in the seer dimensions—or keep you out of the seer dimensions altogether. For the sake of accuracy, and our own well-being, we need to walk in emotional stability. We can't move by what we feel emotionally.

Is it possible that we could avoid the extreme highs and lows of the emotional roller coaster if we maintained God's perspective? What if we could wait on the Lord, mount up with wings as eagles and take a prophetic perspective of our lives—then rejoice in the Lord for the victory?

Paul suffered betrayal, frustration, warfare, and persecution. One time the pressure was so great that he even despaired of life itself (2 Corinthians 1:8). But Paul knew how to keep his emotions in check. He kept his mind set on things above, not on the things of this earth (Colossians 3:2).

Paul thought about things that were true, noble, pure, lovely, of a good report, things with virtue and praiseworthiness (Philippians 4:8). He told us to do these things because he knew from personal experience it was a powerful key to stay emotionally grounded. He practiced what he preached. We should also practice what he preached.

When Paul was in prison, up to his waist in sewage, he didn't take on a victim mentality or get discouraged. He rejoiced. When Paul was thrown into prison after casting a devil out of the girl in Thyatria, he sang, prayed, and worshipped God.

Paul experienced the fellowship of Christ's sufferings more than most of us ever will. But he was stable in his calling despite the emotions that surely tried to invade his soul.

I believe the key to Paul's emotional stability was rejoicing in the Lord. No matter which way Paul's emotions were trying to sway him, he remained constant and fearless in the face of his enemies. And because he was emotionally stable through it all, he penned half of the New Testament by revelation, including visual encounters.

PRAYER

Father, in the name of Jesus, would You help me remember to look at You when my emotions want to take me off course? I don't want unruly emotions to keep me from seeing something in the spirit.

JANUARY 12

I SAW THE LORD

Blessed are the pure in heart, for they shall see God.

Matthew 5:8

Any believer can experience a divine vision anytime the Holy Spirit wills. But having a random vision doesn't confirm the seer's calling. Indeed, God can choose many ways to confirm your seer calling. We see one dramatic way in Numbers 12:5-6:

> Then the Lord came down in the pillar of cloud and stood in the door of the tabernacle, and called Aaron and Miriam. And they both went forward. Then He said, "Hear now My words: If there is a prophet among you, I, the Lord, make Myself known to him in a vision...."

Did you catch that? At a certain level in the seer dimensions, God may confirm your gift through making Himself known to you in a vision. That's intense! I've seen the Lord in a vision more than once. You may too!

The Hebrew word for *know* in the verse above is *yada*. It means "to know, learn to know, to perceive and see, find out and discern, to discriminate and distinguish, to know by experience, to recognize, and to make known," according to The KJV Old Testament Hebrew Lexicon.

Beyond these words to Moses and Aaron, there's Isaiah's account. Isaiah saw the Lord in a vision and recorded the encounter in Isaiah 6:1, "In the year that King Uzziah died, I saw the Lord sitting on a throne, high and lifted up, and the train of His robe filled the temple."

Micaiah also saw the Lord in a vision, as described in 1 Kings 22:19, "I saw the Lord sitting on His throne, and all the host of heaven standing by, on His right hand and on His left."

There are many demons in the seer dimensions that cause people to want to shut down their gift. You may indeed see demons, but God doesn't just want you to *only* see the demons. He wants you to see the angels and, at times, He may let you see Him. You can't force God to show up in a vision, but we can ask Him to make Himself known in a vision.

PRAYER

Father, in the name of Jesus, help me to purify my heart so I become a candidate to see You in a vision. Help me to consecrate my seer eyes to Your purposes so I can see You in all Your glory.

JANUARY 13

ACTIVATING YOUR SEER GIFT

Therefore I remind you to stir up the gift of God which is in you through the laying on of my hands.

2 Timothy 1:6

Activating your spiritual eyes is not a one-time event. It's an ongoing process. With each new level comes another activation.

Activate means "to set up or formally institute (as a military unit) with the necessary personnel and equipment; to put (an individual or unit) on active duty," according to *Merriam-Webster's Dictionary.*

Jesus activated the disciples in their impartation in Matthew 10:7-8: "And as you go, preach, saying, 'The kingdom of heaven is at hand.' Heal the sick, cleanse the lepers, raise the dead, cast out demons. Freely you have received, freely give."

We activate a gift through Word study. Romans 10:17 explains, "So then faith comes by hearing, and hearing by the word of God." I like how GOD'S WORD Translation puts it: "So faith comes from hearing the message, and the message that is heard is what Christ spoke."

We also activate a gift through use. When the Lord gives you a gift, He expects you to use it. Second Corinthians 5:7 tells us we walk by faith and not by sight; but in the seer dimensions, we walk by faith into sight.

The reality is if you don't set out to see, you probably won't. I can choose not to look at the person sitting next to me on a plane. If I choose not to look, I won't see them. If I happen to turn my head toward them for a split second, I will catch a glimpse. But when I choose to look with the intention of seeing, I am positioning myself to not only see but notice the finer details of their clothing, countenance, and so on.

As Paul told Timothy, you have to stir yourself up. Second Timothy 1:6 reads, "Therefore I remind you to stir up the gift of God which is in you through the laying on of my hands." He received the impartation, but it still required activation. You can receive a car, but if you don't activate the engine, it won't take you anywhere. My book, *Seer Activations*, is full of such charges, as well as prayers that prime your seer pump.

PRAYER

Father, in the name of Jesus, remind me to stir myself up in my most holy faith. Remind me to stir up the seer gift that You gave me. I want to use my gifts to their greatest potential.

JANUARY 14

THE JOSEPH SEER ANOINTING

And Pharaoh said to Joseph, "I have had a dream, and there is no one who can interpret it. But I have heard it said of you that you can understand a dream, to interpret it."

Genesis 41:15

Joseph is set apart among seers in Scripture for his strategic vision. Not only did he have profound dreams, but he also had the wisdom to interpret the dreams and apply the truth in those dreams strategically. He had a skill to steward what he saw through his dreams in a way that brought salvation to the nations.

Joseph did not immediately understand the far-reaching implications of the dreams he had about his family bowing down to him. Sometimes God hides deeper meanings until the fullness of time. But Joseph continued maturing in his gifting.

Joseph cultivated deep humility and confidence in his God-given seer anointing. When the baker and butler asked him to interpret their dreams, his response was: "Do not interpretations belong to God? Tell me [your dreams], I pray you" (Genesis 40:8 AMPC).

Joseph received accurate interpretations for the baker and butler who each dreamt of their fate while imprisoned. He also received an accurate interpretation of Pharaoh's famine dream, a divine strategy to apply it, and a gift of wisdom to steward it through to complete manifestation.

The Joseph seer anointing, then, is a call to take a revelation from A to Z—to receive it, interpret it, apply it, and see it through to full realization. While some seers receive visual revelation but cannot interpret, or interpret but don't know how to apply it, Joseph was anointed to walk out the whole process. He demonstrated the highest integrity, despite being severely tested.

The Bible says, "Until the time that his word came to pass, the word of the Lord tested him" (Psalm 105:19). Indeed, his making progress was extreme. Some of his early mistakes with the seer anointing landed him in a pit before being sold as a slave. God grew him up in a crucible so he would have the ability to steward the nations. If you are going through severe tests and trials, remember Joseph and take heart. God has called you to something great.

PRAYER

Father, in the name of Jesus, help me learn from the incredible life of Joseph, the dreamer. Help me see his mistakes and successes so that I can avoid the pitfalls and glorify You.

JANUARY 15

KEEP YOUR MIND SET ON THINGS ABOVE

And set your minds and keep them set on what is above (the higher things), not on the things that are on the earth.

Colossians 3:2 AMPC

Paul's words in Colossians 3:2 were not a friendly suggestion. They were a Spirit-inspired command to every believer—and how much more for one who sees on behalf of the Body of Christ? Keeping your mind set on things above takes disciplined emotions and thought life.

Most of us allow the carnal to dominate us. Remember, *carnal* does not necessarily mean sinful. Carnal means living by the natural senses only. As a seer, you need your natural senses, but you don't access the seer dimensions through those senses. In fact, your natural senses can dominate your spiritual senses if you don't discipline your soul and body.

We need our natural senses to relate to the natural world, but we need to develop our spiritual senses to relate to the spiritual world. Remember, the spirit world is more real than the natural world and you are not seeing into the spirit with your natural eyes. Most people are led more by what they see, hear, smell, taste, or touch instead of setting their minds on the spirit realm. Let that not be said of you.

When you keep your mind set on things above, you'll see, for example, the spirit behind a thing. You'll hear the spirit behind the words people speak. You may even see the motives of people's hearts. You'll see multiple dimensions and levels. You'll hear God through the noise.

Many Christians today and some seers spend more time on social media than in the presence of God. They are more interested in hearing church gossip than hearing the word of the Lord. We need to practice keeping our mind set on things above.

I remember a time when someone called me and said, "Go look at what So and So just posted on social media. You won't believe it." When I started to go to social media to see it, the Holy Spirit said to me, "Every time you look at things like that, you diminish your ability to see in the spirit." I immediately abandoned my efforts to hear the latest ministry drama and went into prayer.

PRAYER

Father, in the name of Jesus, would You give me grace to set my mind on things above—the higher things—not on the things of this earth. Help me be heavenly minded so I can see into the spirit world clearly.

JANUARY 16

UNDERSTANDING YOUR SEER MANTLE

Now Elijah took his mantle, rolled it up, and struck the water; and it was divided this way and that, so that the two of them crossed over on dry ground.

2 Kings 2:8

When I was about four years old in the Lord, the Holy Spirit drew me into a time of prayer. In my natural mind, I didn't have time to pray because I needed to head out to Wednesday night Bible study. But I yielded. After a few minutes, I suddenly felt something like a warm heavy blanket resting on my back and shoulders. I felt the glory of God all around me.

I didn't have full understanding of what was happening to me at that moment, but the Lord later showed me what felt like a heavy blanket was actually a prophetic mantle. Soon after that encounter, leaders in my church started recognizing the prophetic anointing on my life.

If you are a seer, you have a seer mantle.

In the Old Testament, prophets were known to wear mantles as a sign of their calling from God. These were physical garments. But the Hebrew word for *mantle* is *addereth*. It means glory, splendor, or cloak, but it also speaks of a prophet's robe. A mantle is a symbol of gifts, callings, anointings, and divine authority. A mantle is a supernatural endowment from God to fulfill your assignment. Some theologians say a mantle is a symbol of the Holy Spirit.

Today, our mantles aren't visible to the natural eye, but they may be visible in the spirit because, well, they are spiritual mantles. And all seer mantles are not the same. Think about it. Ezekiel was different from Zechariah, who was different from Daniel, who was different from John the Revelator. God doesn't make seers like robots with the exact same gifts, graces, and anointings. There are many different types of seer mantles.

Jeremiah had a mantle for travail. He is known as the weeping prophet. Travail is an intense form of prayer. Daniel had a mantle to interpret dreams. While any of us can interpret dreams with the Holy Spirit's help, this was a special grace God gave Daniel. Zechariah had a mantle to see into the end times. He had eight significant visions recorded in Scripture.

When you understand your seer mantle, you can operate as God designed. It's not about pressing into areas where He isn't inviting you, but rather fully honing your skills according to your divine talents. Ask God to show you your seer mantle.

PRAYER

Father, in the name of Jesus, would You show me my seer mantle? Help me understand the gifts, graces, and anointings with which You have endued me to walk in my calling in this season.

JANUARY 17

THIS DISTORTS YOUR VISION

For God has not given us a spirit of fear, but of power and of love and of a sound mind.

2 Timothy 1:7

When I was a kid, I loved to go to the fair. There were carnival rides, food stands with cotton candy, carnival games where I could win prizes and, of course, funhouses. It was, well, fun.

In the funhouses they had wacky mirrors. Wacky mirrors have curved surfaces to warp the reflection you see of yourself or someone else. Some people look taller than they really are. Others look shorter or thinner than they really are. Still others look wider than they really are. These mirrors distort reality.

The distortion can give you a good laugh at the fair, but we don't want to see distorted visions in the seer dimensions. When something is distorted, it means that it's altered from a true, natural, or normal state, shape, or condition. Like a distorted image (think about the wacky mirror) or a distorted view or account of something that happened.

What can cause visual distortions? Many things, from personal agendas and burnout to soul ties and unforgiveness and beyond. But perhaps the most common culprit of distorted visions is fear. When you have a spirit of fear or when you see through the lens of fear, you are seeing a distorted image.

God is the faith God. If you are operating in fear, you will see threats everywhere. Instead of seeing what God is doing, you may only see what the enemy is doing and let it breed anxiety in your heart. If you share that fear-based interpretation with others, you can release fear over other people.

When you see through the lens of fear, you will interpret through the lens of anxiety or terror. God may be trying to give you a warning for the sake of intercession, but you are so scared that you bend toward gloom and doom instead of hope and faith.

It's more difficult for God to use a seer who operates from a place of fear. If you are dealing with a spirit of fear in your personal life, you need to deal with it because it will distort your visions. Ask God to deliver you from all fear, anxiety, and dread so you can see rightly.

PRAYER

Father, in the name of Jesus, would You show me if I have any fear in me? I don't want to look through the lens of fear or any other distorted lens. Please, deliver me from fear.

JANUARY 18

ENTERING THE DREAM DIMENSION

And it shall come to pass in the last days, says God, that I will pour out of My Spirit on all flesh; Your sons and your daughters shall prophesy, your young men shall see visions, your old men shall dream dreams.

Acts 2:17

Within the seer realm lies what I call the "dream dimension." But when people tell you every dream is from God, don't believe them. It's not biblical.

Just like the enemy sowed tares among the wheat, the enemy can sow his images into your sleeping soul (Matthew 13:25). Specifically, the enemy can bring demonic dreams—nightmares, night terrors, and night paralysis—to our unconscious minds.

We can also dream carnal or soulish dreams based on the idolatry in our hearts, what we ate before bedtime, our frame of mind, or the medications we're taking. Solomon warned in Ecclesiastes 5:3 (NLT), "Too much activity gives you restless dreams; too many words make you a fool." The NIV puts it this way, "A dream comes when there are many cares, and many words mark the speech of a fool." (I go into much greater details about this in my book *Decoding Your Dreams*.)

All that said, God is still giving divine dreams and some seers have a bent toward dreams over visions. As I write in *The Seer Dimensions*, dreams are an area seers and seeing people, in particular, need to take seriously. That's because while God speaks to us through dreams, dreams from seers may have broader implications than personal dreams.

Think about it. Some of the most dramatic communications we see the Lord revealing to His people—and even to heathen kings—in the Bible came in the form of dreams. God is the same yesterday, today, and forever (Hebrews 13:8). That means that to Him the dream realm is just as important a mode of communication today as it was thousands of years ago. Ignoring or taking the dream realm lightly is a mistake. You can miss God's will for your life, miss warnings for the Church or world, and much more

Upward of 90 percent of the dreams you dream will feature you as a main character. In the seer realm, though, you should expect to have dreams in which you are an observer—or dreams where you are part of something bigger than yourself. Those dreams are often for intercession or warning.

Are you ready to enter the dream dimension? You can't make God give you a dream, but you can prepare your heart to receive one.

PRAYER

Father, in the name of Jesus, help me not to take my dream life for granted. Help me also not to attribute something from my soul to Your Spirit. Teach me what to do with the dreams I receive.

JANUARY 19

HAVING A SIT-DOWN WITH GOD

For through him we both have access by one Spirit to the Father.
Ephesians 2:18

Have you ever had a discussion with God in a vision? When God encounters you in a vision or a dream, there are times He will initiate a conversation. These moments are priceless and can be life-changing.

Indeed, they come with a great weight or assignment. After all, it's one thing to hear the still small voice of God, which is precious. It's another to have a conversation with the Almighty in the seer dimensions.

Abraham had a discussion with God. Consider the scene in Genesis 15:1-5:

> After these things the word of the Lord came to Abram in a vision, saying, "Do not be afraid, Abram. I am your shield, your exceedingly great reward."
>
> But Abram said, "Lord God, what will You give me, seeing I go childless, and the heir of my house is Eliezer of Damascus?" Then Abram said, "Look, You have given me no offspring; indeed one born in my house is my heir!"
>
> And behold, the word of the Lord came to him, saying, "This one shall not be your heir, but one who will come from your own body shall be your heir." Then He brought him outside and said, "Look now toward heaven, and count the stars if you are able to number them." And He said to him, "So shall your descendants be."

This was not just a one-sentence exchange between Abraham and the Lord. This was a conversation. This was a discussion about Abraham's heirs and his legacy. This is amazing!

Note how the Lord initiated the conversation. That's often the way it is in visions. If the Lord appears to you in a vision, it's most likely to deliver some sort of message personally, and He is usually the first one to speak, but You may also be led to ask Him a question.

Also note how God gave Abraham instructions: "Look toward heaven." I believe this is a key to more heavenly visions. We need to keep our eyes on things above, not on things of this earth.

PRAYER

Father, in the name of Jesus, prepare me for conversations with You in the seer dimensions. I want to follow Heaven's protocol and always reverence You if I encounter You in visions and dreams.

JANUARY 20

SEERS IN THE WILDERNESS

So the child grew and became strong in spirit, and was in the deserts till the day of his manifestation to Israel.

Luke 1:80

Every seer has to walk through a wilderness experience—and some may spend years there for any number of reasons. No one likes wilderness seasons and many times we think it's the enemy holding us and our ministry hostage there. But know this: the Holy Spirit leads you there and the Holy Spirit leads you out. The enemy may meet you there, but he's not putting you there or keeping you there (Mark 1:12).

Don't despise the wilderness. Take on the mindset of John the Baptist. John was the one Isaiah prophesied about in Isaiah 40:3: "The voice of one crying in the wilderness: 'Prepare the way of the Lord; make straight in the desert a highway for our God.'" John spent much of his life in the wilderness. Luke records this about him. "So the child grew and became strong in spirit, and was in the deserts till the day of his manifestation to Israel" (Luke 1:80).

John's public ministry lasted only months after the day of his manifestation to Israel. Herod murdered him, but not before he fulfilled his ministry as a forerunner of Christ. John was not in the wilderness because of anything he was doing wrong. John's manifestation to Israel was a matter of God's timing.

Think about it: John was prepared in the wilderness. He received revelation in the wilderness. He learned humility and obedience in the wilderness. He built a strong relationship with God in the wilderness. If you find yourself in the wilderness right now, take heart—it may be that God is preparing you for something marvelous. Take the time to get to know Him because that relationship will serve you well after your revealing.

That said, you may keep yourself in the wilderness longer than you'd like to stay if you don't cooperate with God. Remember, there's a big difference between being a voice crying in the wilderness in obedience to God and finding yourself stuck in the wilderness, going around the same mountain over and over (and over) because you are complaining about the experience.

PRAYER

Father, in the name of Jesus, I know every seer goes through rejection, pain, and wilderness places. Your written promises are enough to get me through. But I am open to angelic encouragement.

JANUARY 21

VISIONS THAT KEEP YOU UP AT NIGHT

For God will bring every work into judgment, including every secret thing, whether good or evil.

Ecclesiastes 12:14

When I speak of visions that keep you up at night, I am not talking about your average night visions. I am talking about visions that stir your spirit or your soul to the point that you can't sleep. You keep pondering what you saw, sometimes until the rising of the sun.

That could be because you are in awe of the depth of the revelation. Or it could be because the vision—and the instruction that comes with it—pulls you out of your comfort zone. Samuel experienced the latter when he was still very young.

In fact, Samuel's first-ever encounter with God was more than a little bit uncomfortable. The Lord kept calling him in the night, but because Samuel didn't yet know the Lord; he thought the voice he heard was Eli the priest. Every time Samuel heard the voice, he ran to Eli's service and said, "Here I am. You called me." After this happened three times, Eli realized it was the Lord calling Samuel and taught him how to respond.

First Samuel 3:11-15 tells us what happens next:

> Then the Lord said to Samuel: "Behold, I will do something in Israel at which both ears of everyone who hears it will tingle. In that day I will perform against Eli all that I have spoken concerning his house, from beginning to end. For I have told him that I will judge his house forever for the iniquity which he knows, because his sons made themselves vile, and he did not restrain them. And therefore I have sworn to the house of Eli that the iniquity of Eli's house shall not be atoned for by sacrifice or offering forever." So Samuel lay down until morning, and opened the doors of the house of the Lord. And Samuel was afraid to tell Eli the vision.

What a way to get baptized into prophetic ministry! Ultimately, Samuel had to decide if he feared the Lord more than he feared Eli's potential punishment. Every seer must learn to deal with sharing uncomfortable visions. If you are right with God, the fear of the Lord will compel you.

PRAYER

Father, in the name of Jesus, help me develop a healthy fear of the Lord that makes me immune to the fear of man. Help me be willing not to just see for You, but be a mouthpiece for You even when it's uncomfortable.

JANUARY 22

WHAT DOES YOUR VISION REALLY MEAN?

Do not interpretations belong to God? Tell them to me, please.
Genesis 40:8

Receiving a vision from God is not difficult. If you are walking in the Spirit, keeping your mind set on things above, and refusing to be distracted, seeing what God is showing you is actually the easy part. And even if you are distracted, God knows how to get your attention.

Sometimes, the more challenging aspect of visual revelation is accurately interpreting what you see in the spirit. It's true that dreams are often more symbolic and visions are more literal, but that's not always the case. Dreams can have a literal aspect and visions can carry symbols.

Consider the epic vision John had in the book of Revelation. He was caught up in the Spirit on the Lord's day and saw sights that few on the face of the earth ever saw. He used the best words he had to describe what he was seeing, saying, "It looked something like…" more than once. But he couldn't immediately comprehend the fullness of what he was seeing.

I can only imagine the visual overwhelm John experienced during that encounter while exiled on the Isle of Patmos. He needed help from angels to interpret the depth of what he was seeing. Sometimes we do, too.

Know this: the interpretation of your vision is just as critical as the vision itself. If you release a wrong interpretation of the vision, you'll have a wrong application of the vision. If you have a wrong application of the vision, you could make a mess by acting outside God's will or timing. We need to be as intent on understanding what God is showing us in a vision as we are about receiving it and recording it.

Look at 2 Chronicles 26:4-5: "And he did what was right in the sight of the Lord, according to all that his father Amaziah had done. He sought God in the days of Zechariah, who had understanding in the visions of God; and as long as he sought the Lord, God made him prosper."

Zechariah had an understanding of the visions of God. We need the same. That doesn't mean we'll understand everything we see—angels had to help John and Zechariah at times—but we should seek to understand. God gave us the vision for a reason.

PRAYER

Father, in the name of Jesus, would You teach me how to interpret what I am seeing? Remind me to turn to the Holy Spirit and Scripture when I need revelation rather than to my own mind or even my own experience.

JANUARY 23

EATING THE BREAD OF HEAVEN

Then Jesus said to them, "Most assuredly, I say to you, Moses did not give you the bread from heaven, but My Father gives you the true bread from heaven."

John 6:32

You've probably heard it said, "You are what you eat." With that, let me ask you a serious question: How's your seer diet? I'm not talking about a food pyramid or cutting carbs. I'm talking, rather, about your visual diet.

What you set before your natural eyes and ears literally affects your spiritual sight. What you watch with your natural eyes and hear with your natural ears can skew your dreams and visions and other visual revelations. Seers should be eating the bread from Heaven.

What do I mean by this? Bread from Heaven, according to *The Seer's Dictionary*, is daily revelation from the throne room of God. Just as it takes time to prepare and consume a meal, it takes time to prepare your heart for what God wants to show you in the seer dimensions.

We first see the concept of the bread of Heaven in Exodus 16:4, from a natural point of view: "Then the Lord said to Moses, 'Behold, I will rain bread from heaven for you. And the people shall go out and gather a certain quota every day, that I may test them, whether they will walk in My law or not."

Bread from Heaven was God's daily provision to the Israelites, but it was also symbolic of our daily provision as New Testament believers. Jesus taught the disciples to pray, "Give us this day our daily bread" (Matthew 6:11). Jesus was not just talking about sourdough bread or whatever sort of bread you like to eat to sustain your physical body. I believe Jesus was also talking about spiritual bread—the daily revelation we need to walk in victory.

In Matthew 4:4, Jesus brings it home to the seer, saying, "It is written, 'Man shall not live by bread alone, but by every word that proceeds from the mouth of God.'" Seers have to show up to the heavenly food line to receive their daily bread, like manna falling from Heaven.

This is John 4:32 (KJV), "meat to eat that ye know not of." Meat often symbolizes revelation in the seer dimensions. God will give the seer a complete meal—a heavenly sandwich that will satisfy your hunger—as the seer seeks His face. Are you eating your daily bread?

PRAYER

Father, in the name of Jesus, help me understand the importance of my spiritual diet and how what I see with my natural eyes affects my spiritual eyes. Remind me to set my eyes on Your Word so I can receive daily bread.

JANUARY 24

DON'T LET THE ENEMY CHASE YOUR NIGHT VISIONS AWAY

And the king said to them, "I have had a dream, and my spirit is anxious to know the dream...."

Daniel 2:3

Do you ever feel like you are grasping at straws to remember your dreams when you wake up? That can be frustrating, especially when you know (that you know that you know) your dream carries great significance for something going on in your life or in the world.

Let me share a tip: Don't let that frustration get the best of you. That only makes it more difficult to remember. Also, you have to be discerning in these moments because sometimes, God is reserving the fullness of the visual revelation for another season.

In that case, you can wrack your brain trying to remember but you're just wasting your time. On the other hand, sometimes it's the enemy chasing away your night visions. Again, discernment is critical. Always ask the Holy Spirit.

Job 20:7-9 reads, "Yet he will perish forever like his own refuse; those who have seen him will say, 'Where is he?' He will fly away like a dream, and not be found; yes, he will be chased away like a vision of the night. The eye that saw him will see him no more, nor will his place behold him anymore."

How does the enemy chase away your night visions? There are many ways, probably more than we know, but here is something to think about: You might wake up to an immediate distraction. You may be in too big of a hurry to sit before the Lord and wait for Him to help you remember.

If you feel pressured to rush out of bed in the morning, start getting up 15 minutes earlier to give yourself some time to reflect on your night visions. Keep a journal next to your bed so you can immediately write down anything you may remember so you can meditate on it later.

And don't stress. If God gave you that dream or vision, He can help you remember it when you need to remember it. God knows everything. The enemy can't interfere with God's recall. Do your part in making the time with God and He will do His part by offering recollection at the right time.

PRAYER

Father, in the name of Jesus, help me to reject the frustration that comes when I can't remember a night vision. Help me to lean not on my own understanding but to seek Your face instead of giving in to frustration.

JANUARY 25

WHEN GOD PUTS YOU IN A DEEP SLEEP

Now, as he was speaking with me, I was in a deep sleep with my face to the ground; but he touched me, and stood me upright.

Daniel 8:18

Deep sleep is part of the seer dimensions we don't hear much about. Yet it is a repeated occurrence in the pages of Scripture. I am not talking about deep sleep in the context of getting a good night's rest that refreshes your body and soul. I am talking about the spiritual side of deep sleep.

Did you know, spiritually speaking, deep sleep can be a good thing or a bad thing. First, let's look at the positive side of deep sleep. As I write in my book *The Seer Dimensions*, deep sleep is not the dream realm. Rather deep sleep is a deeper state than normal sleep where you do not remember the experience.

Daniel fell into a deep sleep after he saw a great vision that shocked him. "Yet I heard the sound of his words; and while I heard the sound of his words I was in a deep sleep on my face, with my face to the ground" (Daniel 10:9). What followed was an angelic encounter. An angel touched him to bring him out of the deep sleep.

And look at what happened to Abraham in Genesis 15:12-16:

> Now when the sun was going down, a deep sleep fell upon Abram; and behold, horror and great darkness fell upon him. Then He said to Abram: "Know certainly that your descendants will be strangers in a land that is not theirs, and will serve them, and they will afflict them four hundred years. And also the nation whom they serve I will judge; afterward they shall come out with great possessions. Now as for you, you shall go to your fathers in peace; you shall be buried at a good old age. But in the fourth generation they shall return here, for the iniquity of the Amorites is not yet complete."

Like other aspects of the seer dimensions, you can't choose to enter a deep sleep. This is a unique aspect of the seer dimensions just as hearing the audible voice of God is a unique aspect of prophetic dimensions.

PRAYER

Father, in the name of Jesus, help me understand this aspect of the seer dimensions. I am not asking for deep sleep, but I want a revelation of this way You speak to Your people so I can be accurate in the spirit.

JANUARY 26

AWE-INSPIRING SIGHTS

Who is like You, O Lord, among the gods? Who is like You, glorious in holiness, fearful in praises, doing wonders?

Exodus 15:11

When God opens your eyes to what's going on behind the veil, it is an awesome sight. Actually, that is a vast understatement as *awesome* doesn't begin to describe the experience.

Scripture shows us time and again that there are all sorts of spiritual creatures and activity in the seer dimensions. It's not surprising, then, that seers may be awestruck by visions of angels or the four living creatures.

In Revelation 22:8 (KJV), John the Revelator wrote, "And I John saw these things, and heard them. And when I had heard and seen, I fell down to worship before the feet of the angel which shewed me these things." In fact, he did this on two different occasions. Surely, angels are awesome creatures but John also saw horse-like creatures with heads like lions and fire, smoke and sulfur coming from their mouths.

But the most awe-inspiring visual revelation is seeing the Lord. According to *The Seer's Dictionary, awe* is "the feeling or emotion when one sees the Lord in a dream or vision, encounter or out of body experience."

The International Standard Bible Encyclopedia defines *awe* as "Fear mingled with reverence and wonder, a state of mind inspired by something terrible or sublime... This is the characteristic attitude of the pious soul toward God in the Scriptures, especially in the Old Testament. It arises from a consciousness of the infinite power, sublimity and holiness of God, which fills the mind with the 'fear of the Lord,' and a dread of violating His law."

Consider David, who had a deep relationship with God. In Psalm 33:8 (KJV), he writes, "Let all the earth fear the Lord: let all the inhabitants of the world stand in awe of him!" And again in Psalm 68:35 (ESV), "Awesome is God from his sanctuary; the God of Israel—he is the one who gives power and strength to his people. Blessed be God!"

David was in awe of his Maker, without having seen Him. May we all develop the awe of God.

PRAYER

Father, in the name of Jesus, I am in awe of You. Whether or not I ever see You in the seer dimensions like Isaiah or John did, I am in awe. Help me to always stand in awe of You.

JANUARY 27

HOW TO AVOID ERRING IN SPIRITUAL SIGHT

> *Wine is a mocker, strong drink is a brawler, and whoever is led astray by it is not wise.*
>
> Proverbs 20:1

Anyone can make a mistake discerning if a vision is from God, if it is one's own imagination or if it is the enemy. One key to avoid erring in vision is to live a holy life.

Paul admonished us by the Holy Spirit, "And do not be drunk with wine, in which is dissipation; but be filled with the Spirit" (Ephesians 5:18). Seers should be filled with the Spirit, not so full of wine that they can't see straight.

Paul also admonished the church at Corinth about drunkenness—and this was a church known to operate in spiritual gifts:

> Therefore when you come together in one place, it is not to eat the Lord's Supper. For in eating, each one takes his own supper ahead of others; and one is hungry and another is drunk. What! Do you not have houses to eat and drink in? Or do you despise the church of God and shame those who have nothing? What shall I say to you? Shall I praise you in this? I do not praise you (1 Corinthians 11:20-22).

I'm not here to debate whether you drink wine, but the Bible is clear about drunkenness. Consider the warning in Isaiah 28:6-8:

> For a spirit of justice to him who sits in judgment, and for strength to those who turn back the battle at the gate. But they also have erred through wine, and through intoxicating drink are out of the way; the priest and the prophet have erred through intoxicating drink, they are swallowed up by wine, they are out of the way through intoxicating drink; they err in vision, they stumble in judgment. For all tables are full of vomit and filth; no place is clean.

Strong drink is not the only thing that leads us into visual error. Setting your eyes on worthless things such as violent or sexually inappropriate content can also lead you astray. The seer should pursue a life in which the eyes are consecrated.

Consider the flip side. You may not err in vision, but you can err in judgment. Sometimes this just comes through inexperience. You misinterpret the vision because of biases or lack of Bible knowledge. I go deeper into this in the School of the Seers.

PRAYER

Father, in the name of Jesus, would You help me not to engage in any excess. The enemy loves excess. I love You and Your Word. I do not want to err in vision or stumble in judgment.

JANUARY 28

WHEN YOUR VISION IS A BOOK

My heart is overflowing with a good theme; I recite my composition concerning the King; my tongue is the pen of a ready writer.

Psalm 45:1

What if your vision became a book? Think about it for a minute. The book of Revelation is largely the record of an epic vision across 22 jaw-dropping chapters.

The book of Revelation records encounters with Jesus, God's throne, angels, elders, scrolls, trumpets, bowls, judgments, the dragon, beasts, Babylon, the Second Coming, the 1,000-year millennium, the new heaven, new earth, New Jerusalem, and more. Talk about a page-turner! You have to read it many times to even scratch the surface of the depths of John's book.

Jesus told John, "Write the things which you have seen, and the things which are, and the things which will take place after this" (Revelation 1:19). God told Isaiah, "Now go, write it before them on a tablet, and note it on a scroll, that it may be for time to come, forever and ever" (Isaiah 30:8). He told Jeremiah, "Thus speaks the Lord God of Israel, saying: 'Write in a book for yourself all the words that I have spoken to you'" (Jeremiah 30:2).

He also told me to write down my vision. My book *Decoding the Mysteries of Heaven's War Room: 21 Heavenly Strategies for Powerful Prayer & Triumphant Warfare* records Bible-based revelations that empower us to partner with God's purposes and achieve greater victory in our lives. Rick Joyner is known for writing books about his visions. He wrote *The Vision, Army of the Dawn* and other books about visions, dreams, and prophetic experiences.

With that in mind, consider Isaiah 29:10-11: "For the Lord has poured out on you the spirit of deep sleep, and has closed your eyes, namely, the prophets; and He has covered your heads, namely, the seers. The whole vision has become to you like the words of a book that is sealed, which men deliver to one who is literate, saying, 'Read this, please.'"

You may never write a book for publication, but it's a strategic move to record your visions in a book. God may not let you release your visions for years, or He may call you to write a series of books like Rick Joyner did. Ezekiel, Isaiah, and others recorded their visions in books. Aren't you glad they did? Get a nice book with blank pages and begin writing.

PRAYER

Father, in the name of Jesus, would You show me when my visual revelation is book material? Would You show me when You want me to release a book for the generation today and generations to come?

JANUARY 29

DISCERNING FALSE VISIONS QUICKLY

Test all things; hold fast what is good.

1 Thessalonians 5:21

Have you ever had a false vision? Before you answer that question, let me define a false vision.

A false vision is a picture, inner vision or open vision that came from a source other than God. This is dangerous because a false vision can mislead you (or others) into acting on revelation that God didn't breathe. Scripture says a lot about false visions, which can pervert God's truth, character, or ways.

God talked to Jeremiah about this: "Do not listen to the words of the prophets who prophesy to you. They make you worthless; they speak a vision of their own heart, not from the mouth of the Lord" (Jeremiah 23:16). Just as in Jeremiah's day, there is too much of this in the Body of Christ right now, and you don't want to fall prey to this trap.

So while it's exciting to have a vision, we must always, always, always take the time to discern the source of what we are seeing in the spirit. Visions, after all, can come from our unsanctified imagination. Visions can come from the Holy Spirit opening our eyes to the seer dimensions. And visions can also come from the enemy.

We do not want to be responsible for releasing false visions accidentally. (Yet, some are releasing false visions on purpose.) So we need to discern the source of our visions, as well as the source of the visions others share with us. We can't automatically believe everything we see.

Read the account in Jeremiah 14:15, "Therefore thus says the Lord concerning the prophets who prophesy in My name, whom I did not send, and who say, 'Sword and famine shall not be in this land'—'By sword and famine those prophets shall be consumed!'"

This should put the fear of the Lord in us about sharing a vision we haven't tested. God is not going to consume us if we release a false vision, but it opens the door for deception in our lives. Weigh up your visions, no matter how spectacular or spontaneous. You'll be glad you did.

PRAYER

Father, in the name of Jesus, help me to remember to test the source of my visions before I release them publicly. Surround me with people who can help me test what I see in the spirit so I don't lead people astray.

JANUARY 30

THE DISTRACTED SEER

Martha was distracted with much serving....

Luke 10:40

When I got off the train from Belgium to Berlin, I was on my phone trying to find an Uber to take us to the hotel. I wasn't paying attention to what was going on around me. I was distracted.

Thank God, I wasn't so distracted that I missed the Holy Spirit's gentle nudge to "Look up." When I looked up, I saw a truck with the word "ARETEMIS" written in big red letters. The Holy Spirit quickened in my spirit that this ancient principality was a stronghold over the city.

Thank God, I didn't let what was going on in the natural distract me from the supernatural. If I had walked another three feet, I would have missed what the Holy Spirit was trying to show me and been less effective in my assignment in Germany.

One of the enemy's most strategic assignments against your visual revelation is distraction. But it doesn't always start with your sight. It often starts in your devotional life. Scripture, the written Word of God, is a critical part of the foundation for accurate spiritual sight. The enemy knows this, so he will work to distract us from studying the Word.

Look at Mark 4:18-19 (AMPC). Jesus was speaking of the sower sowing the seed, and the seed is the Word of God: "And the ones sown among the thorns are others who hear the Word; then the cares and anxieties of the world and distractions of the age, and the pleasure and delight and false glamour and deceitfulness of riches, and the craving and passionate desire for other things creep in and choke and suffocate the Word, and it becomes fruitless."

The Word can't bear fruit in a distracted heart. Likewise, worry, anxiety, worldly endeavors, and even "good" things can also distract us from what God wants to show us.

Finally, the enemy can distract you with noise in the spirit. Consider Psalm 55:2-3 (AMPC), "Attend to me and answer me; I am restless and distraught in my complaint and must moan, [And I am distracted] at the noise of the enemy, because of the oppression and the threats of the wicked; for they would cast trouble upon me, and in wrath they would persecute me."

Don't allow yourself to be distracted. You never know what visual revelation you could miss.

PRAYER

Father, in the name of Jesus, help me to discern distractions and not bow to them. Help me not to be entangled in the affairs of life to the point that I am too distracted to see what You are trying to show me.

JANUARY 31

DID A SPIRIT JUST PASS BEFORE YOUR EYES?

The spirit stopped, but I couldn't see its shape. There was a form before my eyes.

Job 4:16 NLT

When I was younger in the Lord, my friend talked me into hiking up the Great Smoky Mountains in North Carolina. She said it would take about an hour, but it was about a five-hour hike.

When we arrived, it was almost sundown and starting a fire was our top priority. After we set up camp, I ate some granola and went to sleep. Suddenly, I woke up to some rustling in the camp. I don't know what got into me, but I unzipped the tent to take a look. When I did, something lunged at me and I pulled back in terror.

I thought it was a bear but it wasn't. No physical form was there. What I saw was blacker than black. When I told my mentor about it, she told me I had seen a spirit of fear passing before my eyes. I hope to never see it again. It was truly terrifying!

We see something similar in Scripture. One of Job's friends had an interesting vision–and it frightened him. Listen in to Eliphaz's vision in Job 4:15-20 (NLT):

> A spirit swept past my face, and my hair stood on end. The spirit stopped, but I couldn't see its shape. There was a form before my eyes. In the silence I heard a voice say, "Can a mortal be innocent before God? Can anyone be pure before the Creator? If God does not trust his own angels and has charged his messengers with foolishness, how much less will he trust people made of clay! They are made of dust, crushed as easily as a moth. They are alive in the morning but dead by evening, gone forever without a trace."

Notice Eliphaz's reaction to a spirit passing before his face: His hair stood on end. He probably didn't know exactly what he was seeing at first, but his soul and his physical body had a strong reaction to seeing beyond the veil. But he quickly discerned it was a messenger from God: an angel.

When you see into the spirit realm, remember it can affect your soul and your body. It may be startling or even frightening. That's when you have to take a deep breath of the Spirit and discern what you are seeing so you can respond rightly and apply the revelation that comes out of the encounter.

PRAYER

Father, in the name of Jesus, would You help me understand what spirit I am seeing and not allow it to scare me? Help me discern what is going on before my spiritual eyes and respond in Christ.

FEBRUARY

At Gibeon the Lord appeared to Solomon in a dream by night; and God said, "Ask! What shall I give you?"

1 Kings 3:5

FEBRUARY 1

A GLORIOUS SIGHT

The sight of the glory of the Lord was like a consuming fire on the top of the mountain in the eyes of the children of Israel.

Exodus 24:17

When we think of Ezekiel, we're quick to point to the "blood on your hands" verses, but the watchman prophet was as much a glory watcher as a sin watcher. If you have the ability to see the sin and the demons, you have the ability to see the King of Glory and His angels.

As a matter of fact, before Ezekiel was anointed as the "blood on your hands" watchman, he saw visions of God. This is a critically important point. Too many seers are mesmerized by the dark side despite being citizens of the Kingdom of light.

In Ezekiel 1, the vision starts with a whirlwind coming out of the north. He describes the four living creatures in great detail, as well as a vision of the wheel within a wheel, with rims full of eyes. Finally, he saw the Lord. Let's look at Ezekiel 1:26-28:

> And above the firmament over their heads was the likeness of a throne, in appearance like a sapphire stone; on the likeness of the throne was a likeness with the appearance of a man high above it. Also from the appearance of His waist and upward I saw, as it were, the color of amber with the appearance of fire all around within it; and from the appearance of His waist and downward I saw, as it were, the appearance of fire with brightness all around. Like the appearance of a rainbow in a cloud on a rainy day, so was the appearance of the brightness all around it. This was the appearance of the likeness of the glory of the Lord.

Ezekiel saw the glory of God. I believe God gave him this experience before calling him to deal with the sin in the land so that he would have a proper perspective.

While watchmen deal with a lot of demons, we have to learn how to keep God at the center of our focus. God is omnipresent. We have to be careful not to default to the demonic realm, when there are angels all around us and God is everywhere all the time. If you focus on God, He will show you whatever demons you need to see.

PRAYER

Father, in the name of Jesus, I am willing to see anything You want to show me. But how I long to see what Ezekiel saw! Would You show me what You showed Ezekiel before you sent him out to deal with the sin in the land?

FEBRUARY 2

WRITE THE VISION

Now go, write it before them on a tablet, and note it on a scroll, that it may be for time to come, forever and ever.

Isaiah 30:8

The prophet Habakkuk understood the importance of writing down what he saw in the spirit. Some seers today should take a lesson from his book.

In Habakkuk 2:1-3 he wrote: "I will stand my watch and set myself on the rampart, and watch to see what He will say to me, and what I will answer when I am corrected. Then the Lord answered me and said: 'Write the vision and make it plain on tablets, that he may run who reads it. For the vision is yet for an appointed time; but at the end it will speak, and it will not lie. Though it tarries, wait for it; because it will surely come, It will not tarry.'"

It's critical that you write out your visions. God shares secrets in visions and we may not remember the details if we don't write them down. Think of John's epic vision in the book of Revelation. Before God showed him things that must soon take place, He gave John a specific instruction: "'I am the Alpha and the Omega, the First and the Last,' and, 'What you see, write in a book and send it to the seven churches which are in Asia: to Ephesus, to Smyrna, to Pergamos, to Thyatira, to Sardis, to Philadelphia, and to Laodicea'" (Revelation 1:11).

And again, "Write the things which you have seen, and the things which are, and the things which will take place after this" (Revelation 1:19).

Later on in the epic vision, an angel gave John the same instruction: "And he said to me, 'These are the true sayings of God'" (Revelation 19:9). John wrote down the visions. He chronicled them because He was instructed.

But we don't need any further instruction from God to pen what we see.

While the canon of Scripture is closed, we are living by every word that comes out of the mouth of God. And sometimes those words are visual representations. Write them down. You'll be glad you did, and so will many future generations.

PRAYER

Father, in the name of Jesus, help me get into the habit of walking like Habakkuk, immediately writing down what I see as I watch and pray. Help me to remember to record the visions so I don't forget anything I saw.

FEBRUARY 3

WHEN GOD SHOWS YOU A BURDEN

The burden against Nineveh. The book of the vision of Nahum the Elkoshite. God is jealous, and the Lord avenges.

Nahum 1:1-2

When you think of a burden, you may think of a heavy load, but in seer language it means that and more. Consider Habakkuk's visual revelation. He starts the book that bears his name with, "The burden which the prophet Habakkuk saw" (Habakkuk 1:1).

Habakkuk doesn't immediately go into a detailed explanation about what he saw like Daniel or Ezekiel or John the Revelator did. Perhaps he spared us those details or perhaps the burden was so heavy that he immediately turned to inquire of the Lord rather than writing every minute detail in the moment.

What does it mean to see a burden? We must first understand that "burden" is an intense word in the original language. The Hebrew word for *burden* is *massa* and it means, "load, bearing, burden, utterance, oracle, and carrying."

Put another way, Habakkuk's burden was his oracle, his message. But what he saw wasn't a pleasant vision. What he saw left the prophet with a heavy heart and some questions.

Habakkuk's response to the burden, or oracle, he saw was a complaint to the Lord about the apparent triumph of wickedness among his countryman, offers *Elliot's Commentary for English Readers*. Let's look at Habakkuk 1:2-4:

> O Lord, how long shall I cry, and You will not hear? Even cry out to You, "Violence!" And You will not save. Why do You show me iniquity, and cause me to see trouble? For plundering and violence are before me; there is strife, and contention arises. Therefore the law is powerless, and justice never goes forth. For the wicked surround the righteous; therefore perverse judgment proceeds.

Clearly, Habakkuk was overwhelmed. But the Lord gave the prophet an instruction in verse 5 to look among the nations and watch. It was going to get worse. With that, we bleed into Habakkuk 2:1 where the prophet decided, *"I will stand my watch."*

When you see something in the natural or in the spirit that burdens your heart, it often becomes your message. But it always becomes your prayer assignment. It becomes something to stand watch over and make war over until the Lord releases you. Ask God for your seer burden.

PRAYER

Father, in the name of Jesus, I want you to be able to trust me with Your oracles. I want to see the burden. Make me ready to walk in the type of ministry that Habakkuk experienced even if it's uncomfortable.

FEBRUARY 4

ENTERING THE VISION DIMENSION

I was watching in the night visions, and behold, One like the Son of Man, coming with the clouds of heaven!

Daniel 7:13-14

The seer dimensions are vast, and most of us haven't scratched the surface. When I read about the visions in Scripture, I see what is possible. At the same time, there's a lot of error in the vision dimension. People mistake their own imagination for an epic vision.

If we want to enter the vision dimension accurately, we should be a student of what Scripture says about visions so we can "plumb line" what we see against the inerrant Word of God. Let's start off with the basic question "What is a vision?"

The Hebrew word for *vision* is *chazah*, which means "vision, a sight (mentally), i.e., a dream, revelation, or oracle—vision," according to Strong's Concordance. Brown-Driver-Briggs breaks it down as a "vision, as seen in an ecstatic state"; "vision, in the night"; and "divine communication in a vision, oracle, prophecy."

The Greek word for *vision* is *horasis*, which means "the act of seeing, a vision, appearance," according to the NAS Exhaustive Concordance. Thayer's Greek Lexicon defines *vision* as "the act of seeing; the sense of sight; appearance, visible form, a vision, i.e., an appearance divinely granted in an ecstasy." And Strong's Exhaustive Concordance defines *vision* as "the act of gazing, i.e. (externally) an aspect or (internally) an inspired appearance—a sight, vision."

Simply put, you dream while you are asleep. You have visions when you are awake. You can have a vision within a dream but ultimately a vision within a dream is still part of the dream dimension. In all cases, Holy Spirit-inspired visions are one more way God communicates with His people. God-given visions are supernatural revelations—divine communication from Heaven.

Within the vision dimension, we find pictures, trances, inner visions, and open visions. When you study accounts of trances and visions in Scripture, it primes the pump for you to experience this realm, because faith comes by hearing. I challenge you to dive into the Word and immerse yourself in the vision dimension.

PRAYER

Father, in the name of Jesus, would You give me a supernatural interest in what Your Word says about visions. By Your Holy Spirit, You chose to record specific examples of visions for my instruction.

FEBRUARY 5

SEEING THROUGH THE EYES OF THE HEART

So that you come short in no gift, eagerly waiting for the revelation of our Lord Jesus Christ.

1 Corinthians 1:7

You may never have thought about it this way, but you have two sets of eyes. You have the eyes that everyone can see—the natural eyes on your human face. But you also have eyes no one can see. We call those the "eyes of your heart."

In Ephesians 1:17-18 (AMPC), Paul writes:

> [For I always pray to] the God of our Lord Jesus Christ, the Father of glory, that He may grant you a spirit of wisdom and revelation [of insight into mysteries and secrets] in the [deep and intimate] knowledge of Him, by having the ***eyes of your heart*** flooded with light, so that you can know and understand the hope to which He has called you, and how rich is His glorious inheritance in the saints (His set-apart ones).

What are the eyes of your heart? You might ask, instead, what is the heart? The word *heart* in this verse is not talking about a physical organ that beats in your chest. Rather, it denotes the center, or seat, of your spiritual life. In other words, Paul was talking about the eyes of your spirit. Since the Holy Spirit lives in your spirit, He is able to show you things to come.

While the Holy Spirit can emphasize things in the natural world He wants you to see through your physical eyes, He often shows you what He wants you to see in the spirit through your spiritual eyes. Keep in mind that you are a spirit who has a soul and lives in a body. The Holy Spirit communicates with your spirit—your inner self, your heart.

Humans were meant to see through the eyes of their heart. Adam and Eve saw through the eyes of their heart and fellowshipped with God in the cool of the day. When the serpent deceived Eve, tempting her to eat the forbidden fruit from the Tree of the Knowledge of Good and Evil, mankind stopped seeing through the eyes of their heart and started depending more on the five physical senses. But when we are born again, our spiritual sight was restored.

PRAYER

Father, in the name of Jesus, would You open the eyes of my heart? Enlighten the eyes of my understanding so that I can accurately understand what You are showing me in the seer dimensions.

FEBRUARY 6

THE GAD SEER ANOINTING

Now when David arose in the morning, the word of the Lord came to the prophet Gad, David's seer, saying, "Go and tell David, 'Thus says the Lord: "I offer you three things; choose one of them for yourself, that I may do it to you."'"

2 Samuel 24:11-12

Gad the seer was a prophet in the days of David and was a trusted voice in the king's life. He was known as the king's seer (2 Samuel 24:11). He was part of David's inner circle. Gad carried a boldness to deliver hard messages to David. Consider this message from 2 Samuel 24:11-13:

> Now when David arose in the morning, the word of the Lord came to the prophet Gad, David's seer, saying, "Go and tell David, 'Thus says the Lord: "I offer you three things; choose one of them for yourself, that I may do it to you."'" So Gad came to David and told him; and he said to him, "Shall seven years of famine come to you in your land? Or shall you flee three months before your enemies, while they pursue you? Or shall there be three days' plague in your land? Now consider and see what answer I should take back to Him who sent me."

Gad's seer anointing is also strategic. Gad wasn't just a seer in the spirit, he gave practical advice to David. When a plague came on the land, Gad had advice for the king: "Therefore, the angel of the Lord commanded Gad to say to David that David should go and erect an altar to the Lord on the threshing floor of Ornan the Jebusite. So David went up at the word of Gad, which he had spoken in the name of the Lord" (1 Chronicles 21:18-19).

Gad also had directional advice for David. When David escaped Saul and fled to the cave of Adullum. Everyone who was in distress, in debt or discontented gathered there, about 400 men. He also called for his family. It seems he was setting up camp there. Then Gad had direction from the Lord: "Do not stay in the stronghold; depart, and go to the land of Judah" (1 Samuel 22:5). What did David do? He took his seer's advice. Scripture says he left Adullum and went into the forest of Hereth. We all need a Gad.

PRAYER

Father, in the name of Jesus, impart to me the Gad seer anointing. Give me strategic counsel for my leaders. Forge in me the character that would allow me to be trusted by authority.

FEBRUARY 7

WHEN YOU FEEL LIKE QUITTING

Looking unto Jesus, the author and finisher of our faith, who for the joy that was set before Him endured the cross, despising the shame, and has sat down at the right hand of the throne of God.

Hebrews 12:2

When you carry too much alone, eventually you may break under the pressure. When you are persecuted for doing what is right, you may feel like giving up. When you miss it badly, you may feel like quitting the ministry. When you are emotionally and spiritually spent, you might feel like throwing in the towel.

There are many reasons you may feel like quitting. Indeed, I know all too well what it feels like to want to give up. But let me make this plain: quitting is simply not an option.

So, what do you do when you feel like giving up? Do you go on a sleep marathon, hoping to escape the harsh reality? Do you veg out in front of the television with a bag of potato chips and a pint of ice cream (and put on a few pounds), watching anything that will keep your mind off the pain?

Do you call your friends to rehearse and rehash the drama, hoping they will have a prophetic word? Do you wallow in self-pity? Do you drown your pillow with tears (Psalm 6:6)? I've done all those things, but none of it helps.

So, what should you do when you feel like giving up?

When we feel like giving up, we can take our complaints to God. He can certainly handle it. Like David, we can take our deep sighs to God dusk, dawn, and noon. But ultimately, we have to come to the conclusion that God does hear us (Psalm 116:1), that He is working on the situation (Romans 8:28) and that His grace is sufficient for us (2 Corinthians 12:9). Ultimately, we have to conclude God is trustworthy (Psalm 9:10). Ultimately, we have to keep on our whole armor of God so we are able to withstand the attacks of the enemy against our mind and, having done all, stand (Ephesians 6:13).

Pile your troubles onto God's shoulders. Because He carried David's load and helped David—He won't fail you. As trite as it sounds, set your heart to trust in God, and you will not be disappointed (Romans 10:11). Don't give up. Amen.

PRAYER

Father, in the name of Jesus, would You help me cast down thoughts of giving up? Where would I go, You have the words of life? Strengthen me in my inner being to endure hardships.

FEBRUARY 8

WHAT TO DO WITH WHAT YOU SEE

But someone will say, "You have faith and I have works." Show me your faith apart from your works, and I will show you my faith by my works.

James 2:18

If we don't apply what we see, we can miss God's purpose for sharing the visual revelation. We have to take what we see in the spirit one step further. We have to do something with what we see. Faith without works is dead. If we believe we're seeing, we need to take action on what we see.

God may be showing you something for the future and the application may be partial now and more complete later. How do you know if the visual revelation is for now, later, or both? The God who gave you the dream or vision will help you see what you need to do now and what you need to do in the future if you ask Him. He's not in the business of hiding His wisdom from you.

In fact, James 1:5 assures us, "If any of you lacks wisdom, let him ask of God, who gives to all liberally and without reproach, and it will be given to him."

The challenge with applying the revelation you receive in dreams, visions, and other encounters is often the timetable. God rarely moves as fast as we'd like Him to move. Conversely, sometimes we don't move as quickly as He wants us to.

When applying revelation you receive in dreams and visions—especially concerning things to come—be careful not to try to help what you saw come to pass. Adding works to your faith is one thing, trying to manipulate a situation in order to see your visual revelation manifest is another.

Abram had a prophecy direct from the mouth of God that he would be the father of many nations. Since she was barren, Sarai encouraged him to take a shortcut and had her servant birth Ishmael, who was not the promised son. That caused more than a little trouble in the family dynamic.

With regard to applying the revelation we receive, remember there's a process to get to the promise. David waited more than 20 years between his anointing in front of his brothers and his kingship. Of course the process doesn't always take that long, but we must cooperate with the grace of God despite our frustrations and weariness.

The seer who masters visual revelation application leverages opportunities, stays in God's timing and walks in His perfect will. This is a skill every seer must develop.

PRAYER

Father, in the name of Jesus, help me not to be idle with the visual revelation You share. Help me not put the revelation in a drawer and just wait and see. Help me not to get ahead or lag behind You.

FEBRUARY 9

WHEN THE VISION DRAINS YOUR STRENGTH

And when I saw Him, I fell at His feet as dead. But He laid His right hand on me, saying to me, "Do not be afraid; I am the First and the Last."
Revelation 1:17

There are times when what you see in the spirit will literally take your breath away. This happened to Daniel in Daniel 10:8-10: "Therefore I was left alone when I saw this great vision, and no strength remained in me; for my vigor was turned to frailty in me, and I retained no strength. Yet I heard the sound of his words; and while I heard the sound of his words I was in a deep sleep on my face, with my face to the ground."

Strength in this verse comes from the Hebrew word *koach*. It means human strength. In other words, he literally passed out! What could be so great that Daniel would literally collapse and fall into a deep sleep with his face to the ground?

"Christ appeared to Daniel in a glorious form, and it should engage us to think highly and honourably of him. There remained no strength in Daniel," Matthew Henry's Commentary explains. "The greatest and best of men cannot bear the full discoveries of the Divine glory; for no man can see it, and live; but glorified saints see Christ as he is, and can bear the sight."

In other words, this great vision was a vision of the pre-incarnate Christ. His beauty took Daniel's breath away. I believe this is a normal response to seeing Jesus. It marks you and is not something you share with the many, but the few.

John the Revelator experienced something similar in Revelation 1. John saw a vision of the Son of Man, Jesus. First, he heard Jesus speaking. When he turned to see who was talking, he had a vision of Jesus.

In Revelation 1:14-17 we read: "His head and hair were white like wool, as white as snow, and His eyes like a flame of fire; His feet were like fine brass, as if refined in a furnace, and His voice as the sound of many waters; He had in His right hand seven stars, out of His mouth went a sharp two-edged sword, and His countenance was like the sun shining in its strength. And when I saw Him, I fell at His feet as dead...."

In other words, the sight of Jesus in all His glory drained John's strength. When you have a vision that drains your strength, do not fear. God is with you.

PRAYER

Father, in the name of Jesus, what incredible visions Daniel and John had! I would like to see You in all Your glory. If You choose to appear to me, I will not be afraid even if I am weak in the knees at Your presence.

FEBRUARY 10

ARE YOU DREAM FLUENT?

God speaks in one way, and in two, though man does not perceive it. In a dream, in a vision of the night, when deep sleep falls on men....
Job 33:14-15 ESV

When I was in high school, I took three years of Latin. People don't speak Latin anymore, but if they did, I would have been considered fluent, though I don't remember much beyond, "Veni, vidi, vici," which means "I came, I saw, I conquered."

What's my point? We need to be fluent in dream language, which is easier said than done. To be sure, dreams often carry profound messages that are not easily discerned by the natural mind. Dream language is sometimes literal, but more often it's parabolic and symbolic with multiple layers of revelation to be explored. Becoming fluent in dream language is our goal, and that comes with Bible study, prayer, and experience.

In Job 33:14-16 (AMPC) we're reminded that "For God [does reveal His will; He] speaks not only once, but more than once, even though men do not regard it.... [One may hear God's voice] in a dream, in a vision of the night, when deep sleep falls on men while slumbering upon the bed, then He opens the ears of men and seals their instruction...."

What does it mean that "men do not regard it"? It means they can't understand what He is saying. What a shame! When we get fluent in dream language, we can interpret what He is saying and bring the revelation from the spirit realm to the natural realm where it's useful.

We need to lean on the Holy Spirit, not dream dictionaries. While dream dictionaries can be useful, without the Holy Spirit in the mix we can come up with a wrong interpretation and application.

First Corinthians 2:10 tells us that "God has revealed them to us through His Spirit. For the Spirit searches all things, yes, the deep things of God." As you immerse yourself in the Word, pray in the Spirit, and wait on the Lord, the Holy Spirit will reveal what you need to know. You will become more fluent in dream language.

PRAYER

Father, in the name of Jesus, would You give me the grace to become fluent in the language of dreams? Teach me Your ways in the realm of dream language so I can be accurate in my interpretations.

FEBRUARY 11

WHEN THE VISION DOESN'T MAKE SENSE

Therefore I speak to them in parables, because seeing they do not see, and hearing they do not hear, nor do they understand.

Matthew 13:13

Sometimes, we really can't understand what we're seeing. Often, what we experience with our seer eyes doesn't make sense to our natural minds. Sometimes the visual revelation doesn't make sense because the deeper meanings are for a later time.

The Holy Spirit does not always unpack every level of the revelation He pours out immediately. Other times, the visual revelation is an invitation to seek His Word and His heart for understanding. But still other times, the reason we don't understand what we're seeing is because you are not yet experienced enough to understand how to navigate what you saw—or you haven't sought to educate yourself in this realm.

Think about it this way. If someone is speaking to you in Spanish, you may understand a word or two, like "hola" or "adios" or "gracias." But you are not fluent. You haven't studied the language so you miss large parts of the message. That's one reason why I compiled *The Seer's Dictionary*.

We find an interesting passage of Scripture in Isaiah 29:10-12:

> For the Lord has poured out on you, the spirit of deep sleep, and has closed your eyes, namely, the prophets; and He has covered your heads, namely, the seers. The whole vision has become to you like the words of a book that is sealed, which men deliver to one who is literate, saying, "Read this, please." And he says, "I cannot, for it is sealed." Then the book is delivered to one who is illiterate, saying, "Read this, please." And he says, "I am not literate."

Other translations including AMPC, ESV, NLT, and NIV simply say, "I cannot read."

In this passage, a lack of education was an excuse for not pressing in to gain understanding. *Gill's Exposition of the Entire Bible* offers this insight:

> *In short, the sum of it is this, that neither the learned nor unlearned, among the Jews, cared to read their Bibles, or to search the Scriptures, and the prophecies in them, concerning the Messiah, and that neither of them understood them; these things were hid from the wise and prudent, as well as from the ignorant and unlearned of the people, in common, and were only made known to a few babes and sucklings.*

Seers, let's make sure we engage in continuing education so we can understand the vision. Nobody can study for you. Be diligent in the Word and the ways of God and you will gain more understanding.

PRAYER

Father, in the name of Jesus, I don't want to be spiritually illiterate. Would You give me grace to continually educate myself in Your Word and ways so that I can gain knowledge that leads to understanding?

FEBRUARY 12

DON'T BELIEVE EVERY VISION

Your prophets have seen for you false and deceptive visions....
Lamentations 2:14

I wish I could tell you that everyone who shares a vision is sharing what the Holy Spirit showed them, but just as it was in Jeremiah's day so it is today.

Lamentations 2:14 warns us, "Your prophets have seen for you false and deceptive visions; they have not uncovered your iniquity, to bring back your captives, but have envisioned for you false prophecies and delusions."

Deceptive visions are visions conjured up in the mind of man to intentionally lead people astray. This is different from innocent daydreaming—even daydreaming that we mistake for a divine vision.

If you are part of the seer community, sooner or later you will run into compromised characters who operate in deceptive visions. Jesus warned us that false prophets would arise and "perform great signs and wonders to deceive, if possible, even the elect" (Matthew 24:24 NIV). This includes visions and dreams that look holy yet lead to error. We must discern by the Spirit, asking God to reveal the source of every vision and to guard our hearts against deception.

If you are not careful to discern the true and the false, you could fall prey, or even fall into the practice yourself. Indeed, we must beware of deceptive visions, visions that masquerade as divine but carry seeds of confusion and misdirection.

In this hour, as the Spirit of truth is moving, the enemy is also hard at work, sending false visions to derail God's people. Remember that "Satan himself masquerades as an angel of light" (2 Corinthians 11:14 NIV). Not every vision, no matter how captivating or spiritual it seems, is from God.

How do we guard ourselves? By testing every spirit, as 1 John 4:1 (NIV) instructs: "Do not believe every spirit, but test the spirits to see whether they are from God...." Take each vision to God in prayer, weigh it against His Word, and seek wise counsel. In these last days, staying rooted in truth is our defense. Be vigilant, for the enemy is seeking to deceive even those who love the truth. Stay close to the Lord, and you will not be led astray.

PRAYER

Father, in the name of Jesus, help me stay anchored in the truth of Your Word. Help me discern when others are sharing false visions, no matter how impressive they are. And help me to avoid this trap.

FEBRUARY 13

DEVELOPING SPIRITUAL SENSITIVITY

So it was, when Elijah heard it, that he wrapped his face in his mantle and went out and stood in the entrance of the cave. Suddenly a voice came to him, and said, "What are you doing here, Elijah?"

1 Kings 19:13

Accuracy in the seer ministry doesn't come from a gift alone. It comes from sensitivity to the Holy Spirit. You may have the gift to see in the spirit, but if you haven't developed spiritual sensitivity, you may not discern His leading. You may not receive consistent revelation. Or your interpretation or timing and delivery can be off.

You need to develop sensitivity to the Holy Spirit. Seer sensitivity is the ability to recognize, receive, and respond to the Holy Spirit with precision and purity. Seer sensitivity is the ability to perceive what the Spirit of God is saying, doing, and revealing. Seer sensitivity is being tuned in to the frequency of Heaven—where even the whispers of the Holy Spirit are caught and treasured.

Read 1 Kings 19:11-13 carefully to see a prime example of seer sensitivity:

> Then He said, "Go out, and stand on the mountain before the Lord." And behold, the Lord passed by, and a great and strong wind tore into the mountains and broke the rocks in pieces before the Lord, but the Lord was not in the wind; and after the wind an earthquake, but the Lord was not in the earthquake; and after the earthquake a fire, but the Lord was not in the fire; and after the fire a still small voice. So it was, when Elijah heard it, that he wrapped his face in his mantle and went out and stood in the entrance of the cave. Suddenly a voice came to him, and said, "What are you doing here, Elijah?"

Here are practical, biblical ways to increase your sensitivity to the Holy Spirit. First, spend time being still in His presence. James 4:8 says, "Draw near to God and He will draw near to you...." You have to make the first move. Seer sensitivity requires intimacy. The closer you walk with God, the clearer you will receive His communications. You can't microwave seer sensitivity. It is cultivated in the secret place.

Obey quickly. The more you respond to God's visual revelation—whether intercession, delivering a message, or taking some other action—the more you will hear it. Delayed obedience dulls seer sensitivity. Quick obedience keeps you sharp. Of course, praying in the spirit regularly is a key practice, as is meditating on the Word and fasting.

PRAYER

Father, in the name of Jesus, would You help me to cultivate greater sensitivity to the Holy Spirit who shows me things to come? Give me the grace to do my part so I don't miss Your part.

FEBRUARY 14

WALK IN LOVE

He who does not love does not know God, for God is love.

1 John 4:8

Seer, without love you are nothing. That may sound harsh, but I am not the one saying it. Paul the apostle made it clear in what we call the "Love Chapter" of the Bible. First Corinthians 13 reads:

> Though I speak with the tongues of men and of angels, but have not love, I have become sounding brass or a clanging cymbal. And though I have the gift of prophecy, and understand all mysteries and all knowledge, and though I have all faith, so that I could remove mountains, but have not love, I am nothing. And though I bestow all my goods to feed the poor, and though I give my body to be burned, but have not love, it profits me nothing.
>
> Love suffers long and is kind; love does not envy; love does not parade itself, is not puffed up; does not behave rudely, does not seek its own, is not provoked, thinks no evil; does not rejoice in iniquity, but rejoices in the truth; bears all things, believes all things, hopes all things, endures all things.
>
> Love never fails. But whether there are prophecies, they will fail; whether there are tongues, they will cease; whether there is knowledge, it will vanish away. For we know in part and we prophesy in part. But when that which is perfect has come, then that which is in part will be done away.
>
> When I was a child, I spoke as a child, I understood as a child, I thought as a child; but when I became a man, I put away childish things. For now we see in a mirror, dimly, but then face to face. Now I know in part, but then I shall know just as I also am known. And now abide faith, hope, love, these three; but the greatest of these is love.

Catch that. The greatest of these is love. Meditate on 1 Corinthians 13 daily and let it convict you where you are not measuring up. Let it renew your mind where you are thinking wrong about people. Let it transform you so that you can see through the eyes of love. Your spiritual sight will be more accurate for it. Take my "Love Challenge" at www.schoolofthespirit.tv.

PRAYER

Father, in the name of Jesus, help me to receive Your love so that I have something to give others. Help me to love people like You do. Help me to see people through the eyes of love.

FEBRUARY 15

UPGRADE YOUR SEER ANOINTING

Now to Him who is able to do exceedingly abundantly above all that we ask or think, according to the power that works in us.

Ephesians 3:20

When I fly, I don't book first-class tickets, but sometimes I am pleasantly surprised when I hand the gate agent my ticket and they announce, "You've been upgraded." Who doesn't like an upgrade?

Upgrade means increase, improve, boost, enhance, advance, raise, lift, make better, and move up. Just like God can upgrade your plane ticket, He can upgrade—increase, improve, boost, enhance, advance, raise, lift, make better and move up—the scope of your spiritual sight. And that's better than a first-class plane ride over the Atlantic!

The Lord spoke to me about seers and seeing people receiving dreams and visions with astoundingly accurate interpretations and applications and the proliferation of seer prophets and seeing believers all around the world. It's a rapid rise. Though some will shut down the gift over unbelief, many will see an upgrade. I heard the Lord say:

"I am upgrading the seers in this season. I have not only restored the office, I am restoring the seers who have been shunned and shamed because the body did not understand the gift. I am increasing the distance and widening the field of vision of seers and seeing people who will keep me in view.

"I am doing a thing in the earth among sold-out seers who put my kingdom ahead of personal fame and personal gain. I am making My seers more visible even as I increase what is visible to their spiritual eyes. I am bringing understanding where there has been misunderstanding and a new respect for a gift that has been disrespected.

"Many will be the seers who arise in the days ahead with a blend of accuracy and boldness. Many will be the seers who come out of the caves with restored confidence. Many will be the breakthroughs by the dreams and visions of My seers. I will show them things to come. Disasters will be averted. Tragedies will be avoided. I will do this as part of the new era of the Church. Seers, see!"

Ask the Holy Spirit to upgrade your seer anointing; but before you do, make sure you are walking faithfully in the anointing He has already given you.

PRAYER

Father, in the name of Jesus, help me to walk worthy of my seer calling. Help me exercise my gifts for Your purpose and Your glory. And when I am ready, give me an upgrade.

FEBRUARY 16

THE DANGER OF FALSE ANGELIC ENCOUNTERS

And no wonder! For Satan himself transforms himself into an angel of light.

2 Corinthians 11:14

Did you know entire religions have been birthed based on false angelic visitations? That's kind of scary, but it's true. Joseph Smith appears to have had a false angelic encounter that led to Mormonism. Christian cults have arisen from people's experiences with angels of light. With that, millions of people were led astray because they didn't test the encounter.

Yes, angels really do visit us with messages. An angel visited Zachariah to announce his wife, Elizabeth, would give birth to John the Baptist. An angel visited Mary to announce she would give birth to the Messiah. An angel visited Daniel to interpret his visions. An angel stopped Abraham from sacrificing Isaac. And the list goes on.

Yes, angels really do visit us with messages. But not all angels are sent from God. Angels are ministering spirits sent to minister to the heirs of salvation (Hebrews 1:14). But we know that satan disguises himself as an angel of light (2 Corinthians 11:14). Many people who claim to have seen angels haven't seen angels at all, and some who sincerely believe they have merely fell prey to a false encounter.

Although angels can visit, we have to fall back on the Bible to judge supernatural experiences. Second Timothy 3:16-17 tells us: "All Scripture is inspired by God and is profitable for teaching, for reproof, for correction, and for instruction in righteousness that the man of God may be complete, thoroughly equipped for every good work."

At the end of the day, we must maintain our focus on the God of the angels rather than the angels themselves. If we obsess over angelic visitations, we will find ourselves out of balance and open a door for the enemy to bring deception to our minds. I don't see anywhere in Scripture where people fervently seek out angelic visitations.

We cannot decide to have an angelic visitation any more than we can decide to have a spectacular vision. God may choose to send an angel to offer direction, but angels should not replace the leadership of the Holy Spirit in our lives. When we put more emphasis on angels than we do our Father, Son, and Holy Spirit, we're ripe for deadly error.

PRAYER

Father, in the name of Jesus, I am grateful for angelic messengers, but help me not to prioritize them over Your presence. I would rather hear You speak more than anyone else.

FEBRUARY 17

CALLING ALL POWER SEERS

For the kingdom of God is not in word but in power.
1 Corinthians 4:20

You've probably heard of "power evangelism." A power evangelist doesn't just preach the Kingdom; they demonstrate the Kingdom. Indeed, Holy Ghost power—power even lost souls cannot deny—is part and parcel of soul-winning campaigns in power evangelism. The signs and wonders that follow power evangelists confirm Jesus is alive.

In that sense, Paul was a power apostle. He wrote in 1 Thessalonians 1:5, "For our gospel did not come to you in word only, but also in power, and in the Holy Spirit and in much assurance, as you know what kind of men we were among you for your sake." He also noted in 1 Corinthians 4:20, "For the kingdom of God is not in word but in power."

But the Holy Ghost power is not relegated to modern evangelists or the apostles of old. God told me He is raising up power seers. I wrote about this in my book, *Power Seers*.

Power seers will see, hear, and say with the accuracy of original Old Testament seers such as Samuel. Holy Spirit boldness will toughen these seers, who will rise up and push back fear of man that tempts too many to keep silent about the prophetic visions He leads them to share. Power seers are not afraid to unflinchingly address sin in the church and call for repentance while praying for mercy.

Power seers will not only walk in signs, they will also become walking, talking signs that prophesy what they see and demonstrate their dreams and visions in prophetic acts that turn the hearts of people back to the Father. Some will be parabolic prophets, such as Ezekiel, who at times will see great visions and at times sacrifice their own dignity to communicate what the Holy Spirit is saying to the Church (Ezekiel 4).

Power seers will speak to kings and those in authority by the greater authority of Jesus Christ. Leaders with a pure heart such as King David will receive God's manifold wisdom through uncompromising power seers. Those with an evil heart such as King Jeroboam will reject the word of the Lord through the mouths of seer prophets.

PRAYER

Father, in the name of Jesus, fill me to overflowing with Your Holy Spirit power so I can be bold, walk in signs and wonders, and speak to those in authority about what I see.

FEBRUARY 18

THE SKILL EVERY SEER NEEDS

...My lord, may the dream concern those who hate you, and its interpretation concern your enemies!

Daniel 4:19

Every seer should develop skills in diplomacy. How people receive your ministry could depend on it. *Diplomacy* "helps us communicate prophetic revelation with tact, without offending the hearers or sparking hostility. Sometimes that's not possible as some will be offended by God's Word," according to *The Seer's Dictionary*.

Being a diplomatic seer means being tactful, rather than insensitive, in the way you communicate your visual revelation. *Tact* is "a keen sense of what to do or say in order to maintain good relations with others or avoid offense."

While your visual revelation can certainly offend people—the truth can be offensive at times—we want to avoid being hurtful or offensive in the way we deliver a message because we lack diplomacy.

Remember, we are ambassadors for Christ, according to 2 Corinthians 5:20. An ambassador is an official envoy, an authorized representative or messenger. How you deliver what you see in the spirit or an encounter can make all the difference in whether or not someone receives it.

If you have to deliver a corrective revelation, for example, it should be released only after much prayer and even grieving or weeping. Delivering words of warning must also be done with diplomacy to avoid perceptions of judgment on a person, as if they are in some way to blame, etc.

Diplomacy in the seer dimensions begins with the way we listen to God. In order to express God's heart in a matter, we need to hear His heart, not just His voice. If we miss God's heart, we can miscommunicate His will and lead people astray or cause them to shut their ears to the message.

When we listen well, we will share responsibly. If we listen to God through the lens of our bias, we will speak with prejudice. If we listen to God through the filter of bitterness, we will speak with judgement. If we listen to God through the ears of grace and mercy, we will speak the bold truth in love.

Ask the Holy Spirit to teach you diplomacy. That doesn't mean watering down or sugar-coating the word. It means prophesying the truth in love.

PRAYER

Father, in the name of Jesus, help me listen to Your heart not just Your words. Teach me to speak with tact not just boldness. Show me how to navigate sensitive matters with Your wisdom.

FEBRUARY 19

WHEN BLIND SPOTS HIJACK INTERPRETATION

Who can understand his errors? Cleanse me from secret faults.
Psalm 19:12

When I was in high school, students were offered a driver's education program. There was classroom instruction but also a car rigged with a brake in the passenger seat so the instructor could hit the brakes if we froze at the wheel.

One of the biggest lessons I remember from the driver's education program was to be aware of the blind spots. A blind spot is any area that you can't see through the front windshield or through the rearview or side mirrors.

You can't see directly in front of the bumper or directly behind the back bumper. You can't see behind the posts between the windshield and the side windows. Cars and pedestrians aren't visible. Blind spots can lead to accidents.

Just like in a car, our natural vision has blind spots. In this instance, a blind spot is a small circular area at the back of the retina where the optic nerve enters the eyeball. No light gets in so that area is darkened. A blind spot is also an area where someone fails to exercise judgment or discretion.

This translates to our seer gift. Be honest. Do you have blind spots? The problem is, you probably wouldn't know if you did. Here's the danger: a blind spot prevents you from seeing accurately and can cause accidents.

For a seer, any time the light doesn't get in—God's light showing us His plans or revealing the enemy's work—we are at a disadvantage. We have a blind spot. We can't see all, or sometimes any, of what God wants us to see. That means we can't share God's will and we can't see the enemy attack brewing.

Are you starting to see the problem here? Blind spots cause accidents. Blind spots cause poor decision making. Blind spots cause us to see partly, as our vision is obstructed by our preference.

What's your blind spot? We all have things that cause us not to see everything accurately all the time. It could be unrecognized sin, faults, or other areas of disobedience. Let's carry the heart posture of David in Psalm 139:23-24, "Search me, O God, and know my heart; try me, and know my anxieties; and see if there is any wicked way in me, and lead me in the way everlasting."

PRAYER

Father, in the name of Jesus, search me. Show me my blind spots. Try me, and see if there is any wicked way in me, and lead me in the way everlasting.

FEBRUARY 20

TELL IT LIKE IT IS

Do not add to His words, lest He rebuke you, and you be found a liar.
Proverbs 30:6

One reason why it's so important to write down what you see in the spirit is so you can report it accurately—without accidentally adding to or taking away from anything the Holy Spirit showed you. On the other hand, some people have a tendency to embellish or exaggerate a visual revelation, whether knowingly or unknowingly. This can be dangerous for the seer.

Jesus said in Revelation 22:18-19 (AMPC):

> I [personally solemnly] warn everyone who listens to the statements of the prophecy [the predictions and the consolations and admonitions pertaining to them] in this book: If anyone shall add anything to them, God will add and lay upon him the plagues (the afflictions and the calamities) that are recorded and described in this book. And if anyone cancels or takes away from the statements of the book of this prophecy [these predictions relating to Christ's kingdom and its speedy triumph, together with the consolations and admonitions or warnings pertaining to them], God will cancel and take away from him his share in the tree of life and in the city of holiness (purity and hallowedness), which are described and promised in this book.

Now, I am in no way saying God is going to lay plagues on you or take away your share in the tree of life. Your salvation does not depend on your seer accuracy, or your seer exaggerations. That said, if you want God to trust you with more revelation, you should walk in the fear of the Lord. You should not add to or take away from what He showed you, unless He tells you to seal part of the encounter.

It's not just the visual revelation, either. It's the instructions in the visual revelation that we need to carry out accurately. In Deuteronomy 12:32, the Lord tells the Israelites, "Whatever I command you, be careful to observe it; you shall not add to it nor take away from it."

If God gives you a calling, an assignment or an instruction during a visual encounter, don't assume you know what He meant. Be clear on His expectations. And don't delay obeying. Delayed obedience is disobedience.

PRAYER

Father, in the name of Jesus, would You help me never to add to what I saw or take away from what I saw? Anybody can get carried away and overstate or hold back things that might bring persecution. Help me never to do that.

FEBRUARY 21

WAS THAT A DREAM OR A VISION?

Then the secret was revealed to Daniel in a night vision. So Daniel blessed the God of heaven.

Daniel 2:19

In the seer dimensions you find dreams, visions, and night visions. What is a vision of the night? It's an important distinction and you need clarity because there is some debate over this in the Body of Christ.

People wonder: Is a dream a vision of the night? Is a night vision a vision you have in the evening hours? Is a night vision something you see when you are in between waking and sleeping states? Is one more symbolic and the other more literal? What is the difference? What does the Bible say?

First, let's look at some Scripture references. Genesis 46:1-3 reads:

> So Israel took his journey with all that he had, and came to Beersheba, and offered sacrifices to the God of his father Isaac. Then God spoke to Israel in the visions of the night, and said, "Jacob, Jacob!" And he said, "Here I am." So He said, "I am God, the God of your father; do not fear to go down to Egypt, for I will make of you a great nation there."

God used the Hebrew word *marah* to describe Jacob's night visions in Genesis. The word means "vision; a mode of revelation." Jacobs's visions of the night in Genesis were not dreams. *Gill's Exposition of the Entire Bible* suggests, "And God spake unto Israel in the visions of the night... He appeared to Jacob as he lay upon his bed in the night season, and with an articulate voice spoke to him...."

Many people lay on their bed without sleeping. If this was a dream, the word *marah,* which means vision, would not have been employed in this verse. The Holy Spirit speaks expressly (1 Timothy 4:1).

Benson Commentary explains, "Visions differed from dreams herein, that God imparted his mind to men in dreams when asleep, but in visions when they were awake. And these visions were sometimes communicated by day, but most frequently by night, whence we read of visions of the night, as Genesis 46:2; Job 20:8; and Job 33:15."

Scripture is clear on the matter, and it's important that you are too so that you can be accurate in recounting your encounters.

PRAYER

Father, in the name of Jesus, thank You for teaching me the difference between these experiences. Would You help me to speak expressly about the types of encounters I have so people have the right context?

FEBRUARY 22

GOD WILL EXPOSE FALSE SIGHT

Thus says the Lord God: "Woe to the foolish prophets, who follow their own spirit and have seen nothing!"

Ezekiel 13:3

We must all be careful not to enter into the seer dimensions without an invitation from the Holy Spirit. In our social media age of likes and clicks—which may drive popularity, conference invites and book deals—some people strive and compete for the latest and greatest visual revelation.

That is dangerous. Let me repeat. That is dangerous. But don't take my word for it. Consider the prophetic words Micah released in Micah 3:6-7 (NLT):

> This is what the Lord says: "You false prophets are leading my people astray! You promise peace for those who give you food, but you declare war on those who refuse to feed you. Now the night will close around you, cutting off all your visions. Darkness will cover you, putting an end to your predictions. The sun will set for you prophets, and your day will come to an end. Then you seers will be put to shame, and you fortune-tellers will be disgraced. And you will cover your faces because there is no answer from God."

Notice how God lumps false seers and prophets in with fortune tellers. Why? The reason is chillingly simple. God speaks of false prophets in the same breath as fortune tellers because they are tapping into the same spirit. They are operating out of a familiar spirit, a spirit of divination, or perhaps some other spirit.

God wants to open your eyes and show you things to come, but it's up to Him to do that. Forcing your way into the seer dimensions leads you into witchcraft and other false spirits that may leave you in bondage. We are coming into a time when the exposure of false seers is going to be public and painful, and yet some will continue following them.

The other side of this is the false seers who oppose you. Some want to compete with your true revelations by releasing false revelations that seem more spectacular. Pray mercy for them, and leave them in God's hands. Don't try to compete with a false seer. You win by staying in God's lane.

PRAYER

Father, in the name of Jesus, help me to wait for Your invitation into the seer dimensions. Likewise, help me never to value the worth of what You showed me based on the popularity—or persecution—it brings.

FEBRUARY 23

WALKING IN YOUR SEER IDENTITY

For we are His workmanship, created in Christ Jesus for good works, which God prepared beforehand that we should walk in them.

Ephesians 2:10

Your identity is in Christ. One pitfall in any ministry—from serving to seeing and beyond—is finding identity in the gift instead of the gift Giver. Our identity should be rooted and grounded in Christ, not in a gift. That said, secondary to your identity in Christ, many will identify you as a seer when you consistently and accurately express your gift.

Identity in this context is a distinguishing character or personality of an individual. It's the unique attributes of a seer's wiring, uniqueness, distinctiveness, and existence. Not all seers are alike, but there are common traits that come along with the gift.

Samuel was a seer, and everyone knew it. Samuel had quite the reputation in the prophetic as one who hears and one who sees. First Samuel 3:19-20 tells us, "So Samuel grew, and the Lord was with him and let none of his words fall to the ground. And all Israel from Dan to Beersheba knew that Samuel had been established as a prophet of the Lord."

Samuel was an ambidextrous prophet: one who could hear as well as he could see and see as well as he heard. First Samuel 9:17-19 reads, "So when Samuel saw Saul, the Lord said to him, 'There he is, the man of whom I spoke to you. This one shall reign over My people.' Then Saul drew near to Samuel in the gate, and said, 'Please tell me, where is the seer's house?' Samuel answered Saul and said, 'I am the seer....'"

Samuel embraced his God-given identity and calling as a seer. He boldly confessed, *"I am the seer."* The flip side of this coin is that he didn't go around announcing to everyone he was a seer. He didn't have a plaque made up in front of his house announcing, "The seer lives here." Humility doesn't make such announcements, but false humility may deny the reality of a gift and calling that is part of our unique identity in Christ.

PRAYER

Father, in the name of Jesus, help me to embrace my identity as a seer without flaunting it. Help me not to try to make a name for myself with the gift You gave me, but to use it to serve as You will.

FEBRUARY 24

PRAYER THAT OPENS YOUR SEER EYES

I will meditate on Your precepts, and contemplate Your ways.
Psalm 119:15

Contemplative prayer is a prayer that opens the eyes of your heart. But what is contemplative prayer and how do you engage at this level?

Well, if you ask ten people what contemplative prayer is, you may get ten different answers. There's no one standard definition. Let's start by understanding the word *contemplative,* which is related to contemplation. *Contemplation* is a concentration on spiritual things as a form of private devotion or a state of mystical awareness of God's being. It's an act of considering with attention, of regarding steadily, with intention and expectation.

Contemplative prayer is an ancient Christian practice that dates all the way back to the early Church and even to the life of King David. The Psalms give proof of David's contemplative prayer life. Contemplative prayer releases the Holy Spirit's supernatural activity in our spirits as we encounter His heart. We enter into enjoyable communion with God that transforms us.

(I write more about this in my book *The Seer Dimensions*, and teach on it in the School of the Seers at schoolofthespirit.tv.)

Contemplative prayer is a thoughtful practice where you focus on the Word of God to the point where you drown out other thoughts, feelings, and temporal distractions. You are focusing on the Father, Son, and Holy Spirit within you rather than the Father, Son, and Holy Spirit outside you. God's voice becomes more clear through this practice.

In contemplative prayer, we behold God's glory and we are transformed into His image (2 Corinthians 3:18). In Psalm 27:4, David said he just wanted one thing: to behold God's beauty. Beholding God's beauty is the same as beholding His glory. Contemplative prayer releases the Holy Spirit's supernatural activity in our spirits as we encounter His heart. We enter into enjoyable communion with God that transforms us.

John of the Cross, a 16th century monk wrote: "For contemplation is nothing else than a secret and peaceful and loving inflow of God, which, if not hampered, fires the soul in the spirit of love."

Get quiet now. Contemplate the Savior. Contemplate the Word. Don't rush it. Watch where it takes you.

PRAYER

Father, in the name of Jesus, I am fascinated by this ancient practice of contemplative prayer. Remind me to make this part of my spiritual practice so I can come to know You and Your Word at a deeper level.

FEBRUARY 25

WHOSE SEER ARE YOU?

Now when David arose in the morning, the word of the Lord came to the prophet Gad, David's seer, saying....

2 Samuel 24:11

I'll always remember when a young woman approached me after I spoke at a conference and boldly announced, "I am your seer." I was taken aback by that statement. I didn't know her from Eve. I certainly did not bear witness to the fact that she was a seer, much less a seer God had assigned to me. Though her motives may have been sincere, she was sincerely wrong.

That said, God does assign some seers to specific people. I have people in my life today that I do consider my seers—or seers God has set in my life to share prophetic intelligence at key moments in my life. This is biblical.

Remember, Gad was David's seer. We see this designation in 2 Samuel 24:11-12, "Now when David arose in the morning, the word of the Lord came to the prophet Gad, David's seer, saying 'Go and tell David, "Thus says the Lord: 'I offer you three things; choose one of them for yourself, that I may do it to you.'"'"

We also see the concept of a seer being assigned to a person in 1 Chronicles 25:5, "All these were the sons of Heman the king's seer in the words of God, to exalt his horn. For God gave Heman fourteen sons and three daughters."

And again in 2 Chronicles 35:15, "And the singers, the sons of Asaph, were in their places, according to the command of David, Asaph, Heman, and Jeduthun the king's seer. Also the gatekeepers were at each gate; they did not have to leave their position, because their brethren the Levites prepared portions for them."

Has God assigned you to be someone's seer? If so, remember that the person God has assigned you to serve with your seer gifting may or may not receive you. If they do receive you, then you will have a direct line in with that person. If they don't receive you—or if you have no way to contact this person—you can still be effective as a seer for that ministry through prayer. But make sure it was really God assigning you!

PRAYER

Father, in the name of Jesus, I am open to serving as someone's seer, if that is Your will. I see how Gad served David and the value of the seer anointing to edify, comfort, exhort, and warn people.

FEBRUARY 26

WHAT IT MEANS TO BE SOMEONE'S SEER

Formerly in Israel, when a man went to inquire of God, he spoke thus: "Come, let us go to the seer"; for he who is now called a prophet was formerly called a seer.

1 Samuel 9:9

Gad was David's seer. You might wonder what it means to be someone's seer. That's a good and right question. I've done an entire teaching on this in my School of the Seers, but let me give you some thoughts to consider.

Being someone's seer means that you have a responsibility in the spirit to watch and pray over their lives. Jesus commands us to *"watch and pray"* in Scripture (Matthew 26:41). What are you watching for? Many things, such as divine opportunities that are just ahead or enemy attacks that are lurking in the shadows. You want to see what God wants to do and how the enemy wants to stop it. Jesus tells us in the same verse, *"so that you will not fall into temptation."*

What if David fell into temptation with Bathsheba because his seer was not watching and praying? I doubt that's the case, but you understand my point. Leaders need seers in their lives because we all have blind spots. David's eyes were blinded by lust—the lust of the eyes, the lust of the flesh, and the pride of life (1 John 2:16). And the enemy brought great harm to his life. His baby died.

Seers should watch over the one they are assigned to so that they can pray more effectively. It's one of the watchman-type functions of a seer. As someone's seer, then, you may fill in the blind spots and stand in the gap for the leader or a friend so they don't get blindsided by the enemy. You may also warn the leader of impending danger from the enemy, from people, or from their wrong thinking.

In some cases, God will assign you to watch and pray for someone you don't know. Therefore you have no way to warn them. That's when you trust the Holy Spirit that if He shows you something and you pray, He will intervene. Of course, what you see is not always dire. You may also see blessings coming and you can get in agreement with God's plan.

PRAYER

Father, in the name of Jesus, thank You for making me aware of this seer function. Would You prepare me to serve as someone's seer, whether a leader, a friend, or seven someone I don't know?

FEBRUARY 27

HOW TO KNOW IF YOU'RE ASSIGNED AS SOMEONE'S SEER

Finally, all of you be of one mind, having compassion for one another; love as brothers, be tenderhearted, be courteous.

1 Peter 3:8

Have you been assigned as someone's seer? How would you know? After all, just because you see something for someone—have a vision or dream concerning them—doesn't mean that they are your permanent assignment.

I've done an entire teaching on this at School of the Spirit (www.schoolofthespirit.tv), but here are some things to consider. If you are assigned to someone, you will feel a responsibility to watch in the spirit for them. But it goes beyond that.

If you are someone's seer, you will have a Holy Spirit burden to pray for them whether or not you are seeing anything in the spirit or dreaming dreams about their life. In other words, the burden remains in good times and bad. It's a commitment to that person's well-being and success in Christ.

Now let's take this a step further. It's often through the intercession for the one to whom you are assigned that you tap into the seer revelation—dreams and visions—for and about the person you are covering. We can't force God's hand for seer revelation. It's up to Him what He shows us about a person. But we can pray without ceasing. In doing so, we show God that we take the assignment seriously and He will give us the insights we need to be more effective in our assignment.

You can also discern the call to be someone's seer if you have divine love for someone, even though you don't know them. The Holy Spirit pours His love in our hearts for them (Romans 5:4-5). You will feel compelled to watch for them. You will have an urgency in your spirit regarding their well-being. You will go to war for them.

If you are someone's seer, you will respect them but also have a spiritual compassion for them. Even if you never have any contact with them, they will keep coming up in your spirit and God will show you things about their life—what He is doing and what the enemy is doing. The bottom line with being someone's seer is intercession. The seer revelation should spur you to pray.

PRAYER

Father, in the name of Jesus, I am willing to serve as someone's seer, but I want to be accurate in the spirit. I don't want to take on a burden You didn't give me. Would You make it clear to me if someone is my assignment?

FEBRUARY 28

THE SINGING SEER

He has put a new song in my mouth—praise to our God; many will see it and fear, and will trust in the Lord.

Psalm 40:3

There are many different seer expressions and singing is one of them. Some prophets, for example, release their gift solely through song. Seers, too, can sing what they see. This is often called the "song of the Lord."

James Goll is a prime example. I have heard him spontaneously sing based on what he has heard and seen. This is one way to release seer revelation into an atmosphere—and it's a powerful expression.

Paul the apostle wrote these interesting words: "...I will pray with the spirit, and I will also pray with the understanding. I will sing with the spirit, and I will also sing with the understanding" (1 Corinthians 14:15). I believe praying in the Spirit can open our spiritual eyes and, if we will yield to the Holy Spirit, we can sing in the spirit. Psalm 40:3 speaks of singing "a new song."

In Revelation 5:8-13, the four living creatures are singing what they see:

> Now when He had taken the scroll, the four living creatures and the twenty-four elders fell down before the Lamb, each having a harp, and golden bowls full of incense, which are the prayers of the saints. And they sang a new song, saying: "You are worthy to take the scroll, and to open its seals; for You were slain, and have redeemed us to God by Your blood out of every tribe and tongue and people and nation, and have made us kings and priests to our God; and we shall reign on the earth." Then I looked, and I heard the voice of many angels around the throne, the living creatures, and the elders; and the number of them was ten thousand times ten thousand, and thousands of thousands, saying with a loud voice: "Worthy is the Lamb who was slain to receive power and riches and wisdom, and strength and honor and glory and blessing!" ...I heard saying: "Blessing and honor and glory and power be to Him who sits on the throne, and to the Lamb, forever and ever!"

It doesn't matter if you don't think you can sing, sometimes God will lead us to sing what we see and it will carry an anointing. It's one way we can tell of His wondrous works.

PRAYER

Father, in the name of Jesus, would You give me songs and hymns and spiritual songs based on what You show me in the Spirit? I don't want to overreach, but I will lift up my voice if You lead me to.

FEBRUARY 29

REFUSING TO COMPROMISE

He who finds his life will lose it, and he who loses his life for My sake will find it.

Matthew 10:39

It seems false prophets and seers in Scripture always had something good to say. They prophesied victory when the Lord was not guaranteeing victory and, in doing so, led people astray.

Consider Ahab's yes men. First Kings 22:6-7 tells us, "Then the king of Israel gathered the prophets together, about four hundred men, and said to them, 'Shall I go against Ramoth Gilead to fight, or shall I refrain?' So they said, 'Go up, for the Lord will deliver it into the hand of the king.' And Jehoshaphat said, 'Is there not still a prophet of the Lord here, that we may inquire of Him?'"

Thank God Jehoshaphat had some discernment! When Ahab called in Michaiah, he reported prophetically about a great defeat, and wound up in prison for his truth-telling.

Throughout Scripture, true seers saw it as it was and were willing to tell it like it is, even if it got them into trouble. We see this reality play out in 2 Chronicles 16:6-10 (NIV):

> Then King Asa brought all the men of Judah, and they carried away from Ramah the stones and timber Baasha had been using. With them he built up Geba and Mizpah. At that time Hanani the seer came to Asa king of Judah and said to him: "Because you relied on the king of Aram and not on the Lord your God, the army of the king of Aram has escaped from your hand. Were not the Cushites and Libyans a mighty army with great numbers of chariots and horsemen? Yet when you relied on the Lord, he delivered them into your hand. For the eyes of the Lord range throughout the earth to strengthen those whose hearts are fully committed to him. You have done a foolish thing, and from now on you will be at war." Asa was angry with the seer because of this; he was so enraged that he put him in prison....

Would you be willing to go to prison for faithfully reporting what you saw in the spirit? Until you get to the point that you love not your life even to the death, you will only go so far and so high and so deep in the seer dimensions. If you want God to trust you with mysteries and revelation, you need to trust Him as you release it.

PRAYER

Father, in the name of Jesus, would You give me courage to report the bad news as well as the good news. Please, grace me with boldness to share what I am seeing without compromise.

MARCH

...I saw the Lord sitting on a throne, high and lifted up, and the train of His robe filled the temple.

Isaiah 6:1 NKJV

MARCH 1

IS YOUR HEAD IN THE CLOUDS?

Then I looked, and behold, a whirlwind was coming out of the north, a great cloud with raging fire engulfing itself; and brightness was all around it and radiating out of its midst like the color of amber, out of the midst of the fire.

Ezekiel 1:4

I was ministering in Nicaragua the first time I saw a "glory cloud." I was a new believer and had never even heard there was such a thing as a glory cloud. What I saw was like a wall of mist that seemed thick, yet translucent. Of course, I didn't fully comprehend what I was seeing. My pastor had to explain it to me later.

We see what we call the glory cloud is one of the first visual manifestations of God's glory in the Bible. Exodus 13:21 (MEV) recounts, "The Lord went before them by day in a pillar of cloud to lead them along the way, and by night in a pillar of fire, to give them light, that they might travel by day and by night."

And in Exodus 16:10: "Now it came to pass, as Aaron spoke to the whole congregation of the children of Israel, that they looked toward the wilderness, and behold, the glory of the Lord appeared in the cloud."

The Bible doesn't stop there. Exodus 24:16 shares, "Now the glory of the Lord rested on Mount Sinai, and the cloud covered it six days. And on the seventh day He called to Moses out of the midst of the cloud."

And Exodus 40:34-35 reads: "Then the cloud covered the tabernacle of meeting, and the glory of the Lord filled the tabernacle. And Moses was not able to enter the tabernacle of meeting, because the cloud rested above it, and the glory of the Lord filled the tabernacle."

Those are just a few of many Scriptures we can point to. While it's true that some people claim glory clouds and orbs do not exist, glory clouds are real and you can see them with your spiritual eyes—and sometimes with your natural eyes when God allows.

That said, I have discovered that not everyone can see the glory clouds I see, which tells me there are times when I am seeing the clouds in the spirit before evidence of His glory manifests in the natural dimension. Maybe you can too.

PRAYER

Father, in the name of Jesus, help me to recognize Your glory in the spirit realm so I can stand in intercession, agreeing with what You want to do in an atmosphere. Help me partner with Your glory.

MARCH 2

EYES ON THE END

Now as He sat on the Mount of Olives, the disciples came to Him privately, saying, "Tell us, when will these things be? And what will be the sign of Your coming, and of the end of the age?"

Matthew 24:3

You don't have to be an end-times seer to see into the end times. Yes, there are some seers who carry an end-times assignment, but God can use you anyway He sees fit if you will yield to Him.

Because of the times we live in, I believe God is opening the eyes of more and more seers to end-times events, including apocalyptic dreams and visions. The curious seers will ask God to show them things to come in the end times.

Joel 2:28-32 tells us: "And it shall come to pass afterward that I will pour out My Spirit on all flesh; Your sons and your daughters shall prophesy, your old men shall dream dreams, your young men shall see visions. And also on My menservants and on My maidservants I will pour out My Spirit in those days. And I will show wonders in the heavens and in the earth: blood and fire and pillars of smoke. The sun shall be turned into darkness, and the moon into blood, before the coming of the great and awesome day of the Lord. And it shall come to pass that whoever calls on the name of the Lord shall be saved...."

Daniel had a vision of the end times. Daniel 12:5-8 (NIV) reads: "Then I, Daniel, looked, and there before me stood two others, one on this bank of the river and one on the opposite bank. One of them said to the man clothed in linen, who was above the waters of the river, 'How long will it be before these astonishing things are fulfilled?' The man clothed in linen, who was above the waters of the river, lifted his right hand and his left hand toward heaven, and I heard him swear by him who lives forever, saying, 'It will be for a time, times and half a time. When the power of the holy people has been finally broken, all these things will be completed.'"

Be a student of end-times Scriptures so that when God gives you these dreams and visions they will not be foreign or scary to you.

PRAYER

Father, in the name of Jesus, I know we are getting closer by the day to Your return and You want to warn Your people of what is ahead. Would You show me end-times visual revelation that prepares Your Bride?

MARCH 3

WHAT EVERY SEER NEEDS TO LEARN FROM EZEKIEL

So the Spirit lifted me up and took me away, and I went in bitterness, in the heat of my spirit; but the hand of the Lord was strong upon me.
Ezekiel 3:14

Ezekiel had some breathtaking visions from God and of God. The types of visions Ezekiel experienced are not an everyday occurrence in the believer's life, but God can choose to open your seer eyes to see divine visions. Ezekiel 8:2-4 offers an incredible account of one of Ezekiel's visions of God.

> Then I looked, and there was a likeness, like the appearance of fire—from the appearance of His waist and downward, fire; and from His waist and upward, like the appearance of brightness, like the color of amber. He stretched out the form of a hand, and took me by a lock of my hair; and the Spirit lifted me up between earth and heaven, and brought me in visions of God to Jerusalem, to the door of the north gate of the inner court, where the seat of the image of jealousy was, which provokes to jealousy. And behold, the glory of the God of Israel was there, like the vision that I saw in the plain.

Through this and other significant visions Ezekiel recorded we can learn plenty. First, God can reveal Himself in difficult seasons and circumstances. Remember, Ezekiel was among the first wave of exiles taken into Babylonian captivity and Judah was wallowing in idolatry.

Second, your commissioning can come in a vision. Ezekiel's stunning vision of God in the first chapter was followed by a commissioning into the prophetic ministry in the second chapter. Third, visions contain a warning that you must proclaim or a call to stand in intercession. Think of Ezekiel 3 and Ezekiel 33 when God called Ezekiel as a watchman to warn Israel. Fourth, visions can contain promises that bring hope in trying times.

What am I saying? Visions are not an end all. It's the message in the vision that matters. The details of the vision can paint a picture that captures people's attention, but ultimately the assignment doesn't end with the vision. Rather, the vision is where the assignment begins.

PRAYER

Father, in the name of Jesus, when You give me visual revelation, would You help me not get so caught up in what I saw that I fail to discern the assignment You are giving me? Help me take the next step.

MARCH 4

WHO DID YOU SHARE THAT DREAM WITH?

But the natural man does not receive the things of the Spirit of God, for they are foolishness to him; nor can he know them, because they are spiritually discerned.

1 Corinthians 2:14

Jesus issued a command in the Sermon on the Mount that applies to every seer: "Do not give what is holy to the dogs; nor cast your pearls before swine, lest they trample them under their feet, and turn and tear you in pieces" (Matthew 7:6).

Your visual revelation, which came from the throne room, is holy. It's like a string of precious pearls. God has shared with you treasures of revelation, insight, and direction through your dreams, visions, and encounters in the seer dimensions. You need to treat them as such.

That means being careful who you share them with. Sharing your pearls with the wrong people can bring massive backlash. People can proverbially turn and tear you to pieces.

Some people turn and persecute you because they don't agree with your revelation. Others will turn and accuse your good name because they are outright offended with what you shared. Still others will turn and criticize or judge you because they are jealous that you walk in such revelation.

Ask Joseph. When he shared his dreams with his brothers, they were jealous and offended. In Genesis 37:5 we read, "Now Joseph had a dream, and he told it to his brothers; and they hated him even more." He should have known better to share the dream with his already-jealous brothers who clearly hated him. He had a gift, but he lacked the wisdom to steward it well. He ended up in a pit and sold as a slave.

You may be excited about your visual revelation, but that doesn't mean anyone else will be. Some may act like swine and trample your precious pearls under their feet. You need to proceed with caution in sharing your pearls, discerning who will be spiritually minded enough to understand. Sharing dreams too soon or with the wrong person can lead to spiritual warfare.

PRAYER

Father, in the name of Jesus, help me to be quick to see but slow to speak. Help me discern who will receive my visual revelation and who will be jealous or offended. Help me share rightly.

MARCH 5

PRAY (AND SEE) IN THE SPIRIT

But you, beloved, building yourselves up on your most holy faith, praying in the Holy Spirit.

Jude 20

Just as I believe God is speaking more than we're hearing (or listening), I also believe the Holy Spirit is trying to show us things to come—or show us what the Father is doing or what the enemy has planned—more than we're seeing. I'm sure you would agree that there is a lot more to see!

Praying in tongues can activate our seer eyes to see what He wants us to see in the spirit. Just like all believers can prophesy according to the will of God, all believers can see in the spirit when God chooses to open their eyes. Seeing is part of the gift of prophecy. It's just another dimension of the prophetic gift mix.

Any believer can manifest any of the gifts of the Spirit anytime God sees fit (1 Corinthians 12:11). The Holy Spirit's nine gifts are to bless people, whether saved or lost. We cannot choose to work a miracle, but we can believe in faith to walk in the miracle realm. We cannot choose to interpret tongues, but we can yield to the Holy Spirit if He chooses to give us an interpretation.

Much the same, we cannot legally force the spirit realm open and take a peek, but we can ask the Lord to open our eyes to show us what He wants us to see and walk with a sensitivity that makes us more aware of what He wants to show us. Praying in tongues opens the eyes of our heart—our spiritual eyes—in conjunction with Paul's prayer in Ephesians 1:18 (NIV): "I pray that the eyes of your heart may be enlightened in order that you may know the hope to which he has called you, the riches of his glorious inheritance in his holy people."

Praying in tongues invites the Holy Spirit to flood your spiritual eyes with the light—opening them to seer dimensions you haven't experienced before. Ask the Holy Spirit to open and activate your seer eyes, then pray in tongues consistently with this in mind and watch what happens! Check out my book, *Tongues of Fire*, for more benefits for seers who pray in the Spirit.

PRAYER

Father, in the name of Jesus, help me remember to pray in the Spirit as much as possible. Would You open my eyes to the diverse benefits of praying in tongues?

MARCH 6

THE ART OF SURRENDER

For it is God who works in you both to will and to do for His good pleasure.

Philippians 2:13

I'll always remember my time in Noah's ark. It was one of the most miserable seasons of my life. I entered Noah's ark after a 40-day spiritual flood swept away everything I had—my home, my car, my job, my dog, my savings.

Of course, I wasn't literally on Noah's ark. I'm not that old! I'm actually talking about Ozark, Alabama. When my daughter was three years old, she thought Ozark was called "Noah's Ark." I didn't realize until 13 years later the prophetic implications of that cute misunderstanding.

God sent me to the backside of the desert, to Noah's ark, Alabama, to start a new life. In fact, I was so miserable that I used to walk down the street to the street drain, sit down and bawl right in the middle of the neighborhood—then get up and walk back home and cry some more. I wasn't sure if I was shipwrecked or floating in a great flood of trial and tribulation.

I hated just about every minute of my time in Noah's Ark. After 13 months passed, my daughter was five years old and it was time to enroll her in elementary school. I dreaded the day because I knew it meant putting down roots in this dreaded place.

I prayed. I cried. I worried and wondered. Finally, I surrendered. I said something like this to God, "Okay, fine. If You want me to stay here in stinky, smelly Noah's Ark for the rest of my life, I'll do it. You win. I give up."

Would you believe it wasn't a week later when I received a call from an aviation magazine in South Florida with a job offer to serve as editor? It was one of my best freelance clients, and the current editor was leaving for a new position. When I surrendered to His will, God provided a way of escape.

Looking back, I am thankful for Noah's ark. That's where I learned to walk with Him and Him alone. I learned to pray. I learned to worship. I learned to study the Bible. I did quite a lot of dying to self. God reprogrammed my life in Noah's ark.

PRAYER

Father, in the name of Jesus, would You give me the grace to surrender to Your will. Help me to not complain about my circumstances, but rather to see the future and hope you have planned for me when I surrender.

MARCH 7

WHAT DO YOU SEE?

And the Lord said to me, "Amos, what do you see?" And I said, "A plumb line...."

Amos 7:8

What do you see? If you read through Scripture you will discover that the Lord asks this question of His seers time and time again. Know this: when God asks you what you see, He's trying to show you something—but He may highlight something in the natural realm before He teaches you a spiritual lesson.

Ultimately when God asks you what you see, He is pulling on that seer aspect of the prophetic gift. He did this with the young prophet Jeremiah at the time of his calling: "Moreover the word of the Lord came to me, saying, 'Jeremiah, what do you see?' And I said, 'I see a branch of an almond tree'" (Jeremiah 1:11). And again, "The word of the Lord came to me the second time, saying, 'What do you see?' And I said, 'I see a boiling pot, and it is facing away from the north'" (Jeremiah 1:13).

But this wasn't the only time God related to Jeremiah this way. In Jeremiah 24:3 (MEV) we read, "Then the Lord said to me, 'What do you see, Jeremiah?' And I said, 'Figs, the good figs, very good. And the rotten, very rotten, that are so rotten they cannot be eaten.'" And Jeremiah wasn't the only prophet to whom God posed this question.

In Amos 7:8 (KJV), we read, "And the Lord said unto me, Amos, what seest thou? And I said, A plumbline. then said the Lord, Behold, I will set a plumbline in the midst of my people Israel: I will not again pass by them any more." You can read other examples in Amos 8:2, Zechariah 4:2, and Zechariah 5:2.

When God asks you what you see, He may be activating your eyes to a new level. You may see something in the spirit you've never seen before. He may also ask you what you see to confirm that you are seeing accurately. He may ask you what you see as a conversation starter or to train your discernment or even to connect what you are seeing with a word of warning or instruction.

What do you see?

PRAYER

Father, in the name of Jesus, I'm intrigued with how You dealt with your prophets in Scripture with such a simple question. Help me to recognize the significance of this question, should You ever ask it of me.

MARCH 8

ARE YOU LISTENING?

He who has ears, let him hear!

Matthew 11:15

When I was a journalist I interviewed people for hours a day. I had to be a good listener. As a seer, you should also learn to listen. Some seers focus more on seeing than hearing, but that's a mistake.

What if Daniel hadn't listened intently to Gabriel as he explained that the prince of Persia was resisting his prayer answers for 21 days. What if John the Revelator hadn't listened to the elders and the angels who spoke to him? We would be missing key revelations that we treasure today.

Consider this. Proverbs 20:12 tells us, "The hearing ear and the seeing eye, the Lord has made them both." If you aren't careful how you listen, you can miss key revelations in the seer dimensions. See, it's not just about seeing. You need to listen for sounds, voices, and listen especially carefully to people you encounter in the spirit, from Jesus to angels to elders.

James 1:19 (AMP) tells us, "...Let everyone be quick to hear [be a careful, thoughtful listener], slow to speak [a speaker of carefully chosen words]...." We can't be quick to listen if we are distracted.

Jesus said in Revelation 3:20 (AMPC), "Behold, I stand at the door and knock; if anyone hears and listens to and heeds My voice and opens the door, I will come in to him and will eat with him, and he [will eat] with Me." Wouldn't you hate to miss a house call from Jesus?

Practice active listening. Active listening helps you focus fully on not just words but nonverbal cues, such as expressions on someone's face. If you see Jesus, for example, you will want to take note of the expression on His face.

Jesus said in Luke 8:18 (AMPC), "Be careful therefore how you listen. For to him who has [spiritual knowledge] will more be given; and from him who does not have [spiritual knowledge], even what he thinks and guesses and supposes that he has will be taken away."

PRAYER

Father, in the name of Jesus, would You help me be an active listener in the spirit? Sometimes, I'm so focused on what I'm seeing that I may not pay close attention to what I'm hearing. Make me ambidextrous in the spirit.

MARCH 9

RULES OF ENGAGEMENT

Let all things be done decently and in order.

1 Corinthians 14:40

Because most churches don't embrace prophetic giftings, many seers coming up the ranks don't have a flesh-and-blood teacher. They are reading books and depending on the Holy Spirit. They are doing the best they can in the school of hard knocks. The unfortunate result is that many lack understanding of vital seer protocols that serve as guardrails for their ministry.

Seer protocols are a set of wisdom-inspired guidelines for operating in the seer anointing that assure one's ministry is safe and effective, according to *The Seer's Dictionary*. A protocol is a code prescribing strict adherence to correct etiquette and precedence, according to *Merriam-Webster*'s *Dictionary*. A protocol outlines the correct way something should be done.

Seer protocols are established by the Word and Spirit of God. Sure, some denominations may have established rigid and even ridiculous protocols for seer ministry that have given protocols a bad name. But the Bible does give us clear guidelines for operating in prophetic ministry and there is wisdom gained from experience.

Yes, there is a right way to operate in seer ministry. The right way blesses the Body of Christ through edification, exhortation, comfort, and at times direction and correction. Yes, there's more than one right way to operate in seer ministry, but there is a "right way." Again, we're not talking about man-made rules and regulations, rather Scriptures and Spirit-inspired wisdom gained through experience.

Of course, there is also a wrong way to operate in seer ministry. The wrong way brings harm to the Body of Christ through presumption, false operations, ill-timed release, and the like. Indeed, there's more than one wrong way to operate in seer ministry, but there is a "wrong way."

Most people who operate the "wrong way" do so innocently, because they haven't been exposed to the right way. No one has trained them. They haven't seen anybody else do it. They don't have a solid mentor. Thankfully, that can easily be corrected by understanding guidelines in my book *Prophetic Protocols & Ethics*.

PRAYER

Father, in the name of Jesus, would You teach me how to follow Your biblical guidelines for sharing what I receive in the seer dimensions? Give me practical wisdom so that I don't operate the wrong way.

MARCH 10

THE SEER'S HOLY PURSUIT

But earnestly desire the best gifts....

1 Corinthians 12:31

Joel released an intense prophecy in the book that bears his name: "And it shall come to pass afterward that I will pour out My Spirit on all flesh; your sons and your daughters shall prophesy, your old men shall dream dreams, your young men shall see visions. And also on My menservants and on My maidservants I will pour out My Spirit in those days" (Joel 2:28-29).

When you meditate on that prophecy, does it stir a zeal in your heart to receive a fresh outpouring of His Spirit? Does it awaken a hunger to receive the divine dreams and visions? Does it spark a desire to pursue what He wants to show you in the seer dimensions? It should.

Paul said we should pursue love and earnestly desire spiritual gifts, especially that you may prophesy (1 Corinthians 14:1). Seers should desire to see in the spirit what God shows us. Seers should actively seek His face, knowing that He will reward us with visual revelation. It's about a heart posture that wants to receive everything He wants to pour out.

That word for *desire* is the Greek word *zeloo,* which means to "burn with zeal." You should pursue God for the manifestation of spiritual gifts, especially prophecy, in your life. While you can't force His hand—that would be witchcraft—you can position yourself to see. You can desire to see. You can expect to see.

While some people are endued with a special gift to see in the spirit without much pursuit, Ezekiel, Daniel, Zechariah, John the Revelator, and others in the Bible saw into the spirit realm without pursuing the gift. Most seeing people need to demonstrate a desire and press into the Lord through prayer to see what He is doing.

But consider these words I wrote in *The Seer Dimensions*, "God has not shut off the seer realm to you. You don't have to be a seer to see—and even seers can't decide to see. All believers are at God's behest when it comes to seeing in the spirit. Your part is to desire spiritual gifts and cultivate a sensitivity in your heart and a faith in your spirit to move in this gift for His glory."

PRAYER

Father, in the name of Jesus, I desire spiritual gifts, especially that I might see in the spirit. Help me continually cultivate that hunger and expectation as I seek Your heart and the visual revelation You want to pour out.

MARCH 11

LESSONS FROM THE SEERS

All Scripture is given by inspiration of God, and is profitable for doctrine, for reproof, for correction, for instruction in righteousness, that the man of God may be complete, thoroughly equipped for every good work.

2 Timothy 3:16-17

I love to read biographies. Biographies, particularly autobiographies, help me understand how people made difficult decisions, responded to crises, and navigated their assignments. I can learn from the mistakes and failures of people who left a legacy. Biographies broaden my worldview and give me new perspectives.

Corrie ten Boom's *The Hiding Place* opened my eyes to sacrificial suffering. Brother Andrew's *God's Smuggler* teaches a lesson in trusting God behind the Iron Curtain. Hudson Taylor's *Spiritual Secret* gave me insights into pioneering.

Many people will tell you that if you want to aspire to greatness, study great people. If you want a role model, read a biography.

The same could be said for the seer dimensions. Samuel was the first one we see in Scripture who was called a seer, but there are others. Zechariah, Ezekiel, and even John the Revelator, who wasn't a seer but who had an epic vision on the Isle of Patmos. Let's not forget Gad, David's seer.

Their stories, or at least part of their ministry storyline, is in Scripture. You can study the visions and dreams they received, observe how they handled the revelation and responded to God, and ask God to show you similar things. You can glean from the successes and failures, as well as their strengths and weaknesses.

Studying the seers in Scripture promotes self-discovery. You may find you have some of the same traits or the same giftings or the same challenges. Studying the seers in Scripture gives you a mentor at a distance. You get a glimpse into their mind. Studying the seers in Scripture allows you to gain a different perspective as well as wisdom and understanding.

Studying the seers in Scripture gives us a glimpse of their anointing in action, and at times their fears and struggles. Studying the seers in Scripture also builds your faith for your own experiences. Faith comes by hearing and hearing by the Word of God (Romans 10:17).

PRAYER

Father, in the name of Jesus, would You give me a spiritual curiosity to study the seers in Scripture? There is so much to learn from their dreams, visions, challenges, and success. Teach me through Your Word.

MARCH 12

STRATEGIC DREAMERS

Through wisdom is a house built; and by understanding it is established; by knowledge the rooms are filled with all precious and pleasant riches.

Proverbs 24:3-4

When I need a prayer strategy, I seek the Lord in prayer. I acknowledge Him as the Master Strategist. And I have faith that He will give me the right strategy at the right time. Sometimes the strategy is delivered by the word of the Lord coming unto me saying. Other times by a dream, vision, or supernatural encounter.

This is a biblical approach. Remember when Jacob needed a strategy? After working for his uncle Laban for 14 years as a dowry for his two daughters, Jacob had no true wealth of his own. Laban was a dishonest man who built his riches on Jacob's back and changed his wages ten times (Genesis 31:7). As Jacob described it:

> If he said thus: "The speckled shall be your wages," then all the flocks bore speckled. And if he said thus: "The streaked shall be your wages," then all the flocks bore streaked. So God has taken away the livestock of your father and given them to me. And it happened, at the time when the flocks conceived, that I lifted my eyes and saw in a dream, and behold, the rams which leaped upon the flocks were streaked, speckled, and gray-spotted. Then the Angel of God spoke to me in a dream, saying, "Jacob." And I said, "Here I am.'" And He said, "Lift your eyes now and see, all the rams which leap on the flocks are streaked, speckled, and gray-spotted; for I have seen all that Laban is doing to you. I am the God of Bethel, where you anointed the pillar and where you made a vow to Me. Now arise, get out of this land, and return to the land of your family" (Genesis 31:8-13).

God gave Jacob a dream that brought justice into this life through a divine strategy. Pay attention to your dreams. God could give you a strategy for your health, your finances, your family, your business, or your ministry.

PRAYER

Father, in the name of Jesus, help me remember to lean on You and not on my own understanding when I need a strategy. And help me to remember the strategies You share with me while I lay on my bed.

MARCH 13

EXPECT YOUR SEER UPGRADE

I am the vine, you are the branches. He who abides in Me, and I in him, bears much fruit; for without Me you can do nothing.

John 15:5

If you are pressing in to God and walking in holiness, you can and should expect seer upgrades at strategic points in your walk with the Holy Spirit.

We aren't pursuing a seer upgrade. We are pursuing the Holy Spirit. The seer upgrade is often the reward of our pursuit of Him, His Word, His ways, and His character. Expect a seer upgrade because your expectation shall not be cut off (Proverbs 23:18).

Consider Amos. He was in the field tending sheep when God called Him to be a prophet who has significant visions. Amos certainly did not see the upgrade coming, but he chronicled the unexpected upgrade for our benefit: "But the Lord took me from tending the flock, and said to me, 'Go, prophesy to my people Israel'" (Amos 7:15 NIV).

What about Jeremiah? He was just a youth who loved the Lord when God encountered Him and upgraded him unexpectedly: "Now the word of the Lord came to me, saying, 'Before I formed you in the womb I knew you; and before you were born I sanctified you, and I ordained you a prophet to the nations.' Then I said, 'Ah, Lord God! Truly, I cannot speak, for I am a youth'" (Jeremiah 1:4-6 MEV). After Jeremiah accepted this calling, God asked him, "What do you see, Jeremiah?" (Jeremiah 1:11 NIV).

Remember Elisha? After Elijah defeated the false prophets at Mount Carmel, Jezebel threatened him and he ran, hid himself in a cave and slept. When he arose, God told him to anoint Elisha to be prophet in his place. Let's read 1 Kings 19:19-20 (MEV): "So he departed from there and found Elisha the son of Shaphat, who was plowing with twelve yoke of oxen before him and he with the twelfth, and Elijah passed by him and threw his cloak on him. He left the oxen and ran after Elijah and said, 'Please let me kiss my father and mother, and then I will follow you....'"

You probably know the story. Elisha served Elijah and got a double portion anointing. He even saw into the bedroom of an enemy king and heard every word spoken (2 Kings 6:12). Expect a visual upgrade!

PRAYER

Father, in the name of Jesus, You are my only good. I want to grow in my seer gift. Would You give me grace to do my part? Help me be diligent in pursuit of Your heart and study of Your Word and ways.

MARCH 14

THE MISUNDERSTOOD SEER

For he supposed that his brethren would have understood that God would deliver them by his hand, but they did not understand.

Acts 7:25

Isaiah was one of the most misunderstood seers in Scripture. Think about it. Part of his God-given assignment was to:

> Go and tell this people, Hear and hear continually, but understand not; and see and see continually, but do not apprehend with your mind. Make the heart of this people fat; and make their ears heavy and shut their eyes, lest they see with their eyes and hear with their ears and understand with their hearts and turn again and be healed (Isaiah 6:9-10 AMPC).

Put another way, they did not understand him. They could not understand him. His messages were misunderstood. Likewise, Moses' motives in killing an Egyptian were misunderstood (Exodus 2:14). And then there's Jesus. He was perhaps the most misunderstood Seer in Scripture.

Think about it. The Israelites were expecting a Messiah who would lead a natural army. Most people didn't understand who Jesus really was or His mission. Even those closest to Him—His family and His friends—did not understand Him. His family thought He was off His rocker (Mark 3:20-21). Before the Cross, He was an embarrassment to His brethren. He was even accused of being demon-possessed (Matthew 12:22-30).

Likewise, you will be misunderstood. You need to accept that reality right now. You need to become an expert at dealing with being misunderstood without developing what I call the "misunderstood syndrome." The misunderstood syndrome taps into self.

It's our "self" that needs to feel understood. It's our "self" that feels rejected. It's our "self" that feels lonely. It's our "self" that gets depressed and wants to have a pity party. We need to get our minds off ourselves and onto God. It's amazing how the burdens lift when you get your mind off yourself.

Ultimately, when people misunderstand us, they are not trying to hurt us, so we shouldn't get angry, resentful, bitter, or unforgiving about it. Maybe they just can't understand because they haven't been in that place. Your assignment is to speak the truth anyway.

PRAYER

Father, in the name of Jesus, I thank You that You understand me. I will not let my life be ruled by feelings. I declare that I am free from the misunderstood syndrome.

MARCH 15

WIRED TO SEE

And He Himself gave some to be apostles, some prophets, some evangelists, and some pastors and teachers, for the equipping of the saints for the work of ministry, for the edifying of the body of Christ.
Ephesians 4:11-12

Some people take exception with the notion of being equipped, taught or trained to see. They say, "You can't make someone a seer." That is absolutely true. Only God can make the seer, nevertheless, even the seer needs to be trained. And all believers have the ability to see in the spirit.

I am a native English speaker. I have the mental ability to learn to speak Spanish, French, or any other language in the world. I know people who speak several languages. But they didn't learn it by impartation alone. They had to study the language. They had to learn the dialects. They purchased courses or bought books to teach them. They were equipped.

In the same way, we need to learn the ins and outs of seeing accurately from a biblical perspective. Without proper training, seers and everyday believers alike may never understand that they have this ability; or worse, they may fall into error because they were not taught what the Word says about the dreams, visions, and encounters. The enemy thrives on our ignorance.

God can equip us Himself through the Word, of course. Paul wrote, "All Scripture is breathed out by God and profitable for teaching, for reproof, for correction, and for training in righteousness, that the man of God may be complete, equipped for every good work" (2 Timothy 3:16-17).

For the seer or seeing person, every good work includes seeing accurately, discerning what you are seeing, interpreting what you are seeing and applying what you are seeing, including praying through what you are seeing. God created seers to do specific works and the Word helps guide us.

But God can also send people to equip us—people who have the experience that we don't have. We can fast-track our growth by sitting under anointed seers and hearing how they practically navigated issues. Jesus said when we are fully trained we can be like our teacher (Luke 6:40). (Be careful who is teaching you!)

Teachers can correct us and show us what to do next time. In fact, that's part of the reason God gave prophets to the Church—to equip people to see and hear. (Check out my School of the Seers at www.schoolofthespirit.tv.)

PRAYER

Father, in the name of Jesus, I thank You that the Holy Spirit can teach me all things. Your Word also instructs me, as well as servants You have ordained. Help me to be equipped for the good work of seeing.

MARCH 16

SEEING WHAT GOD IS SAYING

Blessed is the man who listens to me, watching daily at my gates, waiting at the posts of my doors.

Proverbs 8:34

Habakkuk was a savvy seer. You might say he was savvy in the spirit. By that, I mean he demonstrated perception and comprehension of the ways of God. He had practical know-how from experience in the seer dimensions. He understood what to do with what he saw.

In the second chapter and first verse of the book that bears his name, Habakkuk wrote these wise words: "I will stand at my watch and station myself on the watchtower; and I will keep watch to see what He will say to me, and what I will answer when I am reproved" (Habakkuk 2:1 MEV). The prophet was watching to "see" what God would "say."

How do you see what God would say? First, you have to keep watch. *Watch* in this verse is the Hebrew word *tsaphah*, which means to look out or about, spy, keep watch, and observe. If you want to be a savvy seer, you need to be actively watching. Don't wait for God to randomly show you what He wants to say. Spend time in prayer. Get up on your watchtower and wait on the Lord.

The word *see* in that same verse comes from the Hebrew word *ra'ah*. It means to see, look at, inspect, perceive, consider, have vision, regard, look after, learn about, look upon, look out, find out, give attention to, discern, and gaze at. That's deep! Hosea was not giving what God was showing him a quick glimpse. No, Hosea was waiting on the Lord with anticipation that God would show him what He wanted him to see and what it meant.

This is the heart posture of a savvy seer. Position yourself to see, then look at, inspect, perceive, consider, have vision, regard, look after, learn about, look upon, look out, find out, give attention to, discern, and gaze at what God shows you until you have full understanding of the message.

PRAYER

Father, in the name of Jesus, I want to be a savvy seer. I want to see what You would say to me. Give me grace to stand with a heart posture that watches and waits, no matter how long, to see what You say.

MARCH 17

WHEN PEOPLE ASK YOU TO SEE FOR THEM

Formerly in Israel, when a man went to inquire of God, he spoke thus: "Come, let us go to the seer"; for he who is now called a prophet was formerly called a seer.

1 Samuel 9:9

When people know you are a seer, some will come to you asking you what you see about their lives, their finances, their callings and so on. That's not altogether wrong, but it can be a slippery slope for all involved.

We don't want people to lean on our gift. We want to equip them and point them back to Jesus. After all, part of the Ephesians 4:11 mandate for the prophet, which includes seers, is to equip believers for the work of the ministry.

The seer should stir a hunger in the hearts of believers to press in to see what the Holy Spirit wants to show them. If we become someone's go-to seer every time they are stuck, we are in danger of taking the Holy Spirit's role in their lives. And that grieves the Holy Spirit.

That said, it's not at all wrong for you to share what you see with someone, especially in the context of a relationship. At times, people are hurting, busy, or distracted and they miss what the Holy Spirit wants to show them.

When people seek a vision from you, it may be because they've tried to hear the Lord and cannot or they don't trust what they are seeing because they are going through a trial. Sometimes they are simply seeking confirmation. Other times they can't see because they are in disobedience, like when Saul could not hear the Lord.

Ezekiel 7:25-27 reads:

> Destruction comes; they will seek peace, but there shall be none. Disaster will come upon disaster, and rumor will be upon rumor. Then they will seek a vision from a prophet; but the law will perish from the priest, and counsel from the elders. The king will mourn, the prince will be clothed with desolation, and the hands of the common people will tremble. I will do to them according to their way, and according to what they deserve I will judge them; then they shall know that I am the Lord.

Be open to sharing what the Holy Spirit shows you. But be careful not to get in the middle of what God is doing with someone's life by pressing to exercise your gift. Always point to Jesus.

PRAYER

Father, in the name of Jesus, help me be so sensitive to Your Spirit that I know when to show someone what I am seeing and I know when I just need to keep quiet and pray that they will see it.

MARCH 18

ARE YOU FULLY AWAKE?

...when they were fully awake, they saw His glory and the two men who stood with Him.

Luke 9:32

We can be awake and not be fully awake. Maybe you can relate to this in the natural realm. The alarm goes off in the morning, waking you from a deep sleep (hopefully not a divine dream) and your eyes open. You are technically awake, but you are not fully alert. You may stumble into the shower or toward the coffeepot, depending on your habit.

In the same way, you can be awake but not fully awake to the spirit realm. If your affections are misplaced—if you are more interested in what's on television than what's on God's heart—you are not fully awake. If you are walking in justified sin, God loves you but you are not fully awake. If you have wrong teaching about the seer dimensions, again, you may not be fully awake. There are many things that keep you less than fully awake.

We see the concept of being fully awake from a natural perspective in Luke 9:28-32. But we can also infer something important from these passages in the spiritual realm. Listen in:

> Now it came to pass, about eight days after these sayings, that He took Peter, John, and James and went up on the mountain to pray. As He prayed, the appearance of His face was altered, and His robe became white and glistening. And behold, two men talked with Him, who were Moses and Elijah, who appeared in glory and spoke of His decease which He was about to accomplish at Jerusalem. But Peter and those with him were heavy with sleep; and when they were fully awake, they saw His glory and the two men who stood with Him.

Notice that when the disciples were fully awake, they saw the transfigured Christ, as well as Moses and Elijah. What a sight! When you are fully awake to the seer dimensions, you will naturally see more.

Jesus said in Matthew 24:42 (AMPC), "Watch therefore [give strict attention, be cautious and active], for you do not know in what kind of a day [whether a near or remote one] your Lord is coming." By the same token, watch, for you don't know at what moment the Lord will invite you into the seer dimensions.

PRAYER

Father, in the name of Jesus, help me reach the state of awareness called fully awake. Help me not to walk around half awake, failing to recognize what You want me to see because I'm not alert to Your heart.

MARCH 19

SEEING SOMEONE'S HURTS AND WOUNDS

> *"For I will restore health to you and heal you of your wounds," says the Lord, "because they called you an outcast saying: 'This is Zion; no one seeks her.'"*
>
> Jeremiah 30:17

It's not difficult to see when someone is bitter. Just listen to their words that come out of their mouth. But emotional pain can also be visible.

God can allow you to see someone's wounded heart. He can allow you to see the parts of their soul—the mind, will, emotions, imaginations, reasoning, and intellect—that are damaged because of the suffering they have endured at the hand of people or the enemy.

The seer's path forward in those cases is clear: minister to the person. You don't need to call out their pain or describe the pain you see. In most cases, they know their pain. If they don't, calling out their pain may make them feel embarrassed and they may get defensive and reject your seer gift.

Jesus said God sent Him to heal the brokenhearted (Luke 4:18). And Ezekiel 36:26 tells us, "I will give you a new heart and put a new spirit within you; I will take the heart of stone out of your flesh and give you a heart of flesh." The psalmist said He binds up our wounds (Psalm 147:3).

It's impossible to live on this earth without getting hurt and wounded along the way. Sometimes the wounding happens at the hand of the enemy, but usually people cause our pain—even if the enemy is working through those people. God doesn't want us to walk around like wounded soldiers, unable to fight back against the next attack. He wants to heal our hearts.

Consider what Psalm 34:18 says, "The Lord is near to those who have a broken heart, and saves such as have a contrite spirit." And John 8:32 tells us, "And you shall know the truth, and the truth shall make you free." The reality is, people cannot begin to heal until they forgive. And they need to know the truth that sets them free.

Perhaps it's a word of life. Perhaps it's the comfort of the Holy Spirit through you. Perhaps it's speaking the opposite of the lie they are believing. Always use your seer gift to heal, not harm.

PRAYER

Father, in the name of Jesus, if I can help someone in pain, please show me their suffering. Show me the hurts and wounds in someone's heart and show me the healing strategy.

MARCH 20

SEER VERSUS PROPHET?

Then Jesus said to them, "Truly, truly I say to you, the Son can do nothing of Himself, but what He sees the Father do. For whatever He does, likewise the Son does."

John 5:19 MEV

As mentioned previously, all seers are prophets but not all prophets are seers. You don't have to be a prophet to prophesy and you don't have to be a seer to see. A seer is one who sees, but not occasionally. A seer will have consistent dreams, visions, or other revelatory encounters. A traditional prophet is one who hears. Of course a seer can hear and a prophet can see. But what's the predominant thrust?

You might ask, why does it matter what the difference is if it's just two different types of prophets? Well, when you go to the hospital there are many kinds of doctors. They are all trained in practicing medicine but they specialize in different areas. Some are cardiovascular specialists. Some are ear, nose and throat specialists. Some are orthopedic specialists.

In the writing world, there are journalists, screenwriters, ad copy writers, speech writers, book writers, poetry writers, short story writers. Prophets and seers are two streams of the prophetic anointing but they specialize in different aspects of the anointing. Even within the realm of prophet and seer there are many different distinctions and types of prophetic flows.

Prophets may hear the Lord. Seers may actually see the Lord. Prophets may prophesy an angel is standing in the corner. Seers may see the angel.

Prophets may prophesy they hear the word *prosperity* over someone's life. Seers may see the word. Prophets may hear the Lord tell them a spirit of fear is attacking someone. Seers may see the spirit of fear.

Prophets may hear about future events from the Lord. Seers may see into the future. Prophets can easily communicate what the Lord is saying by repeating it. Seers have to rely on human language to describe what they have seen as best they can. Prophets often have a "now" word. Seers may see something to be revealed at a much later time.

The language of prophets and seers is different. Prophets will use the verbiage, "I heard the Lord say." Seers will relate that "I see" or "The Lord showed me." We need to be accurate in the spirit. Can you see it?

PRAYER

Father, in the name of Jesus, thank You for helping me distinguish between prophets and seers. Would You help me to teach others to understand the difference so they can better receive from Your heart?

MARCH 21

WHAT KIND OF SEER ARE YOU?

But you have an anointing from the Holy One, and you know all things.

1 John 2:20

You can't put a seer in a box. What do I mean by that? Not all seers are the same. There are many different seer anointings and each one has a purpose in God's Kingdom. When you understand your seer anointing, you will be a better steward of the gift of God within you.

Some seers are primarily dreamers. Most of their visual revelation comes while they are sound asleep. Others have the gift of interpreting dreams, like Daniel or Joseph. They can understand what others don't. Still others operate primarily through visions. They see pictures or even have open visions, like John the Revelator.

Some seers activate their seer anointing in intercession. As they pray through a burden from the Lord, they receive visual revelation and prophetic intelligence that helps them stand in the gap more effectively. Some seers have an Issachar anointing that gives them strategic insight into times, seasons, and strategies. Still others see far, far into the future.

Some seers are more interactive with angels than others, like Daniel and Zechariah. Others have encounters in the ecstatic realm, such as out-of-body experiences, traveling in the spirit, or visiting the throne room. Still others have a gift to discern spiritual atmospheres or an anointing to stand as a watchman over cities and nations.

Of course, there are also scribing seers. While every seer should scribe what they see, some have a gift to articulate and teach visual revelation applications in a way that makes it practical. Then there are worshipping seers like the prophet Asaph in 1 Chronicles 25:1. Worshipping seers release the sound of Heaven that can break through hard heavens and shift spiritual atmospheres.

Finally, though this is not an exhaustive list, there are seers whose visual revelation comes through symbols and metaphors or parabolic prophecy. Remember Jeremiah, who saw an almond branch (Jeremiah 1:11). This seer anointing demands strong interpretation and this type of seer is often the most rejected.

Of course, you can operate in any aspect of the seer anointing as the Holy Spirit wills, but usually you will have a predominant flow. Once you see it, steward it well.

PRAYER

Father, in the name of Jesus, would You reveal my specific strengths in the realm of spiritual sight? Help me discern how You've gifted me, specifically, so I can lean into it and not press into something I shouldn't.

MARCH 22

WHEN YOU SEE THE ABOMINATION

And from the time that the daily sacrifice is taken away, and the abomination of desolation is set up, there shall be one thousand two hundred and ninety days.

Daniel 12:11

As we go deeper into the end times, God is going to deal with abominations in the body with a stronger hand. An abomination is something detestable in God's eyes. The word *abomination* is mentioned 144 times in Scripture. Many of these references have to do with things God hates.

Proverbs 6:16-19 (NIV) lists seven things which are also abominations: "haughty eyes, a lying tongue, hands that shed innocent blood, a heart that devises wicked schemes, feet that are quick to rush into evil, a false witness who pours out lies and a person who stirs up conflict in the community."

God may show you visions or you may have dreams of abominations. Ezekiel 8-11 reveals the visions of abominations the prophet had in his day. Here's a sample from Ezekiel 8:7-13:

> So He brought me to the door of the court; and when I looked, there was a hole in the wall. Then He said to me, "Son of man, dig into the wall"; and when I dug into the wall, there was a door. And He said to me, "Go in, and see the wicked abominations which they are doing there." So I went in and saw, and there—every sort of creeping thing, abominable beasts, and all the idols of the house of Israel, portrayed all around on the walls. And there stood before them seventy men of the elders of the house of Israel, and in their midst stood Jaazaniah the son of Shaphan. Each man had a censer in his hand, and a thick cloud of incense went up. Then He said to me, "Son of man, have you seen what the elders of the house of Israel do in the dark, every man in the room of his idols? For they say, 'The Lord does not see us, the Lord has forsaken the land.'" And He said to me, "Turn again, and you will see greater abominations that they are doing."

I believe in these last days, we will see greater abominations than even Ezekiel did. When you see an abomination, it can be hard on the eyes. Why does God show us abominations? Often for two overarching reasons: to warn of judgment for sin and to pray. He wants mercy over judgment and someone has to stand in the gap and blow the trumpet.

PRAYER

Father, in the name of Jesus, if You show me abominations, help me not to react in my soul but to respond by Your Spirit. Give me words to sound the alarm, when needed, and to pray for Your mercy to abound.

MARCH 23

SHARPENING YOUR VISUAL ACCURACY

The Lord said to me, "You have seen correctly...."

Jeremiah 1:12 NIV

Seers should seek pinpoint accuracy in the spirit. As defined in *The Seer's Dictionary*, being accurate in the spirit means freedom from error or influences that would breed error.

Accuracy in the spirit is a state in which we are careful to weigh what we see in the spirit realm against the Word of God, the ways of God and the witness of the Spirit of God. It means to be precise in describing or explaining what we see and hear before sharing prophetic insight.

In other words, it's more than just being accurate in what you see. It's filtering through your dreams and visions to sift out any potential mixture in what you saw, being careful that it does not contradict what God is doing or saying. It's being sure you have the right interpretation before sharing what you saw.

When you have an accurate seer lens, you see things through the eyes of the Spirit instead of your own eyes. When you have an accurate seer lens, you gain wisdom and understanding when it comes to applying what you see in the spirit.

When you have an accurate seer lens, you see beyond the surface level and obtain deeper revelation concerning your dreams, visions, and other encounters in the seer dimensions. In other words, you are spiritually minded instead of carnally minded. You have your sights set on things above and not on the things of this earth.

So how do you develop seer accuracy? I teach on this topic in-depth in my School of the Seers, but accuracy always starts with the Word of God. You need a sure foundation of the Word.

Studying the Word causes growth and maturity. Studying the Word sanctifies our perspective. Jesus prays in John 17:17, "Sanctify them by Your truth. Your word is truth." Studying the Word corrects our perspective and brings righteousness to our perspective.

Remember 2 Timothy 3:16-17 (NIV), "All Scripture is God-breathed and is useful for teaching, rebuking, correcting and training in righteousness, so that the servant of God may be thoroughly equipped for every good work."

PRAYER

Father, in the name of Jesus, I want to be 100 percent accurate in the seer dimensions. Would You help me as I seek to sharpen my seer accuracy so I can better represent You?

MARCH 24

CHARACTER OVER ANOINTING

In all things showing yourself to be a pattern of good works; in doctrine showing integrity, reverence, incorruptibility, sound speech that cannot be condemned, that one who is an opponent may be ashamed, having nothing evil to say of you.

Titus 2:7-8

I always say, "I don't want my anointing to take me where my character can't keep." You might say it this way, "Character over gifts." I didn't make up that saying, but I live by it.

Some believe that just because they can see in the spirit, God doesn't mind their angry outbursts at home. Or because they have angelic encounters, God is giving them a pass on that drinking problem, sexual sin, or whatever else is hidden behind closed doors. No, we don't have to be perfect to see an accurate vision. We don't have to have a flawless character to have divine dreams.

But we need to stop confusing gifts and callings with maturity and character. God can use a stubborn mule to prophesy, and he can use a stubborn believer to see in the spirit. That doesn't mean God endorses stubbornness, which is like the sin of idolatry (1 Samuel 15:23). It just means that God needed a vessel to deliver visual revelation to a person who desperately needed to hear it.

Good character doesn't earn you spiritual gifts and anointings, and poor character doesn't remove them, at least not overnight. The Holy Spirit distributes the nine spiritual gifts—word of wisdom, word of knowledge, gift of faith, gifts of healings, working of miracles, prophecy, discerning of spirits, different kinds of tongues, and interpretation of tongues—to people as He wills (1 Corinthians 12:4-11). It doesn't have anything to do with our will, nor does it validate our character.

If God called you into seer ministry, He isn't going to revoke that call or the gifts that go with it the first time (or even necessarily the 10th or 20th time) you act out or sin. Ultimately, we are the ones who turn our backs on our ministry when we repeatedly disobey God, like Saul did. God is so slow to anger and abounding in mercy (Numbers 14:18) that it may seem like we're getting away with our poor behavior and behind-the-scenes sin. God is just giving us space to repent.

PRAYER

Father, in the name of Jesus, would You help me to focus on building strong character as much, if not more, than I work on developing my seer gifts? I want to be holy even as You are holy.

MARCH 25

CARRYING APOCALYPTIC REVELATION

So the first went and poured out his bowl upon the earth, and a foul and loathsome sore came upon the men who had the mark of the beast and those who worshiped his image.

Revelation 16:2

As we go deeper into the end times, the more God is opening up apocalyptic visions to seers and seeing people. As explained in *The Seer's Dictionary*, apocalyptic visions typically reveal acts in the end times. Daniel and John the Revelator both had apocalyptic visions.

Apocalyptic means, "of, relating to, or resembling an apocalypse; apocalyptic events; forecasting the ultimate destiny of the world: prophetic apocalyptic warnings; foreboding imminent disaster or final doom: terrible; apocalyptic signs of the coming end-times; wildly unrestrained: grandiose; ultimately decisive: climactic," according to *Merriam-Webster's Dictionary.*

There is only one apocalyptic dream in the Bible and it was actually a dream and a vision (Daniel 7). What does that tell you? God's primary way of releasing apocalyptic revelation has not historically been through dreams, but through visions or the spoken word. Therefore, we must be especially careful to test apocalyptic dreams, especially when we're in the middle of a world crisis.

Like prophecy, apocalyptic dreams and visions can come from any one of three sources: you, the enemy, or God. Therefore, it's critical that we judge the source of apocalyptic revelation before releasing it publicly.

First Corinthians 14:29 tells us, "Let two or three prophets speak, and let the others judge." This also applies to dreams and visions, especially apocalyptic dreams and visions that could breed fear in the hearts of people.

Gill's Exposition of the Entire Bible comments, "The other prophets that sit and hear, and all such as have a spirit of discerning, whether what the prophets say comes from their own spirits, or from a lying spirit, from the spirit of antichrist, or whether from the Spirit of God."

While everyone should judge what they hear, when you are dealing in deep seer dimensions such as apocalyptic dreams and visions, wisdom dictates allowing other prophets and seers to be part of the testing of the seer revelation.

PRAYER

Father, in the name of Jesus, I know You are already pouring out apocalyptic dream and visions. Help me not to be rash in sharing these revelations, but to use great wisdom in navigating these truths.

MARCH 26

DISCERNING SECOND-HEAVEN REVELATION

Beloved, do not believe every spirit, but test the spirits, whether they are of God; because many false prophets have gone out into the world.
1 John 4:1

In the seer dimensions, we must be cautious of reporting second-heaven revelation. According to *The Seer's Dictionary*, the second heaven is satan's domain; a sphere above the earth's atmosphere but below Heaven, where God's throne sits.

Common sense informs us if there is a third heaven, there must be a second heaven and a first heaven. The concept of the second heaven is found in Revelation 8:13 (AMPC): "Then I [looked and I] saw a solitary eagle flying in midheaven, and as it flew I heard it crying with a loud voice, Woe, woe, woe to those who dwell on the earth, because of the rest of the trumpet blasts which the three angels are about to sound!"

We see supernatural activity in the midheaven, or second heaven, with other references found in Revelation 14:6 and Revelation 19:17. Spiritual conflicts take place in the second heaven. When the Prince of Persia withstood the angel seeking to deliver Daniel's prayer answers, this skirmish took place in the midheaven. Much of the spiritual warfare with which we are familiar is taking place in the second heaven.

Second-heaven revelation isn't from God or your soul. It's from the demonic realm. Usually, second-heaven revelation depicts evil the enemy plans to do. There is usually vivid detail about death and destruction and it's frightening. The enemy infiltrates the soul and tries to torment you. When you receive word about impending disaster from second-heaven revelation, you may feel helpless to do anything about the impending destruction.

Be careful. The enemy wants to make the prophet his mouthpiece to spew fear all over the Body of Christ. Seers have been deceived by this tactic more than you know. How do you know if it's a second-heaven revelation? I teach more about that in my School of the Seers. However, second-heaven revelation is fear-based and hopeless. When God gives us a dream, He gives us a plan.

PRAYER

Father, in the name of Jesus, thank You for making me aware of second-heaven revelation. I don't want to report something as from Your throne room when it comes from a demonic source. Give me discernment.

MARCH 27

WHAT DOES IT RESEMBLE?

Before the throne there was a sea of glass, like crystal. And in the midst of the throne, and around the throne, were four living creatures full of eyes in front and in back.

Revelation 4:6

At times, there is no human means to describe what you are seeing in the spirit. The unseen realm is filled with creatures or objects or just things you can't explain with earthly language. In that case, seers in Scripture talked about the appearance of a thing.

As described in *The Seer's Dictionary*, appearance is a common word seers use in the pages of Scripture. *Appearance* means "a sense impression of aspect of a thing." An appearance is when one thing resembles, or looks like another thing. You've seen clouds in the sky, for example, that look like a bird or a tree. It's not a bird or a tree, but it has the appearance of a bird or a tree.

We see Ezekiel using this sort of language in both Ezekiel 1. Ezekiel 1:5-9 reads, "Also from within it came the likeness of four living creatures. And this was their appearance: they had the likeness of a man. Each one had four faces, and each one had four wings. Their legs were straight, and the soles of their feet were like the soles of calves' feet. They sparkled like the color of burnished bronze. The hands of a man were under their wings on their four sides; and each of the four had faces and wings. Their wings touched one another...."

We see this again in Ezekiel 1:13, "As for the likeness of the living creatures, their appearance was like burning coals of fire, like the appearance of torches going back and forth among the living creatures. The fire was bright, and out of the fire went lightning."

We see the use of this seer description tactic over and again in the book of Revelation. John described Jesus' hair white like wool (Revelation 1:14) and His feet like fine brass (Revelation 1:15) and His countenance was like the sun shining in its strength (Revelation 1:16). He later said Jesus had eyes like a flame of fire (Revelation 2:18). He described Jesus' voice like a trumpet (Revelation 4:1).

PRAYER

Father, in the name of Jesus, would You help me find the right words to say to describe what I am seeing in the spirit even when there are no human words? Help me describe what it resembles so I can explain it well.

MARCH 28

ASCENDING IN THE SPIRIT

After these things I looked, and behold, a door standing open in heaven. And the first voice which I heard was like a trumpet speaking with me, saying, "Come up here, and I will show you things which must take place after this."

Revelation 4:1

Seers, at times, can ascend in the spirit. Ascend, according to *The Seer's Dictionary*, is the act of going up to the second or third heaven. It also means to rise, climb or go up in the spirit realm. This, of course, is not an everyday occurrence so if it happens, you need to observe, record, analyze, and interpret the encounter with the fear of the Lord.

When seers ascend, they are entering an unseen realm that is very real. In fact, it's more real than the natural world around us. Jacob had a dream in which there was a ladder set up on earth that reached to the top of Heaven. He saw angels of God ascending and descending on it (Genesis 28:12). Seers can also ascend in dreams, but they can literally ascend in the spirit realm through dreams, visions, or out-of-body experiences.

Again, this is not something every seer experiences and is reserved for those with clean hands and a pure heart who have not lifted up their soul to idols or sworn deceitfully (Psalm 24:3-4). I write more about this in my book, *The Seer Dimensions*. You can't try or decide to ascend. This could lead you into counterfeit operations and defy the will of God.

Consider Lucifer. Isaiah 14:13-14 speaks of Him, "For you have said in your heart: 'I will ascend into heaven, I will exalt my throne above the stars of God; I will also sit on the mount of the congregation on the farthest sides of the north; I will ascend above the heights of the clouds, I will be like the Most High.'"

Christ, on the other hand, ascended to the right hand of the Father as the sinless and victorious Son of God (Mark 16:19). Enoch ascended to Heaven (Genesis 5:24). Elijah ascended to Heaven (2 Kings 2:1). When you ascend in the spirit, you will see things from God's perspective as John the Revelator saw. When you ascend in the spirit, it's by God's will, not yours. Judge these experiences wisely.

PRAYER

Father, in the name of Jesus, if You should invite me to ascend in the spirit, through dreams, visions, trances, or out-of-body-experiences, help me to guard these moments and steward them wisely.

MARCH 29

WAITING ON THE WITNESS

...And it is the Spirit who bears witness, because the Spirit is truth.
1 John 5:6

You will witness many things in the spirit world as you continue to follow Jesus. Of course, not everything we witness in the seer dimensions is divine. Indeed, some of it is demonic dressed up as the divine.

So seeing in the spirit, then, is not just about what we witness. It's bearing witness to what we see. In other words, it's allowing the Spirit of truth to confirm if what we are seeing is from His spirit, our soul, or some other spirit.

Paul told us plainly in Romans 8:16, "The Spirit Himself bears witness with our spirit that we are children of God." What does a witness do? Testifies to the truth. In fact, the Greek word for *witness* in that verse is often translated *testifies*, but one interesting definition is "bear joint witness." The New Living Translation says, "testifies with our spirit."

This is an important distinction. The Holy Spirit doesn't bear witness with our mind. We can't reason out in our minds if something is from Him or not. If we use reason alone, we can reason our way right out of valid visual revelation. Imagine if Ezekiel had tried to reason out the wheel within a wheel. He may have thought it was something purely demonic or his imagination gone wild.

The Amplified Bible expounds on that: "The Spirit Himself testifies and confirms together with our spirit [assuring us] that we [believers] are children of God." If the Holy Spirit can bear witness that you are a child of God, do you think He could give you a witness to a true or false message or encounter?

Seer, it's time to develop a sensitivity to the Holy Spirit. He will witness what comes from Jesus and what does not. He will assure us that it is Him showing us even the strangest sights—sights beyond our wildest imagination. Remember, part and parcel of the Holy Spirit's ministry is to testify of Jesus (John 15:26). And the spirit of prophecy is the testimony of Jesus (Revelation 19:10).

PRAYER

Father, in the name of Jesus, would You help me wait for the witness of the Holy Spirit before I share my revelation? Moreover, would You help me discern the witness of the Spirit in my spirit?

MARCH 30

TAKEN UP IN A VISION

It was like the appearance of the vision which I saw—like the vision which I saw when I came to destroy the city. The visions were like the vision which I saw by the River Chebar; and I fell on my face.

Ezekiel 43:3

It's not often that a seer is taken up in a vision by the Spirit while in a vision. When this happens, there is an especially significant message for the seer and we need to chronicle it well and thoroughly pray it through.

Consider what happened to Ezekiel. We read about his visual experience in which the Spirit took him up, in Ezekiel 11:22-29:

> So the cherubim lifted up their wings, with the wheels beside them, and the glory of the God of Israel was high above them. And the glory of the Lord went up from the midst of the city and stood on the mountain, which is on the east side of the city. Then the Spirit took me up and brought me in a vision by the Spirit of God into Chaldea, to those in captivity. And the vision that I had seen went up from me. So I spoke to those in captivity of all the things the Lord had shown me.

Notice how Ezekiel was already seeing the vision. He was seeing the cherubim and the wheels and the glory of God. That, in itself, was an experience. But then, in the midst of this, the Spirit of the Lord caught him up in the vision. He experienced it in a whole new dimension.

In other words, it's one thing to see a vision and it's another thing to get caught up in the vision. When God takes you up into a vision, you gain a different perspective. You gain God's perspective. You see things from His point of view. That experience will help shape your intercession and your assignment. It may affect your emotions, whether that's grief, indignation, or elation at a deeper level. And that, no doubt, shaped how he delivered God's message.

When Ezekiel came out of the vision, he had a message. He was compelled by the Spirit of God to share what happened. But that's not always the case. Once, John was told to seal up things he saw. When you get caught up in a vision like this, it's a special experience. Obey the Lord in the next steps, whether to speak or seal up the vision.

PRAYER

Father, in the name of Jesus, I know I can't decide to get caught up in the vision but I want to get Your perspective. I want to see what You see and feel what You feel. I want to deliver Your messages with passion. Help me.

MARCH 31

WHEN GOD SHOWS YOU SOMETHING DISTRESSING

Be anxious for nothing, but in everything by prayer and supplication, with thanksgiving, let your requests be made known to God.

Philippians 4:6

We all love to see angels show up with a message or Jesus visit us in a vision with an instruction. But we have to be open to anything the Holy Spirit shows, just like Daniel, Isaiah, and John the Revelator. Put another way, we don't get to pick and choose what we see in the spirit.

Many times, God launches us into the seer dimensions with vision and dreams that thrill our heart, but as we mature and He knows we can handle it, we may find ourselves with visual revelation that is distressing.

When that happens, we need not look away. We need to respond rightly.

We can take a page from the prophet Isaiah. He saw the fall of Babylon–recorded in Isaiah 21:1-4:

> As whirlwinds in the South pass through, so it comes from the desert, from a terrible land. A distressing vision is declared to me; the treacherous dealer deals treacherously, and the plunderer plunders. Go up, O Elam! Besiege, O Media! All its sighing I have made to cease. Therefore my loins are filled with pain; pangs have taken hold of me, like the pangs of a woman in labor. I was distressed when I heard it; I was dismayed when I saw it. My heart wavered, fearfulness frightened me; the night for which I longed He turned into fear for me.

Catch that. He was dismayed when he saw it. He still recorded it. His response was not to sit in shock or hide in a corner. Isaiah processed the distressing vision and his response demonstrated his maturity. Verse 5 reads, "Prepare the table, set a watchman in the tower, eat and drink. Arise, you princes, anoint the shield!"

No matter how distressing the vision, the Lord expects us to gather ourselves, pray and respond according to His will. As you mature in your seer gift, it will be easier to do this. Isaiah responded to the distressing vision with wisdom and grace supplied by the Holy Spirit who gave him the vision.

PRAYER

Father, in the name of Jesus, would You help me to "grow up" in the seer dimensions. I am willing to see anything You want to show me, even if it is distressing, and issue a warning to Your people.

APRIL

I was in the Spirit on the Lord's Day, and I heard behind me a loud voice, as of a trumpet.

Revelation 1:10

APRIL 1

BEWARE OF BACKDOOR ACCESS

And the Lord, said to me, "The prophets prophesy lies in My name. I have not sent them, commanded them, nor spoken to them; they prophesy to you a false vision, divination, a worthless thing, and the deceit of their heart."

Jeremiah 14:14

I am sure you would never dream of going through a back door in the spirit, but make no mistake: if you allow people to pressure you to see and you are not seeing, the enemy will tempt you to go into the seer dimensions without the Holy Spirit. This is a dangerous practice.

The Holy Spirit is the One who leads you and guides you into the seer dimensions. The enemy would love to lead you and guide you operating illegally in the seer dimensions. I have seen too many seers compromise their gift for the sake of seeing something new step into witchcraft through a back door. Sometimes they aren't even aware of what they are doing.

What is a back door? According to *The Seer's Dictionary*, a back door is an illegal access point to seeing in the spirit. Backdoor access is an unauthorized method for entering seer realms, such as choosing by your will to check in on someone in the spirit, eavesdrop on conversations, or otherwise cooperate with familiar spirits to see something the Holy Spirit is not trying to show you.

I also call it hacking the seer dimensions. In the natural, hacking is an illegal operation criminals undertake. *Collins Dictionary* puts it this way: "You can use backdoor to describe an action or process if you disapprove of it because you think it has been done in a secret, indirect, or dishonest way."

In the seer dimensions, Jesus is the Gatekeeper. He is the Door. He is the One who guards the gate. The Holy Spirit leads and guides us to and through the gates.

Jesus called Himself the Door more than once. John 10:7, "Most assuredly, I say to you, I am the door of the sheep." Jesus is also the door to the Father. No one goes to the Father except through the gate called Jesus (John 14:6).

The word *door* in John 10:7 comes from the Greek word *thura*, which means "an entrance, a way, or passage; 'an open door' is used as an opportunity of doing something; the door of the kingdom of heaven," according to the *KJV New Testament Greek Lexicon*.

Jesus is the only legal Door to the seer dimensions. Beware of the enemy's temptation to pervert your hunger with a wrong motive to see in the spirit. I teach more about this in my School of the Seers.

PRAYER

Father, in the name of Jesus, would You help me to recognize when the enemy is tempting me to enter the seer dimensions through any door that is not Jesus? Help me discern true and false leading.

APRIL 2

JESUS IS THE DOOR

I am the Door; anyone who enters in through Me will be saved (will live). He will come in and he will go out [freely], and will find pasture.
John 10:9 AMPC

Jesus is the Door to the seer dimensions. He is the only legal Door to enter through. The Holy Spirit invites you through this Door and there is no other way to operate legitimately.

In John 10:9, Jesus said, "I am the door." The NIV says, "I am the gate." While in this context He meant that He is the Door to the Father and the only way to salvation, He is also the only legal door into the supernatural.

Yes, I realize there are shamans, psychics, and mediums who see things in the spirit, but they are going through a back door. They are entering illegally; and not only is it not safe, there are serious consequences.

Jesus said in John 10:1 (AMPC), "I assure you, most solemnly I tell you, he who does not enter by the door into the sheepfold, but climbs up some other way (elsewhere, from some other quarter) is a thief and a robber." The same principle holds true for the seer dimensions. There's a proper door to go through, but there are other ways to get in.

Occult practices may yield accurate information, but they are not a legal door. New Age mysticism may lead you into encounters, but not with the one true living God. I even met a man once who strived to separate from his body in an illegitimate experience and ended up with sudden and lasting symptoms of Multiple Sclerosis.

If you want to be accurate in the seer dimensions, spend time with Jesus. He is the Door. He's not trying to hide anything from you that you need to see. Through the Holy Spirit, He shows you things to come. Entering through Jesus, the Door, is entering in alignment with His will, His ways, and His timing.

Yes, we can position ourselves to enter the seer dimensions through prayer and worship and fasting. We do have a part to play, but if the Door is not open we can't force our way into it. Or if we do, we are acting like a thief and a robber, not like a son or a daughter. The seer dimensions are invitational only. Your job is to discern and respond to the invitation.

PRAYER

Father, in the name of Jesus, help me respect the legal Door into the seer dimensions and not be tempted by the enemy to go in through any other gate. Teach me not to strive to see.

APRIL 3

THE VOICE YOU CAN'T UNHEAR

That the Lord called Samuel. And he answered, "Here I am!"
1 Samuel 3:4

Shortly after I was saved, I heard the audible voice of God. I thought it was my father speaking to me. But it was my Father (capital F) speaking to me. When I heard His voice out loud, it released the spirit of the fear of the Lord. That is a typical response when you hear the audible voice of God in a visual revelation. Consider John's experience in Revelation 1:12-15:

> Then I turned to see the voice that spoke with me. And having turned I saw seven golden lampstands, and in the midst of the seven lampstands One like the Son of Man, clothed with a garment down to the feet and girded about the chest with a golden band. His head and hair were white like wool, as white as snow, and His eyes like a flame of fire; His feet were like fine brass, as if refined in a furnace, and His voice as the sound of many waters.

Catch that. His voice was like the sound of many waters. That's intense! It was roaring aloud. It was a voice with power and authority.

Sometimes when you enter the seer dimensions, you also hear the audible voice of God. As explained in *The Seer's Dictionary*, as opposed to the still small voice you hear internally, the audible voice of God is something you hear from the outside. You won't confuse the audible voice of God for the still small voice of God. These are two entirely different experiences.

While you may hear many voices in the seer dimension—including the Lord, angels, and demons—it's relatively rare to hear the audible voice of God. But beyond John and Samuel, we do know of several other instances in Scripture of people hearing the audible voice of God.

Adam and Eve heard the audible voice of God in the Garden of Eden (Genesis 3:8-10). God spoke to Moses face to face, so it's presumed he heard the audible voice of God (Numbers 12:6-8). When Jesus was baptized, a voice came out of Heaven and spoke audibly (Matthew 3:16-17). Many commentators contend everyone heard it. When Paul was on the Road to Damascus, he heard the audible voice of God (Acts 9).

As you can see by these occurrences, this audiovisual manifestation is reserved for critical times in the lives of believers. And it's an experience you will never forget.

PRAYER

Father, in the name of Jesus, I want to hear Your audible voice. I know it comes with the spirit of the fear of the Lord. Would You speak to me audibly when it serves Your purposes for my life and for Your Bride, the Church?

APRIL 4

ENTERING THE TRANCE DIMENSION

Now it happened, when I returned to Jerusalem and was praying in the temple, that I was in a trance.

Acts 22:17

I was praying for a young man who was visiting our congregation, Awakening House of Prayer in Fort Lauderdale. While I was praying, he fell into a trance for more than 20 minutes. At first, the congregation was still and quiet. After about 10 minutes, I pulled the pulpit around and taught about trances while he was standing behind me, frozen like a statue.

As I write in my book *The Seer Dimensions,* trances are not merely the domain of shamans, New Agers, and DJs with pumping beats. The enemy always works to counterfeit what God is doing, and because of this many have feared to even learn of the trance realm. The reality is, trances are biblical and we need to understand what the Bible says about them. What is a trance? Before we go any further, it's helpful to see various definitions that will lay a foundation for your faith.

Noah Webster's 1828 Dictionary defines trance this way, "An ecstasy; a state in which the soul seems to have passed out of the body into celestial regions, or to be rapt into visions." We only see trances mentioned five times in the Bible, but that is more than enough to set a principle of a way God moves on us and speaks to us. Paul fell into a trance in Acts 22:17-21 when the Lord gave him a warning and a commission to preach the gospel to the Gentiles:

> ...I was in a trance and saw Him saying to me, "Make haste and get out of Jerusalem quickly, for they will not receive your testimony concerning Me." So I said, "Lord, they know that in every synagogue I imprisoned and beat those who believe on You. And when the blood of Your martyr Stephen was shed, I also was standing by consenting to his death, and guarding the clothes of those who were killing him." Then He said to me, "Depart, for I will send you far from here to the Gentiles."

Notice that Paul received instruction in the trance, just as Peter did. Trances, like any other supernatural encounter, are purposeful. God is not random.

PRAYER

Father, in the name of Jesus, I am not asking You to encounter me in a trance, but I would like to understand this trance dimension. Would You show me more about trances and Your purposes in them?

APRIL 5

WHEN YOU DREAM OF THE BOOK OF LIFE

He who overcomes shall be clothed in white garments, and I will not blot out his name from the Book of Life; but I will confess his name before My Father and before His angels.

Revelation 3:5

When Jesus told His disciples they should rejoice that their names are written in Heaven, He was referring to the Lamb's Book of Life. But Jesus wasn't the only, or even the first, to mention this Book of Life.

Also called the Book of Living, a number of Scriptures talk about the Book of Life. Moses was the first to mention this book in Exodus 32:32, "Yet now, if You will forgive their sin—but if not, I pray, blot me out of Your book which You have written." David also mentioned the Book of the Living in Psalm 69:28, "Let them be blotted out of the book of the living, and not be written with the righteous." The keyword *blot* signifies it was indeed the Book of Life of which these men were speaking.

We see the Book of Life mentioned several times in Revelation:

Revelation 3:5 tells us, "He who overcomes shall be clothed in white garments, and I will not blot out his name from the Book of Life; but I will confess his name before My Father and before His angels." Revelation 20:12 offers, "And I saw the dead, small and great, standing before God, and books were opened. And another book was opened, which is the Book of Life. And the dead were judged according to their works, by the things which were written in the books." And Revelation 20:15 warns, "And anyone not found written in the Book of Life was cast into the lake of fire."

Paul may have had a glimpse into the Book of Life. Philippians 4:3 says, "And I urge you also, true companion, help these women who labored with me in the gospel, with Clement also, and the rest of my fellow workers, whose names are in the Book of Life."

As a seer, God can show you anything He chooses to reveal. We need to be careful not to pursue supernatural experiences because the devil may oblige us. Rather, we should stretch our faith to see things in Heaven, even the Lamb's Book of Life. Meditate on these Scriptures about the Book of Life. Ask God about it. Maybe He will show you so you can assure someone of a relative's eternal position.

PRAYER

Father, in the name of Jesus, would You show me the Lamb's Book of Life? I know my name is written there, but seeing into this book could motivate me to preach the gospel or intercede for those whose names are not in it.

APRIL 6

ARE YOU CULTIVATING DISCERNMENT?

But solid food belongs to those who are of full age, that is, those who by reason of use have their senses exercised to discern both good and evil.

Hebrews 5:14

Discernment is part of the seer's gift mix, but like any other spiritual gift it needs to be developed. Think about it practically: your role as a seer doesn't stop with seeing into the spirit realm. You also need discernment to know how to handle what you see. You need to discern the interpretation, the application, and God's timing releasing the visual revelation.

Remember, not every dream, vision, or encounter you have is from God. The enemy is crafty and can try to seep into your visual revelation. You need to discern between the profane and the holy (Ezekiel 44:23). You need to discern true from false encounters. You need to separate the divine from the demonic and your own flesh from the Holy Spirit. In other words, you can't take everything you see at face value. You have to test the spirits (1 John 4:1).

A certain measure of discernment comes from experience. Once you've had true encounters, you have something to compare with the false. And once you've made mistakes, you can learn from them. But you can't rush experience. Use Scripture as your anchor. Get rooted and grounded in the incorruptible, infallible Word of God. Always "plumb line" your visual revelations against what God has already said in the Bible.

Beyond the visual revelation itself, you need to discern if and when you should share what you experienced. God sometimes shares revelation with us that is not ready for prime time. In other words, it's not ready for release. Your revelation may be for the sake of an intercessory prayer assignment or even personal preparation. We don't want to gossip in the name of Jesus because He can't trust us with more if we don't steward well what we already have.

I know what it's like to feel an urgency to share what I've seen, but learning how to wait on the Lord for the seer release is part of your seasoning. Obeying the Lord is worth the wait.

PRAYER

Father, in the name of Jesus, help me cultivate the discernment You have imparted to me. Help me grow in this wisdom to know the source of what I am seeing and what to do with it.

APRIL 7

IS YOUR IMAGINATION SANCTIFIED?

Casting down arguments and every high thing that exalts itself against the knowledge of God, bringing every thought into captivity to the obedience of Christ.

2 Corinthians 10:5

When your spirit was born again, you gained the ability to see all things possible (Mark 9:23) within the bounds of your imagination. Imaginations, therefore, can be good or bad and anybody can have them. But how does that fit into the seer dimensions?

The word *imagination* is found five times in the Old Testament. It generally refers to the human heart. *Imagination* appears in the New Testament three times, and two of those times it refers to the heart. The third reference is "*vain imaginations*" found in 2 Corinthians 10:5 and is often translated reasonings or arguments.

While the enemy tries to use your imagination against you—launching vain imaginations against your mind—you can cooperate with God to use your imagination for His glory. God has an imagination and our imagination is one of His great gifts to humankind. Every great invention, for example, was first found in someone's imagination. Imagination is part of our creative ability.

That said, with the fall of man, our imaginations also became depraved. Genesis 6:5 (KJV) shares, "And God saw that the wickedness of man was great in the earth, and that every imagination of the thoughts of his heart was only evil continually." When we were born again, we received the opportunity to renew our mind, which is the seat of our imaginations. As our mind is renewed we can tap into our illuminated imagination to see what God wants us to see, and we should.

As you seek to enter the seer dimensions through the imagination, be careful to first work to root out corrupted areas of your imagination so you can separate what is your own invention from God's innovation. Ask the Lord to help you enter into seer dimensions through imaging scenes in the Word.

PRAYER

Father, in the name of Jesus, would You sanctify my imagination? Help me to submit my imagination to Your Word. Illuminate my imagination and help me see things that are not visible to the natural senses.

APRIL 8

LET IT RAIN

Let us know, let us pursue the knowledge of the Lord. His going forth is established as the morning; He will come to us like the rain, like the latter and former rain to the earth.

Hosea 6:3

Have you ever seen it raining on the inside? At my first women's conference at Awakening House of Prayer, we saw it raining in the spirit. This was a manifestation of God's glory. The result? Every woman with any kind of infirmity—from back pain to tumors and beyond—was instantly healed. I believe the rain comes out of the glory cloud, whether you see it or not.

Job 37:11 says God loads the thick clouds with moisture. And Zechariah 10:1 (MEV) says, "Ask for rain from the Lord during the season of the latter spring rains. And the Lord will make the storm winds; and He will give them showers of rain; all will have vegetation in the field."

In prophetic encounters—whether in visions, dreams, or moments of deep intercession—rain can be a prophetic sign of the glory of God invading a place. A gentle mist may represent the tender touch of His presence, while a torrential downpour can signal revival breaking out, cleansing from Heaven, or the weighty glory of God descending with force.

When you see unusual rain—rain falling in a dry season, showing up indoors, or manifesting with no clouds in sight—don't dismiss it. That's not natural. That's a supernatural visitation. That's the Spirit of God testifying to divine approval or making Himself known in a visible, tangible way.

Throughout prophetic and Pentecostal history, rain has been a clear metaphor for the outpouring of the Holy Spirit. On the day of Pentecost in Acts 2, the Holy Ghost fell like a mighty rushing wind and fire, but Joel's prophecy called it the latter rain—a final outpouring that brings harvest. That outpouring didn't just bring tongues, it brought the glory.

The rain of His glory doesn't just water the earth, it also shifts atmospheres. So if you're in a moment of worship or prayer and suddenly you sense or even see rain—whether in the spirit or the natural—don't move on too quickly. Stop. Discern. Ask the Holy Spirit, "What are You doing right now?" You may be standing in the glory.

PRAYER

Father, in the name of Jesus, would You make me spiritually sensitive to the rain of Your glory? Even if I don't see it with my spiritual eyes, help me discern it with my discerner. I want to bask in Your glory.

APRIL 9

HAUNTING DREAMS

While Pilate was sitting on the judge's seat, his wife sent him this message: "Don't have anything to do with that innocent man, for I have suffered a great deal today in a dream because of him."

Matthew 27:19 NIV

Have you ever had a dream or vision that you couldn't shake? By that I mean, you couldn't get it out of your head. You keep rolling it over in your mind, even closing your eyes and replaying the visuals revelation in your thoughts?

Eliphaz, a so-called friend of Job, experienced this, and the Holy Spirit saw fit to record it in Scripture for the seer's benefit. Eliphaz bears his heart in Job 4:12-14: "Now a word was secretly brought to me, and my ear received a whisper of it. In disquieting thoughts from the visions of the night, when deep sleep falls on men, fear came upon me, and trembling, which made all my bones shake." That's quite an encounter. I personally have never had a vision that made my bones shake! Have you?

The NIV translation of Job 4:13 says he had "disquieting dreams." *Disquieting* refers to something that is alarming, disturbing, or steals your peace. We know the Holy Spirit is the Spirit of peace—He's not in the peace-stealing business. But sometimes we can allow ourselves to get anxious about what we see in the spirit, especially if it's dark in nature or we just don't understand the encounter.

The Christian Standard and Holman Christian Standard translations of Job 4:13 say he had "unsettling thoughts from visions in the night." The Contemporary English Version puts it plainly: "I was overcome by sleep, but disturbed in my dreams." And the Good News Translation puts it this way: "Like a nightmare it disturbed my sleep."

It's hard to imagine any vision or dream from God manifesting in such a way, so when a vision brings disquieting thoughts we need to turn to Him. We need to take authority over the spirit of fear, anxiety, and every disquieting thought. We need to be still and know that He is God (Psalm 46:10).

Keep in mind that divine visions can also lead to thought disturbances. Some men of God in the Bible fell on their faces in fear when they saw an angel. To be sure, sometimes we are taken aback by what we see and have a fear reaction even though it's not God's intention to scare us.

PRAYER

Father, in the name of Jesus, help me discern the source of my troubled thoughts after a vision. I don't want to shun something You are trying to show me. I refuse to be anxious despite what I see.

APRIL 10

THE SEER'S FAITH BUILDER

Faith comes by hearing, and hearing by the word of God.

Romans 10:17

All believers walk into sight by faith—how much more the seer? Although God alone decides who sees what and when and how—whether by dream, vision, trance, an out-of-body experience, or an encounter—our faith does play a part in how much of what He is showing us we will actually see.

Paul writes in Romans 12:6, "Having then gifts differing according to the grace that is given to us, let us use them: if prophecy, let us prophesy in proportion to our faith." If we prophesy according to our faith, it follows that we see according to our faith.

So, then, how do we build faith to see? Paul gives us the answer to this question in Romans 10:17, "So then faith comes by hearing, and hearing by the word of God."

Next question: How do we apply that to the seer dimensions? The Bible records 21 specific dreams across the Old and New Testaments. When you read the dreams—when you meditate on the dreams and even visualize the dreams with your sanctified imagination—you are building your faith for what is possible. I am not saying that God is obligated to give you similar dreams. I am saying you are building your faith. The same God who gave Jacob dreams that shaped nations can give you dreams that stop wars.

Similarly, there are more than 20 visions in the Bible. Meditating on those visions prepares your spiritual eyes to walk by faith into sight. Even still there are numerous trances and other divine encounters in the Word. Set your eyes on them. And by the way, you can also learn about false dreams and visions, which can help you grow in discernment between true and erroneous visual revelations.

By reading these dreams and visions, you build your faith to enter these dimensions. God shows no favoritism (Acts 10:34). You are a candidate for epic dreams, visions, and encounters. You also gain hunger to see like these men of old saw. You can find a list of all the dreams and visions at the end of my book, *Seer Activations*.

PRAYER

Father, in the name of Jesus, give me a hunger for what Your Word says about dreams and visions. Give me a spiritual curiosity about the dreams and visions the Holy Spirit recorded in the Bible for my instruction.

APRIL 11

VISIONS THAT LEAVE YOU SPEECHLESS

Then I came to the captives at Tel Abib, who dwelt by the River Chebar; and I sat where they sat, and remained there astonished among them seven days.

Ezekiel 3:15

I've had visual encounters that left me absolutely astonished. By astonished, I mean I was astounded. I was surprised. I was filled with holy wonder. I was amazed. Indeed, there are truly some amazing sights in the seer dimensions.

Consider what the Israelites experienced in Exodus 19:16, "Then it came to pass on the third day, in the morning, that there were thunderings and lightnings, and a thick cloud on the mountain; and the sound of the trumpet was very loud, so that all the people who were in the camp trembled."

Likewise, I am sure the Israelites were astonished when Elijah called fire down from Heaven that licked up all the water in the trench surrounding the sacrifice. I'm sure the disciples were astonished when Jesus walked through the wall into the room where they were waiting and when He was taken up in a cloud. That's astonishing!

Ezekiel was astonished by what he saw in Ezekiel 8:1-4 (MSG):

> In the sixth year, in the sixth month and the fifth day, while I was sitting at home meeting with the leaders of Judah, it happened that the hand of my Master, God, gripped me. When I looked, I was astonished. What I saw looked like a man—from the waist down like fire and from the waist up like highly burnished bronze. He reached out what looked like a hand and grabbed me by the hair. The Spirit swept me high in the air and carried me in visions of God to Jerusalem, to the entrance of the north gate of the Temple's inside court where the image of the sex goddess that makes God so angry had been set up. Right before me was the Glory of the God of Israel, exactly like the vision I had seen out on the plain.

Amazement or astonishment is often the result of epic visions or after waking from an epic dream. If you have an astonishing vision, spend time meditating on what you saw over and over. There are probably many details to ponder and much revelation to be had for the sake of intercession.

PRAYER

Father, in the name of Jesus, when I think of what Your people were privileged to witness, it makes me hungry to see in the spirit. Help me to respect the visual revelation You share with me and treat it as holy.

APRIL 12

THE EZEKIEL SEER ANOINTING

The appearance of the wheels and their workings was like the color of beryl, and all four had the same likeness. The appearance of their workings was, as it were, a wheel in the middle of a wheel.

Ezekiel 1:16

Ezekiel was a seer prophet who stewarded his anointing well—so well, in fact, that God kept trusting him with encounters and assignments like few in the Bible experienced. Ezekiel is the classic watchman seer.

Ezekiel's recorded ministry in the Bible lasted 22 years, and his ministry expanded little by little, which is one of the ways of God. When we first meet Ezekiel, he was serving as a priest. The book that bears his name opens with a dramatic vision of God while he was functioning in the priestly anointing.

After faithfully serving as a priest, God activated another level of prophetic anointing in his life and called him to stand in the office of a prophet in Ezekiel 3. Thirteen years later, Ezekiel was called a watchman. Catch that. It was 13 years later. There were 13 years between Ezekiel 1 and Ezekiel 3.

Extraordinary visions and parabolic acts marked Ezekiel's ministry. Think about it. Ezekiel saw the heavens open to reveal the glory of God (Ezekiel 1:10). In another epic vision, he saw the Valley of Dry bones (Ezekiel 37:1-10).

Beyond this, Ezekiel bridged the natural and supernatural realms with his symbolic acts. He spent four hundred and thirty days laying on his side to represent Israel's iniquity. He cooked his food over dung. He consumed small amounts of bread and water to symbolize a famine.

Ezekiel walked in obedience to God, even when it was personally uncomfortable, so he would not have blood on his hands. And because of his assignment, Ezekiel developed boldness rooted in a commitment to speak the truth despite the consequences. The Ezekiel seer anointing, then, is rooted in a call to extraordinary encounters, parabolic expressions, watching, and boldness. Ask God for the Ezekiel anointing.

PRAYER

Father, in the name of Jesus, when it serves Your purpose, would You give me the Ezekiel anointing? I see the three-fold anointing as a priest, prophet, and watchman. I will function in any role You anoint me for.

APRIL 13

ENTERTAINING ANGELS

Don't forget to extend your hospitality to all—even to strangers—for as you know, some have unknowingly shown kindness to heavenly messengers in this way.

Hebrews 13:2 The Voice

Have you ever entertained an angel unaware? You may not know it, or you may not have known at the time but, looking back, you realize it was an angel.

Beyond the Hebrews exhortation in Scripture, we see angels showing up in human form, cloaking their spiritual form, more than once. If God did this in the Old Testament, should we dare think He would not allow this in the New Testament? Jesus Christ is the same today, yesterday and forever (Hebrews 13:8).

In Genesis 18, Abraham looked up and saw three men standing by him. He bowed himself to the ground and showed hospitality with the offer to bring water and food to refresh them. Angels don't need food, so it seems Abraham didn't immediately discern they were angels.

Shortly thereafter, Abraham's nephew Lot entertained two angels unaware: "...When Lot saw them, he rose to meet them, and he bowed himself with his face toward the ground. And he said, 'Here now, my lords, please turn in to your servant's house and spend the night, and wash your feet; then you may rise early and go on your way...'" (Genesis 19:1-2).

The carnal men of Sodom and Gomorrah also thought they were flesh-and-blood men. Genesis 19:4-5 tells us, "Now before they lay down, the men of the city, the men of Sodom, both old and young, all the people from every quarter, surrounded the house. And they called to Lot and said to him, 'Where are the men who came to you tonight? Bring them out to us that we may know them carnally.'"

So it's possible for angels to appear in human form. You may see them with your natural eyes, but if you strengthen your discernment you will know them by the spirit. This is in line with 2 Corinthians 5:16, "Therefore, from now on, we regard no one according to the flesh. Even though we have known Christ according to the flesh, yet now we know Him thus no longer."

PRAYER

Father, in the name of Jesus, I know angels can show up in human form. Help me not to just discern the spectacular in the spirit but to discern when I am entertaining angels so I will not be unaware.

APRIL 14

FINDING YOUR COMPANY OF SEERS

When they came there to the hill, there was a group of prophets to meet him; then the Spirit of God came upon him, and he prophesied among them.

1 Samuel 10:10

You've probably heard of the "company of prophets," but what about a company of seers? And have you found yours?

All seers are prophets, but there is a distinction between a company of prophets and a company of seers. A traditional company of prophets may focus more on *nabi,* or prophets who predominantly hear the word of the Lord. A company of seers focus more on *chozeh,* having visions and dreams.

According to *The Seer's Dictionary*, a company of prophets is a group, family, hub, or school of prophets or seers; a fellowship or network of prophetic people; a camp within the prophetic movement.

In the Old Testament, we see this company rise under the leadership of Samuel. Samuel was not only a seer but a mentor and guide for these prophets, training them to hear from the Lord clearly and consistently.

Scripture says that in those days, "the word of the Lord was rare" (1 Samuel 3:1), yet through Samuel's leadership, God began to raise up a company of prophets, each one set apart to study the Word and some would carry His voice to the nation. These prophets were not in isolation but in community, learning together, challenging each other, and submitting to one another in their pursuit of prophetic accuracy and integrity.

The company of prophets was a prophetic incubator, a safe place to learn and practice the gift. They were called to carry the burden of God's heart, to discern His voice in a world filled with false idols and deceptive voices. They were vigilant, watchful, and ready to stand against the counterfeit prophets who would lead God's people astray.

We see the company of prophets in action in 1 Samuel 10:5, "After that you shall come to the hill of God where the Philistine garrison is. And it will happen, when you have come there to the city, that you will meet a group of prophets coming down from the high place with a stringed instrument, a tambourine, a flute, and a harp before them; and they will be prophesying." We also see the company of prophets in 1 Samuel 10:10 and 1 Samuel 19:20.

Even today, God is raising up modern-day companies of prophets and seers who gather in community to train, equip, and sharpen one another. In a perfect world, you would have the *nabi* and *chozeh* prophets in the same company. But seers benefit from being around other seers. Join my community for seers and other prophetic people at www.ignitenow.org.

PRAYER

Father, in the name of Jesus, I would love to find my company. I would love to be part of a tribe of prophets and seers. Would You help me find other seers to fellowship with, minister with, and discuss revelation?

APRIL 15

CONFIRMING DREAMS AND VISIONS

And the dream was repeated to Pharaoh twice because the thing is established by God, and God will shortly bring it to pass.

Genesis 41:32

Many seers prize the latest revelation from the throne room, and we should. But confirming dreams and visions can often be just as valuable to the seer's revelatory expression.

Think back. Have you ever had the same dream more than once or had a vision about something you heard the Lord say to you, or about what someone else prophesied or experienced in the seer dimensions?

There could be several reasons for this, but one of them is that God is bringing you confirmation that the seer revelation is from His Spirit, and something to be believed and acted upon. We all need confirmation at times.

According to *The Seer's Dictionary*, confirming dreams confirm a circumstance the Lord has been speaking to you or someone else about. Likewise, confirming visions confirm what you already know or believe is true. You can also have a vision that confirms a dream or a dream that confirms a vision. God is awesome!

Confirm means to give approval or to ratify something. It means to make firm or firmer. Confirm means to strengthen. It means to give new assurance of the validity of a thing, and to remove doubt by authoritative act or indisputable fact. We all need confirmation at times.

The principle of confirming is in Scripture. Paul says in 2 Corinthians 13:1, "This will be the third time I am coming to you. 'By the mouth of two or three witnesses every word shall be established.'" While Paul was talking about discipline, the same principle holds true in judging seer revelation. With that said, one way to confirm is by receiving the same revelation in different forms—seeing, hearing, dreaming—or by someone else having similar revelation.

When you seek confirmation on seer revelation, you are obeying 1 John 4:1. Under the inspiration of the Holy Spirit, John the apostle wrote, "Beloved, do not believe every spirit, but test the spirits, whether they are of God; because many false prophets have gone out into the world." Paul echoed this thought in 1 Thessalonians 5:20-21, "Do not despise prophecies. Test all things; hold fast what is good."

With grand visions and dreams—or seer revelations that could impact the masses—wisdom dictates seeking confirmation from God and testing from others.

PRAYER

Father, in the name of Jesus, I do prize fresh revelation, but help me also to prize confirming dreams and visions that give me confidence to move forward with acting on or releasing what You have shown me.

APRIL 16

THE CONSECRATED SEER

For I am the Lord your God. You shall therefore consecrate yourselves, and you shall be holy; for I am holy. Neither shall you defile yourselves with any creeping thing that creeps on the earth.

Leviticus 11:44

Seers must live consecrated lives. If you don't consecrate your eyes, the enemy can deceive you through vain imaginations, false dreams and visions, illegitimate trance experiences or even angels of light.

According to *The Seer's Dictionary*, *consecration* means "to pull away from something in order to draw to God." The dictionary goes on to say, "Seers must consecrate their eyes; that is to set them apart for God's use. It's critical that seers guard their eye gates so that worldly influences don't taint their spiritual vision."

Romans 12:1-2 puts it this way: "I beseech you therefore, brethren, by the mercies of God, that you present your bodies a living sacrifice, holy, acceptable to God, which is your reasonable service. And do not be conformed to this world, but be transformed by the renewing of your mind, that you may prove what is that good and acceptable and perfect will of God."

I heard the Lord say, "Those who are thirsty, come and drink. Those who are hungry, come and eat. Those who are feeble, come and find strength. Those who are confused, come and receive wisdom. Set yourself apart to Me and watch Me bring transformation into areas of your life that you didn't even know needed transformation.

"For the time is short, and I'm beckoning you. Come to Me. I'm urging you. Come to Me. I am beseeching you. Come to Me. Drink from Me. Eat of My flesh and drink of My blood. Be one with Me. I'm waiting for you. You think you're waiting for Me, but I am waiting for you to set yourself apart. I have sanctified you. Now come into the holy of holies.

"Come into the secret place. Come where I am...deeper still. Come and experience My goodness, My love, My joy at levels that you've never even known. Set yourself apart from the ways of the world, from the stressors of daily life. Choose to shun those things and come into My presence. Come away with Me."

PRAYER

Father, in the name of Jesus, help me understand the value and necessity of a consecrated life. I don't just want to consecrate my eyes, but also my ears, my thoughts, and my imagination.

APRIL 17

TAKING TIME WITH THE VISION

At the beginning of your supplications the command went out, and I have come to tell you, for you are greatly beloved; therefore consider the matter, and understand the vision.

Daniel 9:23

It's not enough to see a thing, you also need to consider a thing. When you have visions, especially complex visions, you need to take the time to reflect on what you've seen. You don't want to miss even a tiny bit of the revelation God has for you. Scripture calls this considering the vision.

More specifically, according to *The Seer's Dictionary*, to *consider the vision* means "to meditate, ponder and pray about the vision in order to find deeper meanings and applications." *Consider* means to carefully think about something or to pay close attention. In this way, you are demonstrating that you value the revelation.

The angel Gabriel visited Daniel in response to his prayer for understanding in the ninth chapter that bears his name. In the vision, Gabriel spoke to him and told him to consider the words he was sharing in the vision. Gabriel shared, specifically, about what we now call the 70-Week Prophecy.

The revelation was an answer to Daniel's petition about a prophecy Jeremiah had released about Israel's 70 years of captivity. I imagine Daniel considered the angel's words in that vision for some time, and it gave him understanding.

Catch that! Understanding comes from consideration. Too often, seers have a vision or dream or some other experience and don't take enough time to wring out all the revelation God has for them. This must not be so of today's seers. We must meditate on the revelation so that we can learn of God, His ways, any plans of the enemy that are revealed, and any information we need to obey.

Indeed, we need to think carefully about what the Lord is showing us, leaving no stone unturned. Everything you see in a dream, vision, or encounter has meaning. Nothing is random. Meditate on what you saw. Ask the Lord to show you the vision again, though He may or may not. Considering the vision is also how we judge the source.

Can you see how important it is to consider the vision? When we consider the vision, we are demonstrating to God that we are attentive to His word and hold His communication in high regard. In doing so, we are positioning ourselves to receive more.

PRAYER

Father, in the name of Jesus, help me not to rush to the next visual revelation You release without thoroughly considering the vision. I want to understand the depths of what You are showing me.

APRIL 18

SHAKE THE DUST OFF YOUR FEET

And whoever will not receive you, when you go out of that city, shake off the very dust from your feet as a testimony against them.

Luke 9:5

"Shake the dust off your feet." I wasn't surprised when I heard the Holy Spirit say this—but when I read the Scripture in context, it sent me into intercession for the ones who rejected what the Holy Spirit showed me.

The sad story begins in a local church where I was serving on the pastoral staff. The church's works were good, reaching out to the poor with food, clothing, and shelter. But I discerned a spirit of compromise. Decision after decision was made to please people rather than please God. I could see the fate of the church if they didn't course correct.

The day finally came when the compromise was so blatant that it sent me into weeping and travails. After seeking outside counsel, I confronted the growing cancer in love with scriptural backing. The result: I was held in contempt for speaking the undeniable gospel truth. That's when the Holy Spirit told me to shake the dust from my feet.

Jesus said, "Whoever will not receive you nor hear your words, when you depart from that house or city, shake off the dust from your feet" (Matthew 10:14). Shaking the dust off your feet signals you have obeyed God and are released from the assignment and you want no part of what is going on.

Now, don't take this as a mandate to correct your leadership and walk away if they don't obey your voice. Just because you see something wrong, doesn't mean you are the one to confront it. I had a divine mandate to speak the truth in love. They rejected the word of the Lord many times to maintain the favor of man.

Sometimes we have to shake the dust off our feet and even shake out our garments (Acts 13:51; Acts 18:6). But before we do, we must have a clear conscience. We must do everything we can to reach those to whom God sends us. We must not leave with self-righteousness or anger but with weeping and intercession for those who refuse to hear God's truth. Only then can we say, "Your blood be upon your own heads; I am clean" (Acts 18:6).

PRAYER

Father, in the name of Jesus, I don't want to be in a position to have to correct leaders, but if You choose to send me with a warning, I will pray and I will obey. Help me speak the truth in love.

APRIL 19

SEEING CONVERSATIONS IN THE SPIRIT

And there is no creature hidden from His sight, but all things are naked and open to the eyes of Him to whom we must give account.
Hebrews 4:13

It's one thing to hear a conversation in the spirit. It's another thing altogether to see the conversation unfold before your eyes with stereo sound. I call that seeing conversations in the spirit.

When you see conversations in the spirit, you don't always hear what is being said. Likewise, when you hear conversations in the spirit you don't always see who is talking, though you may recognize their voices. But God will allow seers to see and hear conversations in the spirit.

Conversations in the spirit, according to *The Seer's Dictionary,* are a verbal exchange that can happen between the seer and God, the seer and an angel, the seer and some other spiritual being, the seer and an elder in Heaven, or the seer and a demon. Conversations, the dictionary expounds, are a two-way exchange of information, such as when an angel brings a message and the seer asks for help understanding when the Lord asks the seer what he sees, etc.

We read about a prophet seeing into the enemy's camp in 2 Kings 6:8-12:

> Now the king of Syria was making war against Israel; and he consulted with his servants, saying, "My camp will be in such and such a place." And the man of God sent to the king of Israel, saying, "Beware that you do not pass this place, for the Syrians are coming down there." Then the king of Israel sent someone to the place of which the man of God had told him. Thus he warned him, and he was watchful there, not just once or twice. Therefore the heart of the king of Syria was greatly troubled by this thing; and he called his servants and said to them, "Will you not show me which of us is for the king of Israel?" And one of his servants said, "None, my lord, O king; but Elisha, the prophet who is in Israel, tells the king of Israel the words that you speak in your bedroom."

Through the pages of Scripture, we also see people talking to angels, listening into conversations in the spirit, and John talking to the elders in the book of Revelation. Renew your mind about what is possible.

PRAYER

Father, in the name of Jesus, I love to hear what You tell me and I love to see what You show me. But seeing conversations in the spirit gives me a fuller visual revelation. Would You let me see conversations in the spirit?

APRIL 20

PAYING THE PRICE

Yet indeed I also count all things loss for the excellence of the knowledge of Christ Jesus my Lord, for whom I have suffered the loss of all things, and count them as rubbish, that I may gain Christ.
Philippians 3:8

When God called me into prophetic ministry, He spoke many things to my heart. One of the things He told me was "to count the costs and don't look back."

Some years later, the Lord asked me if I was willing to pay the price to do what He had called me to do. I answered quickly, "Yes, Lord. I am willing." After all, I had already counted the costs when He called me—or at least I thought I had.

The Holy Spirit admonished me, "Don't answer too quickly. Consider the costs." I spent a week praying about this, really pondering what that would mean, and I decided that it was worth it. I gave the Lord my yes. And, indeed, I have paid a heavy price.

Jesus said to His disciples, "If anyone desires to come after Me, let him deny himself, and take up his cross, and follow Me. For whoever desires to save his life will lose it, but whoever loses his life for My sake will find it. For what profit is it to a man if he gains the whole world, and loses his own soul? Or what will a man give in exchange for his soul?" (Matthew 16:24-26).

There is a price to pay to go deep into the seer dimensions. It comes by invitation and pursuit. But the pursuit often comes before the invitation. There is a cost. There is a price to pray in prayer and consecration—in meditating on the Word and His person.

According to *The Seer's Dictionary*, the cost is "the price to pay to operate in high levels of the seer anointing." Are you willing to pay the price? Have you counted the costs?

Jesus speaks of counting the costs in Luke 14:26-30: "If anyone comes to Me and does not hate his father and mother, wife and children, brothers and sisters, yes, and his own life also, he cannot be My disciple. And whoever does not bear his cross and come after Me cannot be My disciple. For which of you, intending to build a tower, does not sit down first and count the cost, whether he has enough to finish it—lest, after he has laid the foundation, and is not able to finish, all who see it begin to mock him, saying, 'This man began to build and was not able to finish?'"

PRAYER

Father, in the name of Jesus, I am willing to pay the price, though I don't fully understand what it will cost me. Help me remember to stand on the promise when it comes time to pay the price for sharing truth.

APRIL 21

ENTERING HEAVEN'S COURTROOM

God presides over heaven's court....

Psalm 82:1 NLT

No one likes to go to court, unless it's the courts of Heaven. That's because the courts of Heaven are where accusations that hold back your breakthrough are overturned.

Although not a phrase used in the Bible itself, the concept of the courts of Heaven is biblical. Revelation 12:10 shares, "Then I heard a loud voice saying in heaven, 'Now salvation, and strength, and the kingdom of our God, and the power of His Christ have come, for the accuser of our brethren, who accused them before our God day and night, has been cast down.'"

Going to the courts of Heaven is not just a method of praying. It's a dimension of the spirit. Seers may find themselves there for any number of reasons, including the sake of intercession. Let's look at the courts of Heaven in Scripture.

Daniel the prophet saw the courts of Heaven. Let's look at Daniel 7:9-10:

> I watched till thrones were put in place, and the Ancient of Days was seated; His garment was white as snow, and the hair of His head was like pure wool. His throne was a fiery flame, its wheels a burning fire; a fiery stream issued and came forth from before Him. A thousand thousands ministered to Him; ten thousand times ten thousand stood before Him. The court was seated, and the books were opened.

Also look at Daniel 7:26 (TLB), "But then the Ancient of Days will come and open his court of justice and take all power from this vicious king, to consume and destroy it until the end."

And Psalm 82:1-3 (TLB), "God stands up to open heaven's court. He pronounces judgment on the judges. How long will you judges refuse to listen to the evidence? How long will you shower special favors on the wicked? Give fair judgment to the poor man, the afflicted, the fatherless, the destitute."

If you ever find yourself seeing or dreaming about the courts of Heaven, that means God wants to overturn something the enemy is holding against you or someone else. Always ask the Lord how to pray and then act swiftly.

PRAYER

Father, in the name of Jesus, I thank You that Jesus is my Advocate and the blood speaks a better thing than the accuser. Help me to navigate courts of Heaven encounters strategically and accurately.

APRIL 22

A GLIMPSE OF THE CROWN OF LIFE

...Be faithful until death, and I will give you the crown of life.
Revelation 2:10

Have you seen your crown? Believers who persevere through trials will receive what Scripture calls the *"crown of life."* God can show you a glimpse of this crown to encourage you or others to continue pressing onward toward the prize.

The crown of life is mentioned twice in Scripture. The first mention is in James 1:12, "Blessed is the man who endures temptation; for when he has been approved, he will receive the crown of life which the Lord has promised to those who love Him."

We see the crown of life mentioned a second time in the context of rewards in the book of Revelation. Revelation 2:10 offers encouragement to the persecuted saints in Smyrna. This is part of one of the seven letters Jesus wrote to the churches in Asia. Jesus advised, "Do not fear any of those things which you are about to suffer. Indeed, the devil is about to throw some of you into prison, that you may be tested, and you will have tribulation ten days. Be faithful until death, and I will give you the crown of life."

Noteworthy is the Greek word for *crown* in these New Testament verses. The word is *stefanos*, which carries a meaning beyond a crown you might see on a modern monarch. It means, "a mark of royal or (in general) exalted rank" that is "given as a prize to victors in public games."

Hebrews 12:1 speaks of running our race with endurance and Jesus plainly said those who endure to the end shall be saved (Matthew 24:13). *Stephos* is also a metaphor for the eternal blessedness that is given as a prize to genuine servants of God.

Beyond encouragement to continue persevering, a seer may see the crown of life over someone who has gone home to be with the Lord to comfort those who mourn. The crown of life, then, often represents the believer's entrance into eternal life.

PRAYER

Father, in the name of Jesus, I am in awe at the many ways You can encourage Your people with visual revelation. I would love to see the crown of life that You have prepared for me. I will cast it at Your feet.

APRIL 23

DISCERNING DARK DREAMS AND VISIONS

Then You scare me with dreams and terrify me with visions.
Job 7:14

If it were strictly up to me, I'd prefer to dream about Jesus, talk to angels in a vision, or see eternity in a trance. But it's not completely up to me. We have an enemy who works to infiltrate our dreams or show us terrifying visions.

So while you may also prefer to dream about Heaven's plans, the throne room, or experience angelic encounters in our dreams, the truth is seers sometimes have dark dreams. It comes with the territory.

Dark dreams are dreams marked by the presence of evil. According to *The Seer's Dictionary*, "Dark dreams often reveal spiritual warfare, hopeless situations, or depressing circumstances. Dark dreams can reveal the enemy's plans to attack finances, relationships, health, or other areas of a person's life. It's vital that you discern the source of these dreams and stand against the enemy's plans."

Dark dreams can torment seers who are younger in their gift because they may not understand that they have authority over the enemy—and authority over dark dreams. Other seers who haven't been trained may believe God gave them dark dreams and they yield to fear or oppression. Seasoned seers, on the other hand, understand that the enemy is attacking their God-given gift.

Make no mistake, the enemy will work to disrupt your divine dreams at some point. Why? Because the enemy is trying to tempt you to forsake the gift. Dark dreams can be beyond terrifying, with no life or light in them.

But know this: God is light, and there is no darkness in Him (1 John 1:5). While God can show you dreams where darkness has invaded a person, city, church, or nation, divine dreams are redemptive in nature. In such encounters, God is shining a light on the darkness so you can intercede. But these dreams don't produce the fruit of soulish fear and oppression.

Think of the very definition of dark: devoid of light, wholly black, dismal, gloomy, not clear to the understanding. Jesus is the light of the world (John 8:12). If you are having dark dreams, ask the Holy Spirit to show you if you have an open door through which the enemy has a right to enter. Pray and plead the blood of Jesus over yourself. But, remember, the enemy doesn't need an open door to attack. Sometimes he attacks to open a door.

PRAYER

Father, in the name of Jesus, I would rather see what You show me, so help me to secure my gates so the enemy can't sneak in with dark dreams. But if he does, please help me discern them and shut them down.

APRIL 24

SURVIVING THE DARK NIGHT OF THE SOUL

Unto the upright there arises light in the darkness; He is gracious, and full of compassion, and righteous.

Psalm 112:4

Have you ever walked through a dark night to the soul? Indeed, you may have done so without understanding what was happening to you. The dark night of the soul is something seers must typically endure—and perhaps not just once in a lifetime.

According to *The Seer's Dictionary*, the dark night of the soul is "a spiritual crisis of sorts, in which you don't seem to feel God's presence, hear His voice, or see what He is doing in our life. Different from a wilderness experience, a dark night of the soul is a transition into a deeper union with God by faith."

I've walked through dark nights more than once. It can feel like an attack from the pit of hell—and the enemy can certainly take advantage during these seasons—but you can choose how you respond. You can choose to view the dark night of the soul as an invitation to greater intimacy and yield to God's transforming power.

I realize that may sound contrary to the one walking through this dark night, since God is often silent and your visual revelation may have ghosted you. For me, it is stressful not to hear a clear word from God. Like David who cried out, "My God, my God, why have You forsaken me," I have felt abandoned at times. But He is always with me—and you. These dark nights refine us.

Know this: God is not punishing you. He's purifying your motives. He's stripping away any self-reliance. He's bringing you to the end of yourself so that your faith is not in your ability—or even your gift—but in Him alone. Like silver in the furnace, the dross brings a fire that brings pride, pain, and hidden fears to the surface so that you can surrender it all to Him and come out seeing more clearly than ever.

Indeed, the dark night of the soul prepares you to step into greater accuracy in the seer dimensions. When you yield to the process, you'll walk in greater authority and revelation out of a deeper sensitivity to the Holy Spirit who shows you things to come. When the light returns, you will have wisdom that can only be forged through the dark nights. It's worth the journey.

PRAYER

Father, in the name of Jesus, I would not choose to go through the dark night of the soul based on what I have heard others say. But based on what I know You do in me through it, I will yield to You.

APRIL 25

WAGING WAR WITH WHAT YOU SEE

> *This command I commit to you, my son Timothy, according to the prophecies that were previously given to you, that by them you might fight a good fight.*
>
> 1 Timothy 1:18 MEV

In this season, I believe there's wind on a strategy Paul gave his spiritual son, Timothy. But it's not just prophetic words with which we can war. We can also war with the visual revelation we see.

Think of Daniel. He had a prophetic vision that took him into prayer and fasting for three whole weeks. That prophetic vision, prayer, and fasting was followed by an angelic encounter from which we can learn plenty. The angel told Daniel from the first day he started praying out that prophetic vision, God heard his words and an angel came because of his words.

> ...For from the first day that you set your heart to understand this and to humble yourself before your God, your words were heard, and I have come because of your words. But the prince of the kingdom of Persia withstood me for twenty-one days. So Michael, one of the chief princes, came to help me, for I had been left there with the kings of Persia (Daniel 10:12-13 MEV).

Angels are still warring in the heavenlies. God can dispatch them—Jesus said He could pray and God would send twelve legions (that's 72,000 angels) to rescue Him (Matthew 26:47-54.) God told Moses He would send an angel before him to drive the enemies out of the land (Exodus 33:2). But angels also obey the voice of His word (Psalm 103:20). That includes the written Word and true visual revelation.

So, we see that waging warfare with the proven visual revelation we've received is scriptural—and that angels hearken unto the voice of His word. The question is, how do we wield this weapon? We pray it through. We decree it. We declare it. We meditate on it so that it gets down so deep in our spirit that when we pray it, decree it, and declare it, it carries authority that comes through faith.

Scripture is the final authority and it's our sword, but tested visual revelations are like arrows in our quiver that we can shoot into the spirit realm to hit the target of God's revealed will. It's time to go back and review some of your visual revelation and rise up against the enemies that are standing in the way of your destiny.

PRAYER

Father, in the name of Jesus, thank You for this spiritual warfare strategy. Help me find the right sword tucked away in my visual revelation that I can war with to see Your will come to pass.

APRIL 26

THE FEELING SEER

...But Paul, greatly annoyed, turned and said to the spirit, "I command you in the name of Jesus Christ to come out of her." And he came out that very hour.

Acts 16:18

Some seers see angels, demons, or even Jesus. Others feel before they see. Put another way, they feel someone coming, or feel that someone has arrived. Those feelings can be almost imperceivable or they can be completely overwhelming.

I am not talking about a natural feeling. I am talking about spiritual feeling, when our spirit senses something that causes us to have an emotional or physical reaction. Feeling in the spirit can cause the hair on the back or your neck to stand up or can allow you to experience the Holy Spirit's emotions.

If you experience these sensations, you may be a feeler. Simply put, a feeler is one who feels in the spirit realm. It's like a spiritual antenna, a sensory organ that you can't see but receives information from the Holy Spirit. This spiritual antenna gives you a special sensitivity or receptiveness. The feeler is often tied in with the gift of discernment, which is tied in with the seer gift.

Not all seers are feelers and not all feelers are seers but both feeling and seeing are part of the realm of discerning of spirits. A seer discerns visually. A feeler discerns with feelings and sensations. In this context, feeling is like an impression but it's stronger than an impression. Most impressions are faint. Feelers have stronger impressions rather your typical "check in the spirit."

Another way to put it is that feelers have spiritual sensations. At times, this can manifest like with the feeling of pain in your body, which would signal someone else has pain. We've called this a manifestation of the word of knowledge, which it is, but it comes in tactical form. Feelers can be moved with strong emotion, but it's not their emotion.

There is a reason for what you are feeling, but that doesn't always mean you will respond. The reason could be for intercession over a person, place, thing, or for when you need to speak up and comfort someone or warn someone.

The feeler gift may operate when you need to battle against something you can't see before it overtakes you, or when you are ministering deliverance on someone. Through the felt gift you may discern the presence of angels or God. I teach more on this in my School of the Spirit.

PRAYER

Father, in the name of Jesus, would You help me see what You see and feel what You feel about what is going on in the spirit realm? Would You help me feel Your presence, angels, or demons so I can respond rightly?

APRIL 27

WITNESSING THE DAY OF THE LORD

For the day of the Lord upon all the nations is near....

Obadiah 1:15

John the Revelator was caught up in the Spirit and saw the Day of the Lord. What is the Day of the Lord?

Also called "that day," the Day of the Lord is the Second Coming of Jesus Christ; a time of salvation and judgment; the culmination of the end of the age, according to *The Seer's Dictionary*. We can read John's account in Revelation 19:11-16:

> Now I saw heaven opened, and behold, a white horse. And He who sat on him was called Faithful and True, and in righteousness He judges and makes war. His eyes were like a flame of fire, and on His head were many crowns. He had a name written that no one knew except Himself. He was clothed with a robe dipped in blood, and His name is called The Word of God. And the armies in heaven, clothed in fine linen, white and clean, followed Him on white horses. Now out of His mouth goes a sharp sword, that with it He should strike the nations. And He Himself will rule them with a rod of iron. He Himself treads the winepress of the fierceness and wrath of Almighty God. And He has on His robe and on His thigh a name written: KING OF KINGS AND LORD OF LORDS.

Luke 21:27 offers some insight from Christ Himself, "Then they will see the Son of Man coming in a cloud with power and great glory." Matthew 16:27 (NIV) offers, "For the Son of Man is going to come in his Father's glory with his angels, and then he will reward each person according to what they have done."

Matthew 24:30 also records Christ saying, "Then the sign of the Son of Man will appear in heaven, and then all the tribes of the earth will mourn, and they will see the Son of Man coming on the clouds of heaven with power and great glory."

Imagine that. Close your eyes and see that. What a sight!

PRAYER

Father, in the name of Jesus, I don't know if I will see the day of Your return in my lifetime. But as I meditate on Your Second Coming, would You help me see what John the Revelator saw?

APRIL 28

A WORD TO THE DAYDREAMING SEER

Thus says the Lord God: "Woe to the foolish prophets, who follow their own spirit and have seen nothing!"

Ezekiel 13:3

Children may daydream about going to Disneyland or what they are going to be when they grow up, but seers need to mature in the realm of visual revelation so they don't mistake their own imagination for a vision from the Lord. In other words, you need to discern between your imagination and God's revelation.

Was that a revelation or a daydream? You should have the ability to tell the difference—or not, and find yourself on the wrong side of the truth.

Daydreaming isn't always a bad thing, but be careful not to call it a Holy Spirit-inspired visual revelation. There is an essential difference between truly seeing something in the spirit versus seeing something in our imagination. We don't want to prophesy based on visions of our own heart, even if those visions reveal good things!

Jeremiah 23:16 says, "Do not listen to the words of the prophets who prophesy to you. They make you worthless; they speak a vision of their own heart, not from the mouth of the Lord."

Not all internal visions are Holy Spirit information. Our minds are not completely renewed yet and can conjure up images based on our biases or even idolatry. Just like some people hear what they want to hear, we can see what we want to see!

That doesn't mean that our imaginations are purely evil. It's healthy to imagine verses coming alive when you are meditating on the Word of God, but it's not right to attribute what you are seeing to a Spirit-inspired revelation. So what's the answer? We need to submit our imaginations to God. Our imaginations need to be sanctified, just like our minds need to be renewed.

David says in Psalm 119:15, "I will meditate on Your precepts, and contemplate Your ways." Setting our imaginations on the Word gives birth to faith and establishes us in truth. And God can certainly give you legitimate visions while you are setting your imagination on the Word, but you still need to test the source of the revelation.

PRAYER

Father, in the name of Jesus, sanctify my imagination. Help me to submit my imagination to Your Word. Please, illuminate my imagination and help me see things that are not visible to the natural senses.

APRIL 29

SEEING SPIRITUAL ALLEGORIES

...A great eagle with large wings and long pinions, full of feathers of various colors, came to Lebanon and took from the cedar the highest branch.

Ezekiel 17:3

God often shows us visual revelation in an allegory. An allegory is an expression of truth using symbolic figures or actions. If you are familiar with Aesop's Fables, you'll catch on quickly.

Consider his fable titled *The Ant and the Grasshopper*. The ants represented people who were diligent and planned ahead for the next season. They worked hard every day so they would have plenty for the future. By contrast, the grasshopper represented those who lived in the moment. They were irresponsible, seeking temporary pleasure. When the winter came, the ants had plenty and the grasshoppers suffered lack.

That's an allegory. God may show seers allegories in either dreams or visions, or during trances or even out-of-body experiences.

Joseph's dreams of his brothers' sheaves bowing down to his sheaf was an allegory, as was his subsequent dream of the sun, moon, and stars bowing to him. The allegory represented his ascent to a powerful position to which they would ultimately submit during the famine.

Likewise, Pharoah's dream in Genesis 41 with the fat cows eating up the skinny cows, followed by seven thin ears of corn consuming the seven healthy ears of corn was an allegory depicting the famine itself.

In Psalm 80, a vine is personified as Israel. In Ezekiel 17, we see an eagle capture the vine, representing Israel's exile in Babylon. Although God spoke these words to Ezekiel, allegories can play out in dreams and visions.

When you see allegories, it takes more time to discern the meaning as it's less literal and more symbolic. Start by asking the Lord what it means. He surely knows and is inviting you to ask. Keep the context in mind. Context is critical in discerning the meaning of allegories in your visual revelation.

Of course, you should search the Scriptures for anything similar that was recorded for your learning. And keep in mind that while allegories can be symbolic, there can sometimes be a literal interpretation. Ultimately, if you break down the allegory piece by piece and pray it through, you'll position yourself for wisdom and revelation.

And if the meaning is not clear, record it and wait. God may give you more revelation later. Sometimes God shows you things now that are for years or decades later. If He gave you the whole meaning now, you may not understand it. But the meaning will become clear when the time is right.

PRAYER

Father, in the name of Jesus, would You help me recognize when You are showing me an allegory so I don't take what is allegorical and try to fit it into a literal box? Help me understand Your visual allegories.

APRIL 30

SPIRITUAL ENCOUNTERS IN DEEP SLEEP

As the sun was setting, Abram fell into a deep sleep, and a thick and dreadful darkness came over him.

Genesis 15:12 NIV

It's one thing to get a good night's rest and to have a deep sleep. But sometimes deep sleep is a supernatural experience. According to *The Seer's Dictionary*, deep sleep is a state of sleep when God escorts you into a seer dimension, and you may or may not remember the entire encounter.

To be sure, entering into a deep sleep in the seer dimensions is an ecstatic encounter that few speak of. We see God put Adam in a deep sleep when he pulled out a rib to form a woman. We also see Abraham and Daniel enter this kind of encounter, as I share in my book, *The Seer Dimensions*.

Look at what happened to Abraham in Genesis 15:12-14: "Now when the sun was going down, a deep sleep fell upon Abram; and behold, horror and great darkness fell upon him. Then He said to Abram: 'Know certainly that your descendants will be strangers in a land that is not theirs, and will serve them, and they will afflict them four hundred years. And also the nation whom they serve I will judge; afterward they shall come out with great possessions.'"

For some seers, this deep sleep can come suddenly, even unexpectedly, leaving them with a powerful, vivid revelation upon waking. Job speaks to this, saying, "For God may speak in one way, or in another, yet man does not perceive it. In a dream, in a vision of the night, when deep sleep falls upon men, while slumbering on their beds" (Job 33:14-15).

This is a relatively rare experience in the seer dimensions, but there are times when seers will find themselves in a divinely inspired deep sleep. We know God is a God of purpose. He's not at all random. So what is the purpose of God putting the seer in a deep sleep? Often it's to reveal mysteries that the natural mind cannot understand without His help.

PRAYER

Father, in the name of Jesus, I'm intrigued by the concept of deep sleep. I know that I cannot enter into this at will and may never experience this, but I am hungry to understand Your mysteries and submit to Your will.

MAY

…your young men shall see visions, your old men shall dream dreams.

Acts 2:17

MAY 1

CRUCIFYING THE CARNAL MIND

Because the carnal mind is enmity against God; for it is not subject to the law of God, nor indeed can be.

Romans 8:7

Carnal seers are not necessarily false seers, but all false seers are carnal seers. Any true seer can turn into a false seer, so we don't want to open the door to carnality in our seer ministry because that can eventually open the door to deceiving spirits.

Carnal seer operations are dangerous because they glorify the flesh. Paul wrote in 1 Corinthians 1:29, "that no flesh shall glory in His presence." Paul also says in Galatians 6:8 (NIV), "Whoever sows to please their flesh, from the flesh will reap destruction [corruption]."

Carnal seer operations are dangerous because they drive jealousy, which breeds strife. Paul wrote in 1 Corinthians 3:3 (NLT), "For you are still controlled by your sinful nature. You are jealous of one another and quarrel with each other. Doesn't that prove you are controlled by your sinful nature? Aren't you living like people of the world?"

Carnal seer operations are dangerous because it can kill your seer reputation. Paul wrote in Romans 8:6 (NLT), "So letting your sinful nature control your mind leads to death. But letting the Spirit control your mind leads to life and peace." Carnal seer operations are dangerous because you may be prophesying the opposite of what God wants for someone. Paul said in Romans 8:7 (NLT), "For the sinful nature is always hostile to God. It never did obey God's laws, and it never will."

Carnal seer operations are dangerous because you are in danger of getting into witchcraft, according to Galatians 5:20. Carnal seer operations are dangerous because you may fall into evil works, according to Galatians 5:17. Carnal seer operations are dangerous because your seer ministry is not pleasing to God, yet you are using His name.

How do you avoid carnal seer operations? Crucify your flesh and renew your mind from worldly influences, including competition, lust, greed. Basically, kill the lusts of the flesh, the lust of the eyes, and the pride of life (1 John 2:16).

PRAYER

Father, in the name of Jesus, I don't want to be a carnal seer. Please, give me grace to crucify my flesh. Help me put to death carnal lusts that could open the door to deception.

MAY 2

SERVE A SEER

And whosoever will be chief among you, let him be your servant.
Matthew 20:27 KJV

One of the secrets to my seer success is service. I have always had a heart to serve my elders and peers. When you serve, you gain access to impartations you may never otherwise receive.

When you serve, you are acting like Jesus. In Matthew 20:27-28 Jesus said, "And whoever desires to be first among you, let him be your slave—just as the Son of Man did not come to be served, but to serve, and to give His life a ransom for many."

It's not about being a butler or a maid. It's a mindset and intentional actions to serve and honor another seer. There is a reward in serving and honoring those who came before you. The writer of Hebrews offered these insights: "For God is not unjust to forget your work and labor of love which you have shown toward His name, in that you have ministered to the saints, and do minister" (Hebrews 6:10).

Think of Elisha. He served Elijah faithfully from the day the prophet threw his mantle on him until the day he was caught up into Heaven and threw his mantle down from the whirlwind. When Jehoshaphat was looking for a true prophet in the land to confirm the Lord's will about going into battle with Ahab, someone told him: "Elisha the son of Shaphat is here, who poured water on the hands of Elijah" (2 Kings 3:11).

What does it mean he "poured water on the hands of Elijah." It's just an ancient way to say that he served Elijah in humble and practical ways. Elisha wasn't just looking for an opportunity to prophesy. He was committed to serving Elijah. The result: Elisha received a double portion of the anointing that was on Elijah's life and did twice as many recorded miracles.

So, seer, remember what Jesus said in Matthew 23:11, "He who is greatest among you shall be your servant." Find a seer to serve.

PRAYER

Father, in the name of Jesus, help me be selfless, serving others. Give me a servant's heart. Teach me the value of being a serving seer. Show me creative ways I can serve my elders and peers.

MAY 3

LIFE-CHANGING LIGHT

Arise, shine; for your light has come! And the glory of the Lord is risen upon you.

Isaiah 60:1

When my daughter was very young, I prayed in her room to evict evil spirits. Immediately after I said, "in Jesus' name, amen," a bright white light shone through the blinds. This was no ordinary light. It was brilliant! God was manifesting His glory as an outward sign that His light displaced the darkness.

One definition of *glory* is light, so it's not surprising that God would manifest His glory as bright white light. We see the glory of the Lord connected with light in Ezekiel 10:4: "Then the glory of the Lord went up from the cherub, and paused over the threshold of the temple; and the house was filled with the cloud, and the court was full of the brightness of the Lord's glory."

Before he was Paul the apostle, Saul the Pharisee had a glory encounter I'm sure he'll never forget. We read it in Acts 9:3-9:

> As he journeyed he came near Damascus, and suddenly a light shone around him from heaven. Then he fell to the ground, and heard a voice saying to him, "Saul, Saul, why are you persecuting Me?"
>
> And he said, "Who are You, Lord?" Then the Lord said, "I am Jesus, whom you are persecuting. It is hard for you to kick against the goads." So he, trembling and astonished, said, "Lord, what do You want me to do?"
>
> Then the Lord said to him, "Arise and go into the city, and you will be told what you must do." And the men who journeyed with him stood speechless, hearing a voice but seeing no one. Then Saul arose from the ground, and when his eyes were opened he saw no one. But they led him by the hand and brought him into Damascus. And he was three days without sight, and neither ate nor drank.

When you see the light of God's glory, you will never be the same.

PRAYER

Father, in the name of Jesus, I know You are the light of the world. Your light shines in the darkness and the darkness cannot overcome it. Lord, I want to witness the light of Your glory. Would You open my eyes?

MAY 4

WHEN SEERS DISAGREE

Then the contention became so sharp that they parted from one another. And so Barnabas took Mark and sailed to Cyprus.
Acts 15:39

Hananiah and Jeremiah had a prophetic showdown of sorts. We see the dramatic encounter in Jeremiah 28. Hananiah told Israel that God had broken the yoke of the king of Babylon. He prophesied, "Within two full years I will bring back to this place all the vessels of the Lord's house..." (Jeremiah 28:3).

That didn't sit well with Jeremiah. Look how he responded, "Amen! The Lord do so; the Lord perform your words which you have prophesied.... Nevertheless hear now this word that I speak in your hearing and in the hearing of all the people: The prophets who have been before me and before you of old prophesied against many countries and great kingdoms—of war and disaster and pestilence" (Jeremiah 28:6-8).

Clearly, they were in disagreement. But it didn't end there. Hananiah made a show of it. He proceeded to take the yoke off Jeremiah's neck and break it, saying, "Thus says the Lord: 'Even so I will break the yoke of Nebuchadnezzar king of Babylon from the neck of all nations within the space of two full years'" (Jeremiah 28:11).

What happened next? Jeremiah walked away and Hananiah died. Not all seer disagreements are so dramatic. In fact, many disagreements are not a matter of someone seeing wrongly. It could be the interpretation or the application that isn't accurate. Sometimes two seers can have dramatically different visual revelations that mean the same thing, but they don't recognize that God is just speaking truth in two different ways.

So how do you handle a seer disagreement? In humility. Don't assume that you are right and the other seer is wrong. You each may have a piece of the larger picture. Paul tells us plainly in 1 Corinthians 13:9, "For we know in part and we prophesy in part." The Holy Spirit is not confused, but strife can quench His revelation.

If you are in relationship with the seer, don't publicly come against them to defy them like Hananiah did with Jeremiah. That shows arrogance rather than cooperation. If you want to know the truth, pray together in humility and wait for the Lord to show you what you both need to say. If you are at a stalemate, present the visual revelation to others in the Body of Christ who have the ability to judge. Strife kills the anointing.

PRAYER

Father, in the name of Jesus, would You help me walk in humility with other seers who have seemingly conflicting visions and dreams? Give me the grace to listen and pray so that we can all come into agreement.

MAY 5

THE DETAIL-ORIENTED SEER

And I saw a beast rising out of the sea, with ten horns and seven heads, with ten diadems on its horns and blasphemous names on its heads.

Revelation 13:1 ESV

If attention to detail is an important quality in writing a book, baking a cake, or painting a house—and it is—how much more important is it to what you see in the spirit? Indeed, one of the most critical skills you can develop as a seer is disciplining your eyes to pay attention to every detail of your dreams, visions, and other experiences in the seer dimensions.

Think about it this way: The Holy Spirit doesn't waste any detail. Nothing is random in your seer experience. He speaks through colors, numbers, movements, objects, and more. If you want to tap into the diverse layers of revelation in what you see, it's important to pay attention to and record every detail you remember.

The less experienced seer may not understand that the Holy Spirit is dropping breadcrumbs, hints and clues that will lead you to deeper truths. Paying attention to details is part of spiritual curiosity and it will be rewarded with revelation; if not now, then when you need it.

Leave no details unrecorded or unstudied. Even if you don't understand it now, it means something and God will reveal it at the right time.

But don't just record them. Meditate on what you saw. Pray about it. Ask God to reveal the meaning of the details and how it all fits together. Study the Word for parallels. You will hit gold, so to speak, if you keep digging. You'll gain more than insight. You may get the wisdom and strategy you need.

What if John hadn't recorded those details in Revelation 13? It's the same with Ezekiel's vision of God on the throne, Daniel's vision of the four beasts or Isaiah's vision of God's glory. Those details bless us today, giving us revelation most of us would never otherwise have. So do not forget that even the tiniest of details can contain the weight of Heaven's strategy and direction. This practice is critical for every seer to walk in accuracy and clarity with their calling.

PRAYER

Father, in the name of Jesus, help me not only to see what You are showing me clearly, but also to pay close attention to every detail. If I forgot part of what I saw, please remind me so I can record it accurately like John.

MAY 6

DON'T GO TO ENDOR

Give no regard to mediums and familiar spirits; do not seek after them, to be defiled by them: I am the Lord your God.

Leviticus 19:31

King Saul goes down in Bible history as a failure in many ways. He was disobedient to the Lord more than once and the kingdom was stripped from him and given to another.

But perhaps his greatest failure was going to a medium to gain seer intelligence. Samuel was gone and he could not hear from the Lord, so he entered into yet another compromise. First Samuel 28:8 reveals: "So Saul disguised himself and put on other clothes, and he went, and two men with him; and they came to the woman by night. And he said, 'Please conduct a séance for me, and bring up for me the one I shall name to you.'"

Saul knew this was an illegal operation. Indeed, the medium knew full well the king had "cut off the mediums and the spiritists from the land" (1 Samuel 28:9). Still in disguise, Saul assured her no punishment would come to her and she agreed to bring up Samuel.

> When the woman saw Samuel, she cried out with a loud voice. And the woman spoke to Saul, saying, "Why have you deceived me? For you are Saul!" And the king said to her, "Do not be afraid. What did you see?" (1 Samuel 28:12-13).

What do you see? That's a question the Lord asks prophets sometimes. In this case, the king was asking a witch what she saw through her divination. "And the woman said to Saul, 'I saw a spirit ascending out of the earth'" (1 Samuel 28:13).

Saul didn't stop there. He asked her for more details. "And she said, 'An old man is coming up, and he is covered with a mantle.' And Saul perceived that it was Samuel, and he stooped with his face to the ground and bowed down" (1 Samuel 28:14).

Here's one of many lessons in this passage—if you are so desperate for seer intelligence that you are willing to compromise, you may see familiar spirits and pervert your gift.

PRAYER

Father, in the name of Jesus, help me to never compromise the seer gift You have given me. Help me never to cross the line from directional revelation to pure divination. I only want to see what You show me.

MAY 7

ENTERING THE ECSTATIC DIMENSION

> *Now it happened, when I returned to Jerusalem and was praying in the temple, that I was in a trance and saw Him saying to me, "Make haste and get out of Jerusalem quickly, for they will not receive your testimony concerning Me."*
>
> Acts 22:17-18

The ecstatic realm is a realm marked by ecstasy. We have relegated that word to a feeling of the flesh. There's even a hallucinogenic drug called ecstasy that gives extreme feelings of euphoria. Indeed, the world has hijacked the word, but ecstasy is actually a biblical concept. It's one of many mystical aspects of the prophetic.

To understand the ecstatic realm, you have to understand mystics, which is just another word for mysteries. *Merriam-Webster's Dictionary* defines *mystical* as "having a spiritual meaning or reality that is neither apparent to the senses nor obvious to the intelligence." The Greek word for *ecstasy* is *ekstasis* and means "standing outside oneself."

Although some high-profile Christians have given a bad name to mystics, Christian mystics of more than 1,000 years ago were men and women of great revelation who left behind understandings into the mysteries of God and His Word such as:

> *Truly it is a trustworthy word and deserving of every welcome, your almighty Word, Lord, which in such deep silence made its way down from the Father's royal throne and speaks to us better by its silence. Hear what this loving and mysterious silence of the eternal Word speaks to us. He speaks peace for the holy people upon whom reverence for him and his example impose a religious silence. —Guerric of Igny, an 11th century Cistercian abbot*

Paul, who wrote two-thirds of the New Testament by direct revelation, spoke of mystic concepts again and again in the Bible. If we are rooted and grounded in the Bible in the mystic realm, including trances, being caught up in the spirit and transported in the spirit, we can engage with the whole counsel of God and understand better the mysteries of the Kingdom.

The Holy Spirit is the Revealer. He is the One who revealed Christ to our heart and convicted us, drawing us to our Savior. That was just the beginning. The Holy Spirit wants us to come to the knowledge of the mystery of God, which unlocks treasures, wisdom, and knowledge. Sometimes he reveals mysteries through His Word, sometimes through a still small voice, and sometimes through the seer dimensions.

PRAYER

Father, in the name of Jesus, I would love to enter the ecstatic realm. Help me to unlearn wrong teachings that paint this as New Age or demonic. I am willing to follow the Holy Spirit anywhere He leads me.

MAY 8

THE COMPARISON TRAP

For we dare not count or compare ourselves with those who commend themselves. They who measure themselves by one another and compare themselves with one another are not wise.

2 Corinthians 10:12 MEV

Don't compare your seer flow with anyone else's seer flow. God moves differently through different seers. You don't need to see like anyone else—nor should you try to. God has given you a unique sight, a unique style, and a unique message. You have a unique seer expression.

You may not see angels, but you may have epic dreams. You may not see over nations, but your visual revelation may encourage the masses. You may not interpret dreams, but you may see revelation in the spirit and understand how to apply it to benefit the Body of Christ. Be willing to go deeper, but be comfortable with how God moves through you while you hunger for more in a healthy way.

Second Corinthians 10:12 (AMP) reminds, "We do not have the audacity to put ourselves in the same class or compare ourselves with some who [supply testimonials to] commend themselves. When they measure themselves by themselves and compare themselves with themselves, they lack wisdom and behave like fools."

Catch that. It's not wise to compare yourself with anyone else in any area, but particularly in the realm of spiritual gifts. If you compare yourself to someone else and decide you are "more anointed," you could get puffed up with pride and fall. Paul wrote in Romans 12:3, "For I say, through the grace given to me, to everyone who is among you, not to think of himself more highly than he ought to think, but to think soberly, as God has dealt to each one a measure of faith."

The flip side of that is you might think less of yourself than you ought. You may not feel like you are as anointed or accurate or prolific or "fill-in-the blank." God made you the way you are and you are growing. Don't toxify your seer flow with comparisons.

If we are going to compare ourselves with anyone in the seer ministry, it should be Jesus. He is the prototype Seer. We will never live up to His accuracy, wisdom, and grace, but we can safely look at Him as the model. Remember, you can get into a lot of trouble—and error—trying to be something prophetically that you are not. Be confident in who you are while God keeps making you into a better you.

PRAYER

Father, in the name of Jesus, help me to always take the advice Paul shared by Your spirit. Help me not to compare my seer ministry with anyone else's. I am content with who You've called me to be.

MAY 9

WALKING BY FAITH INTO SIGHT

While we do not look at the things which are seen, but at the things which are not seen. For the things which are seen are temporary, but the things which are not seen are eternal.

2 Corinthians 4:18

Paul said we walk by faith, not by sight; but we also walk by faith into sight. Just like we prophesy according to the proportion of our faith, we step into the seer dimensions through the door of Jesus according to the proportion of our faith (Romans 12:6).

So how do we cultivate faith to see into the spirit realm? It often begins by rooting out wrong teaching—teaching that insists only seers can see in the spirit realm. Or worse, that no one today can see into the spirit realm. If you have doubt, fear, or unbelief in your heart, it's hard to see through the eyes of your heart. Once you've laid an axe to the root of these obstacles, you can work to build yourself up in your most holy faith to see in the spirit.

I'm big on praying in the Spirit, or what we call praying in tongues. Jude 20 tells us that we can build ourselves in our most holy faith by praying in the Spirit.

Holy faith is sanctified faith. It's pure faith. Reading accounts of seers in the Bible is another way to build faith. Exploring the visions of Ezekiel and Daniel and the dreams of Joseph and other seers builds faith because, "Faith comes by hearing, and hearing by the word of God" (Romans 10:17).

Along with that, stop confessing that you can't see in the spirit. You should be confessing that you can see what God wants you to see in the spirit realm; that He is opening your eyes wide to spiritual things and giving you spiritual vision; and that you have a prophetic spirit. Confess that you have prophetic dreams and visions. Call those things that are not as though they are (Romans 4:17).

Every day, ask God to open the eyes of your heart. In Ephesians 1:18-19, Paul prayed that the eyes of our heart would be enlightened so we would know the hope of our calling. When the eyes of your heart are enlightened, you can see and know many things in the spirit. You receive revelation, wisdom, understanding, discernment, and more.

PRAYER

Father, in the name of Jesus, I commit to building my faith to see into the unseen realms. Help me remember to keep my heart right, my mouth right, and my faith high by meditating on Your Word.

MAY 10

RIGHT DREAM, WRONG APPLICATION

And they said to him, "We each have had a dream, and there is no interpreter of it." So Joseph said to them, "Do not interpretations belong to God? Tell them to me, please."

Genesis 40:8

You can have the most accurate dream or vision a seer has ever received. You can even have the right interpretation of what you saw in the spirit. But without the right application, you can make a mess. Or worse, you can unintentionally lead others astray. Indeed, applying the revelation is where some seers miss the mark.

Of course, not all dreams have an immediate application. God may be showing you something for the future, or the application may be partial now and fuller later. Likewise, God may give you the dream, give someone else the interpretation, and give yet a third person the interpretation. That's the beauty of a company of seers.

If you don't know how to apply what you've seen in the spirit, James 1:5 (AMPC) assures us, "If any of you is deficient in wisdom, let him ask of the giving God [Who gives] to everyone liberally and ungrudgingly, without reproaching or faultfinding, and it will be given him."

Sometimes, the Holy Spirit gives us an application in measures. Dreams or visions you have today may have one application now and a deeper application in the future. If He gave you all the applications now, you might get ahead of Him. This is what I call the progressive application of your visual revelation.

In other words, when you received revelation in a dream or vision you applied it the best way you knew how at the time. That application wasn't wrong, but it may not have been the fullness of God's prophetic intent. Often, it takes years for a dream or vision to realize its full manifestation, as we saw in the life of Joseph.

The same is true for corporate visual revelation. You may receive one application now, but that doesn't mean there's not more to the story that will unfold later. That's why we don't take a "one-and-done" approach to applying what God shows us. We need to keep a journal and review our revelations and the applications. But remember, just like the interpretation belongs to the Lord, so does the application.

PRAYER

Father, in the name of Jesus, show me how to apply the visual revelation You have given me. Remind me that application can come in stages. Bring to my memory things You've shown me in the past that are relevant now.

MAY 11

SUPERNATURAL VISITATIONS

Therefore take heed how you hear. For whoever has, to him more will be given; and whoever does not have, even what he seems to have will be taken from him.

Luke 8:18

Seers often focus on the seeing aspect of their gift, but many times God will also speak words of truth in a vision. (In fact, God speaking in a vision instead of a still small voice is one way we distinguish between a prophet and a seer.)

The word of the Lord can come to you in a vision, even if you don't see the Lord. While God does not speak in every vision—sometimes you see Him moving, or see a vision of a future event, or even a visual word of knowledge—we need to open our spiritual ears to what He might want to share. We need to activate all of our spiritual senses.

Consider Abaham's experience in Genesis 15:1, "After these things the word of the Lord came to Abram in a vision, saying, 'Do not be afraid, Abram. I am your shield, your exceedingly great reward.'"

First, catch the context: After what things? What happened right before the Lord came to Abram in the vision and what can we learn from this? This vision came to Abram right after Abram tithed to Melchizedek, the priest of God Most High. It came right after Abram refused any reward from the king of Sodom. It came after extreme selflessness and obedience.

Second, read the verse again. The Lord came to Abram in a vision. It wasn't just a picture. The Lord spoke clearly to Him. He didn't have to spend a year deciphering the message. It was plain as day.

God rewards those who diligently seek Him (Hebrews 11:6). The willing and obedient will eat the good of the land (Isaiah 1:19). Abram showed himself faithful and God visited him in a vision with a promise and reward greater than any other: "I am your exceedingly great reward."

God doesn't just appear in visions to anyone. And we can't conjure up a visitation—nor should we seek one. When we seek supernatural visitations, satan may disguise himself as an angel of light and deceive us. Also keep in mind God didn't regularly visit Abram in visions. These are special encounters.

That said, if we want to position ourselves for supernatural visitations from our supernatural God, we should be diligent seekers of His heart, selfless and generous. In other words, we should walk with Him and obey Him. Are you willing?

PRAYER

Father, in the name of Jesus, help me to sharpen my spiritual senses so that I can glean the fullness of the messages that come through visions, dreams, and other encounters. Give me ears to hear.

MAY 12

THE READY HEART

Keep on asking and it will be given you; keep on seeking and you will find; keep on knocking [reverently] and [the door] will be opened to you.

Matthew 7:7 AMPC

As I always say, "God is speaking more than we're listening." It's also true that God wants to speak to you in dreams more than you are receiving. Yes, God wants to speak to you in dreams. It's part of how He wired you as a seer. The wise seer prepares to receive divine dreams.

What am I saying? We need to prepare our heart to receive His messages while we're asleep. That means cultivating a heart posture to receive divine revelation in your dreams before your head hits the pillow. If you are serious about receiving and remembering the dreams He gives you, then do your part. You don't want to miss warnings, information, and the mysteries He wants to share.

How do you prepare your heart to receive dreams? Before you go to sleep, pray. Ask the Holy Spirit to share anything He would like you to see that night. Ask Him to help you remember anything He shares.

Jeremiah 33:3 (NIV) says, "Call to me and I will answer you and tell you great and unsearchable things you do not know." You can pray that Scripture back to Him knowing that it is His will. After inviting Him to release divine dream downloads, expect to dream.

Proverbs 23:18 (AMP) says, "...your hope and expectation will not be cut off." I'm not suggesting you w he spiritual side, repent for any sins you've committed that day. Cast all your cares on Him. Cleanse your heart and mind of the clutter from the day. We want clean hands and a pure heart as we lay down to sleep.

Worshipping or meditating on Scripture before you call it a night is also wise if you want to prepare your heart to receive prophetic dreams. When you engage with Him at this level, you are sowing to the spirit and positioning yourself to reap from the spirit realm.

PRAYER

Father, in the name of Jesus, I take the dream realm seriously. Help me to prepare myself to receive divine dreams while I sleep. Help me build a holy expectation to dream the dreams of God.

MAY 13

THE SAMUEL SEER ANOINTING

Samuel answered Saul and said, "I am the seer. Go up before me to the high place, for you shall eat with me today; and tomorrow I will let you go and will tell you all that is in your heart."

1 Samuel 9:19

Samuel was dedicated to the Lord from his mother's womb. He was a miracle child from the tribe of Levi and the last judge in Israel. This seer prophet anointed Israel's first two kings, Saul and David. His name literally means "name of God" or "heard of God."

Samuel's prophetic ministry was marked by uncanny accuracy. When Saul came to the seer inquiring about his father's donkeys, Samuel had detailed knowledge, "As for your donkeys that were lost three days ago, do not be anxious about them, for they have been found..." (1 Samuel 9:20).

Further, 1 Samuel 10:1-8 demonstrates just how specific Samuel was. The seer gave Saul extremely specific signs that would unfold on his way back home. Samuel prophesied Saul would meet two men near Rachel's tomb to confirm the donkeys were found, meet three men at the great tree of Tabor, each carrying specific items, and meet up with a company of prophets playing the harp, tambourine, flute lyre. Samuel also prophesied that the Spirit of God would come upon Saul and he would prophesy. Everything came to pass in exact detail.

First Samuel 3:19 tells us, "So Samuel grew, and the Lord was with him and let none of his words fall to the ground." The NLT says, "everything Samuel said proved to be reliable." And The Living Bible says, "people listened carefully to his advice." That's quite a reputation, and quite an anointing!

That's an accurate and precise seer anointing. Samuel also raised up other prophets and seers in his schools, shaping the future of the prophetic movement his mother birthed when he was born. He was a mentor to kings whose words carried the weight of Heaven. But he was also an intercessor, standing in the gap for a sinful nation and calling them to repentance. The Samuel anointing is one of purity, precision, and perseverance.

PRAYER

Father, in the name of Jesus, would You impart to me the Samuel seer anointing? Help me walk in the fear of the Lord he displayed while releasing words of judgment. Raise me up to impart truth to other seers.

MAY 14

TESTING YOUR VISUAL ACCURACY

The hearing ear and the seeing eye, the Lord has made them both.
Proverbs 20:12

When I was growing up, we had eye exams at school every year. It wasn't exhaustive like the eye exams you get when you go to the ophthalmologist, but they did use a Snellen chart. You know, the one with the big E at the top and the letters that get smaller and smaller toward the bottom so that you have to squint to see them.

When I was 13 years old, I failed the test! Honestly, I knew the letters on the chalkboard were blurry, but when I squinted I could see just fine. I didn't think I needed glasses and didn't want them, but my parents insisted on taking me to the mall to get confirmation of my visual problems and prescribe a fix. That fix came in the form of glasses with some pretty thick lenses!

Why am I telling you this? Because just as I was deceived into thinking my natural eyesight was just fine when it wasn't, you may think your spiritual eyesight is just fine when it's not. You don't want to deceive yourself when you are seeing for the Lord, and you don't want to be deceived by the enemy either.

That's why testing your visual accuracy in the spirit is just as important, if not more important, than testing your natural vision. If your natural vision is not strong, you need a prescription to fix it. If your spiritual vision is dim or you are seeing wrongly, the prescription is the Word and the Spirit.

So how do you test your visual accuracy in the seer dimensions? How do you know if you are seeing rightly?

There are a battery of tests you can perform, but here's the main one: a vision from God will not violate Scripture, but should somehow glorify God by showing you His will, revealing the enemy's plans, or spurring you to press in to Him or pray. The more you stay in the Word and fellowship with the Spirit, the more accurate you will be.

PRAYER

Father, in the name of Jesus, would You remind me, from time to time, to take a spiritual eye exam. I know there are many things that can damage my spiritual eyesight. I want to see rightly.

MAY 15

INTIMATE INTERPRETATIONS

He who has knowledge spares his words, and a man of understanding is of a calm spirit.

Proverbs 17:27

God is personal in how He speaks. He knows exactly how you think and process information, and in His wisdom, He tailors His communication to reach you in the way you best receive it. That's why ten people can have the same dream and accurately draw ten different meanings from it—God is speaking to each of them through the lens of their own life and experience.

Here's a great example. If you are a dog lover, God may use a dog in your dream to symbolize loyalty. But if you were attacked by dogs as a youth, a dog will mean something much different to you—old Fido would not be a welcomed sight. As you can see, dream language is subjective.

Here's another example. If you have been through a painful divorce, a dream in which you are getting married may mean something totally different to you than to someone who is longing for a mate. And marriage doesn't always mean actual marriage. It could mean a covenant or partnership. Again, it's subjective.

By subjective, I mean particular to your worldview. We all have personal preferences—even biases. We have unique backgrounds and life experiences. Even within the same family, parents relate to individual children in subjective ways. Dad may relate differently to his son than his daughter, and differently to his firstborn than his last born based on their personalities or what he has learned over the years.

God knows our emotional makeup better than we do. God knows our knowledge base. God knows our personal experiences. And He knows we're going to filter any and all communications through a uniquely colored lens. While we must always turn to the Bible for interpretation, sometimes the interpretation is more subjective than biblical—but will never violate Scripture.

Dreams, then, are not only symbolic and parabolic, at times they are subjective. When you are interpreting dreams other people have—whether it's about you or about something related to your own life—you can't filter it through your own dream code. Our heavenly Father speaks to us in a way that is intimate between us and Him.

PRAYER

Father, in the name of Jesus, thank You for speaking to me personally. Help me remember the rule of subjectivity so that I don't accidentally interpret someone else's dreams through my personal lens.

MAY 16

WHEN THE VISION IS ALMOST TOO MUCH TO BEAR

So I said: "Woe is me, for I am undone! Because I am a man of unclean lips, and I dwell in the midst of a people of unclean lips; for my eyes have seen the King, the Lord of hosts."

Isaiah 6:5

Also called an amazing vision or a grand vision in Scripture, you may find yourself in the midst of a great vision. Daniel did.

Daniel had many visions, but in Daniel 10 he had something far beyond what we would call a normal vision. Daniel specifically denoted it as a great vision. According to *The Seer's Dictionary*, a great vision is an intense vision; a vision that is large in magnitude; an important vision. While we may see simple visions or pictures, a grand vision is set apart.

The prophet Daniel speaks of a great vision in Daniel 10:8, "Therefore I was left alone when I saw this great vision, and no strength remained in me; for my vigor was turned to frailty in me, and I retained no strength."

Elliot's Commentary for English Readers offers, "Daniel again distinguishes this from former visions: The glory of the man who appeared to him was far in excess of what he had witnessed previously (Daniel 8:7). The effects of the vision upon him are also mentioned. His 'comeliness was turned,' or, he grew pale with terror at what he saw, and fainted."

When you see a great vision, you need to spend more time with it than a simple picture. There are likely layers upon layers of revelation, such as with my vision of the war room in Heaven. You need to meditate on it, and sometimes ask the Lord to show it to you again. Don't be too quick to move on from a great vision.

PRAYER

Father, in the name of Jesus, help me discern the layers upon layers of revelation that often come with a great vision. As I sit with You and wait, show me what everything means that I saw.

MAY 17

SEEING VISIONS WITH YOUR EYES CLOSED

Ears to hear and eyes to see—both are gifts from the Lord.
Proverbs 20:12 NLT

I love when God gives me open visions with vivid images that mark my spiritual senses. These encounters are unforgettable and can even be life changing, like when I saw Jesus with a sword in His hand offering me an invitation to go deeper. But the reality is not all visions qualify as epic. Not all dreams are astounding.

We need to appreciate anything and everything the Holy Spirit shows us in the seer dimensions, including what we call inner visions. Also called a closed vision, an inner vision is "a vision in which one sees with his mind's eye; a vision in which the Holy Spirit shows one something internally rather than an open vision or encounter," according to *The Seer's Dictionary*. Inner visions are more common than open visions, but they can be just as important as any other visual encounter.

An inner vision isn't something you see outwardly. It's a picture or a scene that suddenly appears in your mind. It's almost like an imagination, but it doesn't come from your mind. It comes from the mind of Christ, revealed by the Holy Spirit, and carries significant revelation. Inner visions can manifest out of the blue, but often appear during prayer, worship or meditating on the Word.

Ephesians 1:18 speaks of "the eyes of your understanding being enlightened." Paul wasn't talking about your natural eyes. He was talking about your spiritual eyes that can see what God wants to reveal. When you close your natural eyes, you can still see in the spirit because your spiritual eyes aren't closed!

In fact, when you close your natural eyes it can sometimes be easier to see in the spirit because you aren't distracted by everything going on around you in the natural realm. In a way, the Holy Spirit has your undivided attention. That's a good time to impress a picture, scene, or symbol that carries a message.

Don't despise inner visions because they seem small. They can reveal guidance, expose warfare or demonic assignments, encourage and strengthen you or someone else, and bring prophetic revelation that you need. As with any revelation, test it against Scripture. Check the fruit of it and, if it's weighty, ask the Holy Spirit for confirmation.

PRAYER

Father, in the name of Jesus, help me focus in with my spiritual eyes. As I pray in the Spirit and my mind is unfruitful, make my spiritual eyes fruitful. Show me something to come. Give me an inner vision.

MAY 18

AN UNPOPULAR SEER ASSIGNMENT

> *"Therefore I will judge you, O house of Israel, every one according to his ways," says the Lord God. "Repent, and turn from all your transgressions, so that iniquity will not be your ruin."*
>
> Ezekiel 18:30

Mature seers are not afraid to boldly address sin in the Church and call for repentance while praying for mercy. Isaiah called Judah to repent in Isaiah 1:16-17, "Wash yourselves, make yourselves clean; put away the evil of your doings from before My eyes. Cease to do evil, learn to do good; seek justice, rebuke the oppressor; defend the fatherless, plead for the widow."

Jeremiah called Israel to repentance in the days of Josiah the king (Jeremiah 3:6). Hosea called for repentance in Hosea 6:1. Joel called for repentance in Joel 2. Ezekiel called the house of Israel to repent in Ezekiel 14:6-7:

> Therefore say to the house of Israel, "Thus says the Lord God: 'Repent, turn away from your idols, and turn your faces away from all your abominations. For anyone of the house of Israel, or of the strangers who dwell in Israel, who separates himself from Me and sets up his idols in his heart and puts before him what causes him to stumble into iniquity, then comes to a prophet to inquire of him concerning Me, I the Lord will answer him by Myself.'"

Those are just a few of the prophetic calls for repentance in the Old Testament. In the New Testament, both John the Baptist and Jesus called for repentance. Can you see the trend line? Calls for repentance go hand in hand with the seer calling.

A call for repentance is a call to return fully to the Lord. It's a call to turn back from sin and go back to God. It's a call to restoration of a right relationship with God. It's turning away from what grieves His heart and putting God back in His rightful place in our lives.

Calling for repentance should be done in humility, not harshness. It's supposed to bring freedom, not resentment. In Acts 3:19, Peter said, "Repent therefore and be converted, that your sins may be blotted out, so that times of refreshing may come from the presence of the Lord." In God's kindness, He leads people to repentance (Romans 2:4).

PRAYER

Father, in the name of Jesus, would You give me the right blend of humility and boldness to call for repentance when repentance is called for? Help me to be led by Your Spirit, never my flesh, when I need to call people to repent.

MAY 19

THE MASTER KEY TO SEEING MORE

O God, You are my God; early will I seek You; my soul thirsts for You; my flesh longs for You in a dry and thirsty land where there is no water.

Psalm 63:1

At our Watchman & Warrior's Summit, God spoke something to me that really moved my heart: "Look at Me and I'll show you everything you need to see."

At times, young seers (and I mean young in the gift, not necessarily young in age) strive to see in the spirit. But striving is always the wrong approach in the seer dimensions. Instead of spending all that energy striving, we should spend it seeking. When we seek, we won't have to strive.

Striving is not faith, but it takes faith to seek. Hebrews 11:6 tells us, "But without faith it is impossible to please Him, for he who comes to God must believe that He is, and that He is a rewarder of those who diligently seek Him." Sometimes, oftentimes in fact, the reward for the seer is a visual revelation.

When we meditate on God—when we gaze upon His beauty—we are priming our visual pumps. Put another way, intimacy with God is the master key to developing your seer anointing. We need to take on David's attitude in Psalm 27:4: "One thing I have desired of the Lord, that will I seek: That I may dwell in the house of the Lord all the days of my life, to behold the beauty of the Lord, and to inquire in His temple."

Invest your time waiting on Him. Study His character, His heart, and His ways. Dialogue with Him. You won't see in the spirit more than you talk with the Spirit. Cultivate a lifestyle of worship. That's how you gain third-heaven revelation. Learn to abide in Him and you will bear much seer fruit.

Paul, an apostle who had dramatic encounters with the Lord, wrote these deep words in Philippians 3:8 (AMPC), "Yes, furthermore, I count everything as loss compared to the possession of the priceless privilege (the overwhelming preciousness, the surpassing worth, and supreme advantage) of knowing Christ Jesus my Lord and of progressively becoming more deeply and intimately acquainted with Him [of perceiving and recognizing and understanding Him more fully and clearly]…." That's our aim!

PRAYER

Father, in the name of Jesus, I repent for any times I entered into striving when I should have entered the simplicity of seeking. I want to know You intimately. Help me set aside the distractions.

MAY 20

STANDING UNDER AN OPEN HEAVEN

When He had been baptized, Jesus came up immediately from the water; and behold, the heavens were opened to Him, and He saw the Spirit of God descending like a dove and alighting upon Him.

Matthew 3:16

When you see the heavens open, God is inviting you to a revelation of Himself that you will never forget. Some seers tend to have more of these types of encounters than others, but even if you never see the heavens open you can read accounts in Scripture and imagine the details of what someone else saw. Indeed, meditating on these accounts can lead you into the seer dimensions.

When I read accounts in the Bible where men of God saw into Heaven, I pay attention to every little detail they scribed. I see both a consistency in the descriptions of the third heaven and new details that are recorded in different encounters that help me paint a more clear, yet obviously incomplete picture, of the heavenly dimension.

Ezekiel saw the heavens opened. So did John the Revelator. So did Stephen the martyr. So did John the Baptist. Only God can initiate such divine encounters, and it's not always an out-of-body experience. Don't just read the accounts I am going to share. Meditate on them. Imagine them.

Revelation 19:11-12 offers John's encounter: "Now I saw heaven opened, and behold, a white horse. And He who sat on him was called Faithful and True, and in righteousness He judges and makes war. His eyes were like a flame of fire, and on His head were many crowns. He had a name written that no one knew except Himself."

Ezekiel wrote, "Now it came to pass in the thirtieth year, in the fourth month, on the fifth day of the month, as I was among the captives by the River Chebar, that the heavens were opened and I saw visions of God" (Ezekiel 1:1).

And here's Stephen's account: "But he, being full of the Holy Spirit, gazed into heaven and saw the glory of God, and Jesus standing at the right hand of God, and said, 'Look! I see the heavens opened and the Son of Man standing at the right hand of God!'" (Acts 7:55-56).

Notice how all of this happens suddenly. These and others who saw Heaven open up didn't merely have an imagination. They had an encounter that was by the will of God, not by their own will. There is jaw-dropping revelation when the heavens open. You can't make it happen, but don't be surprised if it does.

PRAYER

Father, in the name of Jesus, as I meditate on these accounts of the heavens opening, would You show me that they saw? I want to do more than imagine it. I want to see it as they saw it.

MAY 21

THE ABCS OF PRESENTING REVELATION

Joseph had a dream, and when he told it to his brothers, they hated him all the more.

Genesis 37:5 NIV

Every seer needs to master the skill of revelation presentation. That's because the presentation can make all the difference whether your revelation is received or rejected. Whether it's a dream, a vision, or some other seer encounter, you need to take great care in how you share your revelations.

I've crafted what I call the ABCs of revelation presentation to give you a simple way to remember a strategic protocol for seers.

A stands for "Always Get Clarity from the Holy Spirit." Don't share half-baked visual revelation publicly. Spend time in prayer and ask the Holy Spirit to show you the meaning of what you saw and the application. If you are in a hurry to share what you see, you could miss a layer of meaning that is important for the audience for whom the revelation is intended. Rushing to release is often reckless and sometimes what you see is not for public release to begin with. It's for the sake of intercession. In this case, you present petitions back to God in prayer based on the revelation.

B stands for "Be Humble in Your Delivery." Paul said, "Knowledge puffs up, but love edifies" (1 Corinthians 8:1). It's easy for seers to get haughty when they move in revelation. Remember, Paul said a thorn was in his side because of the abundance of revelation, to keep him from being conceited (2 Corinthians 12:7). Remember also that we see in part and know in part (1 Corinthians 13:9). Don't demand people hear you or comply with your revelation. Present it humbly.

C stands for "Communicate Simply." Visual revelation can have layers of complexity that can leave people feeling overwhelmed or confused if you get too granular. Communicate what you saw clearly and concisely in the first presentation. You can always unpack it more deeply if needed. Stick to the core truths in the message and how to apply the revelation practically and people will be more receptive.

PRAYER

Father, in the name of Jesus, would You help me master the art of revelation presentation? I know the way I present what I saw in the spirit matters. Help me not to overcomplicate it.

MAY 22

HOW'S YOUR DREAM RECALL?

Then the secret was revealed to Daniel in a night vision. So Daniel blessed the God of heaven.

Daniel 2:19

Just the other day I woke up knowing that I had a significant dream and couldn't remember it. I knew that I knew that I knew I had a dream, but the recall was just out of my reach. That can be frustrating! I'm sure you can relate. When this happens, it's a problem with what I describe as dream recall.

Dream recall is "the ability to recall a prophetic dream upon waking; a time period after the initial dream when the Holy Spirit brings it to your remembrance," according to *The Seer's Dictionary*.

Dream recall is one of the most critical aspects of stewarding the seer anointing. If you can't remember the dreams God is giving you, you may miss vital pieces of revelation He is trying to communicate. The truth is, God often speaks to us in the stillness of the night when our hearts are at rest and our spirits are more receptive. But how often do we wake up with only fragments or feelings, struggling to piece together what He revealed? This is why developing strong dream recall is so important.

So why don't we remember our dreams? There are too many reasons to list here, but let me give you a few things to think about. It could be God is hiding the revelation in your spirit only to open it at a later time so you don't get ahead of Him. It could be God is depositing a mystery in your heart—hiding it from the enemy—so that the Holy Spirit can bring it to your remembrance at exactly the right moment. It could also be a distracted mind.

Being frustrated won't help you get to the root. Instead, work on mastering dream recall. There are several strategies involved, but here's one to start with: the simple exercise of writing down any little detail you can remember can open up the rest of the dream. If you want to go deeper on this topic, enroll in my School of the Seers at www.schoolofthespirit.tv.

PRAYER

Father, in the name of Jesus, would You help me remember the dreams that You share with me while I lay on my bed? Lead me to sit before You if I am having trouble remembering the divine dreams You've shared.

MAY 23

DISCERNING DUAL MEANINGS

To these four young men God gave knowledge and understanding of all kinds of literature and learning. And Daniel could understand visions and dreams of all kinds.

Daniel 1:17 NIV

Did you know a dream can have more than one meaning? It can have one meaning in the near term and another meaning in the longer term. I learned this the hard way.

I had a dream in which I walked into the Awakening House of Prayer and it was dark inside. People had pillows and were sleeping on the floor. I was shocked. As I looked around, I saw two men dressed in black on either side of the platform. It was surreal and something that would never happen in the natural. Someone came up to me with bad news about the death of someone close to me. I was so hysterical they had to walk me out of the building.

When I woke up, I was troubled. I thought someone was going to die. I prayed and prayed on this and within a few days, our worship leader's son was diagnosed with cancer. I cried out to the Lord to spare his life. But he was not the one. I didn't receive any further revelation from the Lord, so I just asked Him to prepare me for what was coming.

Well, within a few months someone I had known for 20 years got offended over something silly and left the ministry in a huff. She refused to speak to me about it. It was the death of a relationship. I thought it was a physical death but it was a relational death. (Back then, I was still learning how to interpret dreams.) But I had peace about this woman leaving. It was a supernatural peace. It made no sense but it felt like a heavy weight came off my shoulders. I thought the dream ended there, but I was sorely mistaken.

A few years later came the death of another significant relationship in my life. And it was upsetting. It was life altering. It came with attacks and persecution and it distracted me for months. Then the Holy Spirit reminded me of the dream. Dreams can have a "now" meaning and a "later" meaning. He may not always tell you, but He will remind you when you need to know.

PRAYER

Father, in the name of Jesus, help me not to dismiss the possibility that a dream may have one meaning for now and another meaning for later. Please, remind me of old dreams that still have meaning.

MAY 24

YOU ASK NOT, SO YOU SEE NOT

...Yet you do not have because you do not ask.

James 4:2

When you discern something happening in the spirit realm, do you ask the Lord to show you what is happening? You should, because that discernment is an invitation to press in for more revelation. If you ask more, you will position yourself to see more.

Jesus said, "Keep on asking and it will be given you; keep on seeking and you will find; keep on knocking [reverently] and [the door] will be opened to you. For everyone who keeps on asking receives; and he who keeps on seeking finds; and to him who keeps on knocking, [the door] will be opened" (Matthew 7:7-8 AMPC).

Seers should develop a lifestyle of asking, seeking, and knocking. When you respond to the Holy Spirit's prompting through your spiritual senses, you could find yourself walking into seer dimensions you haven't experienced before.

Let me give you a practical example. Let's say you discern a spirit in operation or an angel in your midst. Ask the Lord to let you see it. He may or may not let you see it, but He's not going to rebuke you for asking. Jesus said, "...now ask and keep on asking and you will receive, so that your joy (gladness, delight) may be full and complete" (John 16:24 AMPC).

When you abide in Him, you will receive more revelation. *Abiding* means to continue to be present with the Lord; to wait on Him. Jesus said in John 15:7, "If you abide in Me, and My words abide in you, you will ask what you desire, and it shall be done for you." That's quite a promise. Of course, your desires have to be in line with His desires and you have to ask with the right motives.

James put it this way in James 4:3 (AMPC), ["Or] you do ask [God for them] and yet fail to receive, because you ask with wrong purpose and evil, selfish motives. Your intention is [when you get what you desire] to spend it in sensual pleasures." If you ask so you can have a good story to tell (or for any other reason that doesn't ultimately glorify God) don't expect Him to open your eyes. Ask Him to purify Your motives.

PRAYER

Father, in the name of Jesus, I am grateful for discernment, but I am curious to see the fullness of what is going on behind the scenes. Would You show me in the spirit what my natural eyes can't see?

MAY 25

NAVIGATING REVELATORY OVERWHELM

When my spirit was overwhelmed within me, then You knew my path....

Psalm 142:3

Sometimes what you see—or the volume of visual revelation you are receiving in a season—can feel absolutely overwhelming. It's not God's intention to overwhelm you. It's the enemy or your unrenewed mind that is overwhelming you.

"Overwhelm" is an enemy I've fought many times over the years, and defeating it starts with understanding what it really is. *Merriam-Webster* defines *overwhelm* as to affect (someone) very strongly; to cause (someone) to have too many things to deal with; to defeat (someone or something) completely. Overwhelm also means upset, overthrow; to cover over completely, submerge; to overcome by superior force or numbers; to overpower in thought or feeling.

For starters, what you see or dream can be overwhelming. But as much as we love to receive visual revelation, there can be seasons when it comes so regularly that trying to record, interpret, apply it, and pray through it can feel overwhelming. Again, that overwhelm is not coming from the Lord.

Overwhelm is the enemy's way to stop up your seer flow. Many overwhelmed seers actually ask God to stop. That is not the right solution.

When revelation comes fast, see it as an opportunity to grow in your stewardship of it. For example, you don't have to go deep on interpreting everything you see immediately. Sometimes, it's enough to record it because the revelation is for a later time. Ask the Holy Spirit what to do with what you receive. He will help you prioritize so you don't get overwhelmed.

Also realize that in seasons when God is pouring out a lot of revelation, the enemy can sneak in and try to bring false revelation. Always take the time to discern the source of the revelation. Was it your own imagination? Was it a pizza dream? Was it a second-heaven revelation? A demon masquerading as an angel of light? Or was it God? Ask Him. He will confirm the source. You can lean into seer elders or a seer company to help you wade through the revelation. That's why we have the Ignite Accelerator.

PRAYER

Father, in the name of Jesus, help me not to get overwhelmed by what I see or dream. Teach me to observe with my spiritual eyes and to lean on Your Spirit to help me process what I am seeing.

MAY 26

ENTERING A COLLECTIVE VISION

And they saw the God of Israel [that is, a convincing manifestation of His presence], and under His feet it was like pavement of bright sapphire stone, like the very heavens in clearness.

Exodus 24:10 AMPC

It's one thing when a seer has a vision. It's another thing when two or more people have the same vision at the same time. I call that a collective vision, and it's not as uncommon as you may think. The first time I see this in Scripture is in Exodus 24:9-11: "Then Moses went up, also Aaron, Nadab, and Abihu, and seventy of the elders of Israel, and they saw the God of Israel. And there was under His feet as it were a paved work of sapphire stone, and it was like the very heavens in its clarity. But on the nobles of the children of Israel He did not lay His hand. So they saw God, and they ate and drank."

Then consider the Transfiguration of Jesus in Mark 9:2-6: "Now after six days Jesus took Peter, James, and John, and led them up on a high mountain apart by themselves; and He was transfigured before them. His clothes became shining, exceedingly white, like snow, such as no launderer on earth can whiten them. And Elijah appeared to them with Moses, and they were talking with Jesus. Then Peter answered and said to Jesus, 'Rabbi, it is good for us to be here; and let us make three tabernacles: one for You, one for Moses, and one for Elijah'—because he did not know what to say, for they were greatly afraid."

The disciples also watched as Jesus was taken up and angels appeared in Acts 1:9-11: "Now when He had spoken these things, while they watched, He was taken up, and a cloud received Him out of their sight. And while they looked steadfastly toward heaven as He went up, behold, two men stood by them in white apparel, who also said, 'Men of Galilee, why do you stand gazing up into heaven? This same Jesus, who was taken up from you into heaven, will so come in like manner as you saw Him go into heaven.'"

Collective visions are purposeful. God can use them to bring people into unity, to establish a truth with two or three witnesses, leave a memory of a corporate moment or turning point, or for many other reasons. If you experience a collective vision, be sure to seek the fullness of God's purpose behind it. God is not random.

PRAYER

Father, in the name of Jesus, thank You for showing me examples in Scripture of collective visions. If You open a collective vision to me, would You help me steward it well and help me to understand Your purpose?

MAY 27

EAT THE SCROLL

Moreover He said to me, "Son of man, eat what you find; eat this scroll, and go, speak to the house of Israel."

Ezekiel 3:1

You've probably heard it said, "You will eat your words!" Seers in the Bible ate God's word, literally. It's called eating the scroll. This is a high level seer function that is reserved for messengers with hard assignments.

Eating the scroll, also called "a little book" in some translations of the Bible, metaphorically means digesting a difficult word of the Lord, according to *The Seer's Dictionary*. Receiving revelation can be exciting, but the gravity of seer revelation can be disturbing. That's why we must process the revelation before sharing it.

In a vision, Ezekiel saw a hand stretched out toward him and the scroll of a book was in it. Ezekiel 2:9-10 tells us there was writing on the inside and on the outside, and written on it were lamentations and mourning and woe. Talk about a difficult assignment! But what we read next shows how the messenger sometimes becomes one with his message.

In Ezekiel 3:1-3 we read, "Moreover He said to me, 'Son of man, eat what you find; eat this scroll, and go, speak to the house of Israel.' So I opened my mouth, and He caused me to eat that scroll. And He said to me, 'Son of man, feed your belly, and fill your stomach with this scroll that I give you.' So I ate, and it was in my mouth like honey in sweetness."

Ezekiel was not the only one. In Revelation 10:9-10, we read of John the Revelator's similar experience: "So I went to the angel and said to him, 'Give me the little book.' And he said to me, 'Take and eat it; and it will make your stomach bitter, but it will be as sweet as honey in your mouth.' Then I took the little book out of the angel's hand and ate it, and it was as sweet as honey in my mouth. But when I had eaten it, my stomach became bitter."

Sometimes you see things so awful and terrible, as *Matthew Henry's Commentary* says, that it leaves a bitter taste in your mouth. Seeing them can be painful to the soul. But still, when the Lord instructs, we must eat the scroll.

PRAYER

Father, in the name of Jesus, I understand that I may see things that hold great weight for many people. Help me to stop and process the revelation with You so I can deliver it in a way that it can be received.

MAY 28

WHEN YOUR DREAMS AND VISIONS ECHO

> *Then he had another dream, and he told it to his brothers. "Listen," he said, "I had another dream, and this time the sun and moon and eleven stars were bowing down to me."*
>
> Genesis 37:9 NIV

Have you ever encountered a seer echo? "Seer echo" are the words to describe the phenomena when visual revelation repeats itself one or more times. Some call it repetitive dreams but they can also be visions or other encounters in the seer dimensions.

We see repetitive dreams in Scripture. Sometimes the same person has the exact dream more than once. Sometimes they have a dream with a similar message that is essentially the same dream communicated in a different way. The dream has different symbols but it has the same story line or outcome. Again, the same can happen with visions.

Joseph had the same dream twice. So did Pharoah. The elements were different but the message was precisely the same. There are at least seven reasons I could dig out with the help of the Holy Spirit as to why we have seer echoes. I can't lay them all out here but I teach about it in my School of the Seers (www.schoolofthesprit.tv). But I want to give you one that many seers miss.

You may experience a seer echo in your dreams, visions, or encounters because God is giving you an urgent warning for the future. He is trying to get your attention because you need to start preparing now. Such was the case with Pharoah. Pharoah didn't understand his consecutive dreams, so he sent for all the magicians and sorcerers to get an interpretation. None of them could help, but God gave Joseph wisdom to connect the dots.

Remember, God had already trained Joseph in the realm of seer echoes in his own life. Here was Joseph's wisdom to Pharaoh in Genesis 41:28-31:

> This is the thing which I have spoken to Pharaoh. God has shown Pharaoh what He is about to do. Indeed seven years of great plenty will come throughout all the land of Egypt; but after them seven years of famine will arise, and all the plenty will be forgotten in the land of Egypt; and the famine will deplete the land. So the plenty will not be known in the land because of the famine following, for it will be very severe.

Think back. Have you experienced a seer echo?

PRAYER

Father, in the name of Jesus, would You help me remember if I have had a seer echo? Since the visual revelations can have different symbols, I may not have recognized it. I don't want to miss what You are showing me.

MAY 29

HOW'S YOUR MENTAL HEALTH?

Why are you cast down, O my soul? And why are you disquieted within me? Hope in God, for I shall yet praise Him for the help of His countenance.

Psalm 42:5

Many seers tend to have melancholy personalities. That's one thing, but suffering from depression, anxiety, or other mental health issues is another story. Everyone struggles with their mental health at times, but we need to recognize the onset and deal with it in Christ.

Now, I didn't say mental illness. I said mental health, which includes your emotional, psychological, and social well-being. Our mental health affects how we think, feel, and act and helps determine how we handle stress, relate to others, and make choices. It can also affect how we see in the spirit.

God wants us to give Him all our worries, cares, and concerns. He wants us to set our mind on Him so we can find peace instead of turmoil, confusion, depression, anxiety, and burnout. But it's not always easy. It can be even more difficult for a seer who has disturbing dreams and visions as part of their gifting.

Mental health challenges can be rooted in the demonic, such as generational curses or in genetic predispositions to certain struggles. Mental health issues can be rooted in chemical imbalances in the brain, relational stress, growing up in toxic family structures, being rejected by friends, and trauma. In 2020, the Holy Spirit told me a spirit of trauma was loosed in the earth. So it's no surprise that mental health issues have proliferated.

Lifestyle factors are also involved. One hundred years ago we averaged nine hours of sleep. Today, the average is 6.8 hours. Our bodies and minds need rest we aren't getting. There's also a lack of human connection and an increase in social media, which studies show brings insecurity, comparison, and can cause anxiety and depression. More people are reporting loneliness than ever before.

The biggest issue is disconnection from God. It's possible in times of crises or even busyness to feel disconnected. Jesus is the answer. But many believers are too ashamed to admit they are facing mental health issues. If you are struggling with mental health, run to Jesus. But also reach out to someone you trust. If you want your seer gift to prosper, you need your soul to prosper because seeing isn't just about what you see, but how you interpret it.

PRAYER

Father, in the name of Jesus, if I am struggling with mental health issues, from anxiety to loneliness to emotional pain, please remind me to run to You immediately. Send people in my path to help me.

MAY 30

SEEING INTO SOMEONE'S BOOK OF LIFE

Declaring the end from the beginning, and from ancient times things that are not yet done, saying, "My counsel shall stand, and I will do all My pleasure."

Isaiah 46:10

When you prophesy about someone's destiny, you are essentially drawing revelation from the book of their life. Have you ever seen into the book of someone's life? Did you even know there was one? What is the book of someone's life?

According to *The Seer's Dictionary*, the "book of someone's life" is simply, "the book God has written about a person's life."

Psalm 139:16 (NLT) says, "You saw me before I was born. Every day of my life was recorded in your book. Every moment was laid out before a single day had passed." We can also surmise that David was talking about the book of his life when we read, "You number my wanderings; put my tears into Your bottle; are they not in Your book?" (Psalm 56:8).

What is this book? *Cambridge Bible for Schools and Colleges* offers, "Each day of his life with all its history was pre-determined by the Creator and recorded in His book, before one of them actually was in existence:—a clear expression of the truth that there is an ideal plan of life providentially marked out for every individual."

Keep in mind, Ephesians 2:10 (AMP) offers, "For we are His workmanship [His own master work, a work of art], created in Christ Jesus [reborn from above—spiritually transformed, renewed, ready to be used] for good works, which God prepared [for us] beforehand [taking paths which He set], so that we would walk in them [living the good life which He prearranged and made ready for us]."

Clearly, God has a plan. These Scriptures suggest God has written those plans in a book about your life—and it would seem everyone has such a book written of them in Heaven. *Barnes' Notes on the Bible* relates, "Perhaps the allusion here would be to the book of an architect or draftsman, who, before his work is begun, draws his plan, or sketches it for the direction of the workmen."

God can allow seers to look into the pages of the book of someone's life to minister life to the person. Have you ever asked Him to show you someone's book? He will only show you what is helpful.

PRAYER

Father, in the name of Jesus, would You show me what You have written about people to whom I am ministering in the book of their life? I want to encourage people to follow Your plan by sharing what I see.

MAY 31

I SAW THE SCARS ON HIS BACK

Who Himself bore our sins in His own body on the tree, that we, having died to sins, might live for righteousness—by whose stripes you were healed.

1 Peter 2:24

The glory of God fell during worship at my church. Suddenly, I was in a different dimension. I was in the seer dimensions. I felt the presence of God in a way that I can't describe with words.

With my eyes closed in deep devotion, I saw Jesus standing above me looking down on the congregation. As I gazed upon His beauty, He extended His arm and I saw the scars in His hands.

Thomas had a similar experience. Doubting Thomas, as he is often called, refused to believe the other disciples when they told him they had seen the Lord. He said to them, "Unless I see in His hands the print of the nails, and put my finger into the print of the nails, and put my hand into His side, I will not believe" (John 20:25). The difference was, Thomas saw Jesus in a bodily way. I saw Him in the Spirit.

> And after eight days His disciples were again inside, and Thomas with them. Jesus came, the doors being shut, and stood in the midst, and said, "Peace to you!" Then He said to Thomas, "Reach your finger here, and look at My hands; and reach your hand here, and put it into My side. Do not be unbelieving, but believing" (John 20:26-27).

I was deeply moved when I saw the scars in Jesus' hand, then He pulled back His robe and showed me the scars on His back—scars He took at the whipping post before He was crucified. I began to weep. I was overwhelmed with the love and healing power of God.

Though I had another message planned, I knew what Jesus wanted me to do. He wanted me to share the vision and heal the sick. I preached impromptu on Isaiah 53:5, "But He was wounded for our transgressions, He was bruised for our iniquities; the chastisement for our peace was upon Him, and by His stripes we are healed."

When you have a vision, you need to discern what the Lord wants you to do. If I had missed that moment, people who came sick would have left the same way. By discerning this as a corporate instruction to heal the sick, many left completely healed.

PRAYER

Father, in the name of Jesus, help me not to get so caught up or overwhelmed by what I see that I miss the moment to release Your will. Help me discern Your agenda and cooperate with it.

JUNE

Then he dreamed, and behold, a ladder was set up on the earth, and its top reached to heaven; and there the angels of God were ascending and descending on it. And behold, the Lord stood above it....

Genesis 28:12-13

JUNE 1

ENTERING THE SECRET DIMENSION

The secret things belong to the Lord our God, but those things which are revealed belong to us and to our children forever, that we may do all the words of this law.

Deuteronomy 29:29

Everyone—even God—has secrets. Choosing whether to—and to whom—a secret is revealed rests solely in the power of the secret holder. In the secret dimension, God is the revealer of secrets (Daniel 2:47). We know God reveals His secrets to two different types of people: His servants the prophets (Amos 3:7) and those who fear Him (Psalm 25:14).

You have the inherent potential to enter the secret dimension of the seer realm as a born-again believer. Deuteronomy 29:29 (NIV) tells us, "The secret things belong to the Lord our God, but the things revealed belong to us and to our children forever, that we may follow all the words of this law."

According to *The Seer's Dictionary*, the secret dimension is a dimension in the spirit where God reveals His secrets to those who fear Him. God can share His secrets with us through a still small voice or through the seer dimension—encounters, trances, dreams, and visions. The unfortunate reality is few will enter into the secret dimension because they are unaware of its existence or won't pay the price to cultivate a lifestyle that positions them for access.

The secret dimension is not simply a place of revelation, it is a sacred invitation. This is where God unveils His plans, His strategies, and even His heart. Isaiah 45:3 calls this realm the place of "hidden treasures, riches stored in secret places." To enter this dimension, you must pursue intimacy with God. The more time you spend in His presence, the more He will trust you with His mysteries.

Living a holy and consecrated life positions you to access the secret dimension. Secrets are given to those who walk in obedience and humility. As you press into the heart of God, He will share what is necessary for your calling, your prayers, and your purpose.

The secret dimension is waiting for those who are willing to pay the price. Will you seek to enter the sacred space where God's mysteries are revealed? Heaven's secrets are waiting to be unveiled!

PRAYER

Father, in the name of Jesus, help me to always seek first the Kingdom and Your righteousness. Help me to position myself to receive secrets from Your throne room. And help me steward them well.

JUNE 2

GOLD AND GLORY

As for the earth, from it comes bread, nut underneath it is turned up as by fire; its stones are the source of sapphires, and it contains gold dust.

Job 28:5-6

Have you ever seen gold dust in the spirit? Some people call this "glory dust." It may manifest like a haze or fog in the spirit realm, but sometimes you can also see the evidence of it in the physical realm. To the natural eyes, it typically looks like very fine gold dust. This is truly a sight to behold.

I believe the glory dust comes often out of the glory clouds, whether you ever see the cloud or not. While some people have admittedly faked these encounters—not all dust you see in the spirit carries a positive connotation—glory dust is an authentic spiritual sign of God's presence.

This is biblical. And I speak from experience. We've had glory dust appear in our Bibles at Awakening House of Prayer, my Fort Lauderdale church. There was glory dust on the pulpit!

Let's look at Scripture. Isaiah 60:2 (MEV) tells us, "For the darkness shall cover the earth and deep darkness the peoples; but the Lord shall rise upon you, and His glory shall be seen upon you." God's glory can manifest on you in many forms. You'll recall Moses' face shone so brightly after being in Jehovah's presence that he had to wear a veil over his face (Exodus 34:33).

But God's glory can also manifest as dust on your hands, your face, your Bible, etc. Job 28:5-6 (NLT) tells us, "Food is grown on the earth above, but down below, the earth is melted as by fire. Here the rocks contain precious lapis lazuli, and the dust contains gold."

Of course, as I mentioned, dust can also have a negative connotation, representing grieving or sin (sitting in sackcloth and ashes) or representing the need to reject a person or a place and walk away (shake the dust off your feet). So when you see dust in the spirit, don't assume everything that glitters is gold. Ask the Holy Spirit to show you the source of the dust.

PRAYER

Father, in the name of Jesus, I know the spirit realm is more real than the natural realm. Would You give me a glimpse of the glory dust that sometimes accompanies Your presence? Help me discern the dust.

JUNE 3

DREAMING OF DIVINE CONNECTIONS

We can make our plans, but the Lord determines our steps.

Proverbs 16:9 NLT

I'm grateful for the many divine connections God has brought into my life. I've been blessed with many godly relationships that have strengthened me, opened doors for me, and imparted wisdom that would have otherwise taken me decades to glean.

You can't make a divine connection happen. Only God can do that. But He can unlock a divine connection through your dreams. I encountered a man I did not know in a dream with a direction to consult him for advice. This was some years after I received a prophetic word about a Third Great Awakening coming to America.

In my dream, I was preparing to minister in a new platform. It was the biggest opportunity I ever had. As I was preparing for the opportunity, this man of God was standing in the background watching me. After a little while, he called me over to him and offered some advice: "I've been where you are going. I know the way. Trust me. Just give them one or two things. That's all they can handle." Then he repeated himself.

Of course, just because we see someone in a dream doesn't mean we'll ever meet them. But in my case, I knew someone who knew him and I asked them to see if he would speak with me. He agreed. I shared with him the dream and the prophetic word I received about a Third Great Awakening coming to America.

He asked me to share it a second time. Then he asked me where I lived. I told him and he said, "Maybe we're supposed to do something together in your city." He then asked me if I knew one of his friends, a man of God who lived near me. I told him I didn't but immediately reached out to connect. Within a week I was sitting at lunch with both men—that dream and following through with the dream set the stage for many of the open doors in that phase of my ministry.

Again, you can't make a divine connection happen, but when you have a divine connection dream, pray it through. Take action in the natural where possible. God opens doors that no one can shut (Revelation 3:7).

PRAYER

Father, in the name of Jesus, help me to value the divine connections You bring into my life, especially among the company of seers. Show me to whom You are connecting me.

JUNE 4

WHEN YOUR EYES GROW DIM

> *...Woe to us, for we have sinned! Because of this our heart is faint; because of these things our eyes grow dim.*
>
> Lamentations 5:16-17

When your natural eyes grow dim, you notice you have to squint to see far away. But when your spiritual eyes grow dim, you may not immediately notice—and that's a scary thought. Consider Eli's reality in 1 Samuel 3:1-2:

> Now the boy Samuel ministered to the Lord before Eli. And the word of the Lord was rare in those days; there was no widespread revelation. And it came to pass at that time, while Eli was lying down in his place, and when his eyes had begun to grow so dim that he could not see.

Notice how the word of the Lord was rare in those days. You can see the spiritual parallel to the natural condition. Not only had Eli's eyes grown dim in the natural, his eyes (and ears) had grown dim in the spirit. The King James Version of 1 Samuel 3:1 says, *"there was no open vision."*

Eyes growing dim is "a state in which it is difficult to see because of compromised emotions or sinful acts. Consider the dimmer on a light. As you dim the light, it becomes more difficult to see in the natural. As darkness invades the seer's spiritual sight, it can be more difficult to see in the spirit," according to *The Seer's Dictionary*.

In Matthew 6:22-24, Jesus tells us: "The lamp of the body is the eye. If therefore your eye is good, your whole body will be full of light. But if your eye is bad, your whole body will be full of darkness. If therefore the light that is in you is darkness, how great is that darkness!"

If a seer looks upon sinful things, his spiritual eyes will grow dim. The psalmist said more than once not to look on worthless or wicked things, and even asked for God's help to do it.

"Turn away my eyes from looking at worthless things, and revive me in Your way" (Psalm 119:37). And again, "I will set nothing wicked before my eyes; I hate the work of those who fall away; it shall not cling to me" (Psalm 101:3).

Eyes can grow dim because of unresolved emotional issues, such as grief or trauma. Keep your eyes on the Word and they won't grow dim!

PRAYER

Father, in the name of Jesus, I don't want my eyes to grow dim in the spirit. I want to be spiritually sharp so I don't miss anything You try to show me. Help me take precautions to avoid dim spiritual eyes.

JUNE 5
LIVING IN THE SPIRIT

But I say, walk and live [habitually] in the [Holy] Spirit [responsive to and controlled and guided by the Spirit]; then you will certainly not gratify the cravings and desires of the flesh (of human nature without God).

Galatians 5:16 AMPC

Kathryn Kuhlman, a miracle worker who lived in the 20th century, lived in the spirit. She breathed in the spirit. She prayed in the Spirit. She said:

> *I pray all the time because if I limited the Holy Spirit to a certain number of hours a day, I would be in danger of using Him for my own purpose. If, for instance, I spent one hour a day in prayer, I would expect the Holy Spirit to reward me for that hour. I would begin to feel that it was that hour in prayer that caused the "anointing" in the meeting. No, I cannot use the Holy Spirit in that way. I must practice His presence all of the time.*

Before her meetings, her staff relates that Miss Kuhlman could be seen "pacing back and forth, head up, head down, arms flung into the air, hands clasped behind her back with her face covered in tears."

Oral Roberts succinctly tells us of the intensity of her prayers, he says, "It was like they were talking back and forth to each other, and you couldn't tell where Kathryn started and the Holy Spirit left off. It was a oneness." Kuhlman said, "I surrendered unto Him all there was of me; everything! Then for the first time I realized what it meant to have real power."

If you want to see more in the spirit, set your heart to live in the Spirit. Living in the Spirit is living under the control of the Holy Spirit instead of the control of the carnal nature, which is your flesh and your unrenewed mind. How do you do this? If you cultivate the fruit of the Spirit, you will live in the Spirit.

Galatians 5:16-17 (NLT) tell us, "So I say, let the Holy Spirit guide your lives. Then you won't be doing what your sinful nature craves. The sinful nature wants to do evil, which is just the opposite of what the Spirit wants. And the Spirit gives us desires that are the opposite of what the sinful nature desires. These two forces are constantly fighting each other, so you are not free to carry out your good intentions."

PRAYER

Father, in the name of Jesus, I want to live in the Spirit and see what the Spirit sees. Would You help me to intentionally walk in the Spirit and cultivate the fruit of the Spirit?

JUNE 6

GUARD YOUR EYE GATES

I will refuse to look at anything vile and vulgar. I hate all who deal crookedly; I will have nothing to do with them.

Psalm 101:3 NLT

I was on an international flight and I was uneasy in my spirit. I was pondering where the agitation was coming from when I accidentally saw the TV monitor in the row in front of me through the small space in between the seats. What they were watching was pornographic. I was aghast! I had to stick one of my pillows in the crack between the seats to avoid seeing it again.

I am careful what I look at in the natural because I understand the spiritual ripple it can have on my visual revelation. David put it this way in Psalm 101:3 (AMPC), "I will set no base or wicked thing before my eyes. I hate the work of them who turn aside [from the right path]; it shall not grasp hold of me."

You have a choice what you look at. If you are watching unseemly television shows, playing violent video games, or reading trashy romance novels, you are setting your eyes on base and wicked things. You are filling your eyes with darkness.

Consider the words in red. In Matthew 6:22 (MEV), Jesus said, "The light of the body is the eye. Therefore, if your eye is clear, your whole body will be full of light." And in Matthew 5:29, He went on to say: "And if your right eye causes you to sin, pluck it out and throw it away. For it is profitable that one of your members should perish, and not that your whole body be thrown into hell."

Seers, perhaps it's time to make a covenant with your eyes (Job 31:1). Like David, we need to pray this prayer, "Turn my eyes away from vanity [all those worldly, meaningless things that distract—let Your priorities be mine], And restore me [with renewed energy] in Your ways" (Psalm 119:37 AMP).

What if you accidentally see something vile like I did? That's not your fault, but it is your responsibility to ask God to cleanse your lens. Ask Him to purge the image of the vile thing from your heart.

PRAYER

Father, in the name of Jesus, turn my eyes away from vanity, all those worldly images and meaningless things that distract me, and give me a hunger to gaze upon Your beauty. Cleanse my lens.

JUNE 7
PURIFYING FIRE

Blessed are the pure in heart, for they shall see God.

Matthew 5:8

If you want to keep the eyes of your spirit wide open, you need to embrace the purifying fire when it comes. Keep in mind, God doesn't send purifying fire unless something needs to be purified. At times, whether you realize it or not, our eyes need to be purified. We live in a fallen world.

I heard the Lord say, "A purifying fire is coming to the prophetic ministry—a baptism of fire is coming for those who will embrace it and let My fire do its perfect work. Those who resist the fire will be sidelined in the next season. Those who embrace My fire will be led into new realms of prophetic revelation and new levels of accuracy in the Spirit. Those who understand the purifying work of My fire—the work of My fire to judge sin in your heart and refine you—will enter in willingly. They will walk into the fire freely, knowing that they are coming closer to My heart in the process. I am bringing My fire to the Church. Embrace my fire. Don't resist my purifying work in your heart. I have great things stored up for you in the days ahead, but the path is for those holy hearts to walk on."

This is biblical and essential for seers. We don't want defiled eyes. We want pure eyes. Don't resist the fire. When you go through the fire, you will come out into a place of abundant revelation (Psalm 66:12). I speak from experience. No one likes the fire, but after we suffer a little while, the God of all grace will restore, confirm, strengthen, and establish us (1 Peter 5:10).

The purifying fire helps our faith, which is key to seeing in the spirit. Peter spoke of the "...genuineness of your faith, being much more precious than gold that perishes, though it is tested by fire, may be found to praise, honor, and glory at the revelation of Jesus Christ" (1 Peter 1:7). Purifying fire always leads to greater revelation of Jesus. Embrace it.

PRAYER

Father, in the name of Jesus, I am willing to walk through the purifying fire. Purify my spiritual eyes. Cleanse my eyes and mind from unrighteousness. I want to walk in greater revelation.

JUNE 8

KEEPING WATCH OVER THE NATIONS

Look among the nations and watch—be utterly astounded! For I will work a work in your days which you would not believe, though it were told you.

Habakkuk 1:5

Just as there are prophets to the nations, there are seers to the nations. In fact, when God called Jeremiah, He asked him, "What do you see?" (Jeremiah 1:11).

Of course, God sees everything and can show us anything. Psalm 66:7 speaks of God as the ultimate watchman over the nations: "He rules by His power; His eyes observe the nations."

Seers to the nations have a gift and an assignment to watch over nations. This is a weighty call and something you grow into over time, if it's part of God's assignment for you.

In other words, God doesn't typically start you out with authority to watch and pray over nations.

That's because keeping watch over the nations demands a spiritual sensitivity and sharpness that is cultivated with experience. Keeping watch over the nations demands a heart that is fully aligned with Kingdom purposes, not personal biases.

God raises up seers to partner with Him to watch over nations—not just watch but watch and pray. Seers who watch over nations are looking for what satan's army and God's angels are doing, how the spiritual climates are shifting, how legislation is being crafted and more. The visual revelation is connected to intense intercession for God's will in a nation.

Proverbs 15:3 tells us, "The eyes of the Lord are in every place, Keeping watch on the evil and the good." A seer to the nations can often see what God sees in their territorial assignment—the evil and the good.

Watching over nations can mean watching over people groups. Praying rightly means tapping into the mind of Christ and the heart of God for His will, which may lead to breaking strongholds or praying in God's redemptive purposes or laboring in intercession for the lost.

This is not a position of striving. Seeing at this level comes through a revelation that "there is no creature hidden from His sight, but all things are naked and open to the eyes of Him to whom we must give account" (Hebrews 4:13). When God calls you as a seer to the nations, He opens your eyes to see what you need to know to steward your assignment well.

PRAYER

Father, in the name of Jesus, I am willing to watch over the nations, but I know this is not a call all seers carry. Nevertheless, would You teach me to watch and pray over my nation?

JUNE 9

HEALING THE EYES OF THE SEERS

He heals the brokenhearted and binds up their wounds.

Psalm 147:3

Just because spiritual eyes have been restored to the body doesn't mean those eyes are completely healthy. Many seers have felt the sting of betrayal, rejection, or other forms of trauma throughout their life before they ever walked in their gift. In fact, these painful experiences are often part of the enemy's strategy to keep you out of your calling. That's why the Holy Spirit is actively healing spiritual eyes.

Think about it. Seers, sages, and mystics have been under attack for thousands of years. From Bible days to modern days, the enemy is afraid of the seeing eye because the seeing eye discerns, exposes, and rallies an army to defeat his plans on earth.

As God emphasizes the eyes of the Church, we can expect the attacks against seers and seeing people to continue and even escalate. But we can also expect God to heal the eyes of the seers who have suffered from rejection, persecution, and misunderstanding in past and current seasons. For some especially bold seers, wounding will come through persecution and they will need to visit the healing well often—but they also need to develop thick enough skin to withstand people's words and the lies of the enemy.

Temptation seems to be the common theme of spiritual eye injury. The Philistines gouged out Samson's eyes after Delilah tempted and nagged him to expose the secret of his great strength (Judges 16:21). The Delilah spirit is still working against seers and seeing people today, luring them in, betraying their hearts, and blinding their spiritual eyes. Delilah defiles the discernment of the discerners who should see through the deception but are tempted with a desire to look at what seems good to their natural eyes.

God is removing spiritual eye infections from the seers who will submit their eyes to Him fully. He's healing blurred vision. He's healing tunnel vision. He's healing eye strain. He's healing vision loss. I see Him now putting His hands on the eyes of seers and seeing people. Dare to look up again as He restores your eyesight so you can see clearly again (Mark 8:25). For more on this, check out my book, *Power Seers*.

PRAYER

Father, in the name of Jesus, would You heal my eyes and the eyes of other seers who have been through painful experiences? Help me stand against the onslaught the enemy brings. You are my Healer.

JUNE 10

THE DANIEL SEER ANOINTING

As for these four young men, God gave them knowledge and skill in all literature and wisdom; and Daniel had understanding in all visions and dreams.

Daniel 1:17

Daniel had one of the most remarkable seer anointings in Scripture. He saw events thousands of years before they took place. He also carried the ability to interpret dreams.

Indeed, the Daniel seer anointing is unique in Scripture as he didn't just interpret dreams, encounter angels, or see in the spirit, he also had extraordinary wisdom in applying what he saw in the spirit. Daniel advised four kings over the length of his storied life. Few seers had as much influence on world events as Daniel.

Daniel 1:17 (AMPC) tells us, "As for these four youths, God gave them knowledge and skill in all learning and wisdom, and Daniel had understanding in all [kinds of] visions and dreams." Nebuchadnezzar described the prophet this way, "But at last Daniel came before me (his name is Belteshazzar, according to the name of my god; in him is the Spirit of the Holy God), and I told the dream before him..." (Daniel 4:8).

All seers have the ability to receive visual revelation, but Daniel was set apart because he could decode dreams, visions and riddles with divine accuracy. He unraveled mysteries that no one else in his day could. And he was able to communicate the revelation in a way that was easily understood. His seer ministry shifted the courses of kingdoms. He influenced several spheres of society.

Beyond all this, Daniel was a seer who fasted and prayed. He had an intimate relationship with God and refused to compromise His faith for any reward. His spiritual discipline of praying three times a day, for example, despite the threat of being thrown into a lion's den demonstrated his unwavering integrity even in the midst of captivity.

And when Daniel ended up facing the lions, his unwavering faith in the God who saves delivered him. When King Darius went to check on the fate of his friend, Daniel didn't hold a grudge. He announced, "My God sent his angel and shut the lions' mouths, and they have not harmed me, because I was found blameless before him; and also before you, O king, I have done no harm..." (Daniel 6:22 ESV).

PRAYER

Father, in the name of Jesus, I know there will never be another Daniel. But please help me to learn the lessons from his life. Help me to walk in integrity like he did and glean from his unique anointing.

JUNE 11

MARKED TO BE A SIGN

Then the Lord said, "Just as My servant Isaiah has walked naked and barefoot three years for a sign and a wonder against Egypt and Ethiopia."

Isaiah 20:3

Power seers will see, hear, and say with the accuracy of original Old Testament seers like Samuel. Holy Spirit boldness will toughen these seers, who will rise up and push back the fear of man that tempts too many to keep silent about their prophetic visions.

Like the apostles in the early Church, their prayer will be, "Now, Lord, look on their threats, and grant to Your servants that with all boldness they may speak Your word, by stretching out Your hand to heal, and that signs and wonders may be done through the name of Your holy Servant Jesus" (Acts 4:29-30).

Like John the Baptist or Jesus Himself, power seers are not afraid to unflinchingly address sin in the Church and call for repentance while praying for mercy. They will cry, "*Repent, for the kingdom of heaven is at hand!*" (Matthew 3:2).

Power seers will not only walk in signs, but they will also become walking, talking signs who prophesy what they see and demonstrate their dreams and visions in prophetic acts that turn the hearts of people back to the Father. Some will be parabolic prophets like Ezekiel who at times see great visions and at times sacrifice their own dignity to communicate what the Holy Spirit is saying to the Church (Ezekiel 4).

Power seers will speak to kings and those in authority by the greater authority of Jesus Christ. Leaders with a pure heart like King David will receive God's manifold wisdom through uncompromising power seers. Those with an evil heart like King Jeroboam will reject the word of the Lord through the mouths of seer prophets.

Power seers will arise from within prisons and within palaces, from all walks of life and all denominations. They will carry the ability to communicate the same messages to different people groups. Like Paul, power seers will become all things to all people so that by all possible means they may get through to some (1 Corinthians 9:22).

Seers, it's time to move beyond mere dreams and visions and develop a bold voice that cuts through the static. It's time to press into the power of the Holy Spirit to work signs and wonders. It's time to preach the gospel!

PRAYER

Father, in the name of Jesus, would You fill me again with Your Spirit? Give me the power to be a witness to Your soon coming, to Your saving grace, and to the penalties of sin in a fallen world.

JUNE 12

WITNESSING CALAMITY

Thus says the Lord of hosts, the God of Israel: "You have seen all the calamity that I have brought on Jerusalem and on all the cities of Judah; and behold, this day they are a desolation, and no one dwells in them."

Jeremiah 44:2

I was in a condo with floor-to-ceiling windows when I suddenly saw water spirits rising up out of the sea. There were a multitude of people on the beach, but they all seemed too busy, or too blind, to recognize the danger in their midst. I was trying to warn them, but they couldn't hear me. I knew disaster was at hand if they didn't run.

Of course, that was a dream. When I woke up, I knew it was a warning dream of calamity and that my role was to intercede. I would not have chosen to see this, but the Lord showed me so I could stand in the gap. No one likes to see calamity, but seasoned seers are bound to see things they don't want to see at some point.

What is calamity? Calamity is a disastrous event marked by great loss and lasting distress and suffering. Calamities are major misfortunes that cause deep distress or misery. Seers may see calamities through dreams or visions, trances or other encounters.

Jeremiah, also known as the weeping prophet, had word after word of calamity. We see calamity in the writings of Ezekiel, Isaiah, Obadiah, and Amos. In Matthew 25, Jesus the Prophet warned of calamities, such as earthquakes and pestilences and famines. John the Revelator has visions of calamity in the end times, with warfare, plagues, storms and other cataclysmic events.

Jeremiah 44:1-3 tells us, "The word that came to Jeremiah concerning all the Jews who dwell in the land of Egypt, who dwell at Migdol, at Tahpanhes, at Noph, and in the country of Pathros, saying, 'Thus says the Lord of hosts, the God of Israel: "You have seen all the calamity that I have brought on Jerusalem and on all the cities of Judah; and behold, this day they are a desolation, and no one dwells in them, because of their wickedness which they have committed to provoke Me to anger, in that they went to burn incense and to serve other gods whom they did not know, they nor you nor your fathers."'"

The purpose of God showing a seer calamity is to pray and warn the people of what the enemy is planning in the unseen realm so as to avert it. We can't pray away every calamity we see, but we may be able to mitigate or lessen its impact through prayer. And we can certainly warn people to prepare for the calamities ahead.

PRAYER

Father, in the name of Jesus, I am willing to see calamities if You choose to use me as an agent of warning or intercession. Help me process the calamity in peace and pray without ceasing.

JUNE 13

WHAT'S YOUR SEER IQ?

For the Lord gives wisdom; from His mouth come knowledge and understanding.

Proverbs 2:6

Seer intelligence comes with maturity, but some start out with more than others by sheer means of God's gifting. What is seer intelligence? It's seeing with the intention of learning or understanding what you are seeing, according to *The Seer's Dictionary*.

Seer intelligence comes, in part, through seer focus. Seer intelligence helps you comprehend not only what you are seeing, but what it means and how to apply the visual revelation accurately. Again, your seer IQ rises with experience and maturity but some start off with more than others.

Keep this in mind: your seer intelligence—or Seer IQ—is not about your natural intellect. You can have head knowledge and not have seer knowledge. No, your seer intelligence is about the measure of spiritual insight you attain. It goes beyond seeing to include how accurately you judge, interpret, pray through, and act on what you see. A low seer IQ will lead you into many mistakes. A high seer IQ will help you avoid them.

Notice that Proverbs 4:7 (KJV) tells us, "Wisdom is the principal thing; therefore get wisdom: and with all thy getting get understanding." Your seer IQ informs what you do with what you see and is connected not just to how well you see, but how well you hear.

Jesus said, "Take heed what you hear. With the same measure you use, it will be measured to you; and to you who hear, more will be given. For whoever has, to him more will be given; but whoever does not have, even what he has will be taken away from him" (Mark 4:24-25).

So how do you grow in seer intelligence? Seek wisdom and understanding about what you are seeing. Don't assume you know everything. Be humble. Ask questions. Asking is how you gain knowledge, intelligence. Don't passively watch and go about your business. Journal what you see and meditate on it. Show spiritual curiosity and seek the Lord. He is a rewarder of those who diligently seek Him (Hebrews 11:6).

PRAYER

Father, in the name of Jesus, would You help me boost my seer IQ as I seek You? Help me to remain humble and teachable so I can continue to learn and grow in the seer dimensions.

JUNE 14

DISCERNING FALSE SEERS

The prophets prophesy falsely, and the priests rule by their own power; and My people love to have it so.

Jeremiah 5:31

Jesus warned false prophets would rise in the last day and deceive many. Given seers are prophets, lovers of the truth must consider the rise of false seers in this hour.

With the rapid rise of seers in recent years, it should come as no surprise that the enemy would work overtime to bring counterfeit seers into the Church. The deceptive revelations of false seers can do and have done great harm to believers.

So how do you recognize a false seer? I've studied this over the years and while it looks a lot like any other false prophet, there are some distinctions. False seers often glorify themselves instead of glorifying God. They point people to themselves instead of Jesus. The Holy Spirit always points back to Jesus (John 15:26).

False seers often use their gift to manipulate people for greedy gain or some other personal advantage. Their revelations are not grounded in the Word of God. They rely on "deep" extrabiblical revelation to woo the masses who are looking for something spectacular or sensational rather than the simplicity of the gospel. False seers will twist Scripture in efforts to make you believe what they have seen aligns in the Word, but if you know the truth you know it's more than a stretch.

False seers thrive in secrecy. They shun accountability. They resist the efforts of "good Bereans" to see if what they are saying is so (Acts 17:11). They push back when challenged, suggesting they are mystics and their revelation is beyond your capacity to grasp. False seers proudly position themselves as "above" while you are "beneath."

This is food for thought. Ultimately, you will know them by their fruit. Test the spirits. Jesus said in Luke 6:45, "A good man out of the good treasure of his heart brings forth good; and an evil man out of the evil treasure of his heart brings forth evil. For out of the abundance of the heart his mouth speaks."

PRAYER

Father, in the name of Jesus, I know false seers are rising as the enemy works to counterfeit this important gift. Would You give me the wisdom and discernment to judge between the true and false?

JUNE 15

WHEN YOU HAVE TO WALK ALONE

...and lo, I am with you always, even to the end of the age.
Matthew 28:20

When I was young in the Lord, my first mentor gave me some truth that has served me well through decades of prophetic ministry. She said, "Jennifer, as a prophet you have to get everything you need directly from the Lord. Everything." Now, I am telling you. You have to get everything you need directly from the Lord.

Elijah the prophet walked alone at times. When Jezebel attacked him with a word curse, he ran off to a cave and left his servant behind. I am sure he felt lonely in that cave. Elijah sat there wishing he was dead (1 Kings 19:4).

Elijah felt alone. He told God twice, "I have been very zealous for the Lord God of hosts; for the children of Israel have forsaken Your covenant, torn down Your altars, and killed Your prophets with the sword. I alone am left; and they seek to take my life" (1 Kings 19:10).

The voice of loneliness was attacking Elijah. He felt like he was the only one standing up for righteousness in Israel. He felt like he was the only one fighting Jezebel in the land. But God corrected the prophet. He told Elijah that there were 7,000 other righteous ones like him.

I've had friends along the way; some have come and gone. Some betrayed me. Some misunderstood me. Some moved on. But in many seasons of my life, I walked alone. Sometimes we have to get comfortable with life just being you and the Lord.

You have to be able to be alone without getting lonely. You have to find the courage to stand alone with your prophetic word even when people are standing against you. You have to resist the temptation to get lonely because it will skew your seer lens.

What is loneliness, really? It's not being alone, it's feeling the distress of being alone. Loneliness can produce toxic emotions in the soul of a seer. Loneliness, if you're not careful, will cause you to compromise your visual revelation for the sake of belonging to a group.

PRAYER

Father, in the name of Jesus, would You help me get everything I need directly from You? I know You are the Friend who sticks closer than a brother. Help me remember that You are always with me.

JUNE 16

THE SHIFTING SEER

But at midnight Paul and Silas were praying and singing hymns to God, and the prisoners were listening to them. Suddenly there was a great earthquake, so that the foundations of the prison were shaken....

Acts 16:25-26

I'll never forget my first experience with the power of spiritual atmospheres. My daughter needed a special outfit for a band recital, so we went shopping at the mall. It was Halloween night and I was young in the Lord and in my gifting, so I wasn't expecting what happened next.

My friend took my daughter into a store while I waited on a bench outside, watching as people walked by with demonic costumes. Suddenly, I felt the overwhelming presence of demons all around me. Oppression marked the atmosphere. It was unbearable. I went into the store, got my daughter and my friend, and got out of that mall as quickly as I could. Back then, I didn't know seers are atmosphere shifters. I could have shifted that atmosphere.

An atmosphere is a pervading mood, environment, or influence. An atmosphere can be relaxing or tense. It can be conducive to concentrating or distracting. An atmosphere can be demonic and cause feelings of heaviness, fear, anxiety, anger, control, uncleanness, hopelessness, oppression, and unbelief.

God wires some seers to discern what spirits are prevailing in an atmosphere—whether God, angels, or demons. But discerning it is one thing, shifting it is another. But know this: God typically doesn't allow us to discern something just so we can know it. He is expecting us to take action. Many times, that action is prayer.

When Elijah called the showdown at Mount Carmel, he didn't passively stand by and accept the dark atmosphere that the false prophets of Baal were creating. Imagine how dark it was as they cried out to a false God and started cutting themselves. This went on for hours! Elijah watched as they made fools of themselves. When they were done, he shifted the atmosphere of the nation.

Elijah did this by rebuilding the altar, calling on the name of the Lord, and watching as the fire of God came down in a spectacular way. The atmosphere immediately shifted and all of Israel repented.

Seers, you carry a God-given authority to shift atmospheres. After you discern a thing, the Holy Spirit may lead you to pray, decree, worship, or perform a prophetic act. When you follow His leadership, you'll be an atmosphere shifter.

PRAYER

Father, in the name of Jesus, help me discern atmospheres—and then take it a step further. Teach me to be an atmosphere shifter. Give me boldness to stand in prayer to clear atmospheres of anything that hinders Your glory.

JUNE 17

WHEN YOUR DREAM LIFE DRIES UP

And it happened after a while that the brook dried up, because there had been no rain in the land.

1 Kings 17:7

Early in my walk with the Lord, I was a prolific dreamer. But suddenly, seemingly out of nowhere, my dream life dried up and I barely dreamed for many years. God is so good that after I stopped dreaming, He started speaking to me in different ways. He's intent on getting His messages to us, and if we're not responding in one way, He'll use another way.

Still, I was not content with losing my dream life. When I spoke with James Goll about it, he offered to pray for me. After he did, I immediately started dreaming again. But I was determined to find out why I stopped dreaming in the first place because I didn't want my dream life to ever dry up again. Here's what I discovered: I wasn't stewarding my dream life well. Nobody ever taught me how!

Maybe you used to dream a lot and your dream life dried up. There are many reasons for this. It could be an attack. It could be that your sleep habits are poor. But it could be that you didn't steward your dream life well. Scripture speaks over and over about being a good steward, or manager. We need to be good stewards of our dream life.

Peter speaks of stewarding the gifts of grace God gives us in 1 Peter 4:10. Paul talks about stewardship in Romans 12:6-8 when he exhorts us to prophesy, serve, teach, exhort, give, lead, and show mercy according to the grace given to us. In other words, steward the grace.

It's the same with our dream life. Remember Proverbs 25:2 (NIV), "It's the glory of God to conceal a matter: to search out a matter is the glory of kings."

We are responsible for stewarding the revelations or information we receive through this communication mode. No one can steward it for us. Of course, God won't condemn us for being poor stewards, but we can certainly cause ourselves plenty of grief by failing to understand what God was gracious enough to share. Take my course on Dream Keepers at www.schoolofthespirit.tv to learn how to steward your dream life.

PRAYER

Father, in the name of Jesus, I don't want my dream life to ever dry up, so please help me steward what You give me well. Please also help me avoid anything that would cause me not to receive divine dreams.

JUNE 18

KNOW YOUR AUDIENCE

Moreover it is required in stewards that one be found faithful.
1 Corinthians 4:2

Before you release a visual revelation, you need to do more than judge its accuracy. You need to discern whether it's personal or corporate. In other words, is that revelation just for you or is it for a church, a movement, or the broader Body of Christ? It's not wise to paint the Body of Christ with a broad brush when what you saw is just for you or your church. In fact, this misapplication can lead many into error.

I've seen too many seers release a corporate word that was meant solely for them, but because it was a word of correction, they assumed it must be for someone else. Keep in mind that if the revelation is for your church or for the Body of Christ, then it's also for you. Apply the visual revelation to your own life before releasing it more broadly so that you have clean hands and confidence.

So what am I saying? Yes, God may show you visual revelation for churches, denominations, movements, or the entire Body of Christ. But He will also show you things to come for your personal life. We must divide the visual revelation rightly so we don't end up delivering it to the wrong audience.

Habakkuk 2:2 offers wisdom: "...Write the vision; make it plain on tablets, so he may run who reads it." Before you invite others to run with the visual revelation you've received, make sure it's theirs to run with. How do you tell the difference?

First and foremost by the Spirit of God, but also keep this in mind: Personal revelation will deal with things like your personal weaknesses, warnings about attacks against your life, or assignments God is giving you. God may give you a visual revelation that refines you, prepares you, or calls you into deeper fellowship with Him.

Corporate revelation, by contrast, goes beyond you. It may include calling you to stand in the gap in intercession, but it's bigger than you. It affects others. Corporate revelation often comes with an urgency to share, to warn, to prepare a group. When Joseph interpreted Pharaoh's dream, he had an assignment, but the dream wasn't just about him. It concerned the whole world. Always ask the Lord, "Is this personal or corporate?"

PRAYER

Father, in the name of Jesus, please help me discern whether my visual revelation is for me alone, for a specific group of people, or for the whole Church. I don't want to mislead people or deceive myself.

JUNE 19

WHEN THE SEER DECLARES

Declare among the nations, proclaim, and set up a standard; proclaim—do not conceal it— say, "Babylon is taken, Bel is shamed. Merodach is broken in pieces; her idols are humiliated, her images are broken in pieces."

Jeremiah 50:2

Seers don't just see, they also say. Specifically, a seer's prophetic proclamation can be a powerful way to usher in God's will. Based on what you see, you may proclaim a warning, a promise or a prophetic strategy.

Think about Jeremiah. God tasked him with proclaiming Babylon's downfall. Making proclamations based on what you see can shift atmospheres, break strongholds and bring divine alignment among a people group.

What does *proclaim* mean? Here's my definition of a prophetic proclamation: the act of saying something in a public, official or definite way; the act of proclaiming something; an official statement or announcement made by a person in power or by a government.

In Christ, you are that person in power and government. You have the power of the Holy Spirit and you are an authorized Kingdom agent. You have the responsibility, as the Holy Spirit leads, to make prophetic proclamations.

There is power in proclaiming the will of God as expressed through visual revelation. Although what you share may not be a Scripture, per se, if God shows you something in the spirit, you can proclaim the truth behind it. I like to connect the dots of my visual revelation to Scripture. Then, when I share it, I can proclaim the Word of God that is in line with what He showed me.

Hebrews 4:12-13, "For the word of God is living and powerful, and sharper than any two-edged sword, piercing even to the division of soul and spirit, and of joints and marrow, and is a discerner of the thoughts and intents of the heart. And there is no creature hidden from His sight, but all things are naked and open to the eyes of Him to whom we must give account."

What power in the Word of God! When you connect the dots between your visual revelation and the Word of God and make proclamations, you may be exposing things. You may be dividing things. But you may also be healing things and releasing things. Be obedient to make proclamations.

PRAYER

Father, in the name of Jesus, would You give me a revelation of seer proclamations? Give me the boldness and confidence to open my mouth and proclaim what I see into the atmosphere.

JUNE 20

TEST THE FRUIT OF YOUR ENCOUNTERS

You will know them by their fruits....

Matthew 7:16

Every seer needs to be a fruit inspector. You need to test the fruit of your visual revelation—dreams, visions, out-of-body experiences, trances, etc.

What do I mean to "test the fruit"? Well, when you go to the grocery store, you squeeze the avocado to see if it's ripe enough to eat (or too ripe). You don't want an avocado that's rotten inside. Much the same, you don't want to be led by revelation from an encounter that's rotten.

You can't squeeze a dream or a vision, but you can judge the fruit it produces in your heart, which will help you determine if it's true or false. Encounters with God should always bear the fruit of humility. If the encounter produces pride, it's not from God. And, in fact, it's dangerous.

Proverbs 11:2 tells us, "When pride comes, then comes shame; but with the humble is wisdom." And Proverbs 18:12 tells us, "Before destruction the heart of a man is haughty, and before honor is humility." When pride enters, purity leaves. In other words, pride pollutes your gift. And, by the way, spiritual pride is the worst kind of pride. Jonathan Edwards, a key figure in the First Great Awakening, put it this way:

> *The first and worst cause of error that prevails in our day is spiritual pride. This is the main door by which the devil comes into the hearts of those who are zealous for the advancement of Christ. It is the chief inlet of smoke from the bottomless pit to darken the mind and mislead the judgment, and the main handle by which Satan takes hold of Christians to hinder a work of God. Until this disease is cured, medicines are applied in vain to heal all other diseases.*

Ouch!

True encounters with God leave us in awe of who He is. Consider Isaiah's vision of the Lord seated on His throne. We see his reaction in Isaiah 6:5, "Woe is me, for I am undone! Because I am a man of unclean lips, and I dwell in the midst of a people of unclean lips; for my eyes have seen the King, the Lord of hosts."

PRAYER

Father, in the name of Jesus, help me to be an accurate fruit inspector. Help me to notice when the visual revelation I receive is producing pride in my heart instead of inspiring awe for Your Spirit.

JUNE 21

THE ZECHARIAH SEER ANOINTING

Then I raised my eyes and looked, and there were two women, coming with the wind in their wings; for they had wings like the wings of a stork, and they lifted up the basket between earth and heaven.

Zechariah 5:9

Zechariah recorded eight profound night visions in the book that carries his name. This seer prophet saw a rider on a red horse among myrtle trees reporting that the earth was at rest. This was symbolic of God's promises of mercy on Jerusalem and for the rebuilding of Solomon's temple (Zechariah 1:1-17).

Zechariah also had a vision of four horns and four craftsmen. The four horns symbolized the forces that scattered the Israelites, while the four craftsmen symbolized men who would cast down those horns. The message was clear: the nations that judged the Israelites would be judged (Zechariah 1:18-21).

Zechariah's visions include the man with the measuring line that promised God would be a wall of fire around Jerusalem (Zechariah 2:1-13), the cleansing of Joshua the High Priest, symbolizing the removal of guilt from the priesthood and foreshadowing the coming Messiah (Zechariah 3:1-10).

He also saw the golden lampstand with two olive trees concerning the rebuilding of the temple (Zechariah 4:1-14); the flying scroll with written curses in Zechariah 5:1-4, the woman in a basket showing wickedness being removed from the land (Zechariah 5:5-11), and the four chariots between the bronze mountains described as the "four spirits of heaven" (Zechariah 6:1-8). And he scribed all this weighty revelation with immaculate detail.

All in all, God used Zechariah's seer anointing to encourage God's people to rebuild the temple and to step into his prophetic timetable. Translated to modern-day seers, the Zechariah seer anointing offers encouragement and direction through visual revelation. God also used him to motivate God's people to persevere. He was a seer with an end-times bent whose visions pointed to the coming Messiah and the triumphant Kingdom.

Reading Zechariah's visions should challenge you to steward obscure visions with wisdom, to operate in edification, exhortation, and comfort as the Church walks through trying times and to call His people into prophetic timing.

PRAYER

Father, in the name of Jesus, would You help me to learn from Zechariah's ministry? Would You help me steward obscure visions with wisdom, to edify, exhort, and comfort the Church and to steward prophetic timing?

JUNE 22

A WORD FOR THE DISCOURAGED SEER

Now may the God of hope fill you with all joy and peace in believing, that you may abound in hope by the power of the Holy Spirit.
Romans 15:13

I was driving down the highway just as content as I could be when the Holy Spirit started talking to me about discouragement. I listened closely with my spiritual ears, as I always do, but my natural mind didn't understand why my Friend would bring up the topic while I was driving down the highway just as content as I could be.

"The enemy wouldn't bring discouragement to your heart if you weren't doing something he didn't like. He's trying to get you to quit doing what you are doing by making it look like you're not making a difference," the Holy Spirit whispered to my heart in that still small voice. "Don't be discouraged."

Seer, I will say the same to you. Discouragement is a dangerous weapon in the enemy's arsenal. *Merriam-Webster*'s *Dictionary* defines *discourage* as "to make (someone) less determined, hopeful, or confident; to make (something) less likely to happen; to try to make people not want to do (something); to deprive of courage or confidence; to hinder by disfavoring; to dissuade or attempt to dissuade from doing something."

That about sums it up, doesn't it? The enemy comes to steal, kill, and destroy (John 10:10), and discouragement is often part of his strategy to steal your confidence so that your visual revelation won't do more damage to his dark kingdom through your obedient acts of service to God. The devil uses discouragement to tempt you give up and quit.

Discouragement is dangerous because it distracts your eyes from what God is trying to show you. You're not called to walk in discouragement. You're not called to give up and quit. You're not called to look at the world with natural eyes. You *are* called to encourage yourself in the Lord, to press in and press on, and to walk by faith, not by sight in the face of anything and everything the devil throws at you.

If you look at life through natural eyes, you may be discouraged; but when you lean into your spiritual sight, God will show you great and mighty things.

PRAYER

Father, in the name of Jesus, would You help me to recognize the first fruits of discouragement? I don't want to put my attention on earthly things and miss the spiritual truths You are ready to share with me.

JUNE 23

BREAKING TOXIC SOUL TIES

...may your whole spirit, soul, and body be preserved blameless at the coming of our Lord Jesus Christ.

1 Thessalonians 5:23

Toxic soul ties can hinder your accuracy in interpreting what you see in the spirit. While the term *soul tie* is not explicitly used in Scripture, the concept is.

Acts 4:32 says, "The multitude of those who believed were of one heart and one soul...." Paul also prayed for the church at Colossae in Colossians 2:2, "that their hearts may be encouraged, being knit together in love...." Ruth and Naomi had a healthy soul tie, as did Jonathan and David. But Samson's soul tie with Delilah was absolutely toxic and he lost his eyes.

Think about it. Your soul contains your mind, will, emotions, imaginations, intellect, and reasoning.

Your mind is the home of your opinions, your memories, your thoughts, and your perceptions. When you have a soul tie, it affects how you think, how you remember things, and how you view things. Your will is the seat of your choices, your desires, and your determinations. When you have a soul tie, it affects your choices and desires.

Your emotions are your conscious mental reactions, such as anger, fear, or joy, that are experienced as strong feelings. When you have a soul tie, it affects your emotions. Your imagination is your creative ability. It's your ability to form a mental image of something that is not right in front of you. When you have a soul tie, it affects your creative ability. When you have a soul tie, it affects your creative ability.

Your reasoning is the ability to understand something from a natural perspective. When you have a soul tie, it affects the decisions you make. Your intellect is your capacity for knowledge. When you have a soul tie, it affects what you think you know. And that can be skewed.

A toxic soul tie can damage your soul. If your soul is not prospering, the way you judge, interpret, apply, or pray through visual revelation can be skewed. Do you have a toxic soul tie? It's worth asking. Check out my course Breaking Toxic Soul Ties at www.schoolofthespirit.tv.

PRAYER

Father, in the name of Jesus, would You show me if I have a toxic soul tie, even one I don't remember? Help me discern and break every toxic soul tie that could affect how I understand or share what You show me.

JUNE 24

SEEING SOMEONE'S DEATH

The last enemy that will be destroyed is death.

1 Corinthians 15:26

When I was young in the Lord, I saw the death of a close friend's brother. After their mother died, he never stopped grieving. His inability to process the grief in a healthy way opened the door for a spirit of grief to enter. My friend tried to get him to come to church, but he was more uncomfortable. Grief was consuming him.

Some years after I first met him, the Holy Spirit showed me that if he didn't shake off that grief he would die within a year. At first, I didn't say anything to anyone. I didn't want to speak death over him, so I prayed. But eventually he started having heart problems, followed by open heart surgery. At that point, I felt led to tell my friend so we could pray together. Long story short, when we were on the mission field in another country he passed away. He died in his grief, and his sister was not battling grief of her own.

I am not the first one who has seen a revelation of death. You may also have experienced this. If you have, you know that it's troubling. So why does the Lord show us these things? First, for the sake of prayer. You need to discern, then, if what you saw demands intercession to push back the spirit of death or intercession to prepare the loved ones for the loss they are going to face.

Next, you need to discern whether or not to tell the person what you saw, or tell their family members if your relationship is solely with them. Isaiah had a mandate to go straight to the king with a prophetic word. We read in Isaiah 38:1: "In those days Hezekiah was sick and near death. And Isaiah the prophet, the son of Amoz, went to him and said to him, 'Thus says the Lord: "Set your house in order, for you shall die and not live."'"

Why did the Lord lead Isaiah this way? I believe it was because he wanted to spare Hezekiah's life. Hezekiah prayed and wept bitterly and God gave him fifteen more years. I wish that was always the outcome, but it's not. Always, always wait on the Lord with what to do if you see someone dying.

PRAYER

Father, in the name of Jesus, if I should ever see someone dying in a dream or vision, please tell me what You want me to do. I don't want to speak death or scare people, but I don't want to be idle either.

JUNE 25

WHEN YOUR PASTOR DOESN'T WANT TO HEAR IT

He who hears you hears Me, he who rejects you rejects Me, and he who rejects Me rejects Him who sent Me.

Luke 10:16

My friend had a vision of the word *Ichabod* over a church we both attended. She prayed and felt led to share this with the leadership of the church with an interpretation, "The glory of the Lord is going to depart if you don't change your ways." I gave her my two cents: don't do it because they will crucify you. She shared it anyway and was promptly removed from all teaching and intercessory prayer leadership. She was sidelined.

There are two sides to visual revelation. There's the one who delivers the dream, vision, feeling, or other encounter in the seer dimensions. And then there's the one who receives it, or refuses to receive it.

Have you ever delivered a visual revelation that your pastor flat-out refused to receive even though you were convinced it was from God? The visual revelation was pure. It was timely. You judged it and prayed it through before releasing it. You asked God for His timing.

The visual revelation didn't seek to control the pastor. It didn't violate Scripture. The encounter exalted Jesus and was delivered in a spirit of humility. Nevertheless, it wasn't received—and maybe you were even harshly criticized or labeled a false prophet for delivering it.

Don't take the rejection personally. If you are delivering a true visual revelation, the people aren't rejecting you. They are rejecting the Lord's revelation. And there's always a price to pay for rejecting revelation from the Lord.

When you know that you know that you know that God has given you a visual revelation for your pastor (or anyone else for that matter)—and you know, too, that He wants you to actually deliver it, speak it forth boldly with humility, not fearing the consequences, not fearing rejection.

And if your pastor (or anyone else) rejects the dream, vision, or encounter—or rejects you—don't respond in kind. Instead, go into intercession for them. This is the spirit of a true seer.

What about my friend who shared the Ichabod vision? Despite the persecution, she stayed in that church for a season. She was praying for the leadership to receive a direct word of God. They didn't, and the glory left. But her hands were clean.

PRAYER

Father, in the name of Jesus, would You help me not to take it personally if my visual revelation is rejected? Help me to act like Samuel, and continue to make intercession even when leaders make bad decisions.

JUNE 26

GOD STRETCHES HIS SEERS

Enlarge the place of your tent, and let them stretch out the curtains of your dwellings; do not spare; lengthen your cords, and strengthen your stakes. For you shall expand to the right and to the left....

Isaiah 54:2-3

I spend several days a week lifting heavy weights and doing all sorts of crazy new exercises in the gym. Sometimes, I forget to stretch and end up with muscles so tight I can barely walk two days later. That soreness makes me want to skip the next workout. You might say my muscles are weary in well doing.

Lately, I've found myself in God's gym—lifting heavy spiritual weights and doing all manner of uncomfortable new exercises. I don't have to worry about the stretching part. He's doing that too. God's stretching is sometimes as painful on our souls as working over a sore muscle, but it leaves you with a spiritual capacity great enough to move into the next season He's ordained for you.

One thing I've learned in times of pressure is that there's pressure from the inside—what I call Holy Ghost pressure—and pressure from the outside the comes from people, places, things (and some of those "things" include devils). Whether the pressure comes from the hand of God or the enemy, if you just keep pressing through the pressure you not only gain strength, but the pressure will also eventually let up. Through the pressing, you are building spiritual strength and character that will serve you well during the next phase of your journey.

God has purpose for everything He does. Take confidence knowing that He's stretching you so that you can hold more of His power, gain more of His wisdom, more of His character—more of Him. He wants to increase your influence and enlarge your territory.

Let me leave you with this quote from Oswald Chambers, an early 20th century Baptist and Holiness Movement evangelist, who said it better than I can:

Patience is more than endurance. A saint's life is in the hands of God like a bow and arrow in the hands of an archer. God is aiming at something the saint cannot see, and He stretches and strains, and every now and again the saint says, "I cannot stand anymore." God does not heed, He goes on stretching till His purpose is in sight, then He lets fly. Trust yourself in God's hands. Maintain your relationship to Jesus Christ by the patience of faith. "Though He slay me, yet will I trust in Him."

Amen.

PRAYER

Father, in the name of Jesus, I welcome Your stretching. I want to enlarge my spiritual capacity. Help me to cooperate with Your stretching process. Help me get out of my comfort zone.

JUNE 27

THE JOEL SEER ANOINTING

The sun shall be turned into darkness, and the moon into blood, before the coming of the great and awesome day of the Lord.

Joel 2:31

If you read the book of Joel, you'll discover it's sort of like a miniature book of Revelation. It's essentially a condensed version of what John the Revelator saw. Like John's apocalyptic visions, Joel's book is marked by prophetic warnings about the end times and redemptive hope.

The Joel seer anointing calls believers to operate in the Spirit and prepare the Bride of Christ for a never-before-seen outpouring of God's presence and power on earth.

It was Joel, after all, who prophesied these words: "And it shall come to pass afterward that I will pour out My Spirit on all flesh; Your sons and your daughters shall prophesy, your old men shall dream dreams, your young men shall see visions. And also on My menservants and on My maidservants I will pour out My Spirit in those days" (Joel 2:28-29). You are part of this generation—a prophetic movement that crosses generational, gender, and ethnic boundaries.

Joel was also anointed to warn of sin that leads to judgment—but always with redemption. Joel 2:25 prophesies, "So I will restore to you the years that the swarming locust has eaten, the crawling locust, the consuming locust, and the chewing locust, my great army which I sent among you." Seers, remember that God is the God of restoration. Yes, judgment—and even wrath—will mark the end times, but God's heart is always to restore. He is the God of mercy.

Joel was an end-times forerunner. More than 2,000 years ago, he prophesied, "And I will show wonders in the heavens and in the earth: Blood and fire and pillars of smoke. The sun shall be turned into darkness, and the moon into blood, before the coming of the great and awesome day of the Lord" (Joel 2:30-31).

Joel's seer anointing carries a threefold mandate of boldness, urgency, and hope. His ministry was marked by end-times visions that aimed to help align God's people with purpose and prepare them for future glory.

PRAYER

Father, in the name of Jesus, would You give me an appreciation and understanding of Joel's seer anointing. Help me glean from his threefold mandate of boldness, urgency, and hope.

JUNE 28

LET THE WIND BLOW

Then I looked, and behold, a whirlwind was coming out of the north, a great cloud with raging fire engulfing itself; and brightness was all around it and radiating out of its midst like the color of amber, out of the midst of the fire.

Ezekiel 1:4

In the 1970s, Kathryn Kuhlman, who was well-known for the many spontaneous miracles and healings that manifested in the wake of words of knowledge the Holy Spirit shared with her heart, saw an extraordinary manifestation of the Holy Spirit as wind.

It reminds me of John 3:8, "The wind blows where it wishes, and you hear the sound of it, but cannot tell where it comes from and where it goes. So is everyone who is born of the Spirit."

Here's what happened: Kathryn Kuhlman invited a foreign couple to come up to the platform where she was speaking. With her distinct Missouri accent and her flowing gown, she prophesied emphatically: "The Lord has something for you." What happened next, no one could have anticipated.

As the couple started approaching the platform, something unusual happened. A strong wind started blowing, seemingly out of nowhere. The wind was so strong that it was difficult for the couple to keep walking straight ahead. In fact, they had to lean forward so they wouldn't fall over. Not only that, but their clothes were also flapping in the wind!

Making matters more supernatural, the wind was only blowing in the center aisle of the auditorium. Kathryn thought it was funny and told them, "Don't be afraid, dear ones, that's the wind of the Holy Spirit blowing on you."

We know the Holy Spirit can manifest as wind and wind is often a symbol of the Holy Spirit in Scripture. In Acts 2:2, the disciples were sitting in the Upper Room, praying in unity. Suddenly, there came from Heaven a noise like a violent rushing wind and it filled the whole house where they were sitting. They were all baptized in the Holy Spirit.

You can sometimes hear the sound of the wind of the Spirit or see the effects of it. Start looking.

PRAYER

Father, in the name of Jesus, would You make me more sensitive to the wind of Your Spirit blowing in my midst? Would You help me discern Your wind is behind a movement so I can agree with what You are doing?

JUNE 29

SAYING WHAT YOU SEE CLEARLY

So likewise you, unless you utter by the tongue words easy to understand, how will it be known what is spoken? For you will be speaking into the air.

1 Corinthians 14:9

As a seer, your ministry goes beyond seeing—and even beyond praying. There are times when you will need to clearly articulate what you see in the spirit. That can be the hardest part. Seeing, after all, is a freely given gift. Trying to explain what you have seen in the spirit is where many people stumble and even accidentally lead people astray.

Think of Ezekiel's vision of God in Ezekiel 1:4-12:

> Then I looked, and behold, a whirlwind was coming out of the north, a great cloud with raging fire engulfing itself; and brightness was all around it and radiating out of its midst like the color of amber, out of the midst of the fire.
>
> Also from within it came the likeness of four living creatures. And this was their appearance: they had the likeness of a man. Each one had four faces, and each one had four wings. Their legs were straight, and the soles of their feet were like the soles of calves' feet. They sparkled like the color of burnished bronze. The hands of a man were under their wings on their four sides; and each of the four had faces and wings. Their wings touched one another. The creatures did not turn when they went, but each one went straight forward.
>
> As for the likeness of their faces, each had the face of a man; each of the four had the face of a lion on the right side, each of the four had the face of an ox on the left side, and each of the four had the face of an eagle. Thus were their faces. Their wings stretched upward; two wings of each one touched one another, and two covered their bodies. And each one went straight forward; they went wherever the spirit wanted to go, and they did not turn when they went.

Imagine the scene. It must have been overwhelming. Now catch this. The Holy Spirit inspired Scripture, which means He helped Ezekiel articulate what he was seeing and write it down for us to read. The Holy Spirit can help you in the same way. If you haven't picked up a copy of *The Seer's Dictionary* yet, grab it on Amazon or on my website at jenniferleclaire.org.

PRAYER

Father, in the name of Jesus, would You help me to articulate what I see in the spirit? Give me the right words to express what I am seeing so that people can understand and act on the revelation.

JUNE 30

THE END TIMES SEER ANOINTING

...There will be a time of distress such as has not happened from the beginning of nations until then. But at that time your people—everyone whose name is found written in the book—will be delivered.
Daniel 12:1 NIV

Not every seer has an end-times assignment. However, I believe seers in the end times will carry an anointing to discern that the pages of the book of Revelation that John penned are unfolding right before their natural eyes.

I also believe they will see what others can't or don't want to see in the spirit during those last days. With that, I believe end-times seers will be uniquely positioned to urge the Bride on in intercession as the birth pangs lead to the breaking of the seals. If you can see it, you can pray it through.

The end-times seer anointing is what it sounds like: an anointing to discern, interpret, and respond rightly to end-times events, whether they are happening thousands of years from now or right in front of our natural eyes. This anointing comes with the skill to wade through complex dreams, visions, and encounters full of parables and symbols that would otherwise be difficult to understand. The end-times seer anointing carries with it the grace to equip and inspire the Body of Christ to align with God's last-days purposes.

Seers with this anointing can detect the schemes of the enemy and the movement of the Lord and His angels. They receive insight into biblical prophecy and supernatural revelation about the times and seasons, so they can help lead the Church through turbulent times, sort of like how Zechariah and Haggai prophesied to the builders in Ezra's day.

This unique seer anointing will help wake up the Bride, stir the lukewarm Church, and urge a call to holiness before and even while end-times events are actively unfolding. This is where the seer function blends with the watchman function to blow the trumpet and sound the alarm, but also stand in the gap for God's plans to come to pass on earth and for the lost to be saved.

You might call the seer with an end-times anointing a forerunner who shows the way into God's perfect will in the most disturbing times mankind will ever see. Just as John the Baptist prepared the way for Christ's First Coming, I believe seers with an end-times anointing will help prepare the way for His Second Coming.

PRAYER

Father, in the name of Jesus, what a time to be alive! I know many would reject an end-times seer anointing because of the weight of what is seen, but if You call me to it I will embrace the assignment.

JULY

I know a man in Christ who fourteen years ago—whether in the body I do not know, or whether out of the body I do not know, God knows—such a one was caught up to the third heaven.

2 Corinthians 12:2

JULY 1

WHEN THE VISION MAKES YOU SICK

I, Daniel, walked around in a daze, unwell for days. Then I got a grip on myself and went back to work taking care of the king's affairs. But I continued to be upset by the vision. I couldn't make sense of it.

Daniel 8:27 MSG

Have you ever seen in a dream, a vision, or an encounter that literally made you sick to your stomach or feel unwell? Sometimes we can feel the weight of visual revelation in our bodies.

If a vision literally makes you feel sick, take some time to sit with the Lord because this is not an everyday encounter. He is trusting You with a weighty revelation that some could not handle. He is sharing dreams or visions that may overwhelm your soul to the point that you feel it in your body. These revelations demand setting some time aside to work through it with the Holy Spirit.

Daniel experienced this in the third year of King Belshazzar's reign. In his vision, it seemed he was in a palace in the capital of Persia. He saw a ram with two long horns standing beside the river, and the ram butted everything out of his way to the west, north, and south. No one could stand against him or help his victims. Suddenly, a male goat appeared from the west and crossed the land so swiftly that he didn't even touch the ground.

> And I, Daniel, fainted and was sick [for several] days. Afterward I rose up and did the king's business; and I wondered at the vision, but there was no one who understood it or could make it understood (Daniel 8:27 AMPC).

God sent Gabriel to explain to Daniel what he saw. But notice how he was sick for several days after this vision. It shook him to the core. He was physically weak. His body literally felt the weight of the vision.

So what do you do if you have a vision that literally makes you sick? First, note that your emotions are overwhelmed so you need to run to the Lord and put your eyes on Him so peace can return. Ask God for the grace to carry the prayer burden that often comes with such dramatic visual encounters. Ask God for the meaning of what you saw. Ask God about the timing of what you saw.

And, please, don't be too quick to run to social media and share things like this. You could scare people or offer a partial revelation that leaves people without understanding. Remember, God didn't show you something to harm you. He showed you because He's entrusting you to steward it well for His glory. The God who opened your eyes will show you what to do next.

PRAYER

Father, in the name of Jesus, would You help me steward weighty revelations that overwhelm my soul and affect my physical frame? I know You are trusting me to discern how to handle what You show me. Help me.

JULY 2

FACING SEER SETBACKS

Fear not, for I am with you; be not dismayed, for I am your God. I will strengthen you, yes, I will help you, I will uphold you with My righteous right hand.

Isaiah 41:10

"It's just a setback; it's not your future." I remember when the Holy Spirit spoke those words to me some years ago. I had just taken a devastating blow—a one-two (three-four) punch from the enemy.

Have you encountered a setback lately? Maybe you had a counterfeit experience and didn't immediately discern it. Maybe you lost some credibility because your visual revelation was perceived as false or you were publicly corrected and humiliated because your pastor disagreed with you.

See this setback for what it is. Setbacks are delays. Setbacks are hindrances. But setbacks are not necessarily failures. You did not fail because you encountered defeat. You only fail when you choose not to get back up and keep going. It's just a setback. It's not your future.

A setback is a form of feedback. In other words, when you encounter a setback it should cause you to stop and assess your situation. How did you come to this point? Could you have done something differently? How should you respond now? Stop, look, listen, and learn from the Holy Spirit and you will find wisdom.

Henry Ford, founder of the Ford Motor Company, said, "Life is a series of experiences, each one of which makes us bigger, even though sometimes it is hard to realize this. For the world was built to develop character, and we must learn that the setbacks and griefs which we endure help us in our marching onward."

There are countless books on great men and women who faced setbacks on their way to realizing their dreams. Michael Jordan was cut from his high school basketball team. Setback. Thomas Edison failed 1,000 times to invent the light bulb before he found success. Setback. Walt Disney was fired from a newspaper for not being creative enough. Setback. Steve Jobs was fired from Apple. Setback.

Despite the setbacks—all of them rather humiliating—each went on to make their mark on modern history. None of these men allowed their setbacks to become their future. Instead, they turned their mistakes into a coach. Imagine if they hadn't. Beloved, you have something to contribute to the world. Don't let your setbacks define your future.

PRAYER

Father, in the name of Jesus, help me not get stuck in a setback, but to see it as a form of feedback. Remind me to process this perceived setback with You and glean wisdom for my future.

JULY 3

ENJOYING THE SILENT DIMENSION

Be still and know that I am God....

Psalm 46:10

I wake up at 3:45 in the morning—or earlier if the Holy Spirit nudges me. The first thing I do when I wake up is not to check my phone or brew some coffee. The first thing I do is enter the silent dimension.

The silent dimension is a dimension in the spirit where there is absolute silence; it's the destination of one who practices silence as a gateway to the seer dimensions, according to *The Seer's Dictionary*. Yes, silence is the absence of sound, but it's also a dimension in the spirit where one receives revelation from the throne room.

Learning how to remain quiet in soul and calm in spirit in order to discern what is happening in the spirit world and see what the Lord is saying is vital to navigating seer dimensions.

Saint John of the Cross, a major figure in the Spanish Counter-Reformation, is known as a friend of silence. He wrote things such as: "Carve out a day every week, or an hour a day, or a moment each hour, and abide in loving silence with the Friend. Feel the frenetic concerns of life in the world fall away, like the last leaves of autumn being lifted from the tree in the arms of a zephyr. Be the bare tree."

"It is best to learn to silence the faculties and to cause them to be still so that God may speak," he wrote. "What we need most in order to make progress is to be silent before this great God with our appetite and with our tongue, for the language he best hears is silent love."

It's been said by many mystics and seers that silence is God's first language. Silence can be uncomfortable at times but it is a powerful pursuit that brings clarity of vision. Psalm 46:10 tells us, "Be still and know that I am God." This heart posture will position you to enter the silent realm.

PRAYER

Father, in the name of Jesus, help me learn to be still—to quiet my soul from the wandering thoughts that try to distract me from the silent dimension. Teach me to value silence.

JULY 4

SEEING STRANGERS IN THE SPIRIT

Jesus saw Nathanael coming toward Him, and said of him, "Behold, an Israelite indeed, in whom is no deceit!" Nathanael said to Him, "How do You know me?" Jesus answered and said to him, "Before Philip called you, when you were under the fig tree, I saw you."

John 1:47-48

Have you ever seen strangers in a dream or vision—or some other encounter? This can be mysterious to some and unsettling to others. It's not altogether uncommon to see the faces of people that we've never seen or met before. God can sometimes use a stranger in a visual revelation to get your attention.

The question is, what is God trying to show you?

Always operate from the truth that God is not random. If He shows you anything, there is a purpose behind it. Every detail has a meaning. You have to discern that purpose and meaning by the Spirit of God.

Is God showing you a divine connection that's coming in the near future, so you will recognize that person when you see them? Is He showing you a Judas or an Absalom or some other agent of darkness? Was it an angel you saw in human form? If so, did this "stranger" share a message?

What was the stranger doing? What activity were they engaged in? What were they wearing? What colors were their clothes? Did they seem benevolent or dubious? All of these details can shed light on the stranger's purpose in the dream. Pay attention to your emotions in the dream or vision as well.

The Holy Spirit knows what God is trying to show you, so always ask Him. Don't speculate. Meditate. Roll the visual revelation over and over in your mind and ask the Holy Spirit to share the truth He wants you to see. When you show yourself spiritually curious, you will be rewarded with revelation.

Did you wake up with an intercessory prayer burden of some sort? Or prophetic insight? If you woke up with an urge to pray for that stranger, do it. You may be praying for a Christian somewhere around the world. If you woke up with prophetic insight, take action on it. Someone's breakthrough might depend on it.

PRAYER

Father, in the name of Jesus, if I see a stranger in the spirit, would You lead me to press in and get all the details, to discern the reason behind what I am seeing? I don't want to neglect my due diligence.

JULY 5

DEVELOPING THICK SKIN

For do I now persuade men, or God? Or do I seek to please men? For if I still pleased men, I would not be a bondservant of Christ.
Galatians 1:10

I used to have such thin skin you could see my heart through my chest, or at least on my sleeve. Walking in seer ministry, I've had to learn to toughen up, especially in the face of a constant barrage of verbal attacks from religious spirits who don't believe there are seers today. Every time you release your seer revelation, somebody is going to disagree with you or call you false or make accusations against you.

When you worry about what other people think, you are giving them a measure of control over your life that belongs to the Holy Spirit. If you worry about what other people think, you are in danger of becoming a people-pleaser rather than a God-pleaser. If you worry about what other people think, you may even give away some of your seer identity.

I'm not saying that we shouldn't be sensitive to how we present visual revelation. I'm saying when you are confident about what God showed you and you release it in humility, don't worry about what people think—or who doesn't like it. If you make mistake, repent. Constantly worrying about what other people think will hinder your seer flow.

Listen, it doesn't matter what they think. It doesn't matter what they say. It only matters what God thinks and says about you. The Pharisees loved the praise of men more than the praise of God and you see where that got them—rebuked (John 12:42-43). Paul put it this way, "But as we have been approved by God to be entrusted with the gospel, even so we speak, not as pleasing men, but God who tests our hearts" (1 Thessalonians 2:4).

So how do you develop thick seer skin? Know who you are in Christ. My mentor in the prophetic once told me, "Jennifer, you must get everything you need directly from God." I've learned that includes approval. Like Paul said, "What then shall we say to these things? If God is for us, who can be against us?" (Romans 8:31). Make it a point to develop thick skin. You'll be a better seer for it.

PRAYER

Father, in the name of Jesus, would You help me to stop caring so much about what people think of me? Help me to develop thick skin so I am not easily swayed by man's opinion.

JULY 6

THE WILLIAM BRANHAM SEER ANOINTING

Truly the signs of an apostle were accomplished among you with all perseverance, in signs and wonders and mighty deeds.

2 Corinthians 12:12

William Branham, a prophet from southern Kentucky who rose to fame during the Voice of Healing movement and was known for healing manifestations with the help of an angel, had a vision in Georgia.

Branham had a vision of a little boy being raised from the dead. He not only predicted it, but he also described with minute detail what the young boy would look like, right down to his hair style and his eye color. Two years later, Branham was in Finland when he came upon the scene of a deadly car crash. The driver of a car struck two children. One of the children had been dead for about 30 minutes.

Branham said he looked down twice and then asked someone to raise the coat off the boy's lifeless body. At that moment, the Lord replayed in his mind the vision he had seen in Georgia of a little boy being raised from the dead. It was the same boy lying on the ground! Long story short, Branham raised the little boy from the dead.

The William Branham seer anointing saw supernatural encounters, precision words of knowledge and clear signs and wonders. He said an angel stood near him and gave him details of people's sicknesses and present and past circumstances. Miracles and healings often resulted.

The William Branham seer anointing awed people during the Voice of Healing movement. Some of his supporters point to tens of thousands of people healed under his ministry, but others say medical evidence was not always offered. In any case, he goes down in church history as one of the most remarkable seers of all time.

Unfortunately, in his latter years he strayed from sound doctrine. He started teaching that God was not Father, Son, and Holy Spirit, a "serpent seed" teaching that claimed Eve engaged in sexual sin with the serpent and birthed Cain, and determined he himself was Elijah, among other things. This demonstrates why we need to stay "plumb line" to the Word as we ascend.

PRAYER

Father, in the name of Jesus, would You help me learn from the true anointing You placed on William Branham? But likewise, help me learn from his terrible mistakes so I don't fall into error.

JULY 7

SNEAKY FAMILIAR SPIRITS

Give no regard to mediums and familiar spirits; do not seek after them, to be defiled by them: I am the Lord your God.

Leviticus 19:31

Beware the counterfeit Holy Spirit that will usher you into counterfeit revelation. It's called the "familiar spirit" and Scripture warns about it seventeen times.

The term *familiar spirit* comes from the Hebrew word *ōb,* meaning a bottle, necromancer, medium, spiritist or one who communicates with the dead. This word paints a picture of a vessel or container—a person becoming a "bottle" for a spirit to pour through. That's how mediums operate. But familiar spirits don't only manifest through witches and necromancers. They attach to ordinary people—sometimes even seers—who unknowingly entertain their whispers.

A familiar spirit is a specific class of spirit. As its name suggests, it is characterized by familiarity. These are spirits that are familiar with people, family lines, and weaknesses. They target seers to lead them astray. If we don't discern the voice of a familiar spirit, we will align with a counterfeit Holy Spirit and pollute our seer stream.

Familiar spirits are directly tied to witchcraft. Mediums, sorcerers, and necromancers deliberately communicate with them. But you don't have to practice witchcraft to have a familiar spirit or to have a familiar spirit talk to you. But the common denominator between the witch and the unsuspecting seer is communication with a devil—whether you realize it or not.

Familiar spirits can show up looking like Jesus or an angel. They can lead you into what seem like true supernatural encounters, but they are mimicking the truth while leading you into bondage. These spirits appeal to your pride and your flesh, so they may show you spectacular things to puff you up into pride so you are set up for a fall.

If we don't know the Holy Spirit, we can be deceived. That's why intimacy with the Holy Spirit is critical for the seer. Ultimately, the Holy Spirit leads you closer to Jesus, holiness, and truth. A familiar spirit pulls you deeper into self, deception, and bondage. The Holy Spirit produces life while a familiar spirit drains it. Check out my course, Deliverance from Familiar Spirits at www.schoolofthespirit.tv.

PRAYER

Father, in the name of Jesus, would You help me recognize a familiar spirit that is masquerading as Jesus, an angel, or some other being in the spirit realm. Inspire my heart to cultivate true intimacy with You.

JULY 8

THE FASTING SEER

You go, therefore, and read from the scroll which you have written at my instruction, the words of the Lord, in the hearing of the people in the Lord's house on the day of fasting....

Jeremiah 36:6

Fasting is a gate into the seer dimensions. Fasting is abstaining from food or some activity to focus on God. But it's just as much what you do as you fast as it is the fast itself. If you fast and sit on the couch and watch TV all day, you are going on a glorified diet. You will get some of the benefits of fasting but you are missing the spiritual point. Fasting is not a diet. It's a spiritual discipline for the seer.

Andrew Murray, a 19th century South African minister known for his prolific writing, said, "Prayer is reaching out after the unseen; fasting is letting go of all that is seen and temporal. Fasting helps express, deepen, confirm the resolution that we are ready to sacrifice anything, even ourselves to attain what we seek for the kingdom of God."

These are important words for the seer to grasp: fasting is letting go of all that is seen and temporal. When you do, you are better positioned to enter the seer dimensions. Your fasting should be Holy Spirit-led or you won't have grace to fast.

Fasting doesn't change God, but it does change you. Remember, Peter was on the roof, hungry, and waiting for food when he fell into a trance. As such, he was praying in a fasted state when he "saw heaven opened and an object like a great sheet bound at the four corners, descending to him and let down to the earth. In it were all kinds of four-footed animals of the earth, wild beasts, creeping things, and birds of the air. And a voice came to him, 'Rise, Peter; kill and eat'" (Acts 10:11-13). In fact, he saw this three times.

Fasting can help us hear more clearly from God. Fasting can help detoxify your body. Fasting helps cleanse your soul of toxic emotions. And as your flesh decreases, your spiritual sensitivity increases. When the Holy Spirit leads you to fast, ask Him to open your eyes a little wider.

PRAYER

Father, in the name of Jesus, lead me to fast when I need to put my flesh under. Help me deepen and confirm the resolution that I am ready to sacrifice anything to see what You want to show me in the spirit.

JULY 9

SEEING AN ENIGMA

And when the disciples saw Him walking on the sea, they were troubled, saying, "It is a ghost!" And they cried out for fear.
Matthew 14:26

At times, it can be difficult to communicate what you see in the spirit. In fact, it can be difficult to understand what exactly you are seeing in the spirit. There are some pretty wild visions recorded in the Bible. Sometimes, it may feel like you are seeing an enigma.

According to *The Seer's Dictionary*, an enigma is, "something hidden in darkness that can't be clearly recognized or easily expressed; a spirit being, either an angel, a living creature, demon or other creation, that is obscured from plain sight either by the Lord or by demon powers."

Think of Ezekiel who saw the wheel within a wheel or Daniel's vision of the four beasts—or how about most of the book of Revelation that John the apostle authored. These seers were seeing an enigma, or what Paul the apostle referred to as *"seeing through a glass darkly."*

Consider Paul's words in 1 Corinthians 13:12 (KJV), "For now we see through a glass, darkly; but then face to face: now I know in part; but then shall I know even as also I am known." Other translations say, "we see things imperfectly" (NLT) or "We don't yet see things clearly. We're squinting in a fog, peering through a mist" (MSG).

So what do you do when you see an enigma? You write down as many details as you possibly can. You take note of shapes, colors, activities, and sounds—even things you have no human words to describe. You write down any messages associated with the enigma. You ask God to explain the meaning.

Sometimes He will show you right away what you are seeing. Sometimes He will send an angel to explain it to you, like He did for Zechariah. Sometimes sharing the enigma with other seers will unlock deeper meaning.

That said, God is the God of purpose. He's not showing you something for the sake of showing you. It could be for training purposes. It could be a deposit for the future. It could be a piece of a bigger puzzle He's sharing with the seer community. Your part is to record and pray through the enigma. God will make the next move.

PRAYER

Father, in the name of Jesus, there are indeed interesting sights in the seer dimensions for which I don't have words. Help me to understand and communicate these enigmas so that revelation can be released accurately.

JULY 10

DON'T PUT OUT A FLEECE

"A wicked and adulterous generation seeks after a sign, and no sign shall be given to it except the sign of the prophet Jonah." And He left them and departed.

Matthew 16:4

When I was young in the Lord, I used to put out fleeces when I didn't know what to do. I would say, "Lord, if what I am seeing is from You, let there be three greenlights in a row." Then if I got two greenlights, but ran into a red light along the way home, I would say, "Lord, let's try again just in case."

That's called putting out a fleece. A fleece is taking some action or waiting on some event as a sign to confirm God's will. Gideon put out a fleece of wool twice to determine if God was speaking to Him, which is where we get the modern term "fleece." In our practice, we are not drawing lots but looking for outward signs of confirmation, according to *The Seer's Dictionary*.

We see Gideon put out a fleece, looking to make sure he heard right, in Judges 6:36-39:

> So Gideon said to God, "If You will save Israel by my hand as You have said—look, I shall put a fleece of wool on the threshing floor; if there is dew on the fleece only, and it is dry on all the ground, then I shall know that You will save Israel by my hand, as You have said." And it was so. When he rose early the next morning and squeezed the fleece together, he wrung the dew out of the fleece, a bowlful of water. Then Gideon said to God, "Do not be angry with me, but let me speak just once more: Let me test, I pray, just once more with the fleece; let it now be dry only on the fleece, but on all the ground let there be dew."

In the Old Testament, people put out fleeces, but in the New Testament God speaks to us through His Son (Hebrews 1:2). Seers, don't put out a fleece for confirmation of what you saw. Instead, build your faith to see in the spirit, use the Word of God to "plumb line" your visual revelation, and get wise counsel when you need it.

PRAYER

Father, in the name of Jesus, help me to filter my visual revelation by the witness of Your Spirit and the Word of God. I don't want to give the enemy any room to deceive me.

JULY 11

CORRECTING YOUR SPIRITUAL SIGHT

The eye is the lamp of the body. If your eyes are healthy, your whole body will be full of light. But if your eyes are unhealthy, your whole body will be full of darkness....

Matthew 6:22-23 NIV

If you are having problems with your spiritual sight, go to the Holy Spirit for an eye exam. In fact, don't wait until you sense a defect in your eye. Examine yourself regularly and let Him show you if something is amiss.

What is a defect in the eye? *The Seer's Dictionary* defines it as "a spiritual problem, such as a bias or sin, in the seer's eye that skews his vision." Consider this in the context of Leviticus 20:4: "And if the people of the land should in any way hide their eyes from the man, when he gives some of his descendants to Molech, and they do not kill him."

Hear me: You need to keep your spiritual vision clean. Paul said in Galatians 5:9 (NIV), "A little yeast [leaven] works through the whole batch of dough." Get the leaven of your eye before you report to the Body of Christ what you believe God is showing you. That leaven can cloud your vision. What do I mean by leaven? Justified sin. Small compromises. An unhealed wound. Unforgiveness. Bitter roots. All of these can affect the accuracy of your spiritual sight.

If someone is color blind, they are missing important details about the world around them. If someone lacks peripheral vision, their view is seriously limited. Just as a physical flaw in our natural eyes can cause us problems, so can a flaw in our souls affect our spiritual eyes.

Keep in mind that a defect in your eye doesn't just affect you, it affects those you are ministering to. That defect can lead to defective visions, dreams, interpretations, applications, and so on. Can you see the ripple effect? Part of stewarding your seer anointing is taking time to examine yourself.

In Lamentations 3:40, Jeremiah, the weeping prophet, said, "Let us search out and examine our ways, and turn back to the Lord." And David cried out in Psalm 139:23-24, "Search me, O God, and know my heart; try me, and know my anxieties; and see if there is any wicked way in me, and lead me in the way everlasting."

PRAYER

Father, in the name of Jesus, examine me to see if there is any wicked way in me. Help me see my faults so that I can make a course correction swiftly before it affects my spiritual sight and brings harm to others.

JULY 12

A PRAYER EVERY SEER SHOULD PRAY

For the Lord gives [skillful and godly] wisdom; from His mouth come knowledge and understanding.

Proverbs 2:6 AMP

I pray for many things every day. I pray for my family, my friends, my ministry, my nation—and, of course, myself. I pray for protection. I pray for a deeper revelation of God's love over my life. I pray for grace.

But there's one thing I've been praying for more and more lately—and I am convinced that if we would pray more for this one thing we would make better use of our time, live happier lives, and ultimately see more answers to our prayers.

What is this one thing I've been praying for more and more lately? Wisdom. Every seer needs tremendous wisdom on navigating the seer dimensions, judging, applying, interpreting, and sharing visual revelation.

We could all take a hint from Solomon during his visual encounter. You know the story. The Lord appealed to Solomon in a dream and made this invitation: "Ask! What shall I give you?" Can you imagine the Lord coming to you in a dream and making such an invitation? What would you ask God for if you could ask and assuredly receive anything?

It seems Solomon had enough wisdom to ask for the principal thing: wisdom. Solomon replied to God's invitation with these words: "Give to Your servant an understanding heart to judge Your people, that I may discern between good and evil. For who is able to judge this great people of Yours?" (1 Kings 3:9).

God is no respecter of persons—He shows no favoritism (Acts 10:34). You can receive the wisdom you need to walk accurately in the seer dimensions. James clearly stated that "If any of you lacks wisdom, let him ask of God, who gives to all liberally and without reproach, and it will be given to him" (James 1:5). The only catch is, you have to ask in faith, without doubting. That's not much of a catch and it shouldn't be too hard to do. God wants to give you wisdom so you can walk wisely, making the best use of your time because the days are evil (Ephesians 5:15-17).

Wisdom begets wisdom. So, by all means, pray for wisdom.

PRAYER

Father, in the name of Jesus, You said if I need wisdom I should ask for it. So I am asking for wisdom to walk in my seer anointing—and for all other aspects of my life. Thank You for Your wisdom.

JULY 13

SEEING THE PAST IN THE SPIRIT

...And you will find in the book of the records and know that this city is a rebellious city, harmful to kings and provinces, and that they have incited sedition within the city in former times, for which cause this city was destroyed.

Ezra 4:15

Seeing is not all about predicting. In other words, many seers want to see into the future and predict what happens next. But sometimes it's just as strategic to see into the past. Scripture calls it the former times.

Ezra 4:15 reveals a request of the king, "that search may be made in the book of the records of your fathers. And you will find in the book of the records and know that this city is a rebellious city, harmful to kings and provinces, and that they have incited sedition within the city in former times, for which cause this city was destroyed."

Seeing into the former times can help you understand God's purpose, His will, or His ways. You can see spiritual patterns or demonic roots that need to be severed for revival to come to a territory. He can also show you roots in a person's life from past traumas or sins that are giving the enemy a legal right to keep them in bondage.

We have to remember that God is the Father of time and moves in and out of time as we know it. He is the Alpha, the Omega, the Beginning and the End. He sees all things and knows all things and may share with you insight into the former things so you can be an agent of intercession on earth.

If you see former things, ask the Holy Spirit what you are seeing. Ask Him why He is showing you former things. Again, it could be for intercession or to issue a warning or just to teach you or the Body of Christ a lesson. God could also be showing you how history repeats itself and give you a strategy to interrupt the cycle in prayer.

Handling what you see in the former times demands weighing it against Scripture, accountability from elders and humility. It's a privilege to be trusted with such encounters and to partner with Him to accomplish His purposes in the present day.

PRAYER

Father, in the name of Jesus, thank You for helping me understand the power of seeing into the past. Help me understand when I am seeing the past so I don't mistake it for the present or the future.

JULY 14

PIECE BY PIECE

Gifts of knowledge and prophecy are partial at best, at least for now.
1 Corinthians 13:9 VOICE

Dream fragments can be frustrating—or even confusing—to a young seer. But once you gain some experience, you'll understand the power of fragments and how to put the pieces of the prophetic puzzle together so you can see the whole picture.

Just as we should not despise the day of small beginnings (Zechariah 4:10), we should not despise visual fragments. Think of them like bread crumbs that lead you to more revelation as you follow the Holy Spirit.

Fragments are pieces or parts that you remember in a dream or a vision, according to *The Seer's Dictionary*. To some seers, the fragments may seem insignificant at first glance. But rest assured God is purposeful and the person, thing, symbol, number, or color you see has meaning; and if you are faithful over the little you have, you will unlock more revelation.

Remember, God often gives revelation in bits and pieces. It's an invitation to dive deeper. The spiritually curious seer will RSVP. Proverbs 25:2 (CEV) tells us, "God is praised for being mysterious; rulers are praised for explaining mysteries." Mysteries will unravel when seers become active investigators and willing waiters.

If you meditate on those fragments, it's like pulling a string on a shirt that unravels the rest of the garment. The fragment can unravel the dream or vision. Maybe you just saw a word or a picture or a symbol. Think deeply about what you saw and ask the Holy Spirit to help you remember other pieces of the prophetic puzzle and how it connects to what He is trying to show you.

I'm big on patterns. Sometimes the fragment you receive connects to a dream or vision you had in the past. When you are a student of patterns and a student of your dreams, you may see the same fragment that appeared in earlier visual revelations or how one fragment connects to another fragment to offer a more complete message. Be patient and persistent. God wants you to see the bigger picture.

PRAYER

Father, in the name of Jesus, remind me not to get frustrated when I see a fragment. Help me change my perspective and understand You are inviting me to seek You for more revelation and understanding.

JULY 15

SURVIVING THE FURNACE OF AFFLICTION

The refining pot is for silver and the furnace for gold, but the Lord tests the hearts.

Proverbs 17:3

Isaiah 48:10 offers words most seers never want to hear: "I have refined you, but not with silver; I have chosen you in the furnace of affliction."

Some translations say the "furnace of suffering" (God's Word; NLT). The people to whom Isaiah had prophesied these words had just gone through a major enemy attack. They were afflicted. Just to be clear, *affliction* is "a cause of persistent pain or distress, great suffering." It means anguish, grief, sorrow, heartache and woe.

Do you feel like you've been in the furnace of affliction? Listen, there's suffering for what you did wrong and there's suffering for what you've done right, but there's also suffering to become who you are supposed to be.

James tells us plainly, "[As] an example of suffering and ill-treatment together with patience, brethren, take the prophets who spoke in the name of the Lord [as His messengers]" (James 5:10 AMPC).

Here's what I have learned: there's no handle on the door to the furnace of affliction. So don't try to fight your way out. Instead, pray your way through. Keep the end result in mind. Become a house of prayer.

Remember Paul's words in Romans 8:17-18 (KJV), "...if so be that we suffer with him, that we may be also glorified together. For I reckon that the sufferings of this present time are not worthy to be compared with the glory which shall be revealed in us."

God will burn up your pride in the furnace of affliction. God will burn up your fears. God will burn up your wrong motives. God will burn up your false identities and torn mantles others put upon you. God will burn up some unhealthy relationships.

It hurts. It's painful. It's confusing. You grieve for losses of things you thought were important to you that are not important to you. But you will come out the other side stronger—and seeing more clearly than ever before.

PRAYER

Father, in the name of Jesus, no one likes the furnace of affliction, but I am willing to submit to the refiner's fire for the sake of seeing more clearly. Please, give me grace to endure the furnace of affliction.

JULY 16

WHY SEERS SHOULD PRAY IN TONGUES CONSTANTLY

For one who speaks in an [unknown] tongue speaks not to men but to God, for no one understands or catches his meaning, because in the [Holy] Spirit he utters secret truths and hidden things [not obvious to the understanding].

1 Corinthians 14:2 AMPC

I discovered 101 benefits of praying in tongues. (Yes, really! I wrote about them all in my book *Tongues of Fire.*) What I discovered in my study helped me see how important it is for seers to pray in tongues as much as possible. In some way, your tongue is connected to your spiritual eyes. What do I mean?

When we pray in tongues, many things may be happening at the same time. God can be giving us more wisdom and strengthening us simultaneously. We could be building up our faith and growing in the gifts of the Spirit—or the fruit of the Spirit—at the same time. I believe when we pray in tongues with our mind set on a specific purpose, the Holy Spirit helps us release the perfect prayer to bring that God-ordained purpose to pass.

The more I studied what happens—or what can happen—when we pray in tongues, the more inspiration I found to continue the charge and press into the benefits. The fruit of praying in tongues is sometimes immediate. Praying in tongues sometimes serves as what I like to call preventative maintenance. In other words, if you pray in tongues with a mind to cultivate boldness, the boldness will be there when you need it.

Put another way, praying in tongues is sometimes, but not always, about what you need in the moment. The Holy Spirit knows what you need before you need it, and because praying in tongues releases the perfect prayer (Romans 8:26-27), we may be pleasantly surprised with the results even if they don't manifest in the moment.

Praying in tongues brings personal transformation, builds our capacity for God, opens seer revelation, and so, so much more. At the same time, we may not put two and two together. We may not always discern that it was praying in the Spirit that brought the breakthrough. Because we can't always understand what we pray in the Spirit, we often have no idea when the answer shows up. In fact, I believe we pray prayers in tongues that we wouldn't dare pray in English, such as, "Lord, crucify my flesh!"

PRAYER

Father, in the name of Jesus, help me get into the habit of praying in tongues as much as possible so I can reap the diverse benefits of praying perfect prayers. Fill me again with Your Spirit.

JULY 17

SIMON'S SIN

> *Looking carefully lest anyone fall short of the grace of God; lest any root of bitterness springing up cause trouble, and by this many become defiled.*
>
> Hebrews 12:15

Bitter seers can become false seers. Remember Simon the sorcerer. In Acts 8 we see Simon the sorcerer got saved, but he didn't get healed from bitterness and acted on his bitter envying. Peter rebuked him:

> And when Simon saw that through the laying on of the apostles' hands the Holy Spirit was given, he offered them money, saying, "Give me this power also, that anyone on whom I lay hands may receive the Holy Spirit." But Peter said to him, "Your money perish with you, because you thought that the gift of God could be purchased with money! You have neither part nor portion in this matter, for your heart is not right in the sight of God. Repent therefore of this your wickedness, and pray God if perhaps the thought of your heart may be forgiven you. For I see that you are poisoned by bitterness and bound by iniquity" (Acts 8:18-23).

The King James Version says the *gall of bitterness,* which is "an intense animosity that defiles the seer; a harsh, cynical spirit that sees the world through disappointment and pain. This disposition infiltrates the seer's eyes and hinders his perspective in the spirit. A bitter seer is more likely to be bent toward seeing demons everywhere, or have false demon-inspired visions he thinks are from the Lord," according to *The Seer's Dictionary*.

Bitterness, my friend, must be rooted out. If you have bitter envying and strife in your heart, glory not, and lie not against the truth. The Holy Ghost spoke expressly through James that this wisdom is not from God but is earthly, unspiritual, and even devilish. Wherever there is envying and strife, there is also confusion and every evil work (James 3:16).

God is not the author of confusion or evil works. So if what you see is bringing utter confusion, they are not coming from the expressly speaking Holy Spirit (1 Timothy 4:1). Forgive quickly. Search your heart regularly. Root out bitterness so you don't become like Simon.

PRAYER

Father, in the name of Jesus, would You show me if I have any bitterness in me? Help me listen to the words that come out of my mouth and discern if I have hidden bitterness. I don't want to pollute my seer flow.

JULY 18

SEERS IN THE GAP

You have not gone up into the gaps to build a wall for the house of Israel to stand in battle on the day of the Lord.

Ezekiel 13:5

Seers have an anointing not just to stand in the gap, but to see the gaps. When you see the gap, it's not so you can assign someone to stand in it for you. When you see the gap, it's your assignment (although someone may stand in prayer with you).

There's never been a more critical time for seers to stand in the gap. Standing in the gap is a selfless, Christlike posture. Standing in the gap is making a defense against an enemy attack. Standing in the gap is exposing oneself to enemy fire to protect something or someone else.

That may sound somewhat daunting, but when you understand the plan and will of God, it's exhilarating. When you stand in the gap God assigns you to, you are standing in His will and nothing by any means shall harm you. When you stand in the gap God assigns you to, God is fighting for you and with you and you cannot lose. When you stand in the gap God assigns you to, you are surrounded with favor like a shield (Psalm 5:12). He is your rear guard (Isaiah 52:12).

That gap could be prayerlessness, or even deeper sin, in a church. It could be spiritual breaches, open doors, and legal rights in a person's life that they can't see. It could be any vulnerability that leaves space for the enemy. Ask the Holy Spirit for wisdom on whether the gap is a personal issue, a corporate weakness or a territorial matter. Then ask Him for your gap strategy.

God said to Ezekiel, "I looked for someone who might rebuild the wall of righteousness that guards the land. I searched for someone to stand in the gap in the wall so I wouldn't have to destroy the land, but I found no one" (Ezekiel 22:30 NLT). If you are a seer, there's a gap for you to stand in. When you find that gap, you'll be the most effective in your intercessory prayer efforts. Remember, though, that although God may give you specific assignments for specific seasons, He's not a one-issue God. Find your gap.

PRAYER

Father, in the name of Jesus, I am willing to stand in the gap. Show me what gap You have assigned me to stand in and I will pray. Teach me the dynamics of seer intercession.

JULY 19

WHAT YOUR SPIRITUAL WARFARE DREAMS ARE TELLING YOU

Be sober, be vigilant; because your adversary the devil walks about like a roaring lion, seeking whom he may devour.

1 Peter 5:8

I had a spiritual warfare dream in which a group of us from my church, Awakening House of Prayer in Fort Lauderdale, were being chased. We were in a large, tall office building. I cannot remember all the people in the group. We were split up. One of the young women with me went to the bathroom. When she came out she remarked, "It's not too bad in here."

When I went into the bathroom I found a dead body hunched over the toilet. It looked kind of like the young woman from my group who had just walked out. Suddenly, that dead body disappeared. The toilet seat had urine all over it. I tried to clean it up but it soaked through the paper. The urine just kept coming back no matter how much I tried to clean it up.

This was a spiritual warfare dream. Spiritual warfare dreams are dreams in which you are in a conflict of some kind. Sometimes, these conflicts are with people who represent demons and sometimes you'll find yourself wrestling dark creatures. But here's what many seers miss: not every spiritual warfare dream originates in the dark kingdom.

What do I mean? Spiritual warfare dreams are not always negative. You need to discern the source of the dream in order to respond rightly. If you think all spiritual warfare dreams are from the enemy, you can miss valuable divine intelligence. Or you can mistake soulish dreams for divine revelation. Let me drill down into this.

You can have what you think are spiritual warfare dreams from taking medications, eating too late, consuming inappropriate media, or worrying about life. Don't mistake a soulish dream for a true spiritual warfare dream or you will engage in unnecessary spiritual conflict.

Of course, there are demonic warfare dreams. In them, you might be getting chased, beaten, murdered, or otherwise seriously harmed. Dreams of being choked, being engulfed in a fearful, thick darkness, or having a suffocating cloak thrown over you are demonic.

The dream I told you about came from God. The Holy Spirit was showing me that this precious woman had serious heart issues and was a liability on our warfare team. She was an open door of attack. Always judge the source of your warfare dreams.

PRAYER

Father, in the name of Jesus, would You remind me not to write off every spiritual warfare dream as purely demonic. Please, show me clearly when You are using a warfare dream to show me what the enemy has planned.

JULY 20

THE MASTER KEY TO SEEING IN THE SPIRIT

...Men of Galilee, why do you stand gazing up into heaven? This same Jesus, who was taken up from you into heaven, will so come in like manner as you saw Him go into heaven.

Acts 1:11

I heard the Lord say:

Look at me and I will show you everything that you need to see. Look at me. Don't go looking around in the Spirit like a sleuth. Just look at me. For I am the Door. Look at Me, and I will open to you everything you need to see. It's so simple and yet so many in My Church today strive, and push and echo instead of being a voice. And I've called you to be a voice.

I've called you to stand in the company of the remnant, to wait on Me, to know Me, to really know me. For out of that knowing comes revelation. Know Me and you'll know many other things. When you know Me, you will know times and seasons. When you know Me, you will know how to pray, how to fight. When you know Me, you will know what to say and when to say it. When you know Me.

So cultivate that oil of intimacy. That is the oil change I am after. I am calling you out of competition and to cultivate intimacy with My Spirit. So I'm going to break some things, some mindsets, even some religious mindsets. When your mind is free, your eyes are free. And when your mind is free, your mouth is free, your ears are free. No more limited thinking, no more vain imagination encroaching upon the truth I'm trying to transmit to you in the Spirit. When you are free, you are free indeed in every way.

So lean into Me, indeed. Wait on Me, indeed. Yes, I have been waiting on some of you for quite a long while now. I am equipping you. I've called you the remnant and I Myself am equipping you. So allow yourself to be equipped. Allow old mindsets to be stripped away and allow Me to pour in you that new wine to give you a new wineskin to walk in a new mantle, a new way because it is a new day and it's not like the days of old.

PRAYER

Father, in the name of Jesus, I want the new mantle. I want the new wineskin. I want to walk in the freedom of mind and sight that You have prepared for me. I give You my yes. Have Your way.

JULY 21

ASK FOR THE GIFT OF INTERPRETATION

If you abide in Me, and My words abide in you, you will ask what you desire, and it shall be done for you.

John 15:7

The gift of interpreting dreams isn't specifically mentioned among the nine gifts listed in 1 Corinthians 12. However, if God can give someone a spiritual gift to interpret tongues—and He can—then He can give someone a gift to interpret dreams. I dare say interpreting tongues is a more challenging task!

In Scripture, the gift of interpreting dreams seems rare. Joseph had a supernatural ability to interpret the dreams of the baker and the butler while he was in prison. Later, he interpreted Pharaoh's dreams. Likewise, Daniel had the ability to interpret the dreams of King Nebuchadnezzar. We also see how the enemy mimicked this gift in the Old Testament as rulers often turned to their magicians and sorcerers to interpret dreams.

But I submit this to you: because God could endow Daniel and Joseph with the unique ability to interpret symbolic and parabolic dreams for kings and pharaohs who were not filled with the Holy Spirit, how much easier is it for Him to impart this gift to us?

Since the interpretations belong to God as Joseph tells us in Genesis 40:8, and because God is the One speaking in our dreams, He can make the meaning known to us. So why not ask? Start by asking Him to give you the ability to interpret your own dreams. Ask Him to present the meaning to you in understandable terms. Ask Him to define the numbers, colors, names, symbols, and other elements of the dream.

Jesus said in Matthew 21:22 (AMPC), "And whatever you ask for in prayer, having faith and [really] believing, you will receive."

Do you believe God knows the meaning and wants to share it with you? Then ask Him and believe, and then wait on the Lord. Once you get adept at interpreting your own dreams, ask for the wisdom to help others interpret their dreams, and teach them these principles so that people are well-equipped.

PRAYER

Father, in the name of Jesus, please give me the gift of interpreting dreams like You did for Daniel and Joseph. I want to understand what You are saying to me in my dreams. And I want to help others.

JULY 22

HANDLING SEER STRESS

...do not fret—it only causes harm.

Psalm 37:8

Seers face stress, but it's different from what many others experience. Yes, seers can be stressed by the daily affairs of life including bills, relationships, or health. But they also face a stress that many others in the Body of Christ may never face.

Seers can face stress about what they are perceiving in the unseen realm—visual revelation that they can't easily explain or prove. Seers can face stress that comes with the constant expectation to see. That stress can feel amplified when rejection or misunderstandings come.

What's going on? It doesn't take a PhD or even a prophet to see the problem. We're wrestling in our own strength instead of resting in Christ. Truth is that the devil isn't stressing us out. People are not stressing us out.

That's right. You are stressing yourself out. Your seer eyes are no longer on Jesus, so instead of perfect peace you are living with chronic stress. You can't blame anybody around you for being stressed out—and only you can make a decision to end the vicious cycle.

We need a greater revelation of the grace of God. We need to meditate on Scriptures about the peace of God. And we need to rely on one another to pray for us when we are so stressed out we can't verbalize a petition. Never be too proud to ask for prayer.

So with that in mind, what will you do the next time you get stressed out? Keep it simple. Pray. Thank Him. Remember that you belong to Christ. And walk in the peace that passes all understanding. When you do, you are a witness to a stressed-out world—and they will want what you have. Here is Paul's time-tested advice:

> Don't fret or worry. Instead of worrying, pray. Let petitions and praises shape your worries into prayers, letting God know your concerns. Before you know it, a sense of God's wholeness, everything coming together for good, will come and settle you down. It's wonderful what happens when Christ displaces worry at the center of your life (Philippians 4:6-7 MSG).

PRAYER

Father, in the name of Jesus, I repent for allowing myself to get stressed over people's expectations, what I see in the spirit, or even enemy attacks. Help me to keep my eyes on You so I can see in peace.

JULY 23

STRANGE ENCOUNTERS

Then he said to me, "This is the curse that goes out over the face of the whole earth: 'Every thief shall be expelled,' according to this side of the scroll; and, 'Every perjurer shall be expelled,' according to that side of it."

Zechariah 5:3

Can you imagine seeing a flying scroll? What a sight Zechariah saw! To be sure, there are strange phenomena in the seer dimensions. And I don't believe God trusts everyone with such strange encounters. It takes a certain maturity to steward truths in these bizarre visual revelations.

The flying scroll is mentioned one time in Scripture. It's unique to Zechariah's prophetic ministry. Zechariah 5:1-2 says, "Then I turned and raised my eyes, and saw there a flying scroll. And he said to me, 'What do you see?' So I answered, 'I see a flying scroll. Its length is twenty cubits and its width ten cubits.'" This must have left Zechariah scratching his head but he pressed in to receive a profound message from the Most High.

So what do we do if we have strange visions like this? What can we learn from Zechariah? First, we always test the vision. Second, we ask the Holy Spirit for an interpretation. In fact, the stranger the visual revelation, the more we need to lean on Him because there is likely very little precedent for what we saw. In Zechariah's case, an angel was standing by and the angel asked, "What do you see?" (Zechariah 5:2).

Although the visual revelation is strange, don't get into reasoning. Reasoning leads to confusion and God is not the author of confusion (1 Corinthians 14:33). Even if He doesn't reveal the particulars to you right away, trust that He will at the right time.

In the meantime, and in addition to asking for the interpretation, get into the Word. You may be surprised to find Scriptures that are in line with what you saw. Or the Holy Spirit may quicken a Scripture to you that applies somehow to what you saw. Look for similar images and themes in Scripture. The Bible is one of the interpreters of visual revelation.

Another tip is to lean in to purpose. God is not random, so strange encounters typically carry weightier messages for intercession. Ask God, "Why are You showing me this? What do You want me to do with what I've seen?" The same Holy Spirit who opened your eyes will lead you into the truth about how to steward the revelation.

PRAYER

Father, in the name of Jesus, I know if I navigate the seer dimensions long enough, I'm bound to run into some things I find strange. Remind me to lean in to You and Your Word to help me understand what I see.

JULY 24

HOW SEERS GRIEVE THE SPIRIT

And do not grieve the Holy Spirit of God [do not offend or vex or sadden Him], by Whom you were sealed (marked, branded as God's own, secured) for the day of redemption (of final deliverance through Christ from evil and the consequences of sin).

Ephesians 4:30 AMPC

Seers, remember this: the Holy Spirit is the One who shows you things to come. The Holy Spirit also helps us build our faith to see in the spirit. Jude 20 says, "But you, beloved, build yourselves up in your most holy faith. Pray in the Holy Spirit."

The Holy Spirit leads you into all true visual revelation. Jesus Himself said, "But when the Spirit of truth comes, He will guide you into all truth. For He will not speak on His own authority. But He will speak whatever He hears, and He will tell you things that are to come" (John 16:13 MEV).

Given all this and more, we want to be careful not to grieve the Holy Spirit. Ephesians 4:30 (The Voice) says, "It's time to stop bringing grief to God's Holy Spirit; you have been sealed with the Spirit, marked as His own for the day of rescue." *Grief* in this verse means to make sorrowful; to affect with sadness, cause grief, to throw into sorrow; to grieve, offend; to make one uneasy; or to vex, irritate, offend, insult.

What grieves the Holy Spirit? Keep in mind that He is the Spirit of holy. When we sin, we grieve Him. The way we talk can grieve Him. What we watch on TV can grieve Him. Our attitude toward people can grieve Him. Our response to His presence can grieve Him.

Disobedience and rebellion, which is as the sin of witchcraft, grieves Him. We see this mentioned in Isaiah 63:10 (MEV), "But they rebelled and grieved His Holy Spirit; therefore, He turned Himself to become their enemy, and He fought against them." And Psalm 78:40 tells us, "How often they provoked Him in the wilderness, and grieved Him in the desert!"

Failing to walk in love grieves the Holy Spirit (Ephesians 5:2). Strife and division grieve Him. Lies and other forms of corrupt communication grieve Him. Unrighteous anger and unforgiveness grieve Him. Harboring bitterness and resentment grieve Him. Any time we violate Scripture, which He authored, we grieve Him.

The Holy Spirit is pictured in Scripture symbolically as a dove. Why? Doves are associated with purity, peace, gentleness, and innocence. These are characteristics of the Holy Spirit. Let's not grieve Him.

PRAYER

Father, in the name of Jesus, I know that my spiritual sight depends on what the Holy Spirit reveals. I don't want to grieve Him and miss something You want me to see. Make me more sensitive to Your Spirit.

JULY 25

CARRYING SEER BURDENS

Bear one another's burdens, and so fulfill the law of Christ.
Galatians 6:2 MEV

Every seer should have a prayer burden. Why? Because all seers are intercessors. A prayer burden is a spiritual concern on the heart of God. The Holy Spirit imparts that prayer burden to someone He trusts to intercede. In the case of the seer, the prayer burden often comes in response to visual revelation.

A prayer burden can seem overwhelming, but you are not carrying it alone. The Holy Spirit helps us pray (Romans 8:26). The Holy Spirit will strengthen us in the intercession. He will sustain us as we cooperate with His will. There's grace. He is the Spirit of Grace.

Please, don't put off the prayer burden. Don't wait until it's a convenient time to pray. If you receive a prayer burden out of nowhere while you're watching TV or driving to work or talking to a friend or sitting in church, respond. Sometimes you can't stop everything you are doing and pray immediately, but sometimes you can. If you can excuse yourself, do so.

Give your full attention to the prayer burden. You may pray for many things every day, but when the prayer burden first comes it will usually come with such a weight that you may not feel grace to pray for much else. If you don't know how to pray, intercede in tongues over the issue.

Romans 8:26-27: "Likewise the Spirit also helps in our weaknesses. For we do not know what we should pray for as we ought, but the Spirit Himself makes intercession for us with groanings which cannot be uttered. Now He who searches the hearts knows what the mind of the Spirit is, because He makes intercession for the saints according to the will of God."

Hold on in prayer until God lifts the burden and discern when it's time to call for reinforcements. You can't just share every prayer burden with anyone. Some matters are extremely private, but some prayer burdens can be shared. And keep your eyes on Jesus.

PRAYER

Father, in the name of Jesus, would You help me discern prayer burdens? Would You help me divide my soul from my spirit so I can respond quickly to Your call to pray? Please, make me more sensitive to Your Spirit.

JULY 26

KEEP ON LOOKING

I kept looking until thrones were placed [for the assessors with the Judge], and the Ancient of Days [God, the eternal Father] took His seat, Whose garment was white as snow and the hair of His head like pure wool....

Daniel 7:9 AMPC

Daniel models something I wish every seer understood. When you see something in the spirit, you have to keep on looking. Many seers look away before they see everything the Holy Spirit wants to show them because they are overwhelmed, excited, or scared by what they see.

Daniel had a vision of four beasts in the book that bears his name. Reading Daniel 7:4-7 in the New American Standard Bible drives my point home. Take a look:

> The first was like a lion but had the wings of an eagle. I kept looking until its wings were plucked, and it was lifted up from the ground and set up on two feet like a man; a human mind also was given to it. And behold, another beast, a second one, resembling a bear. And it was raised up on one side, and three ribs were in its mouth between its teeth; and they said this to it: "Arise, devour much meat!"
>
> After this I kept looking, and behold, another one, like a leopard, which had on its back four wings of a bird; the beast also had four heads, and dominion was given to it. After this I kept looking in the night visions, and behold, a fourth beast, dreadful and terrible, and extremely strong; and it had large iron teeth. It devoured and crushed, and trampled down the remainder with its feet; and it was different from all the beasts that were before it, and it had ten horns.

After that, Daniel started thinking about what he had seen and he saw yet another troubling vision, but he kept on looking. He didn't allow anything to distract him in the seer dimensions. He just kept watch. Finally, in Daniel 7:9, we read, "I kept looking until thrones were set up, and the Ancient of Days took His seat...."

Think about it. If Daniel had not kept looking, he would not have seen the Lord. If he stopped looking before he saw the Lord, he may have walked away troubled; instead, he walked away with a glimpse of glory. When you see things you don't understand, don't stop looking.

PRAYER

Father, in the name of Jesus, help me keep on looking. Help me not to get distracted, overwhelmed, or so excited about what I see that I start scribing when I should still be watching.

JULY 27

A DEADLY EYE DISEASE

...We know that we all have knowledge. Knowledge puffs up, but love edifies.

1 Corinthians 8:1

The first and worst cause of error that prevails in our day is spiritual pride, so said Jonathan Edwards, a preacher, theologian, and missionary to Native Americans who lived in the 1700s.

As mentioned previously, Edwards went on to say that spiritual pride is the main door by which the devil comes into the hearts of those who are zealous for the advancement of Christ—the chief inlet of smoke from the bottomless pit to darken the mind and mislead the judgment, and the main handle by which satan takes hold of Christians to hinder a work of God. Powerful words!

If that was true in Edwards' day—and it was—then how much more is it true in our day? In Edwards' era, there were no megachurches, no Facebook pages where seers could woo millions of "fans," and no global satellites to broadcast visual revelation to the masses.

In the seer ministry, I've seen spiritual pride because of position, prominence, popularity, even if it's only position, prominence, and popularity in a small local church. To be sure, the spiritually proud seer doesn't need a large kingdom to call his own in order to feel superior.

Spiritually proud seers see themselves as more discerning, more anointed, more eloquent, more revelatory, more important, and otherwise, well, more spiritual than you. Some of the ways spiritual pride manifests include self-righteousness, hypercritical attitudes, hypocrisy, scorning correction or guidance, putting on pretenses, and false humility.

Of course, God hates pride in any form, but I believe spiritual pride is the worst manifestation. It's so deceptive that the ones who walk in spiritual pride are too proud to consider that they may be suffering from this deplorable disease. In fact, spiritual pride mistakes the favor of people for the favor of God.

Edwards concluded that until the disease of spiritual pride is cured, medicines are applied in vain to heal all other diseases. The good news is spiritual pride can be cured. The prescription is a strong dose of conviction, repentance, and humility—and I might say an ongoing effort to cooperate with the grace of God to walk in the fear of the Lord.

PRAYER

Father, in the name of Jesus, would You please help me see if I am at risk of developing this deadly disease? Give me grace to walk in humility even when I walk in an abundance of revelation. Without You, I am nothing.

JULY 28

EXPOSING THE ROOT OF SPIRITUAL BLINDNESS

But He answered and said, "Every plant which My heavenly Father has not planted will be uprooted."

Matthew 15:13

What causes spiritual blindness? There are many roots to consider—and remember, a root takes time to bear fruit. At some level, spiritual blindness can seep in little by little. Think of the slowly boiled frog analogy. You put the frog in room-temperature water, then set the burner on high. Slowly the water heats up and the frog doesn't notice until it's too late.

Also know this: blind people don't see black. They see nothing. If you see nothing, it's concerning. God has given us spiritual eyes to see, to discern the unseen world around us. If you have lost your spiritual eyesight little by little, there's a good chance there is one or more roots causing your eyes to be fruitless.

For example, rejection blinds you to the light of God's love. You may see the dark side but not see what the Lord is doing. Or you may be seeing through the lens of bitterness because people have rejected you or your gift. Pride blinds the light to God's grace. Pride can make your eyes haughty and you see through the lens of condemnation, always seeing people's faults.

Pain blinds you to the light of God's comfort. Offense blinds you to forgiveness. Unforgiveness blinds you to God's will for your life. Negativity blinds you to the light of God's possibility. Betrayals blind you to those you can trust. All of these roots can skew your seer vision and infiltrate your dream life making you less and less accurate until you are all but spiritually blind.

Jesus wants to heal the blind today. Psalm 146:8 (NLT) tells us, "The Lord opens the eyes of the blind. The Lord lifts up those who are weighed down. The Lord loves the godly." And again, "You will open the eyes of the blind. You will free the captives from prison, releasing those who sit in dark dungeons" (Isaiah 42:7 NLT). Ask the Lord to pull out any roots that are blinding your spiritual eyes.

PRAYER

Father, in the name of Jesus, would You help me to check my heart when my spiritual eyes seem blind? I don't want to be blind to issues that are keeping me from receiving visual revelation.

JULY 29

BEHOLDING IN THE SPIRIT

But Stephen, full of the Holy Spirit, gazed steadily into heaven and saw the glory of God, and he saw Jesus standing in the place of honor at God's right hand.

Acts 7:55 NLT

What's your greatest desire? Some of the most accurate seers I know prioritize the delightful loveliness and majestic grandeur of the Lord Himself above all. They have the same mindset as David, who wrote: "One thing I have desired of the Lord, that will I seek: That I may dwell in the house of the Lord all the days of my life, to behold the beauty of the Lord, and to inquire in His temple" (Psalm 27:4).

There is nothing I want to behold more than the beauty of the Lord, which is my anchor in the seer dimensions. But the truth is, we will see many things in the spirit and we should behold them all. *Behold* means "to perceive through sight or apprehension" or "to gaze upon, observe," according to *Merriam-Webster's Dictionary*. Apprehension speaks of the power to perceive or comprehend, and that power comes from God. You can only behold what God opens your eyes to see, but once you see it you should press in to behold it.

Beholding is not a quick glimpse. Beholding is a gaze. *Merriam-Webster* defines *gaze* as "to fix the eyes in a steady intent look often with eagerness or studious attention" and "a fixed intent look." When David says in Psalm 27:4 that his one desire was to gaze upon the Lord, he wasn't taking a quick glimpse. He was seeing with intelligence.

But the Bible definition goes deeper. *Strong's Concordance* translates *chazah*, the Hebrew word for *behold*, as "envisioned in visions, gaze, look, prophesy, saw, see, seeing, seen, sees." This implies that we are to keep on looking. *Brown-Driver-Briggs* defines *gaze* as "to see, see as a seer in the ecstatic state, accusative of the vision seen, with the intelligence." This implies that when we behold a thing, we gain insight and intelligence.

The Greek word for *behold* is *ide*. It carries a more forceful command to see. According to *Strong's Concordance*, it means, literally, "be sure to see" in the sense of "Don't miss this! It is an observable, objective fact!" When God shows you a spiritual truth in the seer dimensions, He wants you to be sure to see it.

These are strong words. When God reveals Himself (or anything else to you) in the seer dimensions, don't give it a quick glance and then rush out to tell people what you saw. Take your time. Behold what God is showing you. Gather details. Stamp it on your memory. Ask God questions about what you are seeing. Behold!

PRAYER

Father, in the name of Jesus, would You teach me the art of beholding? Help me to not be distracted in the seer dimensions with all its activity. Give me the grace to keep looking so I can see everything You want to show me.

JULY 30

SEER EVANGELISM

And a vision appeared to Paul in the night. A man of Macedonia stood and pleaded with him, saying, "Come over to Macedonia and help us."
Acts 16:9

All believers are called to preach the gospel, but many seers are so heavenly minded that showing people the way to Heaven is not their first instinct. I get it. Nevertheless, the Great Commission does not exclude seers. The idea, then, is to leverage our seer gifts to draw people to the Savior.

When most people think of evangelism, they picture a preacher with a microphone on a street corner, a tract tucked under a windshield wiper, or a door-to-door conversation about Heaven and hell.

I'm not against tracts or traditional methods—God has used them and still does. But I believe the Holy Spirit wants to breathe fresh creativity into evangelism in this hour and seers can be part of that company. In fact, I think evangelism teams are even more effective when seers join.

Seer evangelism is about more than reciting the Roman road or following a script. It's about demonstrating that Jesus is alive and that He knows the person He's reaching. It's about presenting the gospel in a way that disarms defenses and reveals the love of God in practical, Spirit-led ways. Seers are primed to do this through visual revelation.

For example, a seer may have a dream or vision of someone they will meet on the outreach the next day or someone they will meet on the train as they head to work. They can pray and ask God for a word for them.

And think of the Macedonian call: a vision Paul had that redirected his second missionary journey. Let's take a look at Acts 16:9-10 (AMPC): "[There] a vision appeared to Paul in the night: a man from Macedonia stood pleading with him and saying, Come over to Macedonia and help us! And when he had seen the vision, we [including Luke] at once endeavored to go on into Macedonia, confidently inferring that God had called us to proclaim the glad tidings (Gospel) to them."

The Holy Spirit could also show you a picture about someone's life on the spot that speaks to a deep desire that only they know about. You can minister to them out of what you see, declaring that God has a good plan for their life. Dream interpretation is another option. You could set up a booth at an outdoor market or on the beach and ultimately lead them to Jesus.

PRAYER

Father, in the name of Jesus, would You give me a burden for the lost—and give me dreams and visions that help me minister to people who don't yet know You? Teach me to be an effective minister of the gospel.

JULY 31

THE JEREMIAH SEER ANOINTING

Then I said, "I will not make mention of Him, nor speak anymore in His name." But His word was in my heart like a burning fire shut up in my bones; I was weary of holding it back, and I could not.

Jeremiah 20:9

Jeremiah's calling into the prophetic was dramatic. Before his eyes were opened, his ears were opened. That made him what I call an ambidextrous prophet to the nations. In other words, he could hear, see, and say. It's sort of like being able to write or shoot a basketball with either hand.

But beyond Jeremiah's gifting was his courage. Though he was young, God empowered him with boldness to confront the sin in the land of Israel. He issued one judgment prophecy after another with great boldness despite the potential consequences. Jeremiah is known as the weeping prophet because he didn't just see, hear and say—he felt deeply as he spoke forth the heart of God. Put another way, Jeremiah's seer anointing combines many of the spiritual senses.

Consider Jeremiah 1:9-10, "...Behold, I have put My words in your mouth. See, I have this day set you over the nations and over the kingdoms, to root out and to pull down, to destroy and to throw down, to build and to plant." Notice how God told him twice to see—"Behold" and "See." God set him in place with a different kind of fivefold anointing.

Jeremiah had the ability to see the root of a thing. You can't uproot something that you can't see. He was also called to destroy and throw down. This points to the ability to see what the enemy has done and demolish it. In his case, it was the idolatry and false prophets in the land. He stood strongly against it all.

But take note that three of the edges of his ministry were coming against what the devil had constructed. He was also called to build and plant. He had to see and say what God wanted planted. This is the ambidextrous anointing of Jeremiah, which matched the difficult assignment God gave him. His seer anointing uprooted deception, exposed sin, and laid the foundation for God's restorative power.

PRAYER

Father, in the name of Jesus, help me to be ambidextrous in the spirit realm. Like Jeremiah, anoint me to see, hear, say, root out, tear down, destroy, overthrow, build and plant.

AUGUST

He stretched out the form of a hand, and took me by a lock of my hair; and the Spirit lifted me up between earth and heaven, and brought me in visions of God to Jerusalem....

Ezekiel 8:3

AUGUST 1

DO YOU HAVE GOOD TIMING?

Then one of them, named Agabus, stood up and showed by the Spirit that there was going to be a great famine throughout all the world, which also happened in the days of Claudius Caesar.

Acts 11:28

Agabus had good timing. The revelation about the coming famine helped people prepare. If he did not release the revelation ahead of time, the church would not have sent the relief to their brethren before the famine hit. By contrast, false prophets in the Bible had bad timing. They proclaimed peace when they should have been issuing warnings.

When it comes to visual revelation, the timing of your release is almost as important as the visual itself. Sharing what you saw prematurely—apart from the leadership of the Holy Spirit who opened your eyes—can invite rejection or other types of unnecessary warfare.

Ecclesiastes 3:7 reminds us there is "a time to be silent and a time to speak." I understand the temptation to share a visual encounter right after you receive it. It's exciting to receive fresh revelation from God. But you can do yourself—and the revelation at hand—a disservice by sharing outside of God's timing. When I received the revelation of the war room in Heaven, I didn't share it for two years. I processed it. I interpreted it. I aligned it with Scripture. I prayed it through.

Think about Mary. The angel Gabriel revealed that she would bear the Messiah. She didn't run around Israel telling everyone. The three wisemen confirmed that the baby she had given birth to was indeed the Messiah. Luke 2:19 (AMPC) tells us, "Mary was keeping within herself all these things (sayings), weighing and pondering them in her heart." She didn't share what she knew with everyone; she just waited for God's plan to unfold.

By contrast, sharing visual revelation too late—which may mean when it's too late to prepare or even after the fact—can damage your credibility or give you the reputation of a hindsight seer. Sharing what you saw or dreamed too late can leave people without the revelation they need to make wise decisions. That can breed resentment.

When you receive visual revelation, ask the Holy Spirit for His timing on the release. His timing is always perfect. Until then, ponder it in your heart. But when He gives you the green light, don't hesitate.

PRAYER

Father, in the name of Jesus, would You help me develop good timing in releasing what I see in the spirit? I don't want to lag behind You and leave people unprepared, but I don't want to get ahead of You either.

AUGUST 2

THERE ARE MANY ROOMS IN HEAVEN

There are many homes up there where my Father lives, and I am going to prepare them for your coming....

John 14:2 TLB

Just behind the veil, I saw one of the many rooms in Heaven. Yes, there are many rooms in Heaven. Most believers haven't meditated on this spiritual reality but Jesus gave His disciples insight into these heavenly rooms while He walked the earth.

Jesus told His disciples there are *"many rooms"* in His Father's house. There are even secret rooms that fewer see. At least one of those rooms contains hidden knowledge. I saw it with my own seer eyes.

"There are many rooms in my Father's house. I wouldn't tell you this, unless it was true. I am going there to prepare a place for each of you" (John 14:2 CEV). The NLT puts it this way, "There is more than enough room in my Father's home. If this were not so, would I have told you that I am going to prepare a place for you?"

We know Jesus went ahead of us to prepare a place for us, but beyond the rooms reserved for Christians who go on to glory, there are other rooms in Heaven. The Bible leaves records for the generations to explore, and many believers throughout the ages have seen these rooms in the Spirit.

The Holy Spirit showed me there are secret rooms in Heaven. It's not unlike hidden rooms in a home. You may have seen them in movies. False walls give entrance to secret rooms. Even when I sat writing this, I saw a hand reaching out beckoning me to a secret room.

At first, the light was bright and I was disoriented. In this secret room, which appeared to be a storage room, I saw innovations from past generations. These were innovations at which many marveled when they were first released, but have since been disregarded or taken for granted. They appeared to be antiques. Some of them were rusty because they hadn't been used in many years.

Samuel Rutherford, a 17th century Scottish pastor, wrote, "Go up beforehand and see your lodging. Look through all your Father's rooms in heaven; in your Father's house are many dwelling-places. Men take a sight of lands ere they buy them. I know Christ hath made bargain already: but be kind to the house you are going to, and see it often."

For more on the rooms in Heaven, check out my book, *Decoding the Mysteries of Heaven's War Room.*

PRAYER

Father, in the name of Jesus, I can only imagine how many rooms there are in Heaven. If it suits Your purposes, I would love to take a glimpse. Nevertheless, let Your will be done.

AUGUST 3

SEEING THE HORROR OF HELL

But the cowardly, unbelieving, abominable, murderers, sexually immoral, sorcerers, idolaters, and all liars shall have their part in the lake which burns with fire and brimstone, which is the second death.
Revelation 21:8

Beyond the demonic realm is hell. Many seers and seeing people have visited hell or looked into this realm. A good number of books have resulted from these horrifying encounters. It's normal to be shaken to the core by these encounters. I have never encountered hell nor do I ever want to. I have heard stories of people being out of commission for days and even weeks after such visitations.

While many Christians don't believe in a literal hell, which is shocking, the Bible speaks of the reality of hell as a place of torment and separation from God. Jesus described it vividly in Luke 16:23-24: "And being in torments in Hades, he lifted up his eyes and saw Abraham afar off, and Lazarus in his bosom. Then he cried and said, 'Father Abraham, have mercy on me, and send Lazarus that he may dip the tip of his finger in water and cool my tongue; for I am tormented in this flame.'"

Yes, hell is real, just like Heaven is real. We do have some images of hell from the pages of Scripture. We know hell (sheol) is a place of sorrow (2 Samuel 22:6). Hell is a place of utter darkness (2 Peter 2:17). Hell is a place of eternal destruction (2 Thessalonians 1:9). Hell is a place with no rest, day or night (Revelation 14:11). Hell is a place of suffering in a lake of burning sulfur (Revelation 19:20). Hell is a place where inhabitants are eternally separated from God, and that is ultimately what makes it so horrifying.

If you see into the realm of hell, as many have, you are likely to have the imagery burned on your soul forever. You will be shaken by images of death, sorrow, pain, and destruction. If you enter the hell realm, you will feel fear. You may feel the separation from God. Clearly, this is not something we want to see, but God can choose to open our eyes to this realm for His purposes. His purposes, in these cases, is usually tied to evangelism and a love for the lost—for intercession.

Beloved, hell is real, and eternity hangs in the balance. As seers, we must carry these revelations with reverence, boldness, and a heart to turn many back to God.

PRAYER

Father, in the name of Jesus, I don't want to see hell. I'd rather see Heaven. But if You choose to show me this dimension, I am willing to see it. Use me for Your glory.

AUGUST 4

THE OIL IS FLOWING DOWN

And he poured some of the anointing oil on Aaron's head and anointed him, to consecrate him.

Leviticus 8:12

Oil represents the anointing of God, which is the Holy Spirit. Jesus said the Spirit of the Lord anointed Him in Luke 4:18-19: "The Spirit of the Lord is upon Me, because He has anointed Me to preach the gospel to the poor; He has sent Me to heal the brokenhearted, to proclaim liberty to the captives and recovery of sight to the blind, to set at liberty those who are oppressed; to proclaim the acceptable year of the Lord."

Scripture also speaks of anointing the sick with oil in James 5:14-15: "Is anyone among you sick? Let him call for the elders of the church, and let them pray over him, anointing him with oil in the name of the Lord. And the prayer of faith will save the sick, and the Lord will raise him up. And if he has committed sins, he will be forgiven."

But sometimes we see manifestations of oil in the natural realm. When we do, it can serve as a clear manifestation of what is happening in the spirit realm. Of course, you don't have to see the oil to know it's flowing. We believe by faith the Holy Spirit is present to heal and deliver.

Likewise, we have to be cautious not to glorify these types of manifestations because the enemy can show off strange oil that mimics a true move of God. Put another way, we must be careful not to reject a true manifestation of the Holy Spirit while not accepting a false one. We must discern.

You may see the oil flowing in the seer dimensions, or you may see natural manifestations of oil. Just remember, one of the Holy Spirit's main assignments is to exalt Jesus. Don't get too hung up on the oil. Christ has the preeminence. If you see oil in the spirit, it should point to the work of Christ manifesting.

PRAYER

Father, in the name of Jesus, let Your oil flow in our midst as You move among us. Would You help me to discern the oil flowing in the Spirit, and if it serves Your purposes, in the natural? Help me discern strange oil.

AUGUST 5

WHEN GOD HIDES THINGS FROM YOU

"My thoughts are nothing like your thoughts," says the Lord. "And my ways are far beyond anything you could imagine."

Isaiah 55:8 NLT

My worship leader was sick for a week. She didn't tell me, and even though I prayed for her daily, the Lord didn't show me either. I would have prayed more specifically if I had known she was sick. Then I thought of Elisha.

In 2 Kings 4, we read of the woman to whom Elisha prophesied a son. The son was born but died in an accident in the field with his father. Second Kings 4:25-27 reads:

> And so she departed, and went to the man of God at Mount Carmel. So it was, when the man of God saw her afar off, that he said to his servant Gehazi, "Look, the Shunammite woman! Please run now to meet her, and say to her, 'Is it well with you? Is it well with your husband? Is it well with the child?'" And she answered, "It is well." Now when she came to the man of God at the hill, she caught him by the feet, but Gehazi came near to push her away. But the man of God said, "Let her alone; for her soul is in deep distress, and the Lord has hidden it from me, and has not told me."

There are times when God hides things from you on purpose. He may hide it for the sake of someone's privacy or because you are not ready to see it or for any other reason He sees fit. I have had this happen to me a number of times, and I was always surprised when I later saw what I had not seen. But His ways are higher (Isaiah 55:8-9).

Especially when it comes to people close to us, it can seem strange when God throttles our prophetic vision and discernment. In our minds, we would have intervened to help someone in distress. But He has a reason for hiding some things from us.

Still, it must have seemed strange to Elisha for God to hide it from him. After all, God did not hide the day of Elijah's departure to Heaven from the young prophet. Look at 2 Kings 2:5, "Now the sons of the prophets who were at Jericho came to Elisha and said to him, 'Do you know that the Lord will take away your master from over you today?' So he answered, 'Yes, I know; keep silent!'"

PRAYER

Father, in the name of Jesus, help me remember that You only show me what I need to know. I am on a need-to-know basis. I trust You to show me what You want me to see.

AUGUST 6

SEEING HIDDEN SNARES

...In the way in which I walk they have secretly set a snare for me.
Psalm 142:3

The enemy lays snares in our path of the righteous, hoping to trap us and isolate people so he can execute his ministry of stealing, killing, and destroying without much resistance (John 10:10). His snares are disguised and invisible to the naked eye, but they can be discerned (or seen) in the Spirit.

Job 18:8-10 reveals the enemy's snare strategy: "For he is cast into a net by his own feet, and he walks into a snare. The net takes him by the heel, and a snare lays hold of him. A noose is hidden for him on the ground, and a trap for him in the road."

Notice how the enemy's target walked right into the snare. What is a snare? According to *The Merriam-Webster Dictionary,* a snare is something by which one is entangled, involved in difficulties, or impeded. A snare is often something deceptively attractive. Snare also means "to capture by or as if by use of a snare." In that way, a snare could be the enemy's bait, lure, decoy, or trick to put people in bondage.

What does a snare look like practically speaking? A snare could be a covenant with the wrong person, such as a business partner or a marriage. Exodus 34:12 (ESV), "Take care, lest you make a covenant with the inhabitants of the land to which you go, lest it become a snare in your midst" (ESV).

A snare could be an offense, or the love of money, which is a root of all evil. First Timothy 6:9 warns, "But those who desire to be rich fall into temptation and a snare, and into many foolish and harmful lusts which drown men in destruction and perdition." There are all kinds of demonic snares. If we can see them, we can avoid them.

I've avoided many snares through visual revelation I received in prayer. I've avoided snares set by false prophets, snares set by Jezebelic believers, snares set by tempting devils, and more. Ask the Lord to show you any snares the enemy has set for you or others—then don't ignore the revelation. Proceed with wisdom.

PRAYER

Father, in the name of Jesus, help me see the snares the enemy has set for me and those around me. I don't want to fall into the enemy's trap and I want to warn others so they can avoid attack.

AUGUST 7

ENTERING THE HOLY OF HOLIES

You shall hang up the veil under the clasps, so that you may bring in the ark of the testimony within the veil; and the veil shall serve for you as a partition between the holy place and the Most Holy.

Exodus 26:33 MEV

The Holy Spirit wants to show you things that your eyes have not seen and tell you things your ears have not heard, but sometimes greater revelation demands a new level of consecration. I heard the Lord say:

You must cooperate with the grace of holiness. You must cooperate with the grace that is inside you. His name is Holy Spirit and He will sanctify you. He will bring you to the place of holiness that you have not yet seen. For there are measures of holiness and you walk in a measure.

For I have not called you to live with drama and trauma, but I have called you to live with peace and joy, no matter your circumstances. So, let your heart not be troubled. Press in for holiness because I want to make you into My Son's image.

I want to form you, mold you, and shape you so that you can walk as He walked. As He was in this world, so you can be now. Faith is now, and if you'll use your now faith to believe Me for the grace of holiness, you will see that things that bothered you don't bother you anymore. Yet other things will bother you because they are not congruent with My holiness.

You will begin to love what I love and hate what I hate and you will be an instrument of honor in My house. I will use you in a great and mighty way, and you will come to know that it was worth it to lay aside the childish things and put away the secret sin, the besetting sin, and all the weights. You will come to know that it was worth it to let them go.

Give Me your weights. Cast your cares on Me. I care for you so cast them on Me. Once and for all, cast them on Me because I care for you. Focus on holiness for I am holy, and I will take you to the deeper place when you prepare your heart to see what I want to show you.

PRAYER

Father, in the name of Jesus, I want to enter the holy of holies. Help me lay aside the weights and distractions that keep me from seeing and experiencing what You have for me.

AUGUST 8

SEEING THE THRONE ROOM

In the year that King Uzziah died, I saw the Lord sitting on a throne, high and lifted up, and the train of His robe filled the temple.
Isaiah 6:1

There is a literal throne room in Heaven. You can read about it and meditate on it in Revelation 3:12 and Revelation 4:1. Indeed, the book of Revelation gives us some awesome insights into appearance and activity in the throne room. Revelation 4 shows us:

> After these things I looked, and behold, a door standing open in heaven. And the first voice which I heard was like a trumpet speaking with me, saying, "Come up here, and I will show you things which must take place after this."
>
> Immediately I was in the Spirit; and behold, a throne set in heaven, and One sat on the throne. And He who sat there was like a jasper and a sardius stone in appearance; and there was a rainbow around the throne, in appearance like an emerald. Around the throne were twenty-four thrones, and on the thrones I saw twenty-four elders sitting, clothed in white robes; and they had crowns of gold on their heads. And from the throne proceeded lightnings, thunderings, and voices. Seven lamps of fire were burning before the throne, which are the seven Spirits of God.
>
> Before the throne there was a sea of glass, like crystal. And in the midst of the throne, and around the throne, were four living creatures full of eyes in front and in back. The first living creature was like a lion, the second living creature like a calf, the third living creature had a face like a man, and the fourth living creature was like a flying eagle. The four living creatures, each having six wings, were full of eyes around and within. And they do not rest day or night, saying: "Holy, holy, holy, Lord God Almighty, Who was and is and is to come!"
>
> Whenever the living creatures give glory and honor and thanks to Him who sits on the throne, who lives forever and ever, the twenty-four elders fall down before Him who sits on the throne and worship Him who lives forever and ever, and cast their crowns before the throne, saying: "You are worthy, O Lord, to receive glory and honor and power; for You created all things, and by Your will they exist and were created."

Meditate on this passage. Maybe God will show you, too.

PRAYER

Father, in the name of Jesus, I can only imagine the activity around Your throne. Thank You for telling John to write down what he saw so that I could get a glimpse. Would You show me Your throne room?

AUGUST 9

UNLOCKING SEER MYSTERIES

As to the hidden meaning (the mystery) of the seven stars which you saw on My right hand and the seven lampstands of gold: the seven stars are the seven angels (messengers) of the seven assemblies (churches) and the seven lampstands are the seven churches.

Revelation 1:20 AMPC

"God will unlock mysteries to you, and when you write out these mysteries they will become revelations," a notable apostle prophesied those words over me decades ago. Suddenly, one day his words started coming to pass. God started revealing mysteries in the seer dimensions.

John also saw mysteries that became revelation. Paul gained revelation of the mysteries of Christ (Ephesians 3:3). Can you see how revelation and mysteries run together in the seer dimensions?

The English word *mystery* in Ephesians 3:3 comes from the Greek word *musterion*. According to the *KJV New Testament Greek Lexicon*, it means, "hidden thing, secret, mystery, generally mysteries, religious secrets, confided only to the initiated and not to ordinary mortals, a hidden or secret thing." It means, "not obvious to the understanding, a hidden purpose or counsel, the secret counsels which govern God in dealing with the righteous, which are hidden from ungodly and wicked men but plain to the godly in rabbinic writings, it denotes the mystic or hidden sense, a saying, an image or form seen in a vision, dream."

Sometimes, we are too quick to brush over what we don't readily understand. But when we seek to understand Kingdom mysteries, we position ourselves for awesome revelations. Indeed, biblical curiosity and spiritual hunger opens doors to eye-opening discoveries. After all, He is a rewarder of those who diligently seek Him (Hebrews 11:6). I believe the Holy Spirit not only shows us things to come, but shows us things that were and should be again. Some of these are mysteries.

Jesus wants His disciples to know the mysteries of the Kingdom of Heaven. In fact, He clearly said to His disciples, "...it has been given to you to know the mysteries of the kingdom of heaven..." (Matthew 13:11). The GWT puts it this way, "Knowledge about the mysteries of the kingdom of heaven has been given to you. But it has not been given to the crowd."

PRAYER

Father, in the name of Jesus, would You show me some of the mysteries that would help me in my walk and my assignment? Give me that spiritual hunger and biblical curiosity to meditate on Your Word.

AUGUST 10

THE APOSTOLIC SEER

According to the grace of God which was given to me, as a wise master builder I have laid the foundation, and another builds on it. But let each one take heed how he builds on it.

1 Corinthians 3:10

Seers are not just sent to expose—they are sent to establish. Remember, Jeremiah didn't just pluck up, root out, destroy, and throw down. He also built and planted (Jeremiah 1:10). While warring seers may be bent toward rooting out and destroying, apostolic seers may be bent more toward building and planting. We, of course, need both!

Moses was a prophet but many consider him a type of an apostle. You might also call him an apostolic seer. We know he saw in the spirit. He saw God in the spirit, speaking to Him face to face! It was also a seer's anointing that enabled him to receive the divine blueprint for the tabernacle on the mountain (Exodus 25:9,40).

In Exodus 25:9, we see God speaking to Moses: "According to all that I show you, that is, the pattern of the tabernacle and the pattern of all its furnishings, just so you shall make it." Then in Exodus 25:40, God told Moses, "And see to it that you make them according to the pattern which was shown you on the mountain."

In confirmation that he built according to what he saw in the spirit, Hebrews 8:5 reveals, "who serve the copy and shadow of the heavenly things, as Moses was divinely instructed when he was about to make the tabernacle. For He said, 'See that you make all things according to the pattern shown you on the mountain.'"

God literally showed Moses something in the spirit. It wasn't just "explained" verbally, it was revealed in a visionary form. The tabernacle was not Moses' invention. It was a heavenly pattern God shared visually.

This demonstrates the very essence of an apostolic seer's assignment: to see God's will and build it on earth. God gives apostolic seer visual blueprints. Apostolic seers may receive specific, detailed patterns that must be carefully followed according to God's plan.

PRAYER

Father, in the name of Jesus, would You give me an apostolic edge? I want to be a Kingdom builder. Show me the blueprints and plans that You want me to execute in my life and ministry.

AUGUST 11

A SEER TO LEADERS

Now when David arose in the morning, the word of the Lord came to the prophet Gad, David's seer....

2 Samuel 24:11

I value our seers and dreamers at Awakening House of Prayer, my home base in Fort Lauderdale. I appreciate that they see things I do not see. Sometimes, for example, people operating under the influence of spirits like Jezebel hide their wicked works from the leader. Many times people with wrong motives are on their best behavior around me. But my seers see through it!

Just as David had Gad, I believe every leader needs a seer advisor. God will place seasoned seers as wise counsel in leadership circles. Many of them have an anointing like the sons of Issachar. They can see and help leaders understand what to do in response to the changing times (1 Chronicles 12:32). Consider David's relationship with Gad in 1 Chronicles 21:9-13:

> Then the Lord spoke to Gad, David's seer, saying, "Go and tell David, saying, 'Thus says the Lord: "I offer you three things; choose one of them for yourself, that I may do it to you."'" So Gad came to David and said to him, "Thus says the Lord: 'Choose for yourself, either three years of famine, or three months to be defeated by your foes with the sword of your enemies overtaking you, or else for three days the sword of the Lord—the plague in the land, with the angel of the Lord destroying throughout all the territory of Israel.' Now consider what answer I should take back to Him who sent me." And David said to Gad, "I am in great distress. Please let me fall into the hand of the Lord, for His mercies are very great; but do not let me fall into the hand of man."

Obviously, David trusted Gad's voice in his life—and Gad's role was critical in that moment. David wasn't hearing directly from God about what to do in response to his forbidden sin of taking a census, but Gad could see what David could not see. David needed, and I am sure appreciated, his insight.

Of course, it's not always bad news. Seers can partner with leaders who offer visual revelation that confirms or helps them make decisions about direction or strategy. Seers can help the leader discern the season. Of course, this is a trusted position. Don't assume to advise your leader without permission.

PRAYER

Father, in the name of Jesus, I am willing to serve my leadership as a seer advisor, but I don't want to open the door on my own. I am available if You want to speak to my leaders about this.

AUGUST 12

THE MAKING OF A SEER

For whom He foreknew, He also predestined to be conformed to the image of His Son, that He might be the firstborn among many brethren.

Romans 8:29

Without exception, every seer goes through a making process, and it never ends. This making process conforms you into the image of Christ the Seer. Many people are afraid of this process because it often causes suffering. Consider what God said to Jeremiah, a prophet with a seer anointing, in Jeremiah 18:1-4:

> The word which came to Jeremiah from the Lord, saying: "Arise and go down to the potter's house, and there I will cause you to hear My words." Then I went down to the potter's house, and there he was, making something at the wheel. And the vessel that he made of clay was marred in the hand of the potter; so he made it again into another vessel, as it seemed good to the potter to make.

God sent Jeremiah to the potter's house to give him a visual that offered an important lesson for seers. Isaiah also learned this: "But now, O Lord, You are our Father; we are the clay, and You our potter; and all we are the work of Your hand" (Isaiah 64:8).

Catch that. We are the work of His hand. He makes us into the seers He wants us to be. And if we don't cooperate, we can miss our highest calling—or we could miss our calling altogether. Notice how the vessel in Jeremiah 18 was marred in the hand of the potter. The NLT puts it this way, "But the jar he was making did not turn out as he had hoped, so he crushed it into a lump of clay again and started over."

That means if you resist God, if you rebel against His process, if you don't yield to His hand, you may be set on a shelf while God goes to work on someone else who will yield to what He wants to make them.

Paul wrote these Spirit-inspired words in 2 Chronicles 30:9 NLT, "For if you return to the Lord, your relatives and your children will be treated mercifully by their captors, and they will be able to return to this land. For the Lord your God is gracious and merciful. If you return to him, he will not continue to turn his face from you."

PRAYER

Father, in the name of Jesus, help me yield to Your hand. Shape me and make me the kind of seer You want me to be. Not my will, but Yours be done. I will not run.

AUGUST 13

DECODING VISUAL METAPHORS

And Jesus said to them, "I am the bread of life. He who comes to Me shall never hunger, and he who believes in Me shall never thirst."

John 6:35

When Jesus called Himself bread, He was using a metaphor. When Paul called us God's building, he was using a metaphor (1 Corinthians 3:9). When James compared the Word of God to a mirror, he, again, was using a metaphor (James 1:23).

Because the Holy Spirit uses metaphors throughout Scripture, we should not be surprised when we see visual metaphors in the seer dimensions. Decoding visual metaphors is a skill every seer needs to develop in order to discern rightly what they are seeing in the spirit.

While Jesus and the New Testament writers used metaphors as figurative language, a visual metaphor can appear as a symbol. God often uses a symbol to compare two unrelated things and show their similarities. When we say, "Sally has a heart of gold" or "I could eat a horse," for example, these aren't literal statements. They are a way of communicating truth.

While dreams are largely symbolic and parabolic, there are times when an element in a dream is literal. Likewise, visions often have more of a literal meaning, but they often contain metaphors as well. It's critical that we can discern the difference between what is literal and what is metaphorical.

Zechariah had a vision of a lampstand in Zechariah 4:2. This was a metaphor for the work of the Holy Spirit. Isaiah portrayed Israel as a failed vineyard. Ezekiel pictured Israel as dry bones and God as shepherd. David called the word a lamp to his feet. These are all metaphors.

When God gives you a vision or dream with a person you know, don't assume it's literally that person. That person may be a metaphor. The meaning may lie in what they represent. If you see a snake in a vision, it may not be an actual snake. It may represent deception or some sort of enemy attack.

Be a student of the Word and you will be better prepared to discern if what you are seeing is literal or metaphorical, and to interpret the meaning. Ask the Holy Spirit to help you judge what you are seeing in the spirit.

PRAYER

Father, in the name of Jesus, help me master the art of discerning and understanding the literal from the metaphorical in my visual revelations. Help me interpret the metaphors rightly.

AUGUST 14

SEEING IN HIS PRESENCE

You will show me the path of life; in Your presence is fullness of joy; at Your right hand are pleasures forevermore.

Psalm 16:11

While God is omnipresent—He is everywhere all the time—we don't always experience His manifest presence. Seeing in His presence is an altogether different experience.

Moses got a glimpse of God's back as He passed by (Exodus 33). John the Revelator saw in Jesus' presence (Revelation 1). But not all visual revelation comes in His manifest presence. Peter fell into a trance on a rooftop while praying and a Gentile named Cornelius saw an angel while praying at home (Acts 10:1-6).

We can't call on the manifest presence of God, but we can praise and worship our way into it. Psalm 22:3 (KJV) makes it plain, "But thou art holy, O thou that inhabitest the praises of Israel." *Inhabit* in that verse is the Hebrew word *yashab*. It means "to dwell, remain, sit, abide or have one's abode." One Japanese translation puts it this way, "when we praise God we build a big chair for God to sit in." Think about that!

Psalm 92:1 tells us it is good to praise the Lord. Have you ever thought about why? There are many reasons cited in Scripture, particularly in the Psalms, to praise the Lord. For our purposes, we'll focus on those that relate directly to entering into seer dimensions.

As we've seen in the Psalms, praise and worship attracts the Holy Spirit. It's easier to see in His presence. Second, when we draw near to Him, He draws near to us (James 4:8). We are aware of His nearness, we are less aware of the distractions that muddy our spiritual vision.

Third, when we praise and worship God in spirit and in truth, we are operating from our seat in heavenly places (Ephesians 2:6) and are positioning ourselves to enter the holy of holies. Fourth, the Holy Spirit's presence can radically shift an atmosphere and elicit a divine invitation into seer dimensions.

Now, this is not a quick praise break. You may have to enter extended praise and worship to get to this place, and it's only as He wills. Nevertheless, praise and worship is a gate of ascension.

PRAYER

Father, in the name of Jesus, remind me to make praise a lifestyle. You are worthy of my praise. Would You give me a revelation of the power of praise and worship to seeing in Your presence?

AUGUST 15

ACCESSING THE MIND OF CHRIST

For "who has known the mind of the Lord that he may instruct Him?" But we have the mind of Christ.

1 Corinthians 2:16

Seers who want to operate in heavenly wisdom need to learn how to tap into the mind of Christ. The mind of Christ is in your spirit, as He is in your spirit. The mind of Christ is "thinking the way Jesus thinks; to understand how Christ thinks about a particular matter; to be in agreement with the way Christ views an issue," according to *The Seer's Dictionary*.

First John 3:20 plainly tells us He knows everything. When Jesus walked the earth as fully God, fully Man He even knew people's thoughts. Three of the four Gospels recorded this reality. While God knows everything, we are on a need-to-know basis. You can't know everything, but you can know what He wants you to know in your knower.

Proverbs 15:3 tells us, "The eyes of the Lord are in every place, keeping watch on the evil and the good." God sees everything, everywhere all the time. He doesn't miss a thing. There is nothing hidden from His sight. Everything is uncovered and exposed before the eyes of Him to whom we must give account (Hebrews 4:13). Tapping into the mind of Christ is seeing what He wants you to see. You can't see something He doesn't want you to see. Not legally anyway.

Psalm 147:5 says His understanding is infinite. You may not understand what He is showing you with your own wisdom or experience. But when you tap into the mind of Christ, you will gain understanding. Isaiah 55:8-11 tells us His thoughts are higher than our thoughts, but we can tap into the mind of Christ and know some of His thoughts.

Jesus said in John 15:15, "No longer do I call you servants, for a servant does not know what his master is doing; but I have called you friends, for all things that I heard from My Father I have made known to you." So how do you tap into the mind of Christ? Through the Word and praying in the Spirit, which are two gates into the seer dimensions.

PRAYER

Father, in the name of Jesus, thank You that the mind of Christ is in my spirit. Thank You for giving me a way to understand what is in the mind of Christ. Please, make His mind and will known to me.

AUGUST 16

SEE AND TASTE

Oh, taste and see that the Lord is good....

Psalm 34:8

The Lord took me up to Heaven in a dream. It was a scene of an angel who escorted me through some warfare in the second heavens and to a table. On the table were some of the most colorful fruits I've ever seen and especially tasty pink juice. In my dream, I could literally taste it.

When you go deeper into the realm of the spirit, you might not just see—you may also taste. Tasting is not just a natural sense; it's also a spiritual sense.

We see some hints at this in the Scripture. Psalm 34:8 says, "Oh, taste and see that the Lord is good." The Hebrew word for *taste* in that verse is *ta'am,* which means "to taste, perceive, or eat." Tasting is one way we perceive in the spirit. Think of Ezekiel and John the Revelator, who ate the scrolls. They were sweet in the mouth but produced a bitterness in the stomach.

Tasting is an invitation to a different dimension of encounter. Hebrews 6 speaks of tasting the heavenly gift. The Greek word for *taste* in this verse is *geuomai,* which means "to taste, to perceive the flavor of, to partake, to enjoy, to feel, or experience." This isn't always a literal tasting; rather, it's a spiritual tasting. However, some encounters can literally leave a taste in your mouth—good or bad.

When I was eating the fruit and drinking the juice in Heaven, it tasted like joy and left me feeling joyful. I now call it "joy juice." Psalm 119:103 says, "How sweet are Your words to my taste, sweeter than honey to my mouth!" Song of Solomon 1:2 says, "...your love is better than wine." And Peter said, "if indeed you have tasted that the Lord is gracious" (1 Peter 2:3).

Alternatively, some encounters may leave a bitterness in your belly. Jesus spoke of tasting death in Matthew 16:28.

Just as we have natural senses, our spiritual senses can come alive and we can literally taste things in the natural or the spirit. This is part of our discernment and we need to pay close attention to what our spiritual senses tell us.

PRAYER

Father, in the name of Jesus, I would love to experience tasting in the spirit. Would You open up this spiritual sense? Most of all, help me taste and see just how good You are.

AUGUST 17

THE REJECTED SEER

To the praise of the glory of His grace, by which He made us accepted in the Beloved.

Ephesians 1:6

I once believed intercessors were the most misunderstood operatives in the Body of Christ. Many pastors still don't appreciate their contribution to the local church—and prayer is often relegated to the back of the house. Many have labeled intercessors weird, odd, strange, or out there.

But now, I believe seers are the most misunderstood—and perhaps the most rejected. Throughout church history, seers have been at times revered for their gift and at times scorned. Despite the reality of seers in the Bible, the Body of Christ has been less accepting of seeing in the spirit realm through visions, trances, and heavenly encounters. They may accept that you had a dream, but an encounter with an angel or Jesus? Many people will think you are making it up! In fact, many who operate in these realms have been labeled heretics.

Of course, seers have existed since creation and there are still seers today. God created us in His image (Genesis 1:27). He is the ultimate Seer. Now, God is emphasizing seers at a level the modern Church has never witnessed before. If you aren't prepared to deal with rejection, it could sideline you for a season.

If you've walked in seer ministry any length of time, you've probably felt the pain of rejection. Know that you are not alone. Old Testament seers had to deal with the reality that many would not receive their visual revelation. Some would even ridicule and attack them for delivering the oracles of God.

If you refuse to compromise your seer gift, you face a measure of rejection. You may be overlooked as "too far out there." You may be ridiculed and attacked for the God-inspired dreams and visions you share. How you respond could make an eternal difference in your seer ministry.

Whether real or perceived, rejection doesn't just give up. If it can't turn you into a self-pity-toting performer, rejection will puff you up with pride to compensate for your insecurities or lead you to fabricate a protective personality to guard yourself from more rejection. When rejection comes whispering to your soul, telling you that something is wrong with you, reject that thought in the name of Jesus. Your clear vision depends on it.

PRAYER

Father, in the name of Jesus, help me to break free from any rejection mindset I have adopted. Help me not to shrink back from delivering my revelation for fear of rejection. Deliver me!

AUGUST 18

THE JOHN PAUL JACKSON SEER ANOINTING

And Pharaoh said to Joseph, I have had a dream, and there is no one who can interpret it. But I have heard it said of you that you can understand a dream, to interpret it.

Genesis 41:15

John Paul Jackson died a premature death in 2015 at the age of 65, but his ministry continues through the sons and daughters he trained in the seer dimensions. John Paul was well-known as a man who revealed God to His people, awakened an awareness of the deep meanings of visual revelation, particularly dreams, and was a leading voice in biblical dream interpretation.

As the founder of Streams Ministries, you might say John Paul Jackson brought an understanding of the significance of dreams—particularly prophetic dreams—to the 21st century Church through his speaking, books, and television shows. He brought language to dream interpreters.

Jackson explained how dreams are one of mankind's greatest mysteries: "Dreams use a symbolic language. To have a correct interpretation one has to know the dream source and dream code. Imagine if the dream you had last night contained the answer that you had been looking for, and you didn't know it? Knowing the meaning of a dream can be life changing."

John Paul Jackson had a teaching gift, and used it in part to help people understand the difference between prophets and seers. He also raised the bar in prophetic ministry with a focus on character over anointing, integrity, character, accountability, humility, and protocols so that believers and leaders would embrace the prophetic function rather than shunning it.

Jackson was known for issuing warnings and end-times perspectives, including the well-known The Coming Perfect Storm, during which he said, "I see coming to the United States is a combination of more than one element, and when the elements unite, the storm becomes exponentially more dangerous."

He goes down in prophetic history as carrying one of the most impactful expressions of the seer gift in the 20th century. With his media legacy and clear teaching that came from the authority of one who walked in this realm, Jackson is still inspiring and will continue to inspire current and future generations of people to pursue the meanings of their dreams. He truly fulfilled the Ephesians 4 mandate to equip believers.

PRAYER

Father, in the name of Jesus, thank You for the legacy of John Paul Jackson. Would You help me glean from his understanding of dreams and take lessons from his emphasis in character over anointing?

AUGUST 19

NAVIGATING NIGHT VISIONS

In disquieting thoughts from the visions of the night, when deep sleep falls on men.

Job 4:13

Israel (Jacob), Job, Daniel, Zechariah, and Paul had something in common: they had night visions. Not to be confused with dreams, night visions are "visions that occur during the time when one begins to rouse from sleep and the time one is fully awake; that period between sleep and wakefulness," according to *The Seer's Dictionary*.

Jacob had visions of the night (Genesis 46:2). Job had a vision of the night in Job 33:15. Daniel had night visions frequently (Daniel 2:19; Daniel 7:7,13). Isaiah had a night vision (Isaiah 29:7). And Paul had two night visions, or visions of the night (Acts 16:9; 18:9).

But not all night visions—or visions of the night as the Bible also calls them—originate with God. Like any other visual revelation, you have to navigate these spiritual experiences with discernment. Night visions can come from your soul or they can present as demonic interference.

Here's my best advice: When you have a night vision, write it down immediately and judge the source later. If you don't chronicle the night vision, you can forget important aspects of the encounter that help you judge the source. Sometimes the source is clearly demonic. The more difficult aspect of navigating night visions is discerning between your soul and His Spirit—or sometimes your troubled soul and a sneaky demon.

When you aren't sure about the source of the night vision, your strategy shifts to prayer and waiting on the Lord before taking any action. He may show the enemy is meddling in your thoughts. If a night vision breeds fear in your heart, cast it down. If it brings confusion to your soul, bind it up. Plead the blood of Jesus against night visions that originate in the enemy's camp. Never come into agreement with it through your thoughts or words. Instead, take authority over it, in the name of Jesus.

The Holy Spirit may show you what you thought was demonic is really the worries in your heart manifesting as a troubling vision. Or it could be Him warning you about something you need to avoid but you mistake it for the enemy. The source of your night visions is not always immediately clear, which is why it's critical to interpret dreams by the Word of God and the Spirit of God, which will always lead you into truth.

PRAYER

Father, in the name of Jesus, would You help me be careful not to attribute to You something that came from my soul? Teach me to discern between Your Spirit and my soul.

AUGUST 20

ENTERING MYSTICAL DIMENSIONS

He reveals deep and secret things; He knows what is in the darkness, and light dwells with Him.

Daniel 2:22

Jesus wants His disciples to know the mysteries of the Kingdom of Heaven. These realms are largely misunderstood, and error can creep in if we are not rooted in the Word and led by the Spirit. But the reality is the Word has plenty to say about this dimension.

The Bible calls us stewards of the mysteries of God (1 Corinthians 4:1). We can't steward something we haven't unlocked. Mysteries become revelation as God opens the eyes of our heart so we can see what we could not see before.

Proverbs 25:2 reveals: "It is the glory of God to conceal a matter, but the glory of kings is to search out a matter." And Deuteronomy 29:29 says, "The secret things belong to the Lord our God, but those things which are revealed belong to us and to our children forever, that we may do all the words of this law." Jeremiah 33:3 instructs us: "Call to Me, and I will answer you, and show you great and mighty things, which you do not know."

What are these mysteries? I write more about mysteries in my book *The Seer Dimensions*, but here are a few: There's the mystery of the gospel (Ephesians 6:19); the mystery of Christ (Colossians 4:3); the mystery of iniquity (2 Thessalonians 2:7); the mystery of faith (1 Timothy 3:9); the mystery of godliness (1 Timothy 3:16); the mystery of the seven stars (Revelation 1:20).

There are many ways to access the mysteries of the Kingdom of Heaven. They are hidden in the Word. The Holy Spirit can share them with you by direct revelation. You can discover them through teachings from leaders in the Body of Christ and so on. But, as I write in my book *Tongues of Fire*, praying in tongues is one of the fastest ways to access these mysteries. Ask God to show you His mysteries.

PRAYER

Father, in the name of Jesus, would You give me a hunger to search out secret truths and mysteries of Your Kingdom so I can understand Your ways. As I pray in tongues, would You unlock deep mysteries of Your glory?

AUGUST 21

WHAT DO THOSE NUMBERS MEAN?

The secret things belong to the Lord our God, but those things which are revealed belong to us and to our children forever, that we may do all the words of this law.

Deuteronomy 29:29

Numerology, the study of numbers, can take you down a wrong interpretation path in a hurry. We must avoid the world's—or the New Age concept—of numerology like the plague. But biblical numerology is, well, biblical.

It seems obvious to any serious Bible student that God is the God of numbers, though some still debate it. Numbers often have both a theological and symbolic meaning in Scripture and numbers we see in dreams could reveal what God is saying or planning to do in our lives or in the world. Of course, numbers can have more than one meaning in Scripture. There can be a positive or negative connotation.

God can and does still communicate through numbers. He's been doing this since the beginning of the earth. For example, the number seven signifies perfection and completion. We see this in both the Genesis account of the seven days of creation and the Revelation 4:5 picture of the seven spirits of God.

Meanwhile, the number twelve consistently speaks of God's government and authority. Consider the twelve tribes of Israel and the twelve apostles of the Lamb. The number forty speaks of trials and tests. Think of Israel's forty years in the wilderness and Christ's forty days in the desert. So when you see numbers in your dreams and visions, it means something. But don't start searching Google for the meaning or you would wind up in a witch's den. Instead, look to the Word of God to interpret the numbers, knowing that some numbers have a positive and negative connotation. That's why context matters.

Remember, God created numbers and numbers are included in the language of Heaven. God may use a flashing number to get your attention, to bring clarity about a timeline or confirm what He has already said. God could use numbers to emphasize spiritual themes. In any case, the numbers you see in your dreams are purposeful. Don't take them for granted; seek out the Word and the Spirit for revelation. One number could unravel the greater meaning of a dream or vision.

Seers, numbers are one way God communicates. God often uses numbers to confirm His Word or guide us in specific assignments. Study His Word, align your interpretations with Scripture, and allow the Holy Spirit to teach you. When you understand biblical numerology, you will unlock a powerful tool for interpreting the mysteries God reveals to you.

PRAYER

Father, in the name of Jesus, would You help me to understand biblical numerology? There is so much to learn and I don't want to miss what You are saying through numbers I see in my visual revelation.

AUGUST 22

DECODING OBSCURE SIGHTS

I have told you these things in obscure figures of speech; a time is coming when I will no longer speak to you in obscure figures, but will tell you plainly about the Father.

John 16:25 New English Translation

John had some of the most obscure sights in Scripture. Consider the locusts from the abyss in Revelation 9:7-10:

> The shape of the locusts was like horses prepared for battle. On their heads were crowns of something like gold, and their faces were like the faces of men. They had hair like women's hair, and their teeth were like lions' teeth. And they had breastplates like breastplates of iron, and the sound of their wings was like the sound of chariots with many horses running into battle. They had tails like scorpions, and there were stings in their tails. Their power was to hurt men five months.

That's obscure! *Obscure* means "difficult to see, understand or immediately interpret without further revelation," according to *The Seer's Dictionary*. Some visual revelation is easy to understand. For example, Joseph, the husband of Mary, had a dream with clear instructions to keep the baby Jesus safe from Herod's murderous intentions. But we do see plenty of obscure sights recorded in the Bible.

Like Ezekiel, Daniel, and Zechariah, you may experience obscure sights in the seer dimensions. Know this: the message is hidden beneath the surface of the visual revelation. In other words, you need revelation to understand the revelation. This is not the time to grab a dream dictionary, which could lead you in the wrong direction. This is the time to grab hold of the Holy Spirit and press into what He is trying to show you.

Put another way, obscure sights are invitations for supplications. It's a call to prayer for wisdom. When Daniel had an obscure vision of the four beasts coming up from the sea, all different from one another, he did not immediately understand the meaning of the obscure sight. He didn't have an instant flash of revelation concerning the meaning of the four beasts. The vision troubled him.

Daniel needed supernatural help to understand what he saw. As it turns out, the four beasts were four kings. He probably would not have come to that conclusion on his own. We have to be careful not to come to our own conclusions when we see obscure sights or receive any form of visual revelation for that matter. Lean on the Revealer.

PRAYER

Father, in the name of Jesus, help me not to dismiss obscure sights in the seer dimensions. Like Daniel, inspire me to ponder what I see and to seek Your mind for the deeper meanings of what You show me.

AUGUST 23

I SAW THE WAR ROOM IN HEAVEN

And a vision appeared to Paul in the night. A man of Macedonia stood and pleaded with him, saying, "Come over to Macedonia and help us."
Acts 16:9

When I saw the war room in Heaven, it was an open vision. An open vision is a vision that appears sort of like a movie playing out before one's very eyes, according to *The Seer's Dictionary*. The seer's eyes are open and he is almost oblivious to what is going on around him in the natural world. It's like time stops.

The Bible offers accounts of massively dramatic visions that are worthy of closer study. Take another look, for example, of Paul's open vision on the road to Damascus (Acts 9:3-9) and the night when he received the Macedonian call (Acts 16:9). Ponder these things.

Also consider Ezekiel's open vision:

> Then I looked, and behold, a whirlwind was coming out of the north, a great cloud with raging fire engulfing itself; and brightness was all around it and radiating out of its midst like the color of amber, out of the midst of the fire. Also from within it came the likeness of four living creatures. And this was their appearance: they had the likeness of a man. Each one had four faces, and each one had four wings. Their legs were straight, and the soles of their feet were like the soles of calves' feet. They sparkled like the color of burnished bronze. The hands of a man were under their wings on their four sides; and each of the four had faces and wings. Their wings touched one another. The creatures did not turn when they went, but each one went straight forward (Ezekiel 1:4-9). (This vision continues through the first chapter, and Ezekiel had other profound visions as well.)

Dramatic visions did not end in the Bible. Rick Joyner has had some dramatic visions that he published in books. One of them, *Final Quest,* is a panoramic vision of the ultimate quest—the last battle between light and darkness. The late David Wilkerson had a prophetic vision about doomsday that has gone around the world. These and the biblical examples should make us hungry to move deeper into this seer dimension.

PRAYER

Father, in the name of Jesus, I am open to open visions. I know these often come suddenly and without invitation. Would You help me to place a value on this realm of the seer dimensions and position myself for revelation?

AUGUST 24

WHEN THE HEAVENS OPEN

Now it came to pass in the thirtieth year, in the fourth month, on the fifth day of the month, as I was among the captives by the River Chebar, that the heavens were opened and I saw visions of God.

Ezekiel 1:1

South Florida is a tough territory. Some have called it the evangelist's graveyard because the heavens are so hard. The Tri-County area starts in Palm Beach, but the spiritual climate grows heavier moving further south, from Broward to Miami-Dade County. Visiting ministers have told me they fall asleep reading the Bible because the witchcraft is so strong. (I suppose I am used to it after 30 years.)

By contrast, when I go to Moravian Falls, a largely Christian community in North Carolina founded by the Moravians, I find myself in an open heaven. That open heaven set the stage for several angelic encounters. Once, for example, I heard angels playing music every time I opened my Bible. When I closed my Bible, it stopped. When I opened it again, the music started.

Both John the Baptist and Stephen the evangelist experienced open heavens. Matthew 3:16 reads, "When He had been baptized, Jesus came up immediately from the water; and behold, the heavens were opened to Him, and He saw the Spirit of God descending like a dove and alighting upon Him." And when Stephen was being stoned, he said, "Look! I see the heavens opened and the Son of Man standing at the right hand of God!" (Acts 7:56).

In an open heaven, you may feel a strong sense of peace, joy, or reverence. You may experience increased revelation as Ezekiel did: "the heavens were opened, and I saw visions of God" (Ezekiel 1:1).You may have a greater awareness of God's presence like Jacob did: "And Jacob awaked out of his sleep, and he said, Surely the Lord is in this place; and I knew it not" (Genesis 28:16 KJV).

We don't live under an open heaven, so when we discern this blessing we need to pay close attention with our seer eyes. You may see angelic activity, hear God's audible voice, have epic dreams, or see massive breakthroughs. Learn to discern and value open heavens. This is where the seer dimension comes alive.

PRAYER

Father, in the name of Jesus, would You help me quickly discern when I am under an open heaven? Help me not to be distracted with the things of the world when I am enveloped in the atmosphere of Heaven.

AUGUST 25

CAUGHT UP IN THE SPIRIT

I was in the Spirit on the Lord's Day, and I heard behind me a loud voice, as of a trumpet.

Revelation 1:10

John the Revelator was caught up in the Lord's day. Out of this ecstatic encounter came the book of Revelation, with its many overwhelming visions of the end times, angelic activity, and a picture of the return of the Lord Himself. This ecstatic encounter occurred while John was in exile on the island of Patmos. He describes it this way:

> I, John, both your brother and companion in the tribulation and kingdom and patience of Jesus Christ, was on the island that is called Patmos for the word of God and for the testimony of Jesus Christ. I was in the Spirit on the Lord's Day, and I heard behind me a loud voice, as of a trumpet, saying, "I am the Alpha and the Omega, the First and the Last," and, "What you see, write in a book and send it to the seven churches which are in Asia: to Ephesus, to Smyrna, to Pergamos, to Thyatira, to Sardis, to Philadelphia, and to Laodicea." Then I turned to see the voice that spoke with me... (Revelation 1:9-12).

John has four experiences in the book of Revelation where he says he's in this spirit (Revelation 1:10; 4:2; 17:3; 21:10). In one of those instances he says an angel carried him away in the Spirit. What does this phrase "in the Spirit" mean? It means that while John was physically in Patmos, his spirit was also somewhere else. This is the same experience Paul had and the same experience Ezekiel had several times: "Then the Spirit lifted me up, and I heard behind me a loud rumbling sound as the glory of the Lord rose from the place where it was standing. It was the sound of the wings of the living creatures brushing against each other and the sound of the wheels beside them, a loud rumbling sound. The Spirit then lifted me up and took me away, and I went in bitterness and in the anger of my spirit, with the strong hand of the Lord on me" (Ezekiel 3:12-14 NIV).

Another time, Ezekiel records: "He stretched out the form of a hand, and took me by a lock of my hair; and the Spirit lifted me up between earth and heaven, and brought me in visions of God to Jerusalem, to the door of the north gate of the inner court, where the seat of the image of jealousy was, which provokes to jealousy" (Ezekiel 8:3). And again, in Ezekiel 43:5 he writes, "The Spirit lifted me up and brought me into the inner court; and behold, the glory of the Lord filled the temple."

Paul described his own out-of-body experience in 2 Corinthians 12:2-4: "I know a man in Christ who fourteen years ago—whether in the body I do not know, or whether out of the body I do not know, God knows—such a one was caught up to the third heaven. And I know such a man—whether in the body or out of the body I do not know, God knows—how he was caught up into Paradise and heard inexpressible words, which it is not lawful for a man to utter."

PRAYER

Father, in the name of Jesus, I am intrigued by encounters in Your Word where men of God were caught up in the spirit. Give me a revelation of why You choose to catch people up in the spirit. I am ready.

AUGUST 26

BREAKING DEMONIC VEILS

But their minds were blinded. For until this day the same veil remains unlifted in the reading of the Old Testament, because the veil is taken away in Christ.

2 Corinthians 3:14

As God raises up the next generation of seers, the enemy is busy deploying strategies to veil visual revelation. And he has many strategies from which to choose, including demonic cloaking, witchcraft interference, territorial resistance, and soulish distractions. We need to tap into our God-given discernment and use our authority to contend against what's working to veil our vision.

Indeed, sometimes you have to fight the good fight of faith to see what God is trying to show you. You have to engage in spiritual warfare to pierce the dark veil the enemy raises up to hinder or shut down your sight. Think about it like this. God wants to open the eyes of our hearts. The enemy wants us to be spiritually blind. There's a war over your sight.

Demonic veils are devices the enemy uses. Paul wrote in 2 Corinthians 4:4 (NIV), "The god of this world has blinded the minds of unbelievers...." If he blinds unbelievers, you better believe he's trying to cloud the eyes of seers. Of course, the enemy can't completely blind you but he can frustrate your vision and weaken your confidence that you're seeing rightly. He can also tempt you into sin, which weakens your ability to see in the spirit.

What does this look like practically? Beyond witchcraft, there's what I call static. You start to pray, read the Word, or meditate on the Lord and discover it's noisy in the spirit. You may hear voices of accusation or of intimation. You may feel unsettled in your soul for no good reason. You may feel unfocused or have a hard time being still.

Then there's what I call demonic cloaking devices. Proverbs 25:2 tells us, "It is the glory of God to conceal a matter, but the glory of kings is to search out a matter." Just like Heaven can conceal a matter, the enemy tries to cloak his operations.

Cloaking is when the enemy tries to hide what he is doing through distraction or misdirection or what I call blurry vision. Maybe you used to see in high definition. Now it's all cloudy, like you're watching a prophetic movie through a fogged-up windshield. The outlines are there but the details are gone.

Before you engage in warfare, you need to discern what's happening. Not every veil is demonic. Some are divine. God sometimes withholds visual revelation because you are not ready to see it. Remember, Jesus concealed things from His disciples until they could bear them. But know that the enemy is active.

PRAYER

Father, in the name of Jesus, would You help me to get to the root of demonic veils and seer-targeted witchcraft attacks. I know I have authority, but I need accurate revelation to come against what's blocking my sight.

AUGUST 27

LEGISLATING IN THE HEAVENLIES FOR NATIONS

When the Lord began to speak by Hosea, the Lord said to Hosea: "Go, take yourself a wife of harlotry and children of harlotry, for the land has committed great harlotry by departing from the Lord."

Hosea 1:2

We're living in an hour when personal seer ministry alone is not going to cut it. Yes, God uses seers to encourage, edify, and comfort the Church through dreams and visions. But God is looking to raise up seers who are willing to press in and level up to legislating over cities and nations with what they see.

Think about it. The enemy is plotting on a global scale. Nations are in crisis. Governments are shaking. Principalities and powers are stirring wars around the world. God's counter-attack often comes through the seer who says, "Here I am. Send me. I am willing to see and war for the souls in nations."

God wants to use a new breed of seers who is not really a new breed at all. Seers in Scripture shared intelligence with kings, not just saints. Yes, this is by calling and gifting. But it's also by equipping and consecrating. This is high-level warfare and not every seer has matured enough to ascend to those levels. But if you are willing and available, God can use you in ways that your eyes have not seen and your ears have not heard.

Habakkuk said, "I will stand my watch and set myself on the rampart, and watch to see what He will say to me, and what I will answer when I am corrected" (Habakkuk 2:1). This was a seer who was on standby. He was not passive. He was actively watching to see what God would assign him. And remember Elisha, who warned the king of Israel about the enemy's next moves before he made them because he could see into the ruler's bedchambers.

Yes, some seers are called to the local church. That is their high calling. But I believe many who have been faithful in smaller assignments—those who have acted with integrity and consistency—are going to be promoted to greater assignments. I'm talking about national and international intelligence and wisdom to legislate in the spirit.

It's not about being political. It's about being wired to see from a different vantage point. Habakkuk climbed high. If this stirs your spirit, start asking God to use you for the greater seer works.

PRAYER

Father, in the name of Jesus, Here I am. Send me. I am willing to see and war for the souls in nations. Train me if You see fit to deal with demonic strongholds in the spirit.

AUGUST 28

FIRE, OIL, AND GLORY

And another angel came out from the altar, who had power over fire, and he cried with a loud cry to him who had the sharp sickle, saying, "Thrust in your sharp sickle and gather the clusters of the vine of the earth, for her grapes are fully ripe."

Revelation 14:18

When I was in Singapore in 2017, the Lord assigned me fire angels. Ever since then, I've seen the fire of God manifest in my ministry at strategic times. When the fire angels show up, the glory manifests.

We know the Angel of the Lord appeared to Moses in a flame of fire in a bush (Exodus 3:2). And Psalm 104:4 calls angels spirits who are "a flame of fire." In Revelation 14:18, the Bible speaks of an angel who has power over fire.

The Bible makes a direct connection between fire and glory again and again. We first see this in Exodus 24:17: "The sight of the glory of the Lord was like a consuming fire on the top of the mountain in the eyes of the children of Israel."

Fire represents the purifying power of God—holiness. Visions of God in His glory across the pages of the Bible showcase fire. Zechariah 2:5 reveals, "'For I,' says the Lord, 'will be a wall of fire all around her, and I will be the glory in her midst.'"

And Isaiah 10:16 reads: "Therefore the Lord, the Lord of hosts, will send leanness among his fat ones; and under his glory He will kindle a burning like the burning of a fire."

> And when Solomon finished praying, fire came down from the heavens and consumed the burnt offering and sacrifices, and the glory of the Lord filled the temple. And the priests were not able to enter into the house of the Lord, for the glory of the Lord filled the Lord's house. And all the sons of Israel saw when the fire came down and the glory of the Lord came on the temple, and they bowed their faces low to the ground on the pavement, and they worshipped confessing, "The Lord is good, and His mercy endures forever" (2 Chronicles 7:1-3 MEV).

Look for the fire of God in the Spirit. Look for the angels of fire.

PRAYER

Father, in the name of Jesus, let me see Your holy fire and avoid strange fire at all costs. Help me learn to work with angels of fire when You dispatch them to operate on earth.

AUGUST 29

ACTIVATING DISCERNING OF SPIRITS

And this I pray, that your love may abound still more and more in knowledge and all discernment, that you may approve the things that are excellent, that you may be sincere and without offense till the day of Christ.

Philippians 1:9-10

Discernment is part of the seer's package. In fact, some call seers "discerners." But even if you have the gift it still needs to be activated.

People who have the gift of discerning of spirits can perceive and differentiate both good and evil spirits in the unseen world. The gift of discerning of spirits is also translated "the distinguishing of spirits" (New American Standard Bible), "the ability to distinguish between spirits" (English Standard Version), and "discernment of spirits" (New Revised Standard Version).

The late John Wimber, founder of The Vineyard Movement, defined discerning of spirits this way: "Discerning of spirits is the supernatural capacity to judge whether the spirit operating has a source that is human, demonic, or divine. It is a supernatural perception in the spiritual realm for the purpose of determining the source of spiritual activity."

John the Baptist visually discerned the Holy Spirit upon Jesus as a dove as He descended from Heaven. In John 1:32-33 (AMPC), John testified saying, "I have seen the Spirit descending as a dove out of heaven, and it dwelt on Him [never to depart]. And I did not know Him nor recognize Him, but He Who sent me to baptize in (with) water said to me, Upon Him Whom you shall see the Spirit descend and remain, that One is He Who baptizes with the Holy Spirit."

The believers in the upper room discerned the Holy Spirit as the sound of rushing wind and then as tongues of fire resting on their heads (Acts 2:3). Mary saw two angels in the sepulcher where Jesus had been laid to rest in John 20. An angel appeared to Paul on the ship to deliver a message in Acts 27. Peter discerned the wrong motives of Simon the sorcerer.

So how does the seer activate this gift? One way is through praying in tongues. Praying in tongues makes us more sensitive to the Holy Spirit, and the gift of discerning of spirits comes from Him. You can also ask God for more discernment. Renewing your mind will help you discern more accurately because it is a "discerner of the thoughts and intents of the heart" (Hebrews 4:12).

Aside from all that, faith without works is dead. You activate your discernment by putting it to use. Hebrews 5:14 tells us plainly, "But solid food belongs to those who are of full age, that is, those who by reason of use have their senses exercised to discern both good and evil."

PRAYER

Father, in the name of Jesus, would You help me to practice discerning spirits? Help me grow in discernment, both visually and just by the inner witness of Your Spirit as I renew my mind with Your Word.

AUGUST 30

YOUR SEER PEDIGREE

Then he took the mantle of Elijah that had fallen from him, and struck the water, and said, "Where is the Lord God of Elijah?" And when he also had struck the water, it was divided this way and that; and Elisha crossed over.

2 Kings 2:14

What's your seer pedigree? Maybe you've never heard that term so let me define it. A *seer pedigree* is your seer ancestry, according to *The Seer's Dictionary*. It's the lineage of seers or seer anointing impartations you have received from people who went before you.

My seer pedigree includes James Goll, who prayed for impartations into my life. James is a prolific dreamer and has had significant encounters with the Lord. I can tell that some of his anointing rubbed off on me. Bishop Bill Hamon, the father of the modern-day prophetic movement, is also part of my seer pedigree. He ordained me into ministry. His anointing to see shifts in the Church and his equipping bent has also rubbed off on me.

Have you ever considered your spiritual ancestry, which includes impartations and mentorship? Perhaps you will never meet James Goll or Bishop Hamon, but people don't need to know well-known prophets and seers to receive mentorship and impartations these days. Sitting under someone's teaching anointing or reading their books can be part of your pedigree even if you never meet someone in person.

Pedigree, or spiritual heritage, is scriptural. In the Bible we see gifts and mantles passed down through generations. Perhaps the most memorable example is when Elijah threw his mantle on young Elisha (1 Kings 19:19). Later, when Elijah was taken up to Heaven, he threw his mantle down one last time and Elisha received a double portion anointing (2 Kings 2:9-15).

In a way, Samuel was part of Elijah's seer pedigree. Elijah continued the schools of the prophets that Samuel started. He carried on Samuel's legacy, honoring his labor. Your seer pedigree is not just about spiritual impartation it's about wisdom, authority, and responsibility.

And remember, Paul reminded Timothy, "Therefore I remind you to stir up the gift of God which is in you through the laying on of my hands" (2 Timothy 1:6). Paul was a seeing apostle who had dramatic encounters, and he imparted to Timothy. If you don't have these types of relationships, don't let that bother you. Your ultimate seer pedigree is in Christ. He is the Seer and the seer anointing flows from Him.

PRAYER

Father, in the name of Jesus, would You direct me to the people from whom You would like me to learn? Even if I never meet some of the spiritual giants, I know I can glean from watching them and reading their wisdom.

AUGUST 31

SCRIBING WHAT YOU SEE IN THE SPIRIT

And the Lord answered me and said, Write the vision and engrave it so plainly upon tablets that everyone who passes may [be able to] read [it easily and quickly] as he hastens by.

Habakkuk 2:2 AMPC

Seeing is not where your anointing stops. Seers must also scribe what they see. Your anointing is not just for receiving and interpreting visual revelation, in other words, but for writing it down and making it plain.

What if Ezekiel didn't scribe what he saw in the vision of the Valley of Dry Bones? What if Zechariah didn't scribe his encounters with angels? What if John the Revelator didn't scribe what he saw? We would be missing large portions of the Bible, Scriptures that help us understand the end times and the principles of the seer anointing.

You are scribing so you will remember, yes, but it's beyond that. Like Ezekiel, Daniel, and others in Scripture with books named after them, you are scribing for the sake of others: to warn, prepare, inspire, and instruct them. You are, at times, unveiling mysteries, announcing times and seasons, and offering intercessory prayer strategies.

I heard the Lord say:

I am calling My scribes to describe what they see and hear before they say. I am calling chroniclers to rise up and write down what I show them in the day and what they dream at night.

For I am releasing My anointing on a new generation of seers and scribes and they will be faithful to write down the visions, the visitations and the views of the future I show them. They will be articulate with a pen and in speech. Their tongues shall be pens of ready writers. They will distribute what I show them, what they have scribed and chronicled, far and wide through digital media that reaches the nations of the earth.

I am calling the scribes to describe My heart, My ways, My precepts, My principles, My presence, My love and more through the power of the pen and the anointing of My Spirit. I am looking for a few good scribes.

Seers, start scribing. Future seers are relying on your present revelation for future application.

PRAYER

Father, in the name of Jesus, would You make me a seer scribe? Let it dawn on me that the revelations You show me may help others walk more closely with You, even if it's far into the future.

SEPTEMBER

But he became very hungry and wanted to eat; but while they made ready, he fell into a trance.

Acts 10:10

SEPTEMBER 1

ENTERING THE HEAVENLY DIMENSION

After these things I looked, and behold, a door standing open in heaven. And the first voice which I heard was like a trumpet speaking with me, saying, "Come up here, and I will show you things which must take place after this."

Revelation 4:1

You can't choose to have dramatic encounters in Heaven any more than you can choose to have a dream from God. But the Holy Spirit may invite us to see Heaven through Jesus, who is the Door (John 10:7). He can do this through a dream, vision, or encounter. I have seen Heaven. You could, too.

Remember, as born-again believers, we walk in a duality. We are simultaneously walking in the earth realm and seated in the heavenly realm. Consider the Holy Spirit-inspired words of Paul the apostle in Ephesians 2:4-7:

> But God, who is rich in mercy, because of His great love with which He loved us, even when we were dead in trespasses, made us alive together with Christ (by grace you have been saved), and raised us up together, and made us sit together in the heavenly places in Christ Jesus, that in the ages to come He might show the exceeding riches of His grace in His kindness toward us in Christ Jesus.

God has made us sit together in heavenly places in Christ. This is our legal position. It's the position from which we war. It's the position from which we see in the spirit. This is not our practical everyday living condition in the earth realm where we witness death and destruction, sickness and disease, pain and sorrow. Rather, it is our legal position. Is it so strange to think we could, by God's invitation, enter into the heavenly realm?

The AMPC translation of Ephesians 2:6 goes a little deeper: "He raised us up together with Him and made us sit down together [giving us joint seating with Him] in the heavenly sphere [by virtue of our being] in Christ Jesus (the Messiah, the Anointed One)."

If you are in Christ, you are legally seated in heavenly places. While I don't believe we ascend and descend to Heaven at will, I do believe there is a legal right to enter the seer dimensions through dreams and visions and the opportunity to ascend as God wills. Do you have faith for it?

PRAYER

Father, in the name of Jesus, would You help me renew my mind to what the Bible says about heavenly encounters. Your apostles and prophets saw into Heaven. If it suits Your purposes, please show me heavenly scenes.

SEPTEMBER 2

ALWAYS ASK PERMISSION

But all things should be done with regard to decency and propriety and in an orderly fashion.

1 Corinthians 14:40 AMPC

Just as a prophetic evangelist asks a lost soul on the street, "Can I pray for you?" before proceeding to prophesy or release healing power, seers should also ask permission before looking into someone's life.

Permission in this context is "approval from someone to look into their life; authorization for someone to pray and seek to see what the enemy or the Lord is doing in your life," according to *The Seer's Dictionary*.

Remember, seers are also intercessors. God may lead you to intercede for a friend, family member, or even a leader. He may choose to show you things according to His will in those cases for the sake of more strategic intercession. They may never know He allowed you to see it, or allow you to tell them what you saw.

But consider this: we should never presume to start peering into someone's life without permission. Even if our motives are right, it's intrusive. I'll give you a natural example. If you had a friend housesitting for you, would you want them rummaging through your drawers and closets? Or would you consider that a violation of your privacy?

We want to carry the seer anointing with integrity and honor. Doing so means asking permission to look into their life. That's because you might see things that embarrass them, like hidden sin or secrets of the heart. If you seek permission, though, anything the Lord shows you would be to their benefit.

Conversely, if you choose to look into someone's life without the Lord's permission or the person's permission, you could be tapping into what the enemy wants you to see and it may or may not be accurate. If you aren't seeing accurately, then at best you are praying wrongly and at worst you could end up making false accusations as you see things about people that are not true.

This permission principle aligns with Paul's instruction in 1 Corinthians 14:40, "Let everything be done decently and in order." Remember, God authorized Elisha to see into the king's bedchambers in order to protect the Israelites from harm.

PRAYER

Father, in the name of Jesus, help me abide Your Kingdom protocols. I want to operate in divine order. Remind me to ask people for their agreement and permission before I seek to see into their life.

SEPTEMBER 3

SEER PERSECUTION

So they took Jeremiah and cast him into the dungeon of Malachiah the king's son, which was in the court of the prison, and they let Jeremiah down with ropes. And in the dungeon there was no water, but mire. So Jeremiah sank in the mire.

Jeremiah 38:6

Persecution is part and parcel of any prophetic ministry. In my experience, the seer ministry is one of the most persecuted and misunderstood in the Church. That's because of the trances, epic dreams, open visions, and other visual revelation that are still relatively rare in the Body of Christ today.

Seers and prophets in the Church faced persecution in their time, and if we are truly seeing for God so will we face ridicule. Think about it for a minute. Jeremiah's prophetic words were burned. He was mocked. He was beaten. He was thrown into a cistern for prophesying. Daniel, meanwhile, was thrown into a lion's den. John the Revelator was exiled on the Isle of Patmos. Isaiah was sawn in two.

Seers will face more than your typical warfare. You will face persecution from people in the form of false accusations, rejection, slander, and the like. But remember the words in red! Jesus said, "Blessed are you when people insult you, persecute you and falsely say all kinds of evil against you because of me. Rejoice and be glad, because great is your reward in heaven, for in the same way they persecuted the prophets who were before you" (Matthew 5:11-12 NIV).

So what's a seer to do? First, accept that persecution is coming, and refuse to carry a persecution complex when it does. Second Timothy 3:12, "Yes, and all who desire to live godly in Christ Jesus will suffer persecution." Jesus said in John 15:18, "If the world hates you, you know that it hated Me before it hated you."

Next, pray for God to prepare you for the persecution. Ask Him to help you trust Him for the grace to endure persecution. Ask Him to strengthen you in your inner man. Ask Him to help you keep your mind set on things above. Ask Him to help you keep your eyes on Jesus. Ask Him to help you go deeper in your prayer life. And when the persecution comes, rejoice!

PRAYER

Father, in the name of Jesus, would You help me not to take on a victim mentality when the persecution comes. Prepare me to process persecution through Your perspective.

SEPTEMBER 4

WHAT'S YOUR SEER LEVEL?

And when the man went out to the east with the line in his hand, he measured one thousand cubits, and he brought me through the waters; the water came up to my ankles. Again he measured one thousand and brought me through the waters; the water came up to my knees....

Ezekiel 47:3-4

When Jesus walked the earth, He wasn't just baptized in the Holy Spirit at the River Jordan. He actually had the spirit without measure (John 3:34). That means there were no limits.

Of course, He was sinless. We are not. We don't have the Spirit without measure. Instead, we experience levels of the seer anointing. While we can grow in our seer gift, we don't decide the measure or the level. God chooses your level. Let's look at Ephesians 4:11-12, "And He Himself gave some to be apostles, some prophets, some evangelists, and some pastors and teachers, for the equipping of the saints for the work of ministry, for the edifying of the body of Christ."

The highest level of prophetic ministry is the office of the prophet. All seers are prophets, but not everyone who sees is a seer. The seer sees, but also helps believers gain confidence in their ability to see in the Spirit and stirs a hunger for intimacy with God through equipping. Seers also build up the Body of Christ by sharing what the Lord shows them.

Some believers have a stronger seer anointing than others by virtue of God's grace, as well as training and pursuit of the spiritual gift. They are not necessarily standing in the office of the prophet but they receive accurate prophetic words, visions, or dreams on a frequent or consistent basis.

People who operate in seer ministry may also tap into higher realms of the visual revelation, including hearing God's audible voice, experiencing angelic visitations, seeing open visions, or receiving revelation about names, dates, and future events. Again, that doesn't make them a seer. God just chose to open their eyes and ears at a higher level for a specific purpose.

Then there are those who see in the spirit irregularly, and mostly for their personal life. This is equivalent to the simple gift of prophecy. It's important to understand your seer level so you don't go out of bounds or into error. God can choose to elevate you at any time, but we can't elevate ourselves.

PRAYER

Father, in the name of Jesus, would You help me not to move beyond the grace and gifting You have appointed to me? Help me to understand my level and not strive to see into things that You haven't opened.

SEPTEMBER 5

USE DISCRETION, PLEASE

That you may preserve discretion, and your lips may keep knowledge.
Proverbs 5:2

A seer without discretion is like a fool who proclaims everything under the sun. Read that again.

Discretion is a heart attitude that shows restraint about what gets said or done publicly in the interest of protecting and preserving a person's privacy or dignity, or guarding the plans of God. Discretion is also an attribute associated with the discerning person; essential to the success of the ministry of a seer. It's operating in a way that goes unnoticed, below the radar of the enemy, according to *The Seer's Dictionary*.

Think about Nathan the prophet. He used deep discretion when he confronted David about his sin with Bathsheba and ordering the murder of her husband, Uriah, after he got her pregnant. Nathan didn't call a public assembly and he didn't immediately confront the king. In discretion, he shared a parable in private that led David to repentance (2 Samuel 11). That was the best possible outcome, and the wisest way to pursue it.

Discretion isn't just about preserving the dignity of another person and guarding God's plans, it's protecting your anointing and guarding your reputation. People trust a discreet seer who can discern whether their visual revelation demands private intercession, or is a warning or is to be shared with a few or one individual alone.

Think about it. The need to be discreet points to a revelation of sensitive information. Sometimes the person about which you receive that revelation is not ready to hear it. That's why prayer is always the best first response. I imagine Nathan prayed to God to get a strategy for how to bring David to repentance and also prayed that David would receive it. He could have had Nathan hanged!

A mature seer is a discreet seer—and a seer who understands that visual revelation can bring backlash. People may not like what you have to share. That's why part of the definition of *discreet* is "operating in a way that goes unnoticed, below the radar of the enemy." Discretion allows the seer to fulfill their calling to the fullest, so that they bring glory to God and are a help and light to His people.

PRAYER

Father, in the name of Jesus, I want to be a discreet seer. Help me to value discretion as much as discernment. Teach me how to walk in discretion for the sake of successfully fulfilling my assignment.

SEPTEMBER 6

WHEN THE BOOKS ARE SEALED

Now when the seven thunders uttered their voices, I was about to write; but I heard a voice from heaven saying to me, "Seal up the things which the seven thunders uttered, and do not write them."

Revelation 10:4

While God can allow you to look into books in Heaven—I once saw a library in Heaven, as I described in my book, *Decoding the Mysteries of Heaven's War Room*—some books are off limits until He chooses to allow the seal to be broken. According to *The Seer's Dictionary*, the book that is sealed, means "books that cannot be opened."

We see this reality in Revelation 5:1-3:

> And I saw in the right hand of Him who sat on the throne a scroll written inside and on the back, sealed with seven seals. Then I saw a strong angel proclaiming with a loud voice, "Who is worthy to open the scroll and to loose its seals?" And no one in heaven or on the earth or under the earth was able to open the scroll, or to look at it.

John wept because no one was found worthy to open and read the scroll, or to look at it. But an elder told him to stop crying because Jesus prevailed to open the scroll and loose its seals.

Later, in Revelation 5:9 we read: "And they sang a new song, saying: 'You are worthy to take the scroll, and to open its seals; for You were slain, and have redeemed us to God by Your blood out of every tribe and tongue and people and nation."

At other times, God may show you a vision and instruct you to seal it up until He releases you to share it. After Daniel received certain end times revelations, he received firm instructions about this book. Daniel 12:4 reads, "But you, Daniel, shut up the words, and seal the book until the time of the end; many shall run to and fro, and knowledge shall increase."

Isaiah experienced a similar mandate. We know Isaiah heard words of woe to Jerusalem. Then Isaiah 29:11 reads, "The whole vision has become to you like the words of a book that is sealed, which men deliver to one who is literate, saying, 'Read this, please.' And he says, 'I cannot, for it is sealed.'"

PRAYER

Father, in the name of Jesus, I know that not everything You share with me is meant to be shared with others. Help me be obedient to seal those truths that the Church and the world are not yet ready for.

SEPTEMBER 7

THE PRESUMPTUOUS SEER

Thus says the Lord God: "Woe to the foolish prophets, who follow their own spirit and have seen nothing!"

Ezekiel 13:3

If you don't want the reputation of a presumptuous seer, please read this slowly. What is a presumptuous seer, you ask?

In our context, *presumptuous* means "overstepping one's authority in the seer dimensions; one who draws conclusions based on soulish dot connections rather than waiting on the Holy Spirit's help to interpret visual revelation; to offer one's opinion in the name of prophecy," according to *The Seer's Dictionary*.

Deuteronomy 18:20 declares, "The prophet who presumes to speak a word in My name, which I have not commanded him to speak, or who speaks in the name of other gods, that prophet shall die."

While the King James Version of the Bible only mentions the words *presume, presumed, presumptuous* and *presumptuously* 11 times, the act almost always leads to death. Indeed, there are few things worse than a presumptuous seer. Deuteronomy 18:20 (NIV) declares, "But a prophet who presumes to speak in my name anything I have not commanded, or a prophet who speaks in the name of other gods, is to be put to death."

Mercy! Of course, we are living in a time of grace and even the most presumptuous seer won't be struck dead for this sin. Jesus died for the sin of the world, including our occasional presumptions. But we must ask ourselves, what is happening inside us, in our spirits, when we presume? Selah.

Look, the seer ministry is not an experiment in spirituality. It's not a Holy Ghost guessing game. Seers should be statesmen. A US ambassador to China would not presume to speak on behalf of the president just because a roundtable of delegates expected him to deliver some governmental wisdom. The ambassador could cause a war with his words if he speaks out of order.

Presumption can be a subtle trap. You can avoid presumption by taking every visual revelation to God in prayer and asking Him what He wants you to do with it. Remain teachable. Surround yourself with trusted mentors.

PRAYER

Father, in the name of Jesus, help me never to assume or presume that what I am seeing is from You. Help me not to presume the meaning without consulting You. Help me not to speak without permission.

SEPTEMBER 8

GETTING AHEAD OF THE ENEMY

For we do not wrestle against flesh and blood, but against principalities, against powers, against the rulers of the darkness of this age, against spiritual hosts of wickedness in the heavenly places.

Ephesians 6:12

I found an article I wrote in 2012 when I was editor of *Charisma* magazine. The title was, "Does Everyone Get This Much Spiritual Warfare?" Seers are going to deal with warfare.

As I matured in the spirit and in my understanding of spiritual warfare, which takes time and experience and knowledge of the Word, I began to realize that these attacks didn't just come out of nowhere. There were warning signs. There were dreams. There were inner checks.

But I hadn't been trained to understand this. I hadn't been trained to move before the enemy launched a fiery dart. I didn't know I could strike first. Striking first is what I call preemptive warfare. I started pressing in to see the enemy's weapon forming before it was launched.

When I pressed in for prophetic intelligence, God started training me in preemptive warfare. Now, I strike before the enemy launches. I block his hand before he builds momentum. I dismantle his assignment before it has a chance to manifest. I'm not perfect at it, but I am more strategic than I used to be. All seers need to master the skill of preemptive warfare.

Proverbs 27:12 (ESV) tells us, "The prudent sees danger and hides himself, but the simple go on and suffer for it." Preemptive warfare is Spirit-led, proactive action taken in the realm of the spirit before the enemy's plan is fully deployed. It's discerning a demonic plot before it plays out and launching a counterstrike by the Holy Spirit to dismantle the enemy's momentum in advance. You strike at the seed level—before the full-blown attack happens.

And this isn't just for you. As a seer, God will show you things for other people so you can shut them down in intercession. For example, if you wake up from a dream about a car accident involving a family member. Don't dismiss it—you fast, pray, anoint your house, and cancel the enemy's assignment. The next day, that family member narrowly avoids a wreck. That's preemptive—you struck before the manifestation. Check out my course on Strike First at www.schoolofthespirit.tv.

PRAYER

Father, in the name of Jesus, would You train me up in preemptive warfare? Would You help me see what the enemy is planning before he has a chance to deploy his strategy against me and others?

SEPTEMBER 9

THE ISAIAH SEER ANOINTING

In the year that King Uzziah died, I saw the Lord sitting on a throne, high and lifted up, and the train of His robe filled the temple.

Isaiah 6:1

Isaiah's seer anointing was put on full display in the first chapter of the book that bears his name. He pens a dramatic vision of the wickedness of Judah. But he didn't just see what was wrong. He saw the God who is right.

Isaiah's ministry was marked by encounters with Heaven and spectacular visions of God's glory. He also carried a scribe anointing that helped him record with great detail what he saw and heard. The Isaiah seer anointing comes with a revelation of God's holiness. These five verses marked his ministry forever, displaying his seer function to see the glory of the Lord. Read Isaiah 6:1-5:

> In the year that King Uzziah died, I saw the Lord sitting on a throne, high and lifted up, and the train of His robe filled the temple. Above it stood seraphim; each one had six wings: with two he covered his face, with two he covered his feet, and with two he flew. And one cried to another and said: "Holy, holy, holy is the Lord of hosts; the whole earth is full of His glory!" And the posts of the door were shaken by the voice of him who cried out, and the house was filled with smoke. So I said: "Woe is me, for I am undone! Because I am a man of unclean lips, and I dwell in the midst of a people of unclean lips; for my eyes have seen the King, the Lord of hosts."

Isaiah was issued beautiful Messianic prophecies, foretelling the coming of our Christ. In Isaiah 2, he prophesies about the Messiah's rule and reign seven hundred years before Jesus was born. Isaiah gives us his Messianic title "The Branch" in Isaiah 4. He speaks of the virgin birth in Isaiah 7 and calls him a stumbling stone in Isaiah 8. Indeed, I found twenty-five references, making the Messiah a key figure in his book.

Isaiah's ministry was marked by a blend of humility and boldness, always pointing people back to the majesty of God. Despite all the judgment prophecies in his book, he is known as a prophet of hope.

PRAYER

Father, in the name of Jesus, I want to see what Isaiah saw. There is so much wrong in the world today and so much demonic activity. I want to see the Messiah. Help me become seer of hope.

SEPTEMBER 10

RECEIVING SEER IMPARTATIONS

For I am yearning to see you, that I may impart and share with you some spiritual gift to strengthen and establish you. That is, that we may be mutually strengthened and encouraged and comforted by each other's faith, both yours and mine.

Romans 1:11-12 AMPC

Impartation is both a scriptural concept and a spiritual reality. Impartation is a divine transfer that releases an ability you didn't have before. Through impartation, the Holy Spirit gives or grants you a spiritual gift, revelation, or power that you need to fulfill your purpose.

I've received many impartations that have changed my life and ministry forever. Notice I said "received." You can't learn or earn an impartation. You have to receive impartation by faith. The ministry of impartation is clear in the Bible.

Impart in this context simply means "impart" or "give," according to the *KJV New Testament Greek Lexicon. Merriam-Webster's Dictionary.* defines "impart" as "to give, convey or grant from as if from a store." God has a great storehouse of gifts and He wants to impart what will strengthen you in your calling. *Young's Literal Bible* translates this "to give a share of."

We can receive impartation from God Himself or from anointed men and women through the laying on of hands. Paul told Timothy to stir up the gift he received by the laying on of his hands. Timothy received impartation from Paul through the ministry of laying on of hands, which we see in other parts of Scripture.

Scripture shows at least five areas of impartation: blessings (Genesis 28:1-4); Baptism of the Holy Spirit (Acts 8:14-20); spiritual gifts (1 Timothy 4:14); service (Acts 6:1-8); and healing ministry (Mark 7:27).

Of course, you can receive an impartation directly from God without anyone laying hands on you or teaching the Word. This often comes through asking, seeking, and knocking for more of Him, but can manifest suddenly. More than once, I have felt the weight of glory from a direct impartation from the Lord.

PRAYER

Father, in the name of Jesus, if I need an impartation, I trust You to order my steps to the people who can release it. But also, Lord, help me learn to trust that You can personally give me everything I need.

SEPTEMBER 11

WHEN GOD PRUNES YOU

I am the true vine, and My Father is the vinedresser. Every branch in Me that does not bear fruit He takes away; and every branch that bears fruit He prunes, that it may bear more fruit.

John 15:1-2

In a vision, I saw the Lord standing over a great bush with pruning shears. The silver shears were glistening as light bounced off the blade. He opened and closed the shears quickly, almost as if to send an audible signal to the bush that He was about to perform an unwanted surgery.

In the vision, the Lord began to prune the bush, carefully clipping here and there and then standing back to examine His work. The bush wound up flat on top, like a carefully sculpted work of art, but He didn't stop there. He looked at the base of the bush, the thick woody part that was thrust into the soil. He saw weeds around and about it.

With gardening gloves on, He pulled each weed with precision, pulling up the entire root of the weeds but leaving the base of the bush intact. He then packed fertilizer around the base of the bush, and almost instantly it started sprouting beautiful blooms from the top.

I heard the Lord say, "I am indeed pruning your life. I am pruning your relationships. I am pruning away those things that hinder growth in your life. I am pulling out the weeds and dealing with the little foxes that spoil the vine. As I am cutting them away, you may feel the pain of loss, but understand that the joy of growth will follow the adjustment."

Pruning means to cut off or cut back parts of for better shape or more fruitful growth. This is a biblical concept that seers must learn to embrace if they want to walk in the places God has in mind for them. Jesus said in John 15:1-2, "I am the true vine, and My Father is the vinedresser. Every branch in Me that does not bear fruit He takes away; and every branch that bears fruit He prunes, that it may bear more fruit." Let Him prune you, even when it hurts.

PRAYER

Father, in the name of Jesus, help me to yield to Your pruning process, knowing that You have something more in mind. Help me to discern between Your pruning shears and the enemy's attacks.

SEPTEMBER 12

DON'T QUENCH YOUR SOURCE

Do not quench (suppress or subdue) the [Holy] Spirit.
1 Thessalonians 5:19 AMPC

It's easy to quench the Spirit when you are learning to navigate the seer dimensions. Until you learn how to move in these realms, you may find yourself overwhelmed by what you see. The enemy often tries to get young or less experienced seers to abandon their gift.

What does it mean to quench the Spirit? It's essentially spiritual malpractice in which one interferes or puts a stop to what the Holy Spirit is saying or doing in an atmosphere, according to *The Seer's Dictionary*. First Thessalonians 5:19 simply says, "Do not quench the Spirit." The NLT says, "Don't stifle the Holy Spirit." The GWT puts it this way, "Don't put out the Spirit's fire."

So how do seers, in particular, quench the Spirit? Well, we quench the Spirit when we don't acknowledge Him in our daily life. We quench the Spirit when we don't follow His leading. We quench the Spirit when we ignore Him or pay more attention to other things. We live in a distracted culture, but church is a place where we should give God our undivided attention.

But more specifically to the seer's function, we quench the Spirit when we don't press into what we see because it's inconvenient. When we don't press into what we see because we are too busy, it stifles Him. We quench the Spirit when we shrug off visual revelation that doesn't immediately make sense to our natural mind. Revelation is an invitation to interpretation.

We quench the Spirit when we operate in fear at any level, such as fear of missing it, fear of backlash, fear of man's rejection, or fear of seeing the dark side of the seer dimensions. We quench the Spirit when we rush ahead of Him to share revelation before His timing. There are many ways we quench the Spirit. Let's remember that He is gentle as a dove and yield to Him.

PRAYER

Father, in the name of Jesus, I don't want to quench Your Spirit and I ask You to forgive me if I have. Help me make what You are showing me a priority. Help me to yield to Your Spirit.

SEPTEMBER 13

DON'T IGNORE QUICK FLASHES

Wisdom is the principal thing; therefore get wisdom. And in all your getting, get understanding.

Proverbs 4:7

Have you ever seen a quick flash of something in the seer dimensions? If we aren't careful, if we ignore those quick flashes, we could be missing opportunities to receive deeper visual revelation.

What is a quick flash? It's something you see in the spirit realm for mere seconds. It's something that flashes by, disappearing almost as fast as it appeared, according to *The Seer's Dictionary*. If you are easily distracted, or you are inexperienced in the ways of God in the seer dimensions, you can miss an important message from the Holy Spirit.

In fact, I would dare say that quick flashes are one of the most overlooked ways God invites us into the seer dimensions. We may not think it's significant because of the brevity of the visuals, but those who have eyes to see are summoned to stop and take notice.

I was in Berlin in 2019. I came in on a train from Belgium. When I got off the train, I was on my phone trying to get an Uber when I felt the Holy Spirit nudge me to look up. When I did, I saw a truck that said "Artemis" on the side panels. It was illuminated to me.

That was a quick flash. I discerned from that quick flash that Artemis, which is the goddess Diana, was a stronghold over that city. This is essentially a Jezebelic spirit. When I preached at the prophetic conference in Berlin, I was able to share my experience and it resonated with the congregation.

So what am I saying? The Holy Spirit uses quick flashes—glimpses—to get our attention. Yes, you need to test quick flashes because it could be your imagination. But don't brush them off. Take the time to recognize and respond and you may step into something deeper than you expected. Quick flashes position you for profound spiritual insight.

PRAYER

Father, in the name of Jesus, I don't want to miss even the faintest impression You show me. Help me catch and value those quick glimpses. Help me to pay closer attention in the spirit.

SEPTEMBER 14

KEEPING A QUIET SPIRIT

Whoever restrains his words has knowledge, and he who has a cool spirit is a man of understanding.

Proverbs 17:27 ESV

If you want to observe what's going on in the seer dimensions, you need to have a cool spirit. A cool spirit is a calm and quiet spirit.

Consider the words of the apostle Peter, "Let it be the inward adorning and beauty of the hidden person of the heart, with the incorruptible and unfading charm of a gentle and peaceful spirit, which [is not anxious or wrought up, but] is very precious in the sight of God" (1 Peter 3:4 AMPC).

So what is a quiet spirit? It's a spirit ready in a tranquil state in full readiness to receive revelation from God, according to *The Seer's Dictionary*. It's difficult to see in the spirit when you are anxious, angry, or otherwise disturbed.

Psalm 131:2 reads, "Surely I have calmed and quieted my soul, like a weaned child with his mother; like a weaned child is my soul within me."

A quiet spirit is one that is quick to listen, slow to speak, and slow to anger (James 1:19). Put another way, before you attempt to enter the seer dimensions, you need to take the time to quiet your soul, still your emotions, and focus your attention on God. From this tranquil state, you are positioned to tap into the mysteries of God.

How do you do this practically? Center your mind on God. Practice being still and knowing that He is God. Isaiah 30:15 tells us, "...in quietness and confidence shall be your strength...." The strength of your spiritual vision corresponds, in some degree, to a quiet spirit.

The enemy will try to distract you with anxious or busy thoughts. Don't let him. Bind up anything that disturbs your spirit. It takes practice, but over time it gets easier. Set your mind to be like a weaned child, resting in His presence so you can see clearly what He wants to say.

PRAYER

Father, in the name of Jesus, help me to maintain a cool spirit throughout the day. Help me catch myself when my soul gets disquieted or disturbed in any way. I want to walk in a cool spirit.

SEPTEMBER 15

TRAVELING IN THE SPIRIT

Now when they came up out of the water, the Spirit of the Lord caught Philip away, so that the eunuch saw him no more; and he went on his way rejoicing.

Acts 8:39

You have probably watched science fiction movies that focus on time travel. Traveling in the Spirit is not time travel, but it does interrupt the cycle of time because God can transport someone from one place to another at any given moment in time. Traveling in the Spirit is an ecstatic state. One of the clearest examples of Spirit travel in the Bible is found in the book of Acts.

We see the Holy Spirit whisking Philip away on assignment after he ministered the gospel to the Ethiopian eunuch passing through Jerusalem. After the eunuch was saved, Philip baptized him in water and was suddenly gone: "Now when they came up out of the water, the Spirit of the Lord caught Philip away, so that the eunuch saw him no more; and he went on his way rejoicing. But Philip was found at Azotus. And passing through, he preached in all the cities till he came to Caesarea" (Acts 8:39-40).

Some Bible commentators insist the Holy Spirit merely urged Philip to go to Azotus immediately after this event so he wouldn't be overly invested in the life of the eunuch. But *Matthew Poole's Commentary* reveals, "Philip was suddenly and extraordinarily taken away from the eunuch's sight and company, that thereby the eunuch might be the more assured of the truth of those things which had been taught by him."

And *Gill's Exposition of the Entire Bible* tells us, "The Spirit of the Lord took up Philip, just as he is said to lift up Ezekiel, between earth and heaven, (Ezekiel 8:3) and carried him above the earth as far as Azotus. The Alexandrian copy, and one of Baez's, and some others, read the words thus, 'the holy Spirit fall upon the eunuch, but the angel of the Lord caught away Philip.'"

If Elijah was taken to Heaven—raptured before he died—and he was, then it should not be difficult to believe the same Holy Spirit could take Peter instantly to another city. And it should not be difficult to believe the Holy Spirit can do the same today, since God does not change.

The purpose of traveling in the Spirit is not for a great story, but a great move of God. People can be saved, healed, and delivered through ecstatic encounters of this kind.

PRAYER

Father, in the name of Jesus, I understand I cannot travel in the spirit at will, but I believe this is a possibility. If it's Your will, I am willing to go wherever You send me, like Philip the evangelist.

SEPTEMBER 16

THE KIM CLEMENT SEER ANOINTING

But now bring me a minstrel. And it came to pass, when the minstrel played, that the hand of the Lord came upon him.

2 Kings 3:15 KJV

Kim Clement, the South African seer-prophet-worship leader who passed into glory in 2016 at the age of sixty, experienced dramatic visions and released prophetic words that are still coming to pass in our day.

Kim Clement's seer anointing walked in "multiplied visions." *The Seer's Dictionary* defines multiplied visions as "a season of increase in visions; numerous visions; a strong increase in visions." In other words, the visions seem to multiply. This was the norm for Clement as he worshipped.

Kim Clement had an anointing to ascend to the throne room and see what many others did not. He not only saw, but could interpret what he was seeing in real time. His messages carried weight in the spirit as he looked beyond the veil of space and time. He often saw far into the future and faced criticism for revelation that seemed impossible to come to pass.

On May 18, 2013, Clement had what he called a "very, very clear vision" about the year 2018. The man of God was seeing five years into the future a significant historical event that few at the time likely believed. He saw into 2027 despite passing away in 2016. His visions were extremely accurate.

One of the most interesting examples is how Clement prophesied the election of President Donald Trump—"Trump shall become a trumpet." Trump, as we know, did become president after Clement's passing.

Clement's ministry was also marked by dreams and visions. He once told TBN, "I knew I was a prophet when I had certain kinds of dreams about the future and when I spoke about it, people actually hated me for it. ...I would see futuristic things and it would cause so much stirring." Indeed, Clement had dramatic visions and inspired even *naba* prophets to press into visual revelation.

Kim Clement's prophetic words and visions continue coming to pass after his untimely death, inspiring more prophets to speak forth about what they see.

PRAYER

Father, in the name of Jesus, thank You for using Your servant Kim Clement as an example of what is possible in seer dimensions. Help me learn whatever You would like to me to glean from his ministry.

SEPTEMBER 17

OVERCOMING SEER TRIALS

Beloved, do not think it strange concerning the fiery trial which is to try you, as though some strange thing happened to you.

1 Peter 4:12

Seers face fiery trials like anybody else, but they also face unique trials. When you understand what you may face, you won't think it strange.

Seers can face the trial of missing it, the trial of people telling them they aren't really seeing in the spirit, the trial of demonic activity that overwhelms them, or even the trial of dry seasons where you see nothing.

We need to see our trials the way God sees them. If perception is reality, then a godly perspective of your trials and tribulations can deliver you from your worst enemy: your own unrenewed mind.

I can't tell you how many times I've allowed the perspective of my unrenewed mind to dictate my thoughts, feelings, and emotions in the midst of a trial. I can't tell you how many times I didn't think I could take another step; how many times I felt like giving up, calling it quits, throwing in the towel—and moving to some remote tropical island where the devil was less likely to find me.

Of course, later I realize that things weren't really as bad as they looked with my natural eyes instead of the eyes of the Spirit. Paul put it like this: "For those who live according to the flesh set their minds on the things of the flesh, but those who live according to the Spirit, the things of the Spirit. For to be carnally minded is death, but to be spiritually minded is life and peace" (Romans 8:5-6).

When you want a prophetic perspective—God's perspective—on anything from your daily trials to your future decisions, wait on the Lord. Expect Him. Look for Him. Hope in Him. He will give you a prophetic perspective on your situation so you can see the proverbial forest instead of getting overwhelmed by the trees.

Once your mind is renewed, you will have the peace that passes all understanding—and it will guard your heart and your mind in Christ Jesus. Your perception will still be your reality, but your renewed mind will offer you God's perspective of the victory that is yours in Christ.

PRAYER

Father, in the name of Jesus, help me not to think it strange when fiery trials come. Remind me to seek Your perspective on the seer trials I face so that I can respond rightly instead of feeling like quitting.

SEPTEMBER 18

INTERACTING WITH ANGELS

Now the angel who talked with me came back and wakened me, as a man who is wakened out of his sleep.

Zechariah 4:1

Angelic interventions, encounters, and interactions are not rare. The more we are aware of the presence of God, the more we will be aware of His angels on assignment. There are over three verses in Scripture about angels—far too many to ignore. And it's not enough to agree they exist. We are to work with angels and sometimes that means interactions, including communication.

Lot spoke with angels. In Daniel 8 and 9, the prophet Daniel had a conversation with Gabriel. And Zechariah talked to angels over and over again in conjunction with the visions he had. Consider Zechariah 4:1-2, "Now the angel who talked with me came back and wakened me, as a man who is wakened out of his sleep. And he said to me, 'What do you see?'...." Isaiah interacted with seraphim. The angel put a coal of fire to his mouth. How would you like that kind of angelic encounter?

Gabriel appeared to Zachariah and announced his barren wife, Elizabeth, would bear a son, John the Baptist. After their conversation, Gabriel struck him mute because of his unbelief. Angels appeared to Joseph concerning Jesus several times in dreams. There was no conversation, but there was an interaction—a message. Throughout the book of Revelation, John spoke with angels in visions.

Not all communication from angels comes in the form of a direct sit-down with a member of the heavenly host. Angels speak in many ways. Scripture speaks of tongues of angels in 1 Corinthians 13:1. Angels speak a prophetic language. Angels prophesy and help us interpret dreams and visions. We see this over and over again. They prophesy the word of the Lord. The prophetic announcements from Gabriel were prophetic words.

Angels can speak a parabolic language. Angels can sing over you. Angels can communicate with you through light. There's a lot to learn about communicating with angels. I teach more about this in my School of the Seers in www.schoolofthespirit.tv. But here is the number-one thing you need to know: don't worship angels. If it weren't tempting, John would not have fallen down before them twice in Scripture.

PRAYER

Father, in the name of Jesus, help me to understand the protocols of interacting with angels. Give me revelation from the Scripture through the many examples You've left for my instruction.

SEPTEMBER 19

SEEING BEYOND YOUR TIME

Declaring the end from the beginning, And from ancient times things that are not yet done, saying, "My counsel shall stand, and I will do all My pleasure."

Isaiah 46:10

Kim Clement, John Paul Jackson, and David Wilkerson were all men who saw beyond their time. They had clear dreams, visions, and Holy Spirit intelligence that didn't come to pass until after they died—and some of the manifestations of what they saw are still in the waiting.

I call this long-range sight. What you see is not always for the now. Sometimes it's for later, much later. If you don't know what to do with long-range sight, you may end up confused, frustrated, or discouraged. You may end up releasing something prematurely or releasing it as a now word when the timing is for the future. That can damage your credibility.

Daniel, Joel, and Zechariah saw into the end times. Talk about long-range sight! But they understood it was for a later time. Joseph saw years ahead and likely never realized he would go through thirteen years of betrayal, false accusations, and even prison before he saw the fulfillment of his dreams.

The first step in handling long-range sight is to discern the timing of what you see. Ask the Holy Spirit to show you the timing. Ask for the Issachar anointing to understand the times. Ask Him whether the visual revelation is an urgent word, something to warn about for the future, or something to pray through.

Remember what the Lord said to Habakkuk: "Write the vision and make it plain on tablets, that he may run who reads it. For the vision is yet for an appointed time; but at the end it will speak, and it will not lie. Though it tarries, wait for it; because it will surely come, it will not tarry" (Habakkuk 2:2-3). Take a page from Habakkuk's book. Write it down and wait for it. But don't wait passively. Interpret. Pray. Prepare. Teach.

Visual revelation may feel urgent according to your timeline, but we have to operate on God's timeline if we hope to be effective and accurate. Remember what Peter, inspired by the Holy Spirit, said in 2 Peter 3:8, "...with the Lord one day is as a thousand years, and a thousand years as one day." What if what you see, like Jackson, Clement, and Wilkerson, is not for your lifetime?

PRAYER

Father, in the name of Jesus, help me to understand that not everything I see is for now, or even for my lifetime. Help me to understand the timing of what You show me so I can release the revelation accurately.

SEPTEMBER 20

WHEN WITCHCRAFT CLOUDS YOUR EYES

Now it happened, when Joram saw Jehu, that he said, "Is it peace, Jehu?" So he answered, "What peace, as long as the harlotries of your mother Jezebel and her witchcraft are so many?"

2 Kings 9:22

Every time I have a massive encounter with God, it seems like I get attacked with some expression or assignment of witchcraft shortly after, sometimes the very same day.

At first, I didn't connect the dots, but then after a while I recognized a pattern: when God increases a seer's sight, the enemy often rises to shut it down, unless you shut him down first.

Paul seems to have experienced this phenomenon of attacks after encounters. In 2 Corinthians 12:1-7, he describes being caught up into Heaven—whether in the body or out he did not know. But he was in Paradise and heard inexpressible words. Next we read, "So to keep me from becoming proud, I was given a thorn in my flesh, a messenger from Satan to torment me and keep me from becoming proud" (2 Corinthians 12:7 NLT). Notice that God didn't send the messenger of satan, but he allowed it.

Now that I see the encounter-warfare pattern in my life, I am better equipped to discern and shut down witchcraft retaliation against my seer eyes. And if it slips by me, then I can shut it down quickly before it settles in. When witchcraft attacks, it can lead you into deception. It can make you feel like you've lost your spiritual sight. It can even cause a burning sensation in your natural eyes or physical pain in your body.

In Scripture, we see Queen Jezebel, operating in what we call today a Jezebel spirit, practiced witchcraft. Second Kings 9:22 speaks of Jezebel and her witchcrafts, and one of her primary attacks was shutting down the prophetic voice.

Thank God He has given us authority over all expressions of witchcraft. Jesus tells us in Luke 10:19, "Behold, I give you the authority to trample on serpents and scorpions, and over all the power of the enemy, and nothing shall by any means hurt you." Remember, after you have an encounter, armor up. The enemy wants to steal the seed from your heart.

PRAYER

Father, in the name of Jesus, would You help me not to be ignorant of the devil's devices? Help me to be sober and vigilant. Help me to gird up the loins of my mind so my seer eyes are not attacked.

SEPTEMBER 21

DISCERNING DEMONIC PORTALS

Now I say to you that you are Peter (which means "rock"), and upon this rock I will build my church [congregation], and all the powers of hell will not conquer it.

Matthew 16:18 NLT

It's one thing to sense or feel something off in the spiritual atmosphere, it's another thing to discern the source of what you are feeling. And it's yet another thing—another layer of seer discernment—to understand what is being released that needs to be shut down.

I am talking about demonic portals. We don't see a chapter and verse that calls out demonic portals, but Jesus did say in Matthew 16:18, "...on this rock I will build My church, and the gates of Hades shall not prevail against it." These gates of hell are often associated with a pagan grotto in Caesarea Philippi. People believed this was an entrance to the underworld. A portal.

A demonic portal is an opening in the spirit realm where wicked spirits ascend and descend. It allows a free flow of demonic activity in a home, church, city, business, or nation. It's a corridor for trafficking violence, oppression, confusion, and every evil work. A portal is an open door that we need to shut.

Some seers have more of a spiritual warfare bent and are wired to pick up on these portals before others notice. You may see a vision of the portal or of demonic activity in the second heaven. You may see dark clouds in the spirit working to cloak demonic trafficking. You may see shadows. You may see a literal door in the spirit. Or you may see actual demons moving through the portal.

What you see may not be literal. It could be symbolic or parabolic. Serpents often represent lying or deception, for example, while flies can represent corruption. Fog can represent confusion. Always ask the Holy Spirit what you are seeing. Identify the spirit so you are not, as Paul said, beating the air. We want to be accurate so we can shut it down.

How do you shut it down? Name the function of the portal and command the portal to shut. If it is a portal of fear say, "I command this portal of fear to be closed now, in the name of Jesus." Be specific because the devil is legalistic. Of course, some portals have legal rights that you have to discern before making a command. This is spiritual warfare 101. Check out my spiritual warfare courses at www.schoolofthespirit.tv.

PRAYER

Father, in the name of Jesus, would You help me discern demonic portals? Help me to understand what demons are trafficking through these portals and to take a stand in the name of Jesus to shut it down.

SEPTEMBER 22

DON'T LET ANYONE PIMP YOUR GIFT

And through covetousness shall they with feigned words make merchandise of you: whose judgment now of a long time lingereth not, and their damnation slumbereth not.

2 Peter 2:3 KJV

There was once a young seer with a breaker anointing who could preach down Heaven. He was humble and Christ-centered, but when the speaking circuit saw his ability to raise an offering, he started gaining ground on some of the largest platforms in the Body of Christ. This twenty-something raised millions of dollars. Today, he's operating in a false spirit.

What happened? When people see the gift of God in you, they may do more than celebrate you. They may try to use your gift for their own personal gain. They may exploit your anointing to serve their purposes. I call this pimping the gift. This is a dangerous trap for unsuspecting seers who just want to serve the Lord.

Peter warned of those who merchandise spiritual gifts: "And in their covetousness (lust, greed) they will exploit you with false (cunning) arguments. From of old the sentence [of condemnation] for them has not been idle; their destruction (eternal misery) has not been asleep" (2 Peter 2:3 AMPC).

How do seers fall into this trap? One way is through inexperience. The young seer I mentioned probably had no idea people were using him to gain money. He probably thought he was serving his elders. But seers are also seduced through flattery or straight up manipulation. Eventually, this leads to learned behavior and instead of other people pimping your gift, you start pimping your own gift.

If our motive for ministry is money, our motive is wrong. God is love and everything we do should be to His glory as we seek to advance His Kingdom—not our kingdom. Remember, 1 Timothy 6:10 (AMPC) tells us, "For the love of money is a root of all evils; it is through this craving that some have been led astray and have wandered from the faith and pierced themselves through with many acute [mental] pangs."

Guard your heart. Stay accountable to people in your life who can tell you what you may not be able to see. Stay grounded in the Word of God and pursue humility.

PRAYER

Father, in the name of Jesus, would You help me to guard my gift from people who want to use me for the wrong purposes? Help me discern people's motives and not fall into the trap the enemy sets for me.

SEPTEMBER 23

SEEING THE RANKS OF ANGELS

For by Him all things were created that are in heaven and that are on earth, visible and invisible, whether thrones or dominions or principalities or powers. All things were created through Him and for Him.

Colossians 1:16

Did you know angels have ranks? As a seer, it's important to understand the ranks of angels you may see in the spirit.

Pseudo-Dionysis, a Christian philosopher of the late 5th century, describes angels ranked into three hierarchies and nine orders. As he explains it, the first hierarchy contains seraphim, cherubim, and thrones. The second hierarchy contains dominions, virtues, and powers. And the third hierarchy contains principalities, archangels, and angels.

In his hierarchy, seraphim are the highest order of angels. *Strong's Concordance* defines *seraphim* as majestic beings with six wings, human hands or voices in attendance upon God. You might say these are God's armorbearers who take care of His throne room. Cherubim are second in the first order of angels. *Strong's Concordance* defines cherubim as angelic beings that flank God's throne. We see cherubim appear 66 times in Scripture.

Then there are thrones, which can be either good or evil. Next are dominions. *HELPS Word Studies* offers a slightly different definition: "a power exerting itself in a particular jurisdiction." Moving down the list are virtues. In line with Jewish angelic hierarchies, Pseudo-Dionysis and Saint Thomas Aquinas in his *Summa Theologica* speak of virtues, and point to relation with the Greek word *dunamis* in Ephesians 1:21. One of Strong's definitions of *dunamis* is "power consisting in or resting upon armies, forces and hosts." They believed these angels work with God in signs and miracles in the world.

Then comes the powers. The Greek word for *powers* in this verse is *exousia,* which means, "power, authority, weight, especially: moral authority, influence." We see an angel in the book of Revelation who has the power over fire (Revelation 14:18). After that are principalities. *Vine's Expository Dictionary* reveals that principalities are "supramundane beings who exercise rule."

Finally are archangels and then angels. The most famed archangel—and the only archangel mentioned by name in the Bible—is Michael. Archangels contend with demons (Jude 9). The Greek word for *angel* is *angelos* and in the New Testament takes on the masculine form; there is no corresponding feminine form of the word. Angels are essentially messengers.

PRAYER

Father, in the name of Jesus, I know angels and demons have ranks. Help me to understand the ranks of angels and demons so I can respond rightly and receive their ministry.

SEPTEMBER 24

ANCHOR YOUR SIGHT IN THE WORD OF GOD

The entrance of Your words gives light; it gives understanding to the simple.

Psalm 119:130

Every seer must become a student of Scripture. It's not just knowing what the Bible says. It's about letting the Bible form your internal grid for judging, interpreting, and applying what you see.

Paul wrote these Spirit-inspired words to his spiritual son Timothy, "Study and be eager and do your utmost to present yourself to God approved (tested by trial), a workman who has no cause to be ashamed, correctly analyzing and accurately dividing [rightly handling and skillfully teaching] the Word of Truth" (2 Timothy 2:15 AMPC).

Scripture is the plumb line. Without it, the accuracy of our interpretations are at risk. If you want to grow in seer accuracy, immerse yourself in the Word of God. A seer needs the Word of Christ, the Seer, dwelling in them richly (Colossians 3:16). I dare say the richer you are in the Word, the richer you are in the seer dimensions.

Paul also told Timothy, "Every Scripture is God-breathed (given by His inspiration) and profitable for instruction, for reproof and conviction of sin, for correction of error and discipline in obedience, [and] for training in righteousness (in holy living, in conformity to God's will in thought, purpose, and action), so that the man of God may be complete and proficient, well fitted and thoroughly equipped for every good work" (2 Timothy 3:16-17 AMPC).

The more fluent you are in Scripture, the more precise you'll be in interpreting symbolic language, angelic activity, and panoramic visions. King David wrote, "Open my eyes, that I may see wondrous things from Your law" (Psalm 119:18). Some seers may rather have their eyes opened to see Jesus, but when God opens your eyes to the Word you are seeing one aspect of Jesus, who is the Word.

You are also renewing your mind to truth so that you can avoid error. How can a seer cleanse his way? By taking heed to God's Word (Psalm 119:9).

PRAYER

Father, in the name of Jesus, make me a lover of the truth. Give me a hunger for Your Word. Help me to use the Word as an anchor for my visual revelation in judging, interpreting, and applying what I see.

SEPTEMBER 25

SEE IT AGAIN!

> *But the Helper, the Holy Spirit, whom the Father will send in My name, He will teach you all things, and bring to your remembrance all things that I said to you.*
>
> John 14:26

I had a vision of the war room in Heaven. It was an epic vision with so much detail that there was no natural way I could remember everything I saw. And there was no way I could write down what I was seeing while I saw it or I would lose spiritual focus.

Maybe you can relate. I am sure Daniel faced that dilemma with his epic visions, as did John the apostle when he saw the dramatic events recorded in the book of Revelation. It's impossible to write all that in the moment, so we have to rely on the Holy Spirit who will put us into remembrance of all things. And we can tap into a seer technique I call "reenvisioning."

In Daniel 7:28, after an epic vision, Daniel said, "This is the end of the account. As for me, Daniel, my thoughts greatly troubled me, and my countenance changed; but I kept the matter in my heart." Reenvisioning allows us to treasure what God has shown us and uncover hidden wisdom.

Can you see the value of reenvisioning? This is not as necessary when you see a simple picture, but when you have a profound encounter and you know in your spirit there is more to see than what you could take in, reenvisioning is a strategic tool in your seer toolbox. It's revisiting the revelation until you wring out of it every ounce of what the Holy Spirit wants to reveal.

After the vision of the war room in Heaven, I immediately asked the Holy Spirit to show me the vision again. I recorded every word of what I saw. Honestly, I saw much more the second time than the first, sort of like if you see a movie two or three times and you notice things you didn't see before.

You can also reenvision visual revelation that you've recorded in your journal. If the Holy Spirit reminds you of a vision, go back to your record of it and meditate on it. That's one way you reenvision older revelation. Sit in His presence, still your soul, and ask Him to let you see it again!

PRAYER

Father, in the name of Jesus, help me not to get overwhelmed by the volume of revelation in a dream or vision. Rather, help me take it all in, knowing that You can help me reenvision what I might miss.

SEPTEMBER 26

THIS WILL HINDER YOUR EYES

Who are you to judge the servant of another? To his own master he stands or falls; and he will stand, for the Lord is able to make him stand.

Romans 14:4

Many "sins" will harm your spiritual sight, but judgment and criticism are two of the fastest ways to dim your eyes. Consider Christ's words in Matthew 7:1-5 (AMP):

> Do not judge and criticize and condemn [others unfairly with an attitude of self-righteous superiority as though assuming the office of a judge], so that you will not be judged [unfairly]. For just as you [hypocritically] judge others [when you are sinful and unrepentant], so will you be judged; and in accordance with your standard of measure [used to pass out judgment], judgment will be measured to you. Why do you look at the [insignificant] speck that is in your brother's eye, but do not notice and acknowledge the [egregious] log that is in your own eye? Or how can you say to your brother, "Let me get the speck out of your eye," when there is a log in your own eye? You hypocrite (play-actor, pretender), first get the log out of your own eye, and then you will see clearly to take the speck out of your brother's eye.

Can you see the direct correlation between judgmentalism and hindered sight? Notice the one with the critical spirit is staring at a very small particle in their brother's eye. If you've ever had an irritant in your eye, you know how difficult it can be to locate it.

The implication here is that the judger is putting a magnifying glass on something small to make a big deal out of it instead of walking in love and covering it, praying about it, or speaking the truth in love. This hypocrisy causes a major blind spot in your spiritual sight. Some translations call the beam of timber a telephone pole. Can you imagine seeing anything at all with a telephone pole sticking out of your eye?

Seers and seeing people see things others don't. That doesn't give one a right to criticize or judge—it gives you a responsibility to pray. God is not showing you someone's faults so you can condemn but so you can intercede. God is love and sees through eyes of love—even though He sees our faults.

PRAYER

Father, in the name of Jesus, help me not to take on a critical spirit and call it discernment. Help me to walk in love and compassion and focus on Christ rather than criticizing.

SEPTEMBER 27

REFILLED WITH FRESH OIL

...but ever be filled and stimulated with the [Holy] Spirit.
Ephesians 5:18 AMPC

The Holy Spirit who dwells in you is the ultimate Seer. He sees all things. He is also the One who opens your spiritual eyes and shows you things to come (John 16:13-15). The more room we make for the Holy Spirit in our lives—and the more we yield to Him—the more sensitive we will be to what He is trying to show us.

Sometimes, that means getting filled, or refilled, with His Spirit. It's been said that Christians are sometimes "leaky." That's not exactly how it works but we do see in Scripture that believers in the early Church were filled with the Holy Spirit more than once.

Ephesians 5:18 tells us to be filled with the Holy Spirit. But the Greek word *filled* in that verse is actually the continuous present tense. It actually means, "Be continually filled with the fullness of the Holy Spirit." Wow!

Peter was filled again in Acts 2 with the rest of the believers in the Upper Room, but he was filled again just two chapters later! (See Acts 4:7-9.)

Then we see a little further down in Acts 4 after Peter and John returned to their own company and told the believers what happened.

Let's look at Acts 4:31: "And when they had prayed, the place where they were assembled together was shaken; and they were all filled with the Holy Spirit, and they spoke the word of God with boldness."

Paul was filled with the Holy Spirit as he confronted a sorcerer (Acts 13:8-10). Again, we see a fresh infilling in Acts 13:50-52, "But the Jews stirred up the devout and prominent women and the chief men of the city, raised up persecution against Paul and Barnabas, and expelled them from their region. But they shook off the dust from their feet against them, and came to Iconium. And the disciples were filled with joy and with the Holy Spirit."

Do you need to be filled again?

PRAYER

Father, in the name of Jesus, would You fill me once again with the Holy Spirit? I know I need more and more of You. Help me to decrease so that You can increase and work through me at Your will.

SEPTEMBER 28

NEFARIOUS NOCTURNAL ATTACKS

You shall not be afraid of the terror by night....

Psalm 91:5

For years and years and years, every October, I experienced an onslaught of witchcraft coming against my mind and body. Once I finally learned how to shut down that demonic cycle, the enemy started using a different tactic. Since the spiritual forces of darkness could not slow me down by day, the attacks started coming at night.

Over a two-week period, I had some of the worst nightmares I'd ever had in my life. I wouldn't even speak about them out loud because I didn't want to release the power of death over my life.

I call it nocturnal warfare. This is a phrase that I coined to describe what was happening to me, and others. All demons like the dark, but some night-loving demons are prone to attack after dark.

Simply stated, nocturnal warfare is warfare that happens at night. But it's more than spiritual warfare that happens after dark. It usually happens while you are asleep or while you are trying to sleep. Nocturnal warfare leads to daytime warfare. In other words, it has a ripple effect. The effect of nocturnal warfare seeps into your day. It's like a double whammy as it ripples through your whole life.

With the nocturnal warfare I experienced, the idea was to completely wear me out at night so that I couldn't resist in the day. It also hindered my dream life—or I should say it overtook my divine dream life with demonic visuals. I was exhausted, so it was harder to discern daytime attacks.

We see nocturnal warfare in several Scriptures. Jesus spoke about nocturnal warfare in Matthew 13:24-28, "...The kingdom of heaven is like a man who sowed good seed in his field; but while men slept, his enemy came and sowed tares among the wheat and went his way. But when the grain had sprouted and produced a crop, then the tares also appeared. So the servants of the owner came and said to him, 'Sir, did you not sow good seed in your field? How then does it have tares?' He said to them, 'An enemy has done this.'"

Seers, guard yourself from nocturnal warfare. It's not a matter of if it comes, but when it comes. I have a course titled Nocturnal Warfare at www.schoolofthespirit.tv.

PRAYER

Father, in the name of Jesus, I know the enemy is roaming about like a roaring lion seeking someone to devour. Help me guard myself against nocturnal warfare that can exhaust me and hinder divine dreams.

SEPTEMBER 29

SEEING INTO SEASONS

And He changes the times and the seasons....

Daniel 2:21

Ecclesiastes 3:1 tells us, "To everything there is a season, a time for every purpose under heaven." God is the God of times, seasons, and purposes. A *season* is "a time characterized by a particular circumstance or feature" or "a suitable or natural time or occasion," according to *Merriam-Webster's Dictionary*.

God changes our times and seasons. There was a time for David to sit on the throne, but that came after many years in the wilderness. There was a time for Joseph to rule Egypt, but that came after painful setbacks. We can't change our times and seasons.

There are also seasons for cities, nations, ministries, and so on. The seer can see into seasons. In the natural, we can just check the weather. But we have to start looking into the spiritual climate and the spiritual seasons. Each season has a purpose in the big picture of God's plans. Isaiah 46:10 (ESV) says, "declaring the end from the beginning, and from ancient times the things that are not yet done, saying, 'My counsel [purpose] shall stand, and I will do all My good pleasure.'"

It's important to know the purpose of each season so you can pray the right prayers and get prepared for what the Lord is going to do. If you don't see the season you are coming into or quickly recognize the season you are in, one of five things will happen: You could miss your *kairos* moment. You will get another opportunity but it's a self-imposed delay. You will not be prepared for what God is doing and not realize the maximum benefits for that period in your life. You might stumble into the season and figure it out but you are not maximizing the opportunity. You may not be prepared for what the enemy is doing in your life.

God expects us to discern the seasons. We discern spiritual seasons with our spiritual eyes. There are new seasons. Isaiah 43:18-19 prophesied, "Do not remember the former things, nor consider the things of old. Behold, I will do a new thing, now it shall spring forth; shall you not know it? I will even make a road in the wilderness and rivers in the desert."

Seeing into seasons is critical. Seasons inform your intercession. Zechariah 10:1 says, "Ask the Lord for rain in the time of the latter rain. The Lord will make flashing clouds; He will give them showers of rain, grass in the field for everyone."

PRAYER

Father, in the name of Jesus, would You help me see into seasons so I can prepare myself and prepare the Body of Christ? Give me the ability to see so I can intercede for Your will to be done in any given season.

SEPTEMBER 30

THE SAFE WAY INTO MYSTICAL DIMENSIONS

His delight is in the law of the Lord, and in His law he meditates day and night.

Psalm 1:2

I was meditating on Revelation 4:1 again and again. I read it over and over. I pondered each word. I spoke it out loud. Revelation 4:1 reads, "After these things I looked, and behold, a door standing open in heaven. And the first voice which I heard was like a trumpet speaking with me saying, 'Come up here, and I will show you things which must take place after this.'"

I don't know how long I was meditating on that verse. I lost track of time as I focused in with deeper meditation on a few specific words and phrases in that verse. The words *"looked," "behold," "door standing open"* and *"come up here"* seemed to leap off the page and into my heart, somehow bypassing my natural mind. It was as if the Word was entering my spirit by osmosis.

My thoughts were, *If there is an open door in Heaven, I want to walk through it.* Suddenly, I saw myself walking toward a magnificent castle. I saw a large opening with a walkway that ran directly through the castle. As I walked to the midway point of what seemed to be a sacred path, the castle rolled up and went inside my spirit.

In that moment I heard the Lord say, "The Kingdom of God is within you. Everything you need is within you. All the resources you require are within you. You don't even have to pull it down from Heaven. It is within you. Speak it out of your mouth and you will see it. Christ in you, the hope of glory. The riches in glory in Christ are within you."

Meditating on the Word of God is a safe way to enter the mystical dimension. Throughout the psalms of David, we see his dedication to meditation. He starts off in Psalm 1:2 talking about the godly man: "His delight is in the law of the Lord, and in His law he meditates day and night" (Psalm 1:2). When you set your heart to meditate on His Word day and night, you will find easier entry into mystical dimensions.

PRAYER

Father, in the name of Jesus, I want to enter into the mystical dimensions Your way. Your way is the only safe way. Would You help me meditate on Your Word day and night and delight in Your law?

OCTOBER

...Daniel had a dream and visions of his head while on his bed. Then he wrote down the dream, telling the main facts.

Daniel 7:1

OCTOBER 1

THE JOEL SEER ANOINTING

The sun shall be turned into darkness, and the moon into blood, before the coming of the great and awesome day of the Lord.

Joel 2:31

If you read the book of Joel, you'll discover it's sort of like a miniature book of Revelation. It's essentially a condensed version of what John the Revelator saw. Like John's apocalyptic visions, Joel's book is marked by prophetic warnings about the end times and redemptive hope.

The Joel seer anointing calls believers to operate in the Spirit and prepare the Bride of Christ for a never-before-seen outpouring of God's presence and power on earth.

It was Joel, after all, who prophesied these words: "And it shall come to pass afterward that I will pour out My Spirit on all flesh; Your sons and your daughters shall prophesy, your old men shall dream dreams, your young men shall see visions. And also on My menservants and on My maidservants I will pour out My Spirit in those day" (Joel 2:28-29). You are part of this generation—a prophetic movement that crosses generational, gender, and ethnic boundaries.

Joel was also anointed to warn of sin that leads to judgment—but always with redemption. Joel 2:25 prophesies, "So I will restore to you the years that the swarming locust has eaten, the crawling locust, the consuming locust, and the chewing locust, my great army which I sent among you." Seers, remember that God is the God of restoration. Yes, judgment—and even wrath—will mark the end times, but God's heart is always to restore. He is the God of mercy.

Joel was an end-times forerunner. More than two thousand years ago, he prophesied, "And I will show wonders in the heavens and in the earth: Blood and fire and pillars of smoke. The sun shall be turned into darkness, and the moon into blood, before the coming of the great and awesome day of the Lord" (Joel 2:30-31).

Joel's seer anointing carries a threefold mandate of boldness, urgency, and hope. His ministry was marked by end-times visions that aimed to help align God's people with purpose and prepare them for future glory.

PRAYER

Father, in the name of Jesus, would You give me an appreciation and understanding of Joel's seer anointing. Help me glean from his threefold mandate of boldness, urgency, and hope.

OCTOBER 2

WHEN YOUR REVELATION LEADS TO REBUKE

So he told it to his father and his brothers; and his father rebuked him and said to him, "What is this dream that you have dreamed?"
Genesis 37:10

I've heard and read stories about people getting rebuked for sharing prophetic dreams—even 100 percent accurate prophetic dreams that are truly from the heart of God. Sometimes the rebuke comes from people who have zero discernment or who are trying to hide something. But other times it's the seer's own fault. Such was the case with Joseph.

When Joseph was 17 years old, he had a prophetic dream and rushed to tell his brothers. Joseph must have known his brothers didn't like him, so why did he share the dream? Perhaps he was excited about his visual revelation. It's also possible he was operating in pride. In any case, he was unfamiliar with prophetic protocol. After all, there was no school of the prophets.

Have you ever been rebuked for sharing a true prophetic dream? Many seers have experienced criticism—from people they know and from strangers online—for sharing prophetic dreams. The rebuke stings and can make you second-guess whether you saw accurately if you meditate on it too long. You might even feel the pain of rejection.

Rather than embracing a spirit of rejection when people don't receive your seer ministry, ask the Lord to show you the root of the backlash. It could be people who hear your dream have no discernment. It could be that you missed the mark. It could be that you delivered the message in the wrong spirit. It could be that you misinterpreted the dream when you shared it.

That said, in my experience, one of the most common reasons people reject true prophetic dreams, visions, and words is due to wrong timing. Just because we receive prophetic communication from Heaven doesn't mean we need to immediately share what we saw or heard. That was perhaps Joseph's biggest mistake.

Proverbs 25:11 says, "A word fitly spoken is like apples of gold in settings of silver." If that's true for words, how much more for visual revelation? Timing of the release is almost as important as accuracy in the prophetic. A right word delivered at the wrong time can cause people to reject you—and it can kill your prophetic reputation.

PRAYER

Father, in the name of Jesus, would You help me not to take rejection of my visual revelation personally? In humility, help me examine my heart and my visual revelation to understand why it was met with rebuke.

OCTOBER 3

EMBRACING THE NEXT LEVEL

Then you will call upon Me and go and pray to Me, and I will listen to you. And you will seek Me and find Me, when you search for Me with all your heart.

Jeremiah 29:12-13

As I've studied the Bible and pressed into the Holy Spirit's revelation, He has given me what I believe are key words for seers in this generation and beyond. Here is one prophetic word from God I received before leaving for my life-changing journey through Sweden and London:

I am mantling seers in this season—seers who have turned to see the voice speaking to them, to record the dreams and visions I have revealed to them, and to steward the mysteries I've unlocked to them—with an anointing to enter into a new dimension of My grace, My revelation, and My glory. I am inviting My seers to forget about the persecution of the past and embrace the next level of My calling for them.

I am opening the eyes of believers who have been crying out for their hearts to be enlightened. I will pour out visions, dreams, spiritual encounters, and utterances that eye has not seen nor ear heard. I am calling you to rise up and look again and again and again; to be watchful in the spirit because I will show you things to come in the days ahead. I will show you new dimensions of My glory. I will show you the enemy's operations. I will even show you the intents and motives of hearts.

You can go as deep and far as you choose to go. I am inviting you to study My Word. I am inviting you to study My heart. Your dedication to the study of your gift will unlock more and more, and the mantle will cause you to operate in higher realms. Don't neglect the study of My Word. Stay rooted and grounded in My holy Scripture for this is your safeguard against deception in an hour when I will pour out a new wave of anointing on My seers.

Do not move beyond the boundaries of My Word, but do not reject spiritual experiences without deep study because I am going to do some things in this hour that go beyond milk. I am offering My seers the meat of the Word—deeper revelations many around you will not understand but that you will embrace by faith.

PRAYER

Father, in the name of Jesus, I say yes to Your invitation. Give me the grace to turn to You, record what I see diligently, and steward the mysteries that You share with me. I want to go deeper.

OCTOBER 4

DISCERNING THE ROOT SYSTEM

To another the working of miracles, to another prophecy, to another discerning of spirits, to another different kinds of tongues, to another the interpretation of tongues.

1 Corinthians 12:10

Growing up, one of my chores was to pull the weeds in my dad's garden. I didn't like pulling weeds. It was hard work. So I just twisted off the top. I didn't realize at the time that the root system was still living under ground. Those weeds came right back within a few days!

Through that experience, I learned that it's one thing to deal with the fruit of a problem. It's another to get to the root of why the problem exists. Until you sever the root, you'll continue to be unfruitful. God graces some seers to see the root of a person's, church's, city's, or nation's problems so the enemy's influence can be plucked up and God's will can manifest.

According to *The Seer's Dictionary*, a root is "something unseen that feeds what is seen; Seers can often see the roots of issues in the realm of deliverance." Remember, deliverance is not merely available to people. God delivered the nation of Israel. God heals nations, but not before the root is plucked up.

John the Baptist put it this way: "And even now the ax is laid to the root of the trees. Therefore every tree which does not bear good fruit is cut down and thrown into the fire" (Matthew 3:10). God told Jeremiah "...to root out and to pull down, to destroy and to throw down, to build and to plant" (Jeremiah 1:10). Again, the purpose of uprooting is so God's will can manifest.

As I always say, an enemy exposed is an enemy defeated, but an enemy that is hidden cannot be forbidden. You can't uproot what you don't discern. Symptoms can be misdiagnosed and send you on a wild goose chase in healing or deliverance ministry; but when you can see the root of what is causing depression, addiction, or affliction, you can cut it off in the name of Jesus.

Seers, one of the most vital ways your gift operates is in the realm of healing and deliverance. God often uses seers to expose the hidden roots of bondage that keep people trapped. While others may address surface symptoms, seers have the unique ability to see beneath the surface into the spiritual root systems that fuel oppression, addiction, or affliction.

PRAYER

Father, in the name of Jesus, would You help me to look beyond the fruit of the problems in people's lives, churches, cities, and nations? Help me see the root so I can severe it and set the captives free.

OCTOBER 5

SCHOOL OF THE SEERS

Be diligent to present yourself approved to God, a worker who does not need to be ashamed, rightly dividing the word of truth.

2 Timothy 2:15

When Jesus ascended to the right hand of the Father, He gave gifts. Ephesians 4:11 tells us He gave some to be apostles, some prophets, some evangelists, some pastors, and teachers for the equipping of the saints for the work of service.

One of the primary mandates of a New Testament seer is to equip the saints to hear from God and to see accurately. Every believer has the capacity to see in the spirit. The Holy Spirit shows us things to come (John 16:13). But many believers do not discern what God wants them to see in or about their lives, which is one reason there is an unhealthy dependence on prophets and seers.

Schooling is biblical. Samuel launched the school of the prophets in the Old Testament days. Some Bible translations say, "company of prophets" or "sons of prophets." In 1 Samuel 19:18-24, we see Saul running into one of Samuel's companies prophesying. Samuel was there with them. Suddenly, the Spirit of God came upon the men with Saul and they started prophesying. Then Saul started prophesying.

But the schools of the prophets didn't make someone a prophet. Sure, there were prophets among them. There were also priests who did not prophesy. Think of the Old Testament schools of the prophets as seminaries, of sorts, where those who sensed God's call to service would band together for training.

Again, you can't make yourself into a seer but reputable schools of seers can help you discern how to judge and interpret what you see in the spirit. These schools can help you develop your seer acuity, build accuracy, and operate with safeguards that protect your prophetic credibility.

Seer schools are where your eyes are opened wider to the realms of the spirit. This is where you sharpen your knowledge of the Scripture as it relates to visual revelation. This is where you learn the foundations and advanced levels of cooperating with God in the seer dimensions.

I've discovered that the topic is inexhaustible. There is always more to learn. There are layers of revelation. That's why I started a School of the Seers in February 2018 that is still going on today. Each month, I release a new teaching on the seer dimensions, whether it's dreams, visions, encounters, trances, discernment, angels, seer warfare, or some other topic that's related to the seer ministry. I do this as part of my School of the Spirit (www.schoolofthespirit.tv).

PRAYER

Father, in the name of Jesus, enroll me in Your School of the Seers. Help me study what the Word says, not just about encounters, but how the seers of old carried themselves as they represented You.

OCTOBER 6

SEEING INTO TIMES

The sons of Issachar who had understanding of the times, to know what Israel ought to do....

1 Chronicles 12:32

We often talk about the Issachar prophets, but Issachar seers are rising up as well. First Chronicles 12:32 speaks of "the sons of Issachar who had understanding of the times, to know what Israel ought to do."

Time is a concept every seer needs to grasp. God doesn't move through time the way we move through time. In the temporal realm, time is linear. In the eternal realm, God can step into and out of time at will. He is moving in the spirit realm rather than the earth realm, where God has set the times and seasons. You can see into times through visions or dreams or discernment.

We could be seeing into a single moment or an era. We could be seeing into a day or an age. We could be seeing into the past, present, or future. We could be seeing into an occasion or eternity. We could be seeing into a life or a generation.

Jesus saw what His Father was doing in a present tense, in real time. John 5:19 reveals, "Jesus answered and said to them, 'Most assuredly, I say to you, the Son can do nothing of Himself, but what He sees the Father do; for whatever He does, the Son also does in like manner.'"

This is real-time vision into the seer dimensions. You can see in real time what God shows you about Himself, angels, demons, or anything else in the spirit realm. You could see a picture over someone's life that pertains to the now. Faith is now, and sometimes time vision is now.

Jesus said, "Your father Abraham rejoiced to see My day, and he saw it and was glad" (John 8:56). The AMPC says, "Your forefather Abraham was extremely happy at the hope and prospect of seeing My day (My incarnation); and he did see it and was delighted."

Abraham saw into the future. Abraham actually saw into the times Jesus walked the earth. God can show you anything in the future because there is no future to God. We know Daniel saw into the end times. John the Revelator saw into the end times. Joseph saw into a time of famine through his dreams. Isaiah saw into eternity. Ask God to let you see into times.

PRAYER

Father, in the name of Jesus, would You allow me to see into times past, into current times, and into future times? Would You give me an Issachar anointing and give me strategies?

OCTOBER 7

THE SEER'S PATH

Small is the gate and narrow the road that leads to life, and only a few find it.

Matthew 7:14 NIV

Caught up in the spirit during prayer, I saw a road in the spirit—a pathway. As I kept on looking I noticed something curious. Crosses were laying on the ground. One after another, I saw crosses strewn along this narrow path.

Just then, the Holy Spirit gave me an interpretation about what I was seeing. These crosses were abandoned. Believers who were once on fire for God left their crosses behind when the pressure to be conformed into the image of Christ was too great. Instead of clinging to Him and casting their cares, they cast their cross and turned back to nominal Christianity—or no Christianity at all.

I was shocked as I kept on looking. I saw cross after cross after cross. It almost looked like a graveyard, except instead of death to self, these abandoned crosses represented those who died to their highest calling.

These crosses belonged to people who started down the path to self-denial. These crosses belonged to people who started down the road to the knowledge of the holy. These crosses belonged to people who started down the lane of life—that narrow road that's constricted by pressure—and when that pressure became too great, when the cost became too much, they abandoned the cross and turned back.

I am reminded of Christ's words in Matthew 16:24-26:

> Then Jesus said to His disciples, "If anyone desires to come after Me, let him deny himself, and take up his cross, and follow Me. For whoever desires to save his life will lose it, but whoever loses his life for My sake will find it. For what profit is it to a man if he gains the whole world, and loses his own soul? Or what will a man give in exchange for his soul?"

You can't embrace God at the highest levels if you do not embrace the work of the Cross—and embrace your own cross. Seers walk a narrow path.

PRAYER

Father, in the name of Jesus, would You Help me embrace the work of the Cross? Help me stay on the narrow path that leads to You, so I don't stumble onto the path that leads to destruction. Help me walk circumspectly.

OCTOBER 8

SEEING DEMONS

Then the seventy returned with joy, saying, "Lord, even the demons are subject to us in Your name."

Luke 10:17

From the time I was a small child, I saw in the spirit. Unfortunately, I didn't see angels. I didn't see Jesus. I saw demons. I believe that was the enemy's first attempt to shut down my seer eyes. He wanted me to have a terrifying experience in the seer dimensions so I would not want to have a second look.

The first time I saw demons was when I was about three years old. I remember seeing something that looked like an alligator in my bedroom, hiding in the corner right behind the door. It was so scary I would scream at the top of my lungs. My mother would come running, thinking I was just having a bad dream. I know now that I saw a spirit of fear.

If you've ever seen a demon in the spirit it can elicit several emotions, from surprise to fear to hysteria. You may see demons in dreams or in visions, or during trances or out-of-body experiences. But if God opens your eyes to show you the demonic realm, He has a reason for it. God is not random. He has a purpose for everything He does, and all demons are subject to Him. So we don't have to be afraid.

Scripture points to times when people saw demons in the spirit. So we have scriptural backing for seeing demons in the spirit realm when God opens our eyes to them. The apostle John saw demons in the spirit in a vision in his chronicles we call the book of Revelation.

Don't be afraid of demons. If you fear them, you open yourself to attack. Like dogs, demons smell fear. Also, don't have conversations with demons. Scripture forbids talking to demons, which includes familiar spirits (Leviticus 19:31). And if the demons talk, don't believe what they tell you. They lie. Don't follow instructions from a demon.

Demons will work to lead you astray. Demons will give you evil suggestions. Remember how the snake suggested to Eve in the garden that she would not die if she ate the fruit from the tree of the knowledge of good and evil. She took a demonic instruction. I teach more about seeing demons in my School of the Spirit.

PRAYER

Father, in the name of Jesus, help me not to be afraid if I see demons in the spirit realm, even if it's a fearful sight. You did not give me a spirit of fear, You gave me a spirit of discernment. Help me understand what to do with what I see.

OCTOBER 9

RSVP TO YOUR INVITATION

"Come up here, and I will show you things which must take place after this." Immediately I was in the Spirit; and behold, a throne set in heaven, and One sat on the throne.

Revelation 4:1-2

Have you ever received a direct invitation from Almighty God? By invitation, I mean a request for your presence. At times, God will give you an auditory invitation that sounds something like this, "Come up here." We see John the Revelator receive such an invitation twice.

Revelation 4:1-5 records an invitation to John the Beloved:

> After these things I looked, and behold, a door standing open in heaven. And the first voice which I heard was like a trumpet speaking with me, saying, "Come up here, and I will show you things which must take place after this." Immediately I was in the Spirit; and behold, a throne set in heaven, and One sat on the throne. And He who sat there was like a jasper and a sardius stone in appearance; and there was a rainbow around the throne, in appearance like an emerald. Around the throne were twenty-four thrones, and on the thrones I saw twenty-four elders sitting, clothed in white robes; and they had crowns of gold on their heads. And from the throne proceeded lightnings, thunderings, and voices. Seven lamps of fire were burning before the throne, which are the seven Spirits of God.

I imagine he was glad he accepted the invitation. But notice he didn't even have time to say yes. This, I believe, was a heart yes.

Revelation 11:11-12 records an invitation to the three witnesses who were killed and rose again: "Now after the three-and-a-half days the breath of life from God entered them, and they stood on their feet, and great fear fell on those who saw them. And they heard a loud voice from heaven saying to them, 'Come up here.' And they ascended to heaven in a cloud, and their enemies saw them."

That's intense. Notice how with both invitations, there was an ascension. In some ways, this is as much a command as an invitation. Know this: when you receive such an invitation, your eyes will see wondrous things.

PRAYER

Father, in the name of Jesus, if You call me I will respond. I will lay aside whatever I am doing to answer Your call. Help me to ready myself for Your invitations. Help me prepare for the deeper things and higher places.

OCTOBER 10

RECEIVING THE SECRET COUNSEL OF GOD

For the perverse person is an abomination to the Lord, but His secret counsel is with the upright.

Proverbs 3:32

When I was in the business arena, I always had executive coaches. Coaches are valuable in helping you see what you cannot see and processing opportunities.

After my last coaching program ended, I asked the Lord if I should get another executive coach. He said, "I will be your coach." He has done a much better job and it doesn't cost me a penny. It only costs me time, and it's time well spent because I tap into the secret counsel of God for my life—and sometimes for cities and nations.

What is counsel? Counsel is advice. God has secret counsel for you that will help you succeed in any situation. The Hebrew word for *counsel* in this verse includes the concepts of familiar conversation and intimacy with God.

In Psalm 16:7, David wrote, "I will bless the Lord who has given me counsel...." David was tapping into the secret counsel of God. David was successful in battle because he depended on the secret counsel of God. Think about it. David never lost a battle. God told him when to go fight and gave him strategies. God also gave him the blueprint for Solomon's temple.

Isaiah 9:6 tells us one of the names of God is Wonderful Counselor. Psalm 33:11 tells us His secret counsel is wonderful and His counsel stands forever. Proverbs 19:21 tells us the counsel of the Lord always stands. And Psalm 64:2 records David crying out to the God of secrets to preserve him from the secret counsel of the wicked.

God often gives us counsel in secret so the enemy is not aware of the wisdom He is imparting that prepares us to overthrow his wicked plots. But God can give us private counsel any time we need it. For seers, this often comes as visual revelation. God can show you a picture, envelop you in a life-changing encounter, or speak to you through a dream.

But know this, you need to position yourself for this secret counsel. That means a life of surrender. David understood this saying, "The secret of the Lord is with those who fear Him, and He will show them His covenant" (Psalm 25:14).

PRAYER

Father, in the name of Jesus, help me position myself for the secret counsel You want to share with me. Help me not to lean on my own understanding but rather trust You to show me what I need to see.

OCTOBER 11

WHAT'S YOUR SEER PARADIGM?

O Lord, how great are Your works! Your thoughts are very deep.
Psalm 92:5

We all have a paradigm in life. A paradigm is the lens through which we see life's events. It's our philosophy. For example, some people have a "lack paradigm" that keeps them from taking financial risks and advancing business. Some have a "performance paradigm" that causes them to overextend and people please.

Now let's translate that to the seer dimensions. A paradigm is your theological framework, such as how you view Jesus, prophetic ministry. or the end times, according to *The Seer's Dictionary*. Why does this matter? Because your paradigm affects how you filter, interpret, and apply what you see in the spirit.

If you see God as angry, that filter will cause you to lean toward judgment in your interpretations of what you see—even if judgment isn't on God's heart. If your paradigm is grace, you may do quite the opposite and miss the meaning of what you saw when a warning was in order.

If you grew up in a denominational church, your paradigm may be much different than if you didn't grow up in a church at all. If you believe in a pre-tribulation rapture, your interpretation or how you apply what you see in the spirit may be much different than if you believe in a post-tribulation rapture. Can you see it?

We need to have God's paradigm. In Isaiah 55:8-9 God tells us, "For My thoughts are not your thoughts, neither are your ways My ways.... For as the heavens are higher than the earth, so are My ways higher than your ways and My thoughts than your thoughts."

God's paradigm is the only correct paradigm in the seer dimensions. So how do we get God's paradigm?

Our seer paradigm needs to be rooted in His character, His ways, and His Word. We start by surrendering our thoughts and ways and asking Him to show us the truth—the real truth. We get in the Word without any lens and seek to understand His ways better. We study to get to know His character. He never changes. We renew our minds with the Word. If you want to be accurate in seer ministry, you need His paradigm.

PRAYER

Father, in the name of Jesus, I want to have an accurate seer paradigm. Would You please show me if I am thinking or seeing through a wrong lens? I want to be accurate in how I interpret what You show me.

OCTOBER 12

STRANGE "SEER" FIRE

A little leaven leavens the whole lump.

Galatians 5:9

We are seeing the rise of a new generation of seers, but we are also seeing the rise of false fire. One expression of false fire is seer revelation that appears powerful but is polluted. You need to discern false fire in your midst so you don't come into agreement with false visual revelation. Anyone can tap into false fire.

In Leviticus 10:1-2, the Bible warns us of the cost of false fire: "Then Nadab and Abihu, the sons of Aaron, each took his censer and put fire in it, put incense on it, and offered profane fire before the Lord, which He had not commanded them. So fire went out from the Lord and devoured them, and they died before the Lord."

Some Bible translations call it unauthorized fire, the wrong kind of fire, strange fire, fire that was not holy, and unacceptable fire. God takes the seer dimensions seriously. False fire is no light matter. And it doesn't just affect the one offering it—it can poison an entire atmosphere.

Strange seer fire is revelation that does not originate from the Holy Spirit. It is driven by flesh, emotion, or an impure heart. It mimics true encounters but lacks the anointing. And it often aims to manipulate outcomes or people.

Strange fire clouds discernment. If we tolerate it, we risk confusing emotion with anointing and charisma with authority. This can eventually lead us into false doctrines, counterfeit movements, and dangerous alignments. Know this: the Holy Spirit will not inhabit what is unclean or impure. False fire contaminates the atmosphere and stifles the Holy Spirit. First Thessalonians 5:19-21 tells us, "Do not quench the Spirit. Do not despise prophecies. Test all things...."

When we operate outside of God's Spirit, we enter into unauthorized realms. That's where familiar spirits and divination can gain access—especially in seer ministry. When we offer strange fire, we're stepping into territory that belongs to God alone. It's spiritual trespassing. God judged Nadab and Abihu because they offered what He had not commanded.

PRAYER

Father, in the name of Jesus, would You help me discern when someone is operating in strange seer fire? And, please, help me never cross this line. I want to use my gifts in ways that glorify You.

OCTOBER 13

SEEING HIDDEN TREASURES IN SECRET PLACES

I will give you the treasures of darkness and hidden riches of secret places, that you may know that I, the Lord, who call you by your name, am the God of Israel.

Isaiah 45:3

When I was a kid, I loved going on treasure hunts. We searched for clues that would lead us to a hidden prize. I didn't always find it, but I still enjoyed the search. We can find parallels in the spirit realm.

Spiritual treasures and riches are hidden in the seer dimensions. You can search for them in prayer, but you can only access them as the Holy Spirit opens your eyes. Several Scriptures point us to these realities, which should give us enough spiritual curiosity to ask the Holy Spirit to show us hidden treasures in secret places so we can pray them into the natural realm.

In Isaiah 45:3, for example, God gives us a hint about what's available in the secret dimension: "I will give you the treasures of darkness and hidden riches of secret places...." One of those hidden treasures is likened to wisdom in Proverbs 2:4, which is noteworthy because Job wished God would show his critical friends "the secrets of wisdom" (Job 11:6).

Although God will pour out wisdom on those who ask, there are secrets of wisdom that unlock greater wisdom. These often come in the form of keys in the seer realm. When you see keys, look carefully to see if they are marked wisdom. Often wisdom keys have a large oval handle at the top with a thinner shaft.

In the Parable of the Hidden Treasure, Jesus shares a truth that you can meditate on to enter into this seer dimension: "Again, the kingdom of heaven is like treasure hidden in a field, which a man found and hid; and for joy over it he goes and sells all that he has and buys that field" (Matthew 13:44).

If you are going to go on a treasure hunt in the secret dimension, start with the Word of God. Remember, He is the Revealer of secrets. The secret dimension should be treated with the utmost respect. After all, these are secrets. If He is allowing you to see these secret treasures, He expects you to grab hold of them in faith for yourself and others.

PRAYER

Father, in the name of Jesus, I want to go on a treasure hunt in the seer dimensions. I want to see the treasures You've laid up for me so I can access Your grace through faith in prayer. Help me see the treasures.

OCTOBER 14

GATEKEEPING SEERS

Then the watchman saw another man running, and the watchman called to the gatekeeper and said, "There is another man, running alone!" And the king said, "He also brings news."

2 Samuel 18:26

I heard the Lord say, "The enemy is trying to burn down the gates." In ancient times, this was literal. Now, the Lord is speaking figuratively. The enemy is targeting gates at all levels of society—the seven mountains and beyond.

This is not a new strategy, but it's escalated as the enemy is no longer interested in merely coming through the gates. He wants to burn them completely down so there is no resistance to his wicked plans. He wants to dominate, changing times and laws so that all manner of idolatry and immorality is the norm.

Some seers have a gatekeeping function. A gate is a legal access point. When I go to London, I have to go through passport control on the way in. A gate is a border or boundary. A gate is a portal. It's a place where angels ascend and descend, or through which demons enter in the spirit. A gate intends to stop easy access. In the simplest terms, think of a dog gate in your house that keeps your dog out of the living room.

Spiritually speaking, gatekeepers are a type of intercessor. A gatekeeper is one who guards the gate or one who controls access. An intercessor is one who intercedes or one who stands between the enemy and God's people to forbid access or between God and His people to plead for them. So a gatekeeper intercessor guards access to the gates, opening and closing them, through prayer.

Gatekeeping seers have the keys of the Kingdom, and need to use them strategically after the Lord shows them what is going on in the spirit realm. Jesus said in Matthew 16:19 (AMPC), "I will give you the keys of the kingdom of heaven; and whatever you bind (declare to be improper and unlawful) on earth must be what is already bound in heaven; and whatever you loose (declare lawful) on earth must be what is already loosed in heaven."

Seers, start looking for what to bind and loose. Check out my series on The Gatekeeper anointing at www.schoolofthespirit.tv.

PRAYER

Father, in the name of Jesus, I am willing to be used in any function that helps Your Kingdom. Would You teach me more about the gatekeeper anointing and how it functions in the seer dimensions?

OCTOBER 15

ARE YOU A REMNANT SEER?

Yet I have reserved seven thousand in Israel, all whose knees have not bowed to Baal, and every mouth that has not kissed him.

1 Kings 19:18

Elijah was a remnant prophet who felt like he was the only one for the Lord and His covenant with Israel. In fact, he said so three times in Scripture. God corrected Elijah, saying, "I have reserved seven thousand in Israel, all whose knees have not bowed to Baal, and every mouth that has not kissed him" (1 Kings 19:18). In other words, he was part of a remnant but he was not the only one.

You can't blame Elijah for feeling the way he did, most of the prophets in his day either fled from Jezebel or were hiding in caves. He confronted Ahab alone. He confronted the false prophets at Mount Carmel alone. He didn't have a company of prophets cheering him on.

What are the characteristics of a remnant seer? Like Elijah, remnant seers sometimes feel like they are the only one standing. Remnant seers make themself of no reputation. Remnant seers are often hated. Leonard Ravenhill said, "The prophet in his day is fully accepted of God and totally rejected by men." Jesus is our prototype Seer, saying, "If the world hates you, you know that it hated Me before it hated you" (John 15:18).

Remnant seers don't tickle people's ears. Remnant seers don't always tell people what they want to hear. They tell people what God has shown them, which is another reason they may be hated. Remnant seers like in the 2 Timothy 4:3 (AMP) cause tension:

> For the time will come when people will not tolerate sound doctrine and accurate instruction [that challenges them with God's truth]; but wanting to have their ears tickled [with something pleasing], they will accumulate for themselves [many] teachers [one after another, chosen] to satisfy their own desires and to support the errors they hold.

Remnant seers aren't afraid of persecution. Remnant seers suffer with a smile. James 5:10-11 tells us, "My brethren, take the prophets, who spoke in the name of the Lord, as an example of suffering and patience. Indeed we count them blessed who endure. You have heard of the perseverance of Job and seen the end intended by the Lord—that the Lord is very compassionate and merciful."

PRAYER

Father, in the name of Jesus, I know there is always a remnant in a nation, city, church, or group who doesn't seem to fit in. They stand out and stand up for Your purposes. Help me walk among the remnant.

OCTOBER 16

WHEN YOU SEE SOMEONE'S SECRET SINS

You have set our iniquities before You, our secret sins in the light of Your countenance.

Psalm 90:8

Have you ever seen someone's secret sin? Why would God show you someone's secret sin? Certainty not to judge, gossip, or condemn, though that is what some immature seers do. There are two key reasons why God may show you someone's secrets.

First, for your own protection. It could be that someone is secretly lying to you. They may have wrong motives toward you. They may be plotting to cause you harm or maybe they are just looking to use you as a stepping stone. If you are a leader, they may be planning a church split or a slander campaign. That would qualify as a secret sin.

The second reason God will show you someone's secret sin is for the sake of intercession. In fact, prayer should always be your first response. When God shows you a secret someone is hiding, you need to pray. First, pray for confirmation so the enemy doesn't tempt you to make a false accusation.

Pray for wisdom on what else He may want you to do with what you know. Sometimes, you just need to pray that God will expose it since a dream or vision does not qualify as primary evidence. Other times, He may tell you to approach the person privately about it, especially if they are struggling with personal sin.

The secret sin isn't always some ill-motive toward someone. Sometimes the secret is a hurt or wound in someone's heart or a mental health issue that they are hiding that is leading them into a sinful lifestyle. In this case, they don't want anyone to know how hurt they are so they don't ask for help or prayer, but they have open doors for the enemy. God can show it to you so you can pray for them.

Be very careful. The enemy can easily fool you into projecting your own sin onto another's life. When the Pharisees dragged forth a woman caught in the act of adultery, Jesus was clear: He who has no sin should cast the first stone (John 8:7). Treat these experiences with tremendous wisdom. Be slow to speak and quick to pray.

PRAYER

Father, in the name of Jesus, I don't particularly want to see someone's secret sin, but if it's necessary to protect myself or others, I am willing to see what You want to show me. Help me be a restorer, not an accuser.

OCTOBER 17

BEWARE A BIASED EYE

Then Peter opened his mouth and said: "In truth I perceive that God shows no partiality."

Acts 10:34

If your eye is biased, you may see what other people want you to see rather than what God wants you to see. What's more, if your eye is biased it can affect how you judge, interpret, and apply your visual revelations. Beware a biased eye.

What is a bias? A bias is a bent or a tendency to favor one thing over another. It could be a prejudice, but it could also just be a preference. I am biased toward vanilla ice cream. It's not evil, but it is a bias.

Samuel was a seer who discovered a bias in 1 Samuel 16 when he set out to anoint the next king of Israel. Samuel called Jesse, David's father, to bring his sons before him. God didn't immediately speak to Samuel about which one of them he had chosen to be king.

"When they came, he looked on Eliab, and said, 'Surely the anointed of the Lord is before Him!'" (1 Samuel 16:6). Why did Samuel assume Eliab was the next king? One reason may have been because Eliab was Jesse's eldest son and the blessing was typically conferred upon the eldest. Eliab was also tall and attractive, which signaled strength.

Before Samuel could pour out his horn of oil, the Lord showed the seer his bias. "But the Lord said to Samuel, 'Do not look on his appearance or on the height of his stature, because I have rejected him. For the Lord sees not as man sees. For man looks on the outward appearance, but the Lord looks on the heart'" (1 Samuel 16:7).

A bias can pollute a pure seer flow. Ask the Lord to show you your biases because, by nature, we often don't recognize them. When He does, repent of your biases specifically and renew your mind in the area of your bias. And remain aware of that bias. When we are thinking and moving fast, we are more prone to act or speak out of a bias.

PRAYER

Father, in the name of Jesus, would You show me my biases? I don't want my biases to affect my spiritual sight. I want to see clearly what You are showing me, not what I want to see.

OCTOBER 18

OVERCOMING THE FEAR OF MAN

Whenever I am afraid, I will trust in You. In God (I will praise His word), in God I have put my trust; I will not fear. What can flesh do to me?

Psalm 56:3-4

When I was young in the prophetic, I wanted to have fire in my bones. But instead I had the fear of man in my bones. The spirit of fear was driving the fear of man. The reality is, I could never have gotten to where I am today with the fear of man plaguing my soul. I would never have reached my highest calling with the fear of man in my way.

You may not think you have the fear of man, and maybe you don't. But wisdom would consider these two possibilities. Maybe you haven't discerned that your hesitation is the fear of man. Sometimes it's subtle or maybe you don't have the fear of man at the level you are operating now. Fear of man can hit you when you start releasing more serious visual revelation, so we have to learn to discern it and resist it.

The higher you go into the seer dimensions, the more warfare you will face. Think about Elijah. He didn't have much trouble with Ahab. In fact, he confronted him boldly. There was no fear of man. But when Jezebel threatened to kill him, he wound up sitting under a tree wishing he was dead. Why? Because his anointing took him into high levels of confrontation and there was backlash.

Scripture has plenty to say about the fear of man. Fear of man is like kryptonite for the seer. Proverbs 29:25 tells us, "The fear of man brings a snare, but whoever trusts in the Lord shall be safe." And Deuteronomy 1:17 (NLT) says, "Don't be afraid of anyone's anger, for the decision you make is God's decision."

Jesus said it plainly in Luke 12:4, "And I say to you, My friends, do not be afraid of those who kill the body, and after that have no more that they can do." When you have the fear of man, you won't share what you saw or you won't share all of what you saw. You won't share the parts that are going to bring backlash. That's the primary way to discern this seer plague.

You can't fear the Lord and fear man at the same time. You have to make a decision. If you have the fear of man, repent now.

PRAYER

Father, in the name of Jesus, I repent for any time I have allowed the fear of man to stop me from sharing what You showed me. Forgive me for using wisdom to mask the fear of man. Deliver me from this plague.

OCTOBER 19

WHEN WHAT YOU SEE SENDS YOU INTO TRAVAIL

The Spirit also helps in our weaknesses. For we do not know what we should pray for as we ought, but the Spirit Himself makes intercession for us with groanings which cannot be uttered.

Romans 8:26

In 2016, I went into travail while I was praying about the prophetic movement. God showed me that if there were not more strong equipping, false prophets would start to rise rapidly in the next five years (by 2021). Unfortunately, the latter part of what I saw is manifesting now.

According to *The Seer's Dictionary*, travail is a genuine form of prayer that can break through in warfare or to birth God's will. Travail is intense! In my encounter, I was sweating, crying, and exhausted at the end of the prayer.

The Greek word *travail* is found several times in the New Testament (and many more times in the Old Testament). When Jesus talked about the pregnant woman who had sorrow in travail (John 16:21), He was referring to *tikto*, which means "to bring forth, bear, produce (fruit from the seed); of a woman giving birth; of the earth bringing forth its fruits."

When Paul was talking about interceding for the Thessalonians (1 Thessalonians 2:9), the Greek word for *travail* is *mochthos*, which means a hard and difficult labor, toil, travail, hardship, distress.

Hebrew words for *travail* include *yalad*, which also brings in the connotation of helping: "to cause or help to bring forth; to assist or tend to as a midwife" (Genesis 38:27); *telaah*, which implies seeking deliverance from toil, hardship, distress, weariness (Exodus 18:8); *inyan*, which refers to an occupation, task, job (Ecclesiastes 1:13); *amal* which refers to toil, trouble, labor (Isaiah 23:4); and *challah*, which means to be or become grieved, be or become sorry (Isaiah 53:11).

What tremendous things can be accomplished in the spirit realm by those who give themselves over to travail! You can't work your way into it, but you can quench it. If you feel travailing coming on, lean into it. God may give you visual revelation in the midst of it that marks your ministry—or even changes cities and nations.

PRAYER

Father, in the name of Jesus, I know I can't choose to enter into travail. It is a work of Your Spirit. But would You help me recognize travail when You bring it so I don't quench the Spirit of prayer?

OCTOBER 20

WHEN YOUR REVELATION IS INCOMPLETE

Now we see things imperfectly....

1 Corinthians 13:12 NLT

Many say Agabus, the prophet who prophesied about Paul's fate in Jerusalem, missed it. Others say he saw in part. Let's take a look.

> And as we stayed many days, a certain prophet named Agabus came down from Judea. When he had come to us, he took Paul's belt, bound his own hands and feet, and said, "Thus says the Holy Spirit, 'So shall the Jews at Jerusalem bind the man who owns this belt, and deliver him into the hands of the Gentiles'" (Acts 21:10-11).

Agabus wasn't completely inaccurate, but he didn't see the whole picture. Indeed, Luke's account shows something a little different happened. In Acts 27 we see the Jews seized Paul, dragged him out of the temple and had plans to kill him. The Romans intervened as the Jews were beating Paul.

> Then the commander came near and took him, and commanded him to be bound with two chains; and he asked who he was and what he had done. And some among the multitude cried one thing and some another. So when he could not ascertain the truth because of the tumult, he commanded him to be taken into the barracks (Acts 21:33-34).

Again, Agabus wasn't completely off. He just saw in part. Seeing in part means an incomplete revelation, according to *The Seer's Dictionary*. Often seers will get one part of the spiritual puzzle and other seers will have another part. This is why it's so important to have a community that can deliberate seer revelation.

Paul wrote in 1 Corinthians 13:12 (NLT), "Now we see things imperfectly, like puzzling reflections in a mirror, but then we will see everything with perfect clarity...." God doesn't always give us the full picture. Paul wrote in 1 Corinthians 8:1 that knowledge can puff you up (make you proud.) On the other hand, you might see everything clearly, but you lack the ability to interpret what you see. Without an interpreter, you don't have all the pieces to the visual puzzle.

Seeing in part is not always a failure to discern rightly. At times it's just part of God's way. Every seer has strengths and weaknesses, which, again, is why we need companies of seers—community. We need humility.

PRAYER

Father, in the name of Jesus, help me remember that I may only be seeing in part. Help me to find a company of seers with whom I can share my visual revelation, knowing they may have a missing part to the full picture.

OCTOBER 21

WHEN YOU HAVE A DREAM WITHIN A DREAM

For God speaks again and again, though people do not recognize it.
Job 33:14 NLT

Do you remember the movie *Inception*? It was a 2010 science fiction film about dream stealers that featured lucid dreaming. (I wouldn't suggest watching it, but the concept is interesting.) Sometimes in the movie they had dreams within a dream.

A dream within a dream occurs when you dream that you've awakened, then continue experiencing new events or surroundings, all while still being asleep. Dreams within dreams can be startling because you wake up in the dream only to later realize you were still dreaming.

When you wake up from a dream within a dream it can be a little disorienting because the experience was so realistic. You may initially think the dream within the dream was reality until you are fully awake.

I've had it happen many times. Once, I was actually telling someone about a dream I had—only I was still in a dream. Other times, you might even see yourself dreaming. It's surreal.

If you've had a dream within a dream, you've probably wondered why and how to interpret it. Job 33:14-16 (NLT) tells us, "For God speaks again and again, though people do not recognize it. He speaks in dreams, in visions of the night, when deep sleep falls on people as they lie in their beds. He whispers in their ears and terrifies them with warnings."

Why do we have dreams within dreams? One reason is because God is trying to get your attention. Dreams within dreams are often very important dreams. A dream within a dream can be confirmation of what the Lord is saying. Often a dream within a dream has to do with something going on right now or something soon to take place. A dream within a dream could also be your soul struggling with a matter and God providing you divine communication about the issue.

As we go deeper into the end times, God is increasingly communicating through dreams and visions. So we need to understand the nuances of the dream world, including a dream within a dream. We don't want to miss the message God is sending us. I teach more about this in my School of the Seers.

A dream within a dream is not an everyday occurrence but if you are a dreamer, you will run into this phenomenon. Treat it very carefully.

PRAYER

Father, in the name of Jesus, a dream within a dream is such a fascinating experience. Help me to wring out every bit of revelation You have for me in the dream and then dream within a dream.

OCTOBER 22

I SAW JEZEBEL

Now when Jehu had come to Jezreel, Jezebel heard of it; and she put paint on her eyes and adorned her head, and looked through a window.
2 Kings 9:30

At times, God will allow us to see specific spirits that are attacking us—or plotting to attack us or other people. God does this so we can be better prepared for combat or understand what we are up against so we can use the right weapons.

I saw Jezebel in 2003. I was praying in my living room with someone from church. We knew there was a lot of witchcraft coming against us, but we didn't know where it was coming from. We believed if we cried out to God to show us the source of the witchcraft attacks that He would pour out revelation so we could use our authority in Christ to shut it down.

We prayed for some time and heard nothing. Then it happened. Suddenly I felt an evil presence in the room. When I looked up, I literally jumped back. I saw the spirit of Jezebel hovering over the condo. It was as if Jezebel showed up to intimate us. Instead, she overplayed her hand.

Jezebel can present in many ways in the spirit realm, but what I saw made it unmistakable that this wicked spirit was the source of the witchcraft that was wreaking havoc on me. I saw a thin woman in a long red dress hovering over us. Her face was painted, which is in line with 2 Kings 9:30, "Now when Jehu had come to Jezreel, Jezebel heard of it; and she put paint on her eyes and adorned her head, and looked through a window."

In this vision, Jezebel had long sharp fingernails. She also fangs. When I saw her, she hissed like a snake and disappeared almost as fast as she had appeared before my spiritual eyes. As a young believer at the time, I didn't know 2 Kings 9:22 AMP, "When Joram saw Jehu, he said, 'Do you come in peace, Jehu?' And he answered, 'What peace [can exist] as long as the fornications of your mother Jezebel and her sorceries are so many?'"

In this case, Jezebel was operating through a man who took interest in both me and my friend. Jezebel was using a person to release the witchcraft. Since we don't wrestle against flesh and blood, we took authority over it in the spirit—and the man was exposed.

PRAYER

Father, in the name of Jesus, I know there are many spirits seeking to steal, kill, and destroy. When it's helpful, would You help me see the spirits that are attacking or poised to attack so I can shut them down?

OCTOBER 23

LEARN FROM YOUR MISTAKES

For a righteous man may fall seven times and rise again....

Proverbs 24:16

If you walk in seer ministry long enough, eventually you are going to miss the mark. If not in revelation then in interpretation or delivery, or the timing of your delivery. And if not in interpretation then in application, or with whom you share the visual revelation. There are many ways we can miss it from the time of receiving to the time of release.

James 3:2 (AMPC) tells us, "For we all often stumble and fall and offend in many things. And if anyone does not offend in speech [never says the wrong things], he is a fully developed character and a perfect man, able to control his whole body and to curb his entire nature."

We are all growing in hearing, seeing, and saying. If you obviously missed it—if it was absolutely wrong—admit it swiftly and take the opportunity to learn from your mistake. Many times, we learn more by our mistakes than we do from our successes. We do not aim to make mistakes in the seer realms, but no one is perfect.

If you know you've made a mistake, ask the Holy Spirit exactly how you missed it. Was it a personal bias? Were you moved by the expression, or lack of expression, on someone's face? Did you get part of it right but the wrong part was so off that the person rejected the entire visual revelation? Were you listening to some other spirit than the Holy Spirit when you interpreted the dream? Was it your imagination instead of a true vision?

Again, if you need to repent, repent. People will respect you more for acknowledging you missed it than for trying to defend a word that is clearly wrong. Don't let missing it discourage you. When you learned to ride a bike, chances are you fell down once or twice. Get back on the bike! The righteous fall down seven times but get back up again (Proverbs 24:16).

Don't condemn yourself if you miss it. That will shake your confidence and can hinder your ability to see the next thing God wants to show you. Ask God to teach you a lesson in the mistake. Proverbs 18:15 (AMPC) says, "The mind of the prudent is ever getting knowledge, and the ear of the wise is ever seeking (inquiring for and craving) knowledge."

PRAYER

Father, in the name of Jesus, I know I am not perfect in my seeing, hearing, saying, timing, and so on. Help me recognize when I have made a mistake, be quick to repent, and to learn from the error.

OCTOBER 24

DON'T OVERTHINK IT

Be anxious for nothing, but in everything by prayer and supplication, with thanksgiving, let your requests be made known to God.

Philippians 4:6

While you should judge your seer revelation before releasing it publicly, be careful not to fall into the seer trap called overthinking. Your head can talk you right out of releasing what the Holy Spirit revealed to your spiritual eyes, or in a dream or encounter. In other words, you can talk yourself right out of sharing a valid visual revelation. And that's what the enemy wants.

Judge the accuracy of your visual revelation by the Word and the Spirit, not by your soul. This is part of being led by the Spirit and demonstrates a level of maturity in the seer dimensions. There may be times when you prophesy what you see in visions or receive dreams that seem contrary to what you know, think, or believe about someone.

Why is that? It may be because you are holding that person to who they used to be or because you know of current situations in their life that seem to make the visual revelation unlikely to be accurate from a natural standpoint.

Remember, God looks at everyone through the eyes of love. You are sharing visual revelation that reveals His will and their potential, not necessarily their current reality or condition. God may show you something to encourage people to lay aside weights and sin that are holding them back from their destiny. The visual revelation you release could actually be part of the process that spurs them to go up higher.

Again, don't overthink it. This is called analysis paralysis and will hinder both your seer flow and delivery. Analysis paralysis is based in your soul, not in your spirit. God has given you a mind to reason, but many times you can't reason out a visual revelation.

It may seem strange or wrong or too fantastic to your soul, but God's thoughts are higher than our thoughts (Isaiah 55:8-9). It doesn't have to make sense to you in order to make sense to the person or people with whom you are sharing what you saw or dreamed. Seer revelation taps into His higher thoughts.

PRAYER

Father, in the name of Jesus, would You help me to get out of my head and into Your heart? Help me not to overthink it or talk myself out of a revelation that may bless someone's life.

OCTOBER 25

WHAT'S IN YOUR HEART?

Therefore, my beloved, flee from idolatry.

1 Corinthians 10:14

Just as the Word of God warns us how one sin can lead to another sin, it is also true that one error can lead us into another error. One wrong belief can cause us to believe many wrong things.

After all, the apostle Paul warned us that satan transforms himself into an angel of light (2 Corinthians 11:14). How does deception get its stronghold? Well, one way is ignorance of the Word of God and the ways of God. But I also believe deception finds a doorway in the idolatry of our hearts.

The Bible says the heart is deceitful above all things and desperately wicked (Jeremiah 17:9). If that's true, and it is, then none of us are above deception. If we think we are, then we're deceived already. But the good news is Jesus sent the Holy Spirit to lead and guide us into all truth. If we follow His Spirit and His written Word instead of the idolatry of our hearts, we'll walk in the light.

The apostle Paul lists idolatry as a work of the flesh (Galatians 5:20). But the same apostle, inspired by the Holy Spirit, also told us to flee from idolatry (1 Corinthians 10:14). The Word of God never instructs us to do something the grace of God won't empower us to do. We simply have to get into agreement.

We must partner with the Lord in guarding our hearts with all diligence from deception in these last days. Guarding our hearts from deception means being humble enough to acknowledge that we are capable of being deceived. It also means setting our minds on Christ and putting first the Kingdom. As far as the world is concerned we have died, and our real life is hidden with Christ in God (Colossians 3:3). Guarding ourselves from deception, then, means taking the apostle Paul's advice:

> Kill (deaden, deprive of power) the evil desire lurking in your members [those animal impulses and all that is earthly in you that is employed in sin]: sexual vice, impurity, sensual appetites, unholy desires, and all greed and covetousness, for that is idolatry (the deifying of self and other created things instead of God) (Colossians 3:5 AMPC).

PRAYER

Father, in the name of Jesus, would You show me if I have idols in my heart? I don't want to be deceived into making anything an idol. Please, lead me and guide me into all truth about my heart.

OCTOBER 26

PRACTICE BEING HEAVENLY MINDED

Set your mind on things above, not on things on the earth.
Colossians 3:2

If you want your spiritual eyes to open wider—if you want to see more of what God is trying to show you—then you have to train yourself to rely less on what you can see, hear, smell, and feel with your natural senses and press into your spiritual senses.

Most of us are dominated by our five natural senses. Don't get me wrong. We need those five senses to operate on earth. However, if we are not careful, we will walk by physical sight and hinder our ability to see through the eyes of faith.

What do I mean? Let me point you to the words of Paul in Colossians 3:1-2 (AMPC): "If then you have been raised with Christ [to a new life, thus sharing His resurrection from the dead], aim at and seek the [rich, eternal treasures] that are above, where Christ is, seated at the right hand of God. And set your minds and keep them set on what is above (the higher things), not on the things that are on the earth."

Your legal position in the spirit is this: you are seated in heavenly places in Christ Jesus. Ephesians 2:6 (AMPC) reminds: "And He raised us up together with Him and made us sit down together [giving us joint seating with Him] in the heavenly sphere [by virtue of our being] in Christ Jesus (the Messiah, the Anointed One)."

And Ephesians 1:3 (AMPC) tells us: "May blessing (praise, laudation, and eulogy) be to the God and Father of our Lord Jesus Christ (the Messiah) Who has blessed us in Christ with every spiritual (given by the Holy Spirit) blessing in the heavenly realm!"

Even though you are walking in the earth realm in a physical body, your spirit is also seated at the right hand of the Father in Christ. This is a natural mystery, but also a spiritual reality. Practice setting your mind on things above rather than being distracted by what the enemy is doing or what your circumstances are showing you.

How do you do that? In short, meditate on the Word, fellowship with the Holy Spirit, and pray in other tongues. Sow to the Spirit and you will see in the spirit.

PRAYER

Father, in the name of Jesus, help me practice being heavenly minded. Give me grace to set my mind on things above, not on the things of this earth only. Help me see myself seated in heavenly places in Christ.

OCTOBER 27

BREAKING THE SEAL

Now I saw when the Lamb opened one of the seals; and I heard one of the four living creatures saying with a voice like thunder, "Come and see."

Revelation 6:1

I was meditating on the Word of God when an angel came with a scroll that was tied with a string of gold. When the angel untied the scroll, I saw words written across the top. It was a list of ten things I needed to understand in that season.

Have you seen a scroll in the spirit? Some scrolls are bound by a string while others contain a seal. When the scroll contains revelation from the heavenly realms, you typically do not have the authority to open it. An angel may open it for you. By contrast, an angel once told Daniel to seal a scroll with revelation he received from Heaven (Daniel 9:24 and 12:4-9).

A seal, in this context, is an inscription or impression. It's a symbol that something is confirmed, proved, or authenticated. It's an official document, often related to the end times or God's plans on earth. According to *The Seer's Dictionary*, to break the seal or loose the seal means "to break open the seal that contains visions of the end times. Only Jesus can break the seal. Seers who claim they have broken the seal are in deception."

For example, Revelation 5:1-5 reads:

> And I saw in the right hand of Him who sat on the throne a scroll written inside and on the back, sealed with seven seals. Then I saw a strong angel proclaiming with a loud voice, "Who is worthy to open the scroll and to loose its seals?" And no one in heaven or on the earth or under the earth was able to open the scroll, or to look at it. So I wept much, because no one was found worthy to open and read the scroll, or to look at it. But one of the elders said to me, "Do not weep. Behold, the Lion of the tribe of Judah, the Root of David, has prevailed to open the scroll and to loose its seven seals."

PRAYER

Father, in the name of Jesus, I want to see into the scrolls You have ordained for my season. Would You open my spiritual eyes to Your plans for this season and the future?

OCTOBER 28

THE DEMONIC DIMENSION

Beloved, do not believe every spirit, but test the spirits, whether they are of God; because many false prophets have gone out into the world.
1 John 4:1

The demonic realm is raging in the unseen world. If demons weren't active in the seer realm, John the Beloved would not have warned us to test the spirits, to see if they are from God (1 John 4:1). While we'd all rather see angels or Heaven, the demonic realm is part and parcel of the seer's visual landscape, and God can choose to open it at any time.

I wrote about this extensively in my book, *The Seer Dimensions*. When Jesus walked the earth, He confronted the demonic realm time and time again. Indeed, He cast out demons everywhere He went. In Acts 10:38, Luke chronicled how Jesus went about doing good and healing all who were oppressed by the devil. The Bible gives believers glimpses into the demonic realm—but seers and seeing people sometimes see into this realm with their spiritual eyes.

Jesus describes the moment He saw satan fall from Heaven like lightning (Luke 10:18). I imagine He also saw one-third of the angels who followed Lucifer in his insurrection fall. What a sight! I also imagine Jesus saw the spirit of infirmity, the spirit of epilepsy, the spirit of fear, and other spirits that were plaguing the captives He set free. What a sight the man with the legion of demons must have been!

With regard to the demonic realm, the seer gift works strongly with the gift of discerning of spirits. While discernment should work to discern the Holy Spirit and angels as well as demon powers, some seers and seeing people are more bent to see into the demonic realm than others.

Regardless of a seer's particular bent or assignment in the Body of Christ, seers and seeing people are quick to discern when satan is transforming himself as an angel of light (2 Corinthians 11:14).

PRAYER

Father, in the name of Jesus, I don't care to see the dark side, but if it serves Your purposes I will look. I will yield my spiritual eyes to what You want me to see because I know it serves Your purposes.

OCTOBER 29

STAY IN BOUNDS

We, however, will not boast beyond measure, but within the limits of the sphere which God appointed us—a sphere which especially includes you.

2 Corinthians 10:13

When seers move beyond their supernatural gifting, they can make mistakes at best—or step into divination at worst. Some less experienced seers may look at the elders, or someone who has had encounters they wish they had, and start striving to enter those realms. It's not always intentional. It's just hunger gone wrong.

We can only see what the Lord allows us to see. When we begin to move beyond the seer anointing God has given us, we can hurt people—or hurt ourselves and our reputation. Let me give you a practical example. If you are not a fivefold seer, giving someone highly directional counsel through a vision or dream can spur someone to make a decision that's not based on the Lord's counsel.

What am I saying? A seer is a fivefold gift, but every believer has the inherent ability to see in the spirit. Like the simple gift of prophecy, the lay believer's spiritual sight is often for edification, exhortation, and comfort. You can't do much damage if you stay in the realm of visual edification, exhortation, and comfort. But if you try to be someone you are not, you will step out of God's boundaries for your sight.

Paul put it this way in 2 Corinthians 10:13 (AMPC), "We, on the other hand, will not boast beyond our legitimate province and proper limit, but will keep within the limits [of our commission which] God has allotted us as our measuring line and which reaches and includes even you."

There is a legitimate province and a proper limit on your visual revelations. That limit is set by God. In other words, He has given you an anointing, an assignment, and sometimes a territory in which to operate. If you move beyond His boundaries, you are out of order.

Paul wrote, "But to each one of us grace was given according to the measure of Christ's gift" (Ephesians 4:7). We are working with Christ's gifts and there are often boundaries to those gifts. God can extend those boundaries when He chooses, but it's not up to us to go beyond His boundaries. That's called presumption, even if it's innocent presumption.

PRAYER

Father, in the name of Jesus, please show me where my boundaries are in the spirit. Help me to resist the temptation to go further than You are taking me. Teach me to be content with the seer anointing You have given me.

OCTOBER 30

DEVELOPING SEER CONFIDENCE

Therefore do not cast away your confidence, which has great reward.
Hebrews 10:35

People who are newer to the seer dimensions can be nervous about sharing what they see in the spirit. That's natural and normal. I call it seer stage fright. We have to get over it! If you are going to release your dreams or visions or other visual encounters, you need to work up confidence so people will take what you are saying seriously.

For example, don't release your visual revelation with a wishy-washy tone as if you are not sure you believe it. Don't say, "Well, I am not sure but I think I saw an angel..." or, "I had this dream and I don't know, but I think that bear means something." That's okay in a home group or a private setting while you are learning, but will not instill confidence in those you are sharing with. In fact, it will do just the opposite.

If you are not confident the Lord is speaking, don't release the visual revelation outside your small group. Judge your own revelation before you open your mouth publicly. Remember, we prophesy according to the proportion of our faith (Romans 12:6). If you don't have the faith to release the visual revelation with confidence, wait until you do so that those who hear your utterance hear a word wrapped in faith.

I have a whole course on Developing Confidence in Your Prophetic Voice and I can't rehash all that here. But let me give you some food for thought. You need a mentor. Finding a mentor can be very difficult. I was extremely blessed that I had mentors in the prophetic from a very young age in Christ. I had role models I could look up to.

You also need to surround yourself with other seers. Proverbs 27:17 (NLT), "As iron sharpens iron, so a friend sharpens a friend." Second Peter 1:1 talks about those of like precious faith. The NLT says, "the same precious faith we have." Just because everyone believes in Jesus doesn't mean everyone believes there are seers today–or that you can see in the spirit. You have a "God confidence" about something with no natural explanation as to why.

PRAYER

Father, in the name of Jesus, please help me get over my insecurities. Please help me develop enough confidence in the reality of what You are showing me that I will be willing to step out and share in humble boldness.

OCTOBER 31

THE SEER'S SIXTH SENSE

Let us know....

Hosea 6:3

Have you ever heard someone talk about sixth sense? In the secular world, they are talking about paranormal phenomena like Extra Sensory Perception (ESP). That's witchcraft!

Knowing in the spirit is part of the seer's discernment, and it has nothing to do with familiar spirits or the paranormal. It has to do with the supernatural.

Some say it's not a sense but seers like James Goll call it a sixth sense, redeeming the language the world created as it counterfeited an actual spiritual experience. He says knowing is like a sixth sense.

So what is our definition of knowing from the seer's perspective? Here's my definition: a way of receiving prophetic revelation or intelligence that is not obvious to the other spiritual senses; an awareness in your spirit that translates to knowledge in your mind without any direct communication from God through the five spiritual senses; spiritual perception and understanding without explanation as to how you know what you know.

Knowing can manifest as what the world calls déjà vu. But it's not déjà vu. Déjà vu is witchcraft. Knowing can manifest as a warning. You know not to pick up the phone. You know not to take that job. It's not a feeling. It's knowing. In other words, it's not a check in your spirit. It's not an uneasy feeling. It's just knowing.

When you are a knower, you know what is right or wrong. Remember, knowing is part of discerning and discerning is the ability to know between right and wrong. You know that person is the right one for the job. The candidates are all equally qualified. But you just know. You just know that you know that you know.

Of course, like any type of discernment, you need to judge your knowings. How do you know if it's a knowing or just a thought? How do you know if it's your mind or if it's the mind of Christ? Sometimes you don't. The closer you get to God, the more God confidence you will have. Check out my course, Knowing, at School of the Spirit.

PRAYER

Father, in the name of Jesus, help me to develop this sixth sense called knowing. Help me to lean in to those Holy Spirit knowings and build confidence in this gift. Teach me to discern my knowings rightly.

NOVEMBER

For God may speak in one way, or in another, yet man does not perceive it. In a dream, in a vision of the night, when deep sleep falls upon men, while slumbering on their beds.

Job 33:14-15

NOVEMBER 1

CULTIVATING SEER CULTURE

Be kindly affectionate to one another with brotherly love, in honor giving preference to one another; not lagging in diligence, fervent in spirit, serving the Lord.

Romans 12:10-11

Any local body can choose to cultivate a seer culture. At Awakening House of Prayer, my home base in Fort Lauderdale, we have labored with the Holy Spirit to create an atmosphere where He feels welcomed and can move in power, encounters, visions, and even trances.

What is a seer culture? It's a culture that welcomes, appreciates, honors and celebrates, and takes seriously the revelations seers release. I like to have seers around me. Some pastors are afraid of seers because of messes prophetic people have made in their church, or horror stories they hear from other pastors about seers. Other pastors are afraid that the seer may see their secret sin. Still other pastors do not believe Christians today can see into the spirit realm.

But believing is not enough to cultivate a seer culture. It requires a fivefold seer or teacher who actively teaches on the topics of seeing in the spirit, prophetic ministry, and the Holy Spirit (Ephesians 4:11). It requires church leadership that seeks first the Kingdom of God and His righteousness (Matthew 6:33).

Cultivating a healthy seer culture demands consistent encouragement for members to seek intimacy with God, a strong corporate intercessory prayer and fasting focus, and a worship experience that allows the Holy Spirit to lead the way. Cultivating a healthy seer culture also means developing an atmosphere free from competition and strife, where people honor each other and their gifts. Cultivating a healthy seer culture means encouraging members to write down what they see or dream and share it with leadership—and giving them feedback.

If we are mindful and intentional about creating a healthy seer culture, we will open a portal of Heaven where people who don't normally see will start to have visions or dreams. Healthy seer cultures may "just happen," especially if you have a lot of prophetic people in any given congregation. But without proper training and accountability you'll see fruits, flakes, nuts—and abuses in the Spirit. We must cultivate and protect the prophetic in our revival hubs, houses of prayers, training centers, and churches.

PRAYER

Father, in the name of Jesus, help me be part of the solution. I want to see a healthy seer culture in my church, but I know I can't force it. Teach me to lead by example in love, honor, and reverencing Jesus.

NOVEMBER 2

THE LIFESTYLE OF THE SEER

He has shown you, O man, what is good; and what does the Lord require of you but to do justly, to love mercy, and to walk humbly with your God?

Micah 6:8

All believers are called to walk in love, live holy, and put on Christ; but the lifestyle of a seer often demands an ever narrower road. When you serve as the eyes of the Body of Christ, you need to adopt a lifestyle that guards your vision and helps you stay focused on the unseen realm. That means developing consistent disciplines and intimacy with the Holy Spirit.

The lifestyle of a seer is grounded in prayer. Remember, all seers are intercessors. As I say in *The Prophet's Devotional*, prayer is the prophet's oxygen. It's your lifeline to God. It's a channel of fellowship, intimacy, and visual revelation. I have experienced some of my most dramatic visions during times of prayer.

In 1 Thessalonians 5:17 exhorts us to "pray without ceasing." But what does that mean? As I share in *The Intercessor's Devotional*, "Practically speaking, though, praying without ceasing means praying with frequency. It means praying often. It means not giving up until we see the answer to prayer or sense it's done in the spirit. Praying without ceasing is the intercessor's mandate, and it's possible. It's a mindset and a heart posture that's ready to pounce in prayer." Prayer sharpens your spiritual vision.

Then there's worship. Worship is releasing our adoration toward God. Visual revelation often flows from the throne room, and worship positions you to see from His perspective. Obedience is critical to the seer's lifestyle, and holiness will take you higher.

First Peter 1:16 tells us, "Be holy, for I am holy." Holiness is complete devotion to the work of God. That means we have to constantly purify ourselves and consecrate ourselves for His use. Think about it. Do you think Isaiah would watch some of the trash coming out of Hollywood? Do you think Ezekiel would listen to some of the stuff they play on the radio today? We have to guard our eye gates and ear gates.

I could write an entire book on this topic, but let me leave you with this. Fasting, devotion, discipline, and surrender are all part and parcel of the seer's lifestyle. Ask God for the grace to make adjustments so you can see more clearly.

PRAYER

Father, in the name of Jesus, help me walk worthy of my calling. Help me adopt a lifestyle that paves the way to receive, judge, interpret, apply, and release the visual revelations that You share with me.

NOVEMBER 3

BREAKING OUT OF A SEER FAMINE

"Behold, the days are coming," says the Lord God, "That I will send a famine on the land, not a famine of bread, nor a thirst for water, but of hearing the words of the Lord."

Amos 8:11

You've probably heard the word *famine,* but have you heard of a visual famine? There was both in Samuel's day. The NLT puts 1 Samuel 3:1 this way, "...Now in those days messages from the Lord were very rare, and visions were quite uncommon."

This spiritual famine was impacting the nations. But did you know visual revelation can impact you, personally? I call it a seer famine. There are two sides to this. First, it's when seers in the land are rare, according to *The Seer's Dictionary*, but it's also when visual revelation has dried up in your life.

We don't have a lack of seers today. Thanks to the work of James Goll, John Paul Jackson, and others, seers have risen and are rising. The trouble comes when seers stop seeing; when they enter a seer famine. Why? Because a seer famine exposes a deeper problem.

If you are in a seer famine, you need to check your hunger. Jesus said in Matthew 5:6, "Blessed are those who hunger and thirst for righteousness, for they shall be filled." I believe the hungry seer will also see. If you are disinterested in the Word and prayer and fellowship with His Spirit, don't be surprised if you enter a seer famine. Thankfully, it's easy to fix. Of course, a seer famine can also come from failing to steward the visual revelation He entrusts you with.

Now, when it comes to a seer famine in a church, that is often an even deeper problem. Remember, Samuel was serving the priest Eli from his youth. But Eli's sons were corrupt and immoral. Sin in the camp can cause a seer famine, not because the seer is sinning but because the leadership is compromised. It can be more difficult to see in an atmosphere or culture that grieves the Holy Spirit.

If you face a seer famine in your life, return to the altar of prayer and worship. If it's in your community, return to the altar of intercession. Without judgment, cry out to God for the leadership to turn their hearts back to Him. Pray from a heart of mercy. God hears and answers prayer. The famine can turn back into a flow.

PRAYER

Father, in the name of Jesus, would You help me recognize a seer famine in my life? In my church? I don't want to walk through a season where I am not seeing what You are trying to show me.

NOVEMBER 4

ENTERING AUTOFOCUS MODE

Since we consider and look not to the things that are seen but to the things that are unseen; for the things that are visible are temporal (brief and fleeting), but the things that are invisible are deathless and everlasting.

2 Corinthians 4:18 AMPC

When I was in college, we worked in a dark room to process black and white film using three sets of chemicals in trays. We also used what was called an enlarger that projected an image from a film negative to a photographic paper. The key to a successful print was manually focusing and setting the aperture for the appropriate depth of field. If the photo was out of focus, we couldn't use it.

As seers and seeing people, we can't ignore any part of our being—spirit, soul, or body—but few could be charged with focusing too much on the spirit realm. Few could be blamed for being overly aware of God and His angels. Few could be accused of practicing His presence too often. It's usually quite the opposite.

We need seer focus. Seer focus is a seer skill developed through experience that allows one to focus primarily on what the Holy Spirit wants them to see amid an active spiritual background that could otherwise be overwhelming, according to *The Seer's Dictionary*.

Consider what the Bible tells us about focus: "And set your minds and keep them set on what is above (the higher things), not on the things that are on the earth" (Colossians 3:2 AMPC).

We can focus on many good things, but the more we train our spiritual senses to focus on "God things," the more clearly we'll see in the spirit realm. God wants to bring seers into the dimension I call autofocus. Autofocus is a seer mode you enter when you have cultivated sensitivity to the seer dimensions as a way of life.

When you enter autofocus, your natural and spiritual eyes are not overemphasizing what the enemy is doing or allowing the world to distract you from visual revelations. Instead, you are actively looking for what God wants to show you. It becomes not second nature, but first nature to see through your spiritual eyes and focus on what God wants you to see.

PRAYER

Father, in the name of Jesus, would You help me to enter autofocus mode? I want to shift my vision to focus more on what You want me to see than what my natural eyes can see.

NOVEMBER 5

BEWARE CELEBRITY SEERS

Now John wore a garment of camel's hair and a leather belt around his waist, and his food was locusts and wild honey.

Matthew 3:4 ESV

There are celebrity seers, then there are consecrated seers. Celebrity seers are celebrated for their accuracy and often flaunt it. They settle for the earthly rewards of popularity (Matthew 6:2). It's not about being well-known; it's not about relishing in the fame and making your own name great. This is one way seers lose their anointing and, as a result, end up in divination.

Celebrity seers are part of the Hollywood Christianity Club. They are prima donnas. Here's the problem: the Hollywood Christianity syndrome causes even the most discerning believers to turn a blind eye to the evidence of deep character flaws that could be a symptom of serious sin in a seer's life. If we can't rightly discern and lovingly deal with the visible pride of seer prima donnas, how will we avoid the even greater deceptions coming in the end times?

Celebrity prophets are afraid to be judged and shun even the healthiest criticism. Some morph into people pleasers rather than God pleasers in order to maintain their status. This is not Christlike. Consider Paul's words in Philippians 2:5-7, "Let this mind be in you which was also in Christ Jesus, who, being in the form of God, did not consider it robbery to be equal with God, but made Himself of no reputation, taking the form of a bondservant, and coming in the likeness of men."

Again, that doesn't mean seers can't have a good reputation. Proverbs 22:1 (KJV) tells us, "A good name is rather to be chosen...." Rather, it means they didn't set out to make their name known. They set out to make Christ's name known.

Celebrity seers are all about the look and the style. Celebrity seers often have the slickest graphics, the most numerous photo shoots and the most expensive clothes. I'm not against expensive clothes. It's the spirit behind that exalts clothing over putting on Christ that troubles me. Consider that John the Baptist wore camel's hair and a leather belt and ate locusts and honey out in the wilderness. Consecrated seers are not focusing on the outward appearance of man. They are focused on the heart of God.

PRAYER

Father, in the name of Jesus, help me not to get caught up in the Hollywood Christianity Club. I don't want a membership. I would rather be hidden than hyped. My gifts are from You and to serve Your Kingdom, not mine.

NOVEMBER 6

THE MINISTRY OF SEER GUARD

...David put him over his guard and council.

1 Chronicles 11:25 AMPC

A woman who followed my ministry for years walked up to me after a meeting and said, "I believe the Lord has called me to be your seer guard." I had never heard that term before, so it intrigued me.

What is a seer guard? It's a seer who watches over another person in the spirit, typically for the purpose of warning, warring, and interceding for them, according to *The Seer's Dictionary*. If you are a seer connected to the local church, it's possible God will assign you to be a seer guard over leadership. The key idea is to guard the anointing.

But seer guards, which might also be described as sentinels in the spirit, are not relegated to the local church only. While God typically starts your assignment in a local assembly so that you can learn and grow in a safe environment, some seers are promoted to larger assignments over ministries, cities, or nations. But know this: a seer guard at any level carries significant responsibility in the spirit realm.

As with many other seer functions, intercession is part and parcel of the seer guard's role. Some seers feel compelled to share everything they see with the one they are guarding, but there's a time when it's not right to share because it may distract or bring fear to the leader. The seer guard is called many times to shut things down in the spirit realm before they land on the leader's doorstep—or pass beyond the gates of the city.

Keep in mind that the Holy Spirit could assign you as a seer guard over someone you don't even know. So, again, the ability to communicate with the person you are guarding in the spirit can be helpful at times, but not always possible and not always necessary. Your partnership in prayer with the Holy Spirit can accomplish His purposes.

PRAYER

Father, in the name of Jesus, I am willing to be used as a seer guard over my leadership, my church, or wherever else You need me. Please give me wisdom to guard what you entrust to me.

NOVEMBER 7

DEVELOPING SEER INSTINCTS

Yes, if you cry out for discernment, and lift up your voice for understanding, if you seek her as silver, and search for her as for hidden treasures; then you will understand the fear of the Lord and find the knowledge of God.

Proverbs 2:3-5

When I go into a conference to speak, or a city to minister, I instinctively lean in to discern the spiritual atmosphere. I instinctively press in to discover what the Lord is doing, what the enemy may be doing, and what my response should be. Many times, that leads me to intercession. I call this seer instinct. Seer instincts are the automatic reactions and behaviors that are innate to the seer gifting, such as intercession and discernment, according to *The Seer's Dictionary*. Instincts are your natural (or spiritual) aptitudes, impulses, and capacities. Instincts drive your seer behaviors.

With that said, know this: walking in the seer anointing and navigating the seer dimensions is not just about what you see. It's how you *respond* to what you see. If you have a spirit of fear, you may respond in terror to what you see in the spirit. Your soul condition can affect how you respond to visual revelation. That's why seers need to pursue emotional healing and, if necessary, deliverance ministry.

If you've been to the doctor who used a reflex hammer—a medical instrument with a rubber head and a handle—to tap your knees and elbows, you've experienced a natural instinct. When your nervous system responds with involuntary muscle jerks, your reflexes are healthy. In the same way, your seer instincts are like spiritual reflexes. You don't have to stop and think about what to do when you discern a demon. You go into binding and loosing mode. You don't have to think about what to do when the King enters the room. You worship.

My seer instincts include researching what I see in the spirit immediately upon receiving visual revelation. I instinctively record revelation. I instinctively pray for revelation. I instinctively sift the revelation through the Word of God to find scriptural backing when possible. These are my automatic reactions and behaviors.

Seer instincts may also include intercession, discernment, spiritual awareness in new atmospheres and more. Seer instincts come naturally, to some decree, but you need to lean into them. You need to cultivate them. You need to hone your skills around them. Your seer instincts are how God wired you—or how the world wired you. If you haven't taken the time to notice your seer instincts, start paying attention to your knee-jerk reactions to the atmosphere. Start noticing how you feel when you are around certain people or environments. What is your first response? That's your seer instinct.

PRAYER

Father, in the name of Jesus, help me to clearly see how I instinctively respond to Your presence, or angelic activity, or demonic infiltration. I want to respond on seer instincts, not soulish or carnal instincts.

NOVEMBER 8

WHAT ARE YOUR SEER HABITS?

For the ways of man are before the eyes of the Lord, and He ponders all his paths.

Proverbs 5:21

I am a creature of habit. I have morning habits, workday start habits, exercise habits, eating habits, sleeping habits. A lot of my life is on autopilot. I get up every morning at 3:45 a.m., immediately begin consuming an audio book or podcast, brush my teeth, make my coffee, start studying and praying and, so on.

Seers need to understand the power of a habit. A habit is formed by frequent repetition. God wants to help us break habits that hinder our seer anointing. Likewise, He wants us to develop good habits that position us for the visual revelation He is pouring out.

A Duke University study in 2006 found that up to 45 percent of all our daily behaviors are automatic. Let me put that another way. You spend one out of every two minutes of your life on autopilot. You are walking in your habits. You might be unaware of a lot of your habits. Roman Emperor Marcus Aurelius said, "What we do today, echoes throughout eternity."

The problem is, most of us are unaware of our habits because once a behavior becomes a habit, a different part of our brain is in control. We're no longer thinking about it. It's done at an unconscious level. The right habits increase the accuracy of your spiritual vision. The wrong habits dim your vision.

British Poet Frederick Langbridge said, "We are our own potters; for our habits make us, and we make our habits." If you write every once in a while, you are not a writer. But if you start a habit to write an hour every day, you become a writer.

In the same way, if you make it your habit to get in the Word, be still before Him, pray in the Spirit, and wait on the Lord, you are installing habits that will bear fruit. When you sow to the Spirit, you reap from the Spirit (Galatians 6:8). What are your seer habits?

PRAYER

Father, in the name of Jesus, help me form divine spiritual and seer habits that will serve Your Kingdom. Likewise, help me break bad natural and spiritual habits that hinder what You want me to see and do.

NOVEMBER 9

THE JAMES GOLL SEER ANOINTING

And He Himself gave some to be apostles, some prophets, some evangelists, and some pastors and teachers, for the equipping of the saints for the work of ministry, for the edifying of the body of Christ.
Ephesians 4:11-12

James Goll is a contemporary seer who helped restore spiritual eyesight to the Body of Christ through his strong teaching and scribing anointing. His anointing is marked by deep intimacy with God, throne room revelation, and a passion for equipping the Body of Christ to navigate the seer dimension with the integrity of the Word and the leading of the Spirit.

An international bestselling author with books like *The Seer, The Lifestyle of a Prophet* and *The Discerner,* Goll is a prolific teacher with a significant voice that has activated seers around the world in languages he does not even speak. One of his desires is that a man of God may be complete, equipped for every good work (2 Timothy 3:17).

Goll's supernatural encounters and practical teaching help show others what is possible in the seer dimensions, giving people a sense of identity that they are not "weird," but wired to see what many cannot. He has helped people not only discern what they see in the spirit, but also discern who they are in the spirit.

As a prophet and intercessor, Goll's anointing spans the five spiritual senses, including spiritual sight, spiritual hearing and understanding, spiritual smell, spiritual taste, and spiritual touch. He offers one of the most comprehensive libraries of materials on spiritual gifts in the Body of Christ. The depth and breadth of his revelations fuel his teachings and have prepared him to navigate sometimes difficult-to-comprehend truths to those who have ears to hear.

Goll is generous with his anointing, which is to both encounter and equip. It's not just about the dreams and visions he received, but imparting to the next generation and modeling how a prophetic statesman presents himself and his revelation. He imparts the power of intercession, prophetic ministry, and life in the Spirit, always with the skill to blend supernatural revelation with biblical grounding.

PRAYER

Father, in the name of Jesus, thank You for Your servant James Goll. Would You give me the ability to teach and scribe like James has so that I can equip the next generation and write out the revelations You give me?

NOVEMBER 10

DISCERNING ATTACKS BEFORE THEY MANIFEST

> *...Elisha, the prophet who is in Israel, tells the king of Israel the words that you speak in your bedroom.*
>
> 2 Kings 6:12

In 2005, I had a dream about a conference at a church I was attending. I saw the enemy's plots and plans. Specifically, I saw three men wearing black cowboy hats walk into the sanctuary while the speaker was preaching.

In the dream, I was the only one who saw them. I watched as they walked through the church and into the back toward the children's area. I got up and followed them. Then I woke up, disturbed.

In my spirit, I knew there was some sort of impending danger. Following protocol, I told the house prophet about the dream and they went to war in the spirit. I thought it might be a physical danger, so they put extra security around the children's ministry. The warning was received and the threat was thwarted.

God often reveals the enemy's plans to seers. Seers can be what you might call early-warning systems in the local church and beyond. This is biblical. In 2 Kings 6, Elisha saw into the enemy's camp and warned Israel repeatedly, saving them from ambush. Let's look at 2 Kings 6:8-12:

> Now the king of Syria was making war against Israel; and he consulted with his servants, saying, "My camp will be in such and such a place." And the man of God sent to the king of Israel, saying, "Beware that you do not pass this place, for the Syrians are coming down there." Then the king of Israel sent someone to the place of which the man of God had told him. Thus he warned him, and he was watchful there, not just once or twice.
>
> Therefore the heart of the king of Syria was greatly troubled by this thing; and he called his servants and said to them, "Will you not show me which of us is for the king of Israel?" And one of his servants said, "None, my lord, O king; but Elisha, the prophet who is in Israel, tells the king of Israel the words that you speak in your bedroom."

A seer in position can expose the enemy's plans before they manifest. That's a strategic advantage in warfare.

PRAYER

Father, in the name of Jesus, help me stay in position to see the enemy's plans before they manifest. Teach me to watch and pray consistently so I don't miss anything the enemy is planning.

NOVEMBER 11

AVOIDING SEER BURNOUT

> *Come to Me, all you who labor and are heavy laden, and I will give you rest. Take My yoke upon you and learn from Me, for I am gentle and lowly in heart, and you will find rest for your souls. For My yoke is easy and My burden is light.*
>
> Matthew 11:28-30

If I look at my computer screen too long, my eyes feel tired and weary. Scientifically, that's because the focusing muscles in my eyes literally get fatigued. At its worst, it leads to achy eyes and blurred vision.

Seer burnout can also cause us not to see clearly in the spirit realm. It's not that your spiritual eyes are tired. Rather, your soul can grow weary. I call it seer burnout. It happens when your soul is overwhelmed by constant output and little intake.

If you are always on, so to speak, ministering to people from your seer gift, interpreting dreams for people, or carrying prayer burdens in your own strength, your soul can get weary. And a weary soul can lead to blurry eyes.

The World Health Organization defines burnout as: "feelings of energy depletion or exhaustion; increased mental distance from one's job, or feelings of negativism or cynicism related to one's job; and reduced professional efficacy." Seers, your job, or vocation, is to see, judge, interpret, pray, apply, and deliver visual revelation. But it's hard to do that when your soul is weary.

The Bible warns us not to grow weary, but somehow at times we can't seem to obey that command. The problem is, if you don't know that you're dealing with seer burnout, it's an even worse experience. Sometimes you just don't know what's wrong with you. It's important to discern it so you can sit with Jesus and be restored.

In the early onset of seer burnout, you may just feel tired all the time. Later, you feel physically and emotionally exhausted. Part of the seer's ministry is waiting on the Lord, and if you are truly waiting on the Lord you shouldn't be burning out. You should be fired up.

In the early onset of seer burnout, you may have trouble falling asleep or staying asleep now and again. That may be an enemy attack, but it may also be that you are carrying too much of the burden to the point of burnout.

As seers, we are supposed to watch and pray. When you get burned out, it's harder to focus. It's harder to see and hear because you are exhausted. There is such a thing as spiritual exhaustion. You could even experience physical symptoms in your body. What's the answer? Jesus told us, "Come to Me, all you who labor and are heavy laden, and I will give you rest."

PRAYER

Father, in the name of Jesus, would You help me recognize the first signs of seer burnout so that I don't wind up completely depleted. I want to serve Your Kingdom well. Help me to take on Your easy yoke.

NOVEMBER 12

RECEIVING ANGELIC ASSISTANCE

Are they not all ministering spirits sent forth to minister for those who will inherit salvation?

Hebrews 1:14

My dear friend James Goll, author of *The Seer*, says, "When I move into the 'seer realm,' it often comes with angelic assistance. This is something I have learned over my many years of prophetic ministry," he explains. "When that realm opens up to me in eternal visions and the manifested presence becomes ever so thick, it is in part due to angels on assignment."

At times, we see angels helping men of God interpret what they saw in the spirit or what was going on in the seer dimensions. Daniel fell into a deep sleep on his face, with his face on the ground. The next thing he knew, an angel showed up to explain what was happening.

> Do not fear, Daniel, for from the first day that you set your heart to understand, and to humble yourself before your God, your words were heard; and I have come because of your words. But the prince of the kingdom of Persia withstood me twenty-one days; and behold, Michael, one of the chief princes, came to help me, for I had been left alone there with the kings of Persia. Now I have come to make you understand what will happen to your people in the latter days, for the vision refers to many days yet to come (Daniel 10:12-14).

The prophet Zechariah had several encounters with angels who helped him understand his end-times visions. Zechariah 1:8-9 reads: "I saw by night, and behold, a man riding on a red horse, and it stood among the myrtle trees in the hollow; and behind him were horses: red, sorrel, and white. Then I said, 'My lord, what are these?' So the angel who talked with me said to me, 'I will show you what they are.'" Over and over again we see Zechariah speaking to angels about the interpretation of the revelation.

John the Revelator also accepted angelic assistance. Revelation 17:8 shares, "The beast that you saw was, and is not, and will ascend out of the bottomless pit and go to perdition. And those who dwell on the earth will marvel, whose names are not written in the Book of Life from the foundation of the world, when they see the beast that was, and is not, and yet is."

Don't worship angels, but don't shun their assistance.

PRAYER

Father, in the name of Jesus, help me learn how to work with messenger angels who may come to help me understand what You are showing me. Like Daniel, Zechariah, and John, I want to work well with angels.

NOVEMBER 13

SEER STREAMS

Now I say this, that each of you says, "I am of Paul," or "I am of Apollos," or "I am of Cephas," or "I am of Christ." Is Christ divided?
1 Corinthians 1:12-13

Not all seer streams—or seer camps—are the same. The visual revelation flows from the same throne room, but the expression may be vastly different from one stream to another.

Seer streams are various facets of the seer movement, including dreamers, visionaries, and those known for heavenly encounters and out-of-body experiences, according to *The Seer's Dictionary*. In Scripture, Peter fell into a trance. Paul had an out-of-body experience and Philip traveled in the spirit.

In more modern times, John Paul Jackson, for example, is in the dreams stream. While he had visions and other encounters, he raised up a people—and still does through sons and daughters who carry on his ministry—that strongly emphasized the dream realm. By contrast, Kim Clement was often caught up in the spirit to see far into the future.

Bobby Conner, known for his prophetic ministry, healing, and deliverance, has reported being taken to Heaven, seeing the Ancient of Days and being guided by angels on assignment. Sadhu Sundar Selveraj of Jesus Ministries is known for heavenly visitations from Jesus. Meanwhile, Maria Woodworth-Etter was known for her prolonged trances.

All these streams reveal different ways God communicates in the seer dimensions. They are all flows that any believer can step into, but many tend to operate predominantly in one stream most of the time. When you understand these streams, you can find your tribe—a group of people best suited to understand how you flow. (Check out www.ignitenow.org to join my community.) That said, we have to be careful about getting so entrenched in our camp that we shut off other flows and shut off other streams. We don't want to operate in silos in the seer movement. We want to share revelation and glean from one another.

First Corinthians 13:9 tells us, "For we know in part and we prophesy in part." One may have a dream, another a vision, another a trance, another an out-of-body experience and when the seers from these different flows share their revelations, abundant understanding can result.

Be careful not to be critical of a stream in which you have not dipped your toe. Criticism is not a gift of the Spirit and, in fact, grieves Him. Just because you haven't experienced a dimension of the seer anointing or it sounds strange to you doesn't mean it's not valid.

PRAYER

Father, in the name of Jesus, would You help me to identify my seer stream? Please also teach me how to accurately define other seer streams and learn to collaborate with people who flow differently than me.

NOVEMBER 14

MAYBE YOU ARE JUST NOT READY

I still have many more things to say to you, but you cannot bear them now.

John 16:12 ESV

Have you ever wondered why some seers have such deep visual revelation and you don't? While we don't want to compare our seer flow to another, it's only natural to sometimes wonder why God doesn't show us some of the things that He shows other seers.

There could be several reasons why you are not seeing what others see. First, they may not have seen it at all. False seers literally make up things. Others saw something but it was their imagination and they could not tell the difference between their soul and the Holy Spirit. But what if it was a different reason?

Jesus said to His disciples in John 16:12, "I still have many more things to say to you, but you cannot bear them now." The CEV says, "I have much more to say to you, but right now it would be more than you could understand." And the AMPC gives it a little more depth: "I have still many things to say to you, but you are not able to bear them or to take them upon you or to grasp them now."

Here we see that Jesus wants to share things with us, but we're not ready. We cannot bear them. *Elliot's Commentary for English Readers* offers, "On His side there is the readiness to impart to them as friends all things that He had heard from the Father. But revelation can only be made to the mind which can accept it; and for those who have only in part understood what He has told them there are many things which cannot now be borne."

God knows that sometimes you can't bear the weight of heavier revelation. You may not yet be skilled enough in the seer dimensions to understand what you are seeing. You may not be spiritually mature enough not to get puffed up in pride by what you see. You may not have enough Word in you to anchor your revelation with Scripture. You may carry a heavy emotional load that crushes your soul.

So how do you prepare for the greater revelations? Get to know Him, His Word, and His ways. Pray in the Spirit to edify yourself. And wait. He knows when you are ready.

PRAYER

Father, in the name of Jesus, I am grateful that You will not show me something I can't bear. But I want to grow. I want to be ready. Give me grace to prepare myself for things You want to show me now and in the future.

NOVEMBER 15

WHEN YOU ENTER A SEER SWIRL

The voice of Your thunder was in the whirlwind; the lightnings lit up the world; the earth trembled and shook.

Psalm 77:18

Have you ever entered a seer swirl? You probably have, but you might not have language for it. A seer swirl is a whirl of revelation that turns the seer's head, according to *The Seer's Dictionary*.

Ezekiel found himself in a literal whirlwind of visual revelation. In Ezekiel 1:4 he wrote, "Then I looked, and behold, a whirlwind was coming out of the north, a great cloud with raging fire engulfing itself; and brightness was all around it and radiating out of its midst like the color of amber, out of the midst of the fire."

The rest of what he saw, including four living creatures and a vision of God, is too long to share here. But read the passage of Scripture and you'll know what I mean about a seer swirl. When you are in a seer swirl, there is so much visual revelation it makes your head spin.

Think of John the Revelator. He was caught in the Spirit a number of times. In Revelation 1:10, he was in the Spirit. In Revelation 4:2, he says, "Immediately I was in the Spirit...." In Revelation 17:3, he writes, "So he carried me away in the Spirit...." And in Revelation 21:10, again he writes, "And he carried me away in the Spirit...."

We don't know for sure if this was one continual vision or if it was a series of visions he received over time. Bible scholars are divided. But what we do know is that it was an overwhelming visual experience. If you haven't read the book of Revelation, take some time to explore it. The visual revelation had to make his head spin.

When you are in a seer swirl, visual revelation comes in rapid fire succession and you need to learn how to navigate the whirlwind. You can't make it happen. Seer swirls are God-initiated. But you can quench it. Don't get so overwhelmed by the series of visual revelations that you tune out. Don't allow yourself to be distracted. Seer swirls are not an everyday occurrence and usually contain significant revelation.

If you enter a seer swirl, it's critical to write down everything you see, hear, or feel in the experience so you don't forget anything important. When it's over, set aside some time to process it. Do it immediately. And always test what you see according to Scripture.

PRAYER

Father, in the name of Jesus, help me never to shut down a seer swirl because it feels overwhelming, or even inconvenient. Teach me how to navigate rapid-fire visual revelation.

NOVEMBER 16

WITHSTANDING SEER WARFARE

Put on the whole armor of God, that you may be able to stand against the wiles of the devil.

Ephesians 6:11

Seer warfare is real. Seer warfare is the spiritual warfare particular to seers and seeing people—and every seer will experience it. Yes, seers deal with the same types of everyday warfare that we all face, but there's a different thrust to seer warfare. It's often a different level of visual intensity and it has a clear target: shutting or defiling your eyes.

The enemy may tempt you into sinning with your eyes so he has the right to attack your vision. Jesus said in Matthew 6:22-23 (NLT), "Your eye is like a lamp that provides light for your body. When your eye is healthy, your whole body is filled with light. But when your eye is unhealthy, your whole body is filled with darkness. And if the light you think you have is actually darkness, how deep that darkness is!"

Seers are sometimes targeted with nocturnal warfare, which includes nightmares. And, of course, seers face daytime warfare such as persecution. All of this is meant to combat your seer gift. The enemy doesn't want you to see him, and he certainly doesn't want you to see anything else God wants to show you.

Seer warfare can also manifest as spiritual fatigue. Seer burnout is real, which is why it's critical to fellowship with the Lord without trying to see in the spirit. Many seers forsake the joy of simple fellowship, always waiting for the next revelation. Spend time with God for who He is, not what He can show you.

Distraction is another aspect of seer warfare. Have you ever been watching a movie or television show and you got distracted for just a few seconds and missed something important on-screen? The same thing happens in conversations when you zone out as a friend is talking. And the same can happen in the seer dimensions. Weary or distracted seers are less effective seers.

What many young seers don't recognize is that your gift is a threat to the kingdom of darkness. Like I always say, "An enemy exposed is an enemy defeated, but an enemy that's hidden cannot be forbidden." If he can keep you up at night, get you focused on the criticism, wear you out or distract you, he can sneak by you. Live "armored up" and stay your mind on Christ and you'll overcome every attack.

PRAYER

Father, in the name of Jesus, help me stay aware of the enemy who is roaming around like a roaring lion seeking someone to devour. Remind me to armor up daily.

NOVEMBER 17

STAY IN YOUR OFFICE

For I speak to you Gentiles; inasmuch as I am an apostle to the Gentiles, I magnify my office.

Romans 11:13

When I was coming up as a young Christian, I landed in an apostolic-prophetic church. The leader taught a lot from Ephesians 4. My Bible would literally fall open to Ephesians 4:11-12, "And He Himself gave some to be apostles, some prophets, some evangelists, and some pastors and teachers, for the equipping of the saints for the work of ministry, for the edifying of the body of Christ."

These are what we call the fivefold offices. Since the seer is a prophet and the prophet is an office, the fivefold seer stands in an office. Where is your office? It's in the local church. Even if God gives you an itinerant ministry to the nations, you still have an office in the local church. Many seers miss this and are disconnected from the local church. This is to their detriment. Community is important.

New Testament prophets were found in the local church. Seers and seeing people need other believers around them for accountability, fellowship, and strength. Seers are the eyes of the body, but they also need the other parts. Consider Paul's words in 1 Corinthians 12:20-21: "But now indeed there are many members, yet one body. And the eye cannot say to the hand, 'I have no need of you'; nor again the head to the feet, 'I have no need of you.'"

I find it particularly interesting how Paul focused on what the eye would say. If not careful, seers can get puffed up in pride because of the abundance of revelation. Paul touched on this in 1 Corinthians 8:1 (AMPC), "...knowledge causes people to be puffed up (to bear themselves loftily and be proud), but love (affection and goodwill and benevolence) edifies and builds up and encourages one to grow [to his full stature]."

The seer gift is to edify the Church—that includes the local church. If you are not part of a local community, find one. If you can't find one that accepts the seer gifting, join AHOP.online, a webchurch with true community in the nations. But don't forsake fellowship, especially as we go deeper into the end times (Hebrews 10:25).

PRAYER

Father, in the name of Jesus, thank You for the local church. Help me to value it as much as You do. You are the Head of the church. Help me find a strong church community where my gifts are received.

NOVEMBER 18

DEVELOPING SEER HUNGER

Now eagerly desire the greater gifts....

1 Corinthians 12:31 NIV

The Holy Spirit showed me this: "Divine dreams and visions come to many, but revelation is released to the hungry." The dream, vision, or encounter itself is not the revelation. It's the experience. We need to draw revelation from the experience. We should be hungry to see, yes, but also hungry to understand what we see.

Paul writes in 1 Corinthians 14:1, "Pursue love, and desire spiritual gifts, but especially that you may prophesy." Seeing is a form of prophesying when you have the interpretation of what you see.

Have you ever wondered why the Bible tells us to desire spiritual gifts? We should desire spiritual gifts because God tells us to. We should desire spiritual gifts to bless people. Spiritual gifts, including seeing, bless the Church.

Paul also writes in 1 Corinthians 14:3-4, "But he who prophesies speaks edification and exhortation and comfort to men. He who speaks in a tongue edifies himself, but he who prophesies edifies the church."

We should desire spiritual gifts for the sake of effective evangelism. Yes, seers have a role to play in reaching the lost! Spiritual gifts can open the eyes of the lost.

First Corinthians 14:24-25 says, "But if all prophesy, and an unbeliever or an uninformed person comes in, he is convinced by all, he is convicted by all. And thus the secrets of his heart are revealed; and so, falling down on his face, he will worship God and report that God is truly among you."

We should desire spiritual gifts because they can interrupt the enemy's plan. Discerning of spirits, which is connected to the seer anointing, is vital in spiritual warfare. We should desire spiritual gifts because they demonstrate the goodness and power of God.

Demonstrate your hunger by asking God to help you see, judge, interpret, and apply visual revelation. Practice your love walk because faith works by love. Study seers in the Bible. Pray in the Spirit as much as you can. Get some training—and step out and take a risk.

PRAYER

Father, in the name of Jesus, would You give me the gift of hunger? Make me hungrier for You and Your Word. Make me hungry to operate in spiritual gifts to build up the Church and release the Kingdom.

NOVEMBER 19

WHEN YOU SHUT DOWN THE GIFT

For the gifts and the calling of God are irrevocable.

Romans 11:29

I can't count the number of people I've ministered to who shut down their seer gift—some in early childhood and some later in life. What does it mean to shut down your seer gift and why would someone do that?

Shutting down your seer gift usually happens when the gift becomes overwhelming either by the abundance of revelation or demonic attack. You may have asked God to shut it down or stop the flow. It may be that what you see in the spirit troubles you or that the spiritual warfare that comes with operating in the seer anointing is too great.

In reality, those are just signs that you haven't matured in your gift. It's not a reason to shut it down and there is no condemnation. This is why we need the School of the Seers (www.schoolofthespirit.tv) and local prophetic churches. It takes time, teaching, and mentors to help you steward what you see without overwhelm.

Know this: the overwhelm you feel and the temptation to ask God to shut down your gift is an assignment from the pit of hell to shut your spiritual eyes and take you out of your calling. God is not trying to overwhelm you, but the enemy will nag and prod and push until you are tempted to shut your eyes.

Don't fall for it. And if you're convicted right now because you know you prayed that prayer, however long ago, it's not too late for restoration. Indeed, God is a God of restoration and He understands why you prayed that prayer. He answered it because He loves you and didn't want to see you overwhelmed and upset. You can repent.

Paul wrote in Romans 11:29 (AMPC), "For God's gifts and His call are irrevocable. [He never withdraws them when once they are given, and He does not change His mind about those to whom He gives His grace or to whom He sends His call.]"

So even though your visual revelation may have dried up, the calling is not removed. You can reactive it through repentance and sincere prayer. The Holy Spirit is your Teacher and will show you how to walk in the anointing Jesus gave you. And yes, you also need human teachers. You also need to pray for yourself. Pray for protection over your mind, imaginations, and thoughts. Pray for discernment. Pray that God would help you navigate your calling with integrity.

PRAYER

Father, in the name of Jesus, thank You for the visual revelation You give me. I repent for the times I have asked You to slow down or to shut down my spiritual eyes. Please, restore my vision.

NOVEMBER 20

STEWARDING YOUR SEER ENCOUNTERS

As each one has received a gift, minister it to one another, as good stewards of the manifold grace of God.

1 Peter 4:10

While every believer has the ability to see in the spirit, many never do. When God graces you with a seer anointing, then, His purpose is to use that gift to advance His Kingdom. That means we have to learn how to be good stewards.

Paul wrote, "Having then gifts differing according to the grace that is given to us, let us use them: if prophecy, let us prophesy in proportion to our faith; or ministry, let us use it in our ministering; he who teaches, in teaching; he who exhorts, in exhortation; he who gives, with liberality; he who leads, with diligence; he who shows mercy, with cheerfulness" (Romans 12:6-8).

While Paul doesn't explicitly mention seeing in the spirit, I don't think it's a stretch to say, "if seeing, let us see in proportion to our faith, let us use it in our ministering." Seeing in the spirit, then, is both a privilege and a responsibility—and it's usually not just about you. In other words, most believers who have a vision or dream are seeing for themselves. As a seer, you will see beyond yourself. You will also see for others, such as churches, cities, people, and nations.

Stewarding your seer anointing means using it for His glory, to edify people and dismantle the enemy's plans, and to prepare the way for His coming. With that in mind, we need to steward visual revelation diligently, humbly, and wisely.

That means making it a point to cultivate intimacy with the Holy Spirit. Without close fellowship with Him, you may misinterpret the source of what you are seeing—or the meaning of what you see. Likewise, part of stewarding your seer anointing is renewing your mind with the Word of God and developing a strong prayer life, as God will encounter you through the Word and prayer.

Asking for the grace of humility and being intentional about responding in the fruit of the Spirit are also critical to stewarding your seer anointing. Pride and carnal attitudes will hinder your anointing because it grieves the Holy Spirit in you.

PRAYER

Father, in the name of Jesus, please give me the grace of humility. Help me be intentional about stewarding my seer anointing well. You have given me this gift to serve others. Give me opportunities to serve.

NOVEMBER 21

SMELLING IN THE SPIRIT

Because of the fragrance of your good ointments, Your name is ointment poured forth; therefore the virgins love you.

Song of Solomon 1:3

I'll never forget the first time God allowed me to smell in the spirit. I was attending a conference in Nebraska when suddenly the aroma of fresh flowers filled the room. It was unmistakable and smelled sweeter than any flower I have ever smelled in nature. I learned later that it was the presence of the Lord. Since then, I have smelled in the spirit many times.

Smelling in the spirit is the ability to smell the presence of God or demon spirits. It's an aspect of the gift of discerning of spirits, according to *The Seer's Dictionary*. There are heavenly smells such as frankincense, capers, coriander, cumin, dill, mint, garlic, onion, hyssop, myrrh, cinnamon, saffron, thyme, anise, fennaway.

Consider Song of Solomon 1:3, "Because of the fragrance of your good ointments, Your name is ointment poured forth; therefore the virgins love you." And again 2 Corinthians 2:14, "Now thanks be to God who always leads us in triumph in Christ, and through us diffuses the fragrance of His knowledge in every place."

And again, "Therefore be imitators of God as dear children. And walk in love, as Christ also has loved us and given Himself for us, an offering and a sacrifice to God for a sweet-smelling aroma" (Ephesians 5:1-2). These are just a few Scriptures illustrating smells.

There are also demonic smells like smoke, sulfur, urine, tobacco, manure, sewage, and skunk, to name a few. Paul spoke in 2 Corinthians 2:16 of aromas: "To the one we are the aroma of death leading to death, and to the other the aroma of life leading to life...." Joel 2:20 speaks of a foul smell, "...his stench will come up, and his foul odor will rise, because he has done monstrous things."

How do you smell in the spirit? One way to position yourself is through deep worship, opening your heart completely to Him, asking for nothing and ready to receive anything He might offer, and pursuing His heart with all of your heart.

PRAYER

Father, in the name of Jesus, I would love to smell in the spirit as part of my gift mix. Would You open my spiritual sense of smell? I want to smell the fragrance of Your presence.

NOVEMBER 22

SOLVING SPIRITUAL RIDDLES

This is the interpretation of each word....

Daniel 5:26

Daniel had a spiritual talent beyond dreaming and interpreting dreams. He also had a spiritual gift to solve spiritual riddles. This is a fascinating aspect of the seer dimensions that we don't often see today.

Let's take a look at Daniel's gift in action in Daniel 5. For context, King Belshazzar held a drunken feast that hosted about one thousand people. He commanded his servants to bring the gold and silver vessels that his father, Nebuchadnezzar, took from God's temple in Jerusalem so he could drink from them.

Suddenly, the fingers of a man's hand appeared and wrote on the wall of the king's palace. The evil king literally saw the hand that wrote on the wall. When he did, his knees started knocking.

He immediately called his astrologers and soothsayers and offered a reward to anyone who could interpret the message. None of them could solve the spiritual riddle. Then the queen advised him to call Daniel, who immediately told the king in Daniel 5:23-28:

> ...You have praised the gods of silver and gold, bronze and iron, wood and stone, which do not see or hear or know; and the God who holds your breath in His hand and owns all your ways, you have not glorified. Then the fingers of the hand were sent from Him, and this writing was written.
>
> And this is the inscription that was written: MENE, MENE, TEKEL, UPHARSIN. This is the interpretation of each word. MENE: God has numbered your kingdom, and finished it; TEKEL: You have been weighed in the balances, and found wanting; PERES: Your kingdom has been divided, and given to the Medes and Persians.

That night, everyone knew Daniel's interpretation was correct. Belshazzar was slain and Darius received the kingdom. And guess who Darius selected as his advisor? The one who solved the riddle, Daniel. The ability to solve spiritual riddles goes along with the gift of interpretation. Not all seers carry this inherently, but you can ask for it. I believe in the end times we will see more spiritual riddles. Start asking now.

PRAYER

Father, in the name of Jesus, would You help me solve spiritual riddles? I want to exercise every aspect of the seer dimensions, including unravelling riddles that contain mysteries.

NOVEMBER 23

EXPOSING THE SPIRIT OF ERROR

We are of God. He who knows God hears us; he who is not of God does not hear us. By this we know the spirit of truth and the spirit of error.

1 John 4:6

I once saw a popular preacher on social media saying masturbation can be a weapon against the enemy. This is a shocking statement—and a sad one given his father was a great man of God who surely taught him better. What happened? He strayed from the truth into a spirit of error. Many others have followed suit.

What we're seeing today is part of something I prophesied in 2015: "A tsunami of perversion and all manner of wicked sin is headed toward this nation. You've only yet seen the rumblings of what the enemy has planned. For many in your nation have called good evil and called evil good. Many in this nation have not believed you will reap what you sow."

When you think of perversion you probably immediately think of sexual perversion—and I believe that's part of it. But it became clear to me that the root of this tsunami of perversion is actually the perversion of God's Word itself. We're seeing prominent pastors and entire denominations perverting God's Word, twisting it to defend and justify perversion itself, and suggesting the rest of us are legalistic or unenlightened about the truth.

Here are some examples of the spirit of error in action: praying to saints; believing Jesus came back in AD 79; using one-off Scriptures to justify sin; the doctrine of causationism, which says there are no more miracles or healing today; the practice of putting personal experience above Scripture; and universalism (which says there is no hell). I could go on and on.

How do you avoid the spirit of error? I've taught entire classes on this. Start by asking the Holy Spirit to help you rightly divide the word of truth (2 Timothy 2:15). That comes, in part, through dedicated Bible study. Be a doer of the Word, not just a hearer of the Word so you don't deceive yourself. Ask the Holy Spirit to make you more sensitive to His conviction. Be careful what preachers you listen to and what you read. The spirit of error is subtle.

PRAYER

Father, in the name of Jesus, help me discern error anywhere it manifests, whether through teaching, dreams, visions, prophetic words, encounters, or any other avenue. Help me rightly divide the Word of truth.

NOVEMBER 24

POSITIONING YOURSELF FOR ENCOUNTERS

You will seek Me and find Me when you seek Me with all your heart.
Jeremiah 29:13

Two seers can have equally powerful gifts. One is prolific in his vision. The other scarcely sees a thing. Have you ever wondered why? I submit to you that one reason—and it's not the only reason—is positioning.

Put another way, you have to position yourself for encounters. Think of it like this: Have you ever looked out the window or walked down the street and noticed that it's raining over some houses on one side but not the other? Those houses were positioned for the rainfall.

You have to position yourself for encounters. Yes, it's up to God to open your eyes and let you see in the spirit realm. Yes, He is the Door. He is the Giver of dreams, visions, encounters, trances, and out-of-body experiences. But we do have a part to play.

You have to position yourself for encounters. Now that I have said this three times, let me tell you what it means. Visual revelation often comes when we are intentionally positioned to receive. That doesn't necessarily mean sitting quietly before Him, although that is one position where revelation often flows.

In Revelation 1:10-16, John was "in the Spirit on the Lord's Day" when he saw Jesus in His glory. In Exodus 24:12-18, Moses ascended Mount Sinai to meet God and receive divine revelation. In Luke 19:4-5, Zacchaeus climbed a tree because he was desperate to see Jesus. And Jesus rewarded him with a house visit.

So, then, how do we position ourselves for an encounter with Jesus? Again, you can't make it happen. But you can sow to the Spirit. You can intentionally pursue intimacy with Him. You can seek His face instead of just another revelation. God made this promise to Jeremiah, "You will seek me and find me when you seek me with all your heart" (Jeremiah 29:13 NIV).

Instead of striving for an encounter, position yourself. Encounters are birthed through relationship. Make time and space for Him. Draw near to Him and He will draw near to you (James 4:8). But don't just draw near casually. "Let us draw near with a true heart in full assurance of faith, having our hearts sprinkled from an evil conscience and our bodies washed with pure water" (Hebrews 10:22).

PRAYER

Father, in the name of Jesus, help me to set aside the distractions and the weights that keep me out of position to receive fresh revelation and heavenly encounters. Help me seek first the Kingdom.

NOVEMBER 25

DÉJÀ VU IS NOT PART OF THE SEER DIMENSIONS

For prophecy never came by the will of man, but holy men of God spoke as they were moved by the Holy Spirit.

2 Peter 1:21

Is déjà vu part of the seer dimensions. Absolutely not, but I can see why some people would think so. It's critical that we don't throw around witchcraft words like déjà vu even though it may seem like the best way to describe what we're experiencing. We need to be accurate in the spirit.

Let me explain. Déjà vu is a French phrase that means "already seen." *Merriam-Webster's Dictionary* defines *déjà vu* as "the illusion of remembering scenes and events when experienced for the first time" and "feeling that one has seen or heard something before" and "something overly or unpleasantly familiar."

I've experienced this many times—and you probably have too. Déjà vu can come from mental disorders like anxiety, dissociative identity disorder, or schizophrenia. Déjà vu can come from medical disorders like epilepsy, and some pharmaceutical drugs.

Some seers point to déjà vu as a deep visual experience. Could it be possible that God is using what feels like déjà vu to communicate His truths? Or is it a familiar spirit? Is it witchcraft?

Déjà vu is mentioned nowhere in the Bible, but one thing is certain—it is not a spiritual gift. This is not the gift of prophecy. It's not the word of knowledge. Scripture is very clear that some supernatural communications and expressions come from God's Spirit (1 Corinthians 12:4-11) while others come from evil forces (Deuteronomy 18:10-12).

Could what feels like déjà vu be God showing you something? Yes. Here's where I land on it. Many times God will give us a dream but we don't remember it. At times, it's enemy interference, but at other times it's God hiding the dream in our spirit. He brings it to our remembrance at just the right time.

If you've ever felt like you've seen the scene playing out in front of your natural eyes, it could be that you had a dream about what you are seeing. In other words, the dream is manifesting before your eyes. The purpose is often to get your attention about a natural event. If you experience what feels like what the world calls déjà vu, don't be deceived. God doesn't speak through déjà vu. He speaks by His Spirit. Lean in and ask Him what to do.

PRAYER

Father, in the name of Jesus, help me not to commingle my visual revelation or vocabulary with the ways of the world. I want to see what You show me, not what familiar spirits offer.

NOVEMBER 26

IT LOOKED LIKE THIS...

Like the appearance of a rainbow in a cloud on a rainy day, so was the appearance of the brightness all around it. This was the appearance of the likeness of the glory of the Lord.

Ezekiel 1:28

There are times when you don't have human words to describe what you are seeing in the spirit. That's when we rely on resemblances. A resemblance is "the shape or form of something in the spirit that can be best described by using a natural example," according to *The Seer's Dictionary*.

Ezekiel repeatedly used this mechanism.

In Ezekiel 1:4-5 he writes, "Then I looked, and behold, a whirlwind was coming out of the north, a great cloud with raging fire engulfing itself; and brightness was all around it and radiating out of its midst like the color of amber, out of the midst of the fire. Also from within it came the likeness of four living creatures. And this was their appearance: they had the likeness of a man."

Peter described what he saw while in a trace on the roof this way: "heaven opened and an object like a great sheet bound at the four corners, descending to him and let down to the earth. In it were all kinds of four-footed animals of the earth, wild beasts, creeping things, and birds of the air" (Acts 10:11-12).

John the Revelator used this mechanism repeatedly. In Revelation 4:7, we read: "The first living creature was like a lion, the second living creature like a calf, the third living creature had a face like a man, and the fourth living creature was like a flying eagle." And again in Revelation 8:8, "Then the second angel sounded: And something like a great mountain burning with fire was thrown into the sea, and a third of the sea became blood."

Can you see it? In the seer dimensions you may see creatures or objects that aren't the same as what we know on earth, but if you were forced to describe it you would say, "It kind of looked like this." It's not a natural object, but the best way you can describe it is by referring to an object in the natural that people can relate to. Resemblance, or likeness, is part of the mature seer's vocabulary.

PRAYER

Father, in the name of Jesus, help me use this tool in my seer toolkit. It if worked for the apostles and prophets in Scripture, it will work for me. Help me to find the right language to describe accurately what I see.

NOVEMBER 27

CAN WE SEE THE GREAT CLOUD OF WITNESSES?

We are encompassed with such a great cloud of witnesses....
Hebrews 12:1 MEV

Hebrews 12:1 offers one of the most hotly debated verses in Scripture. As a seer, you need to understand what the Bible says and decide what you believe about seeing the great cloud of witnesses.

Let's look at Hebrews 12:1 in the AMPC version of the Bible: "Therefore then, since we are surrounded by so great a cloud of witnesses [who have borne testimony to the Truth]...." The MSG translation puts it this way: "Do you see what this means—all these pioneers who blazed the way, all these veterans cheering us on? It means we'd better get on with it." And the TLB says this, "Since we have such a huge crowd of men of faith watching us from the grandstands, let us strip off anything that slows us down or holds us back...."

So who are among this great cloud of witnesses? They are people who have passed into glory who are in Heaven with the Lord, according to *The Seer's Dictionary*. The general belief is that they are members of the Hebrews 11 "Hall of Faith" and others who walked with the Lord.

Barnes' Notes on the Bible reads, "The phrase, 'a cloud of witnesses,' means many witnesses, or a number so great that they seem to be a cloud." These witnesses are those who went before us who bore witness to the truth.

There are people in Heaven who don't yet have resurrected bodies. The believers who went before us are in Heaven with spirit bodies. They don't get their resurrected bodies until Jesus returns. For example, we see in the Bible Jesus talking to Moses and Elijah.

In the book of Revelation, we see the elders in Heaven making invitations to John. Revelation 5:4-5 says, "So I wept much, because no one was found worthy to open and read the scroll, or to look at it. But one of the elders said to me, 'Do not weep. Behold, the Lion of the tribe of Judah, the Root of David, has prevailed to open the scroll and to loose its seven seals.'"

It is clear that it is possible to have interactions with those in the great cloud of witnesses. But this is to be judged with great discernment as the last days will bring deceiving spirits that pretend to be angels, Jesus, and others. Proceed with caution.

PRAYER

Father, in the name of Jesus, help me to appreciate the reality of the great cloud of witnesses without making it a major doctrine that risks leading me astray. I am open to any experience You bring me into.

NOVEMBER 28

THE JOHN THE REVELATOR SEER ANOINTING

After these things I looked, and behold, a door standing open in heaven. And the first voice which I heard was like a trumpet speaking with me, saying, "Come up here, and I will show you things which must take place after this."

Revelation 4:1

John called himself the disciple whom Jesus loved, but biblical history also knows him as John the Revelator. The former fisherman recorded epic apocalyptic visions, angelic encounters—and even had a conversation with the resurrected Christ who appeared before him—that are beyond what most of us have ever experienced.

John's eschatological book offers some of the strangest visual revelations in the Bible—and among the most misunderstood and ignored. But when they read the book of Revelation, most seers tend to focus less on eschatological debates about the timing of the tribulation and more on the heavenly encounters, conversations with elders, and end-times events.

John's life was marked by deep intimacy with Jesus. Think about it. He was the one who reclined on Jesus' chest at the Last Supper (John 13:23). John was the one Jesus chose to take care of His mother, instructing him to adopt her as his own while He was dying on the Cross (John 19:27). I believe this intimacy is part of what opened the door to end-times mysteries.

Operating under a seer anointing, John explored some of the deepest realms of the seer dimensions. He received and stewarded revelations that Jesus aimed to prepare the Church for His Second Coming.

But more than that, John's seer anointing opened up to us an unveiling of Christ in His glory. Ultimately, the book of Revelation is not just a revelation of the end of the age but a revelation of Christ as King, coming back to war against evil with saints and angels. It's a revelation of His glorious Kingdom with glimpses into Heaven and the new Jerusalem.

Meditate on this: "Then I turned to see the voice that spoke with me. And having turned I saw seven golden lampstands, and in the midst of the seven lampstands One like the Son of Man, clothed with a garment down to the feet and girded about the chest with a golden band. His head and hair were white like wool, as white as snow, and His eyes like a flame of fire; His feet were like fine brass, as if refined in a furnace, and His voice as the sound of many waters" (Revelation 1:12-15). Can you see it? Keep looking until you do.

PRAYER

Father, in the name of Jesus, help me develop the intimacy with You that John experienced when Jesus walked the earth. I know there is a connection between intimacy and deep revelation. I want to be trustworthy.

NOVEMBER 29

SEEING BEHIND THE VEIL

This hope we have as an anchor of the soul, both sure and steadfast, and which enters the Presence behind the veil, where the forerunner has entered for us, even Jesus, having become High Priest forever according to the order of Melchizedek.

Hebrews 6:19-20

The veil between Heaven and earth still exists, but it's getting thinner. In other words, it's getting easier to see through the veil and into the spirit.

Encounters behind the veil do not come through striving but through seeking God and, often, waiting in silence. Other times they come suddenly, even at inconvenient times. (I write about the silent dimension in my book, *The Seer Dimensions*.)

Hebrews 6:19 speaks of a hope that serves as a strong and trustworthy anchor for our souls. That hope paves the way into His presence behind the veil, since we go there by faith and faith is the substance of things hoped for (Hebrews 11:1). The AMPC puts Hebrews 6:19 it this way: "[Now] we have this [hope] as a sure and steadfast anchor of the soul [it cannot slip and it cannot break down under whoever steps out upon it—a hope] that reaches farther and enters into [the very certainty of the Presence] within the veil."

This hope reaches beyond the curtain into the Throne Room. Let that sink in. Jesus Himself is our hope and gives us the measure of faith to follow Him behind the veil.

One of the mysteries Paul unraveled by revelation is this: when we turn to the Lord, the veil is taken away. When the veil is removed we can behold the glory of the Lord (2 Corinthians 3:16-18). Our legal position is seated in heavenly places with Christ Jesus even now (Ephesians 2:4-5). We are seated behind the veil, even if we don't yet see behind the veil. But, again, the veil is growing thinner as the Second Coming of Christ approaches. We're seeing more people encounter Heaven, hell, and receiving profound visual revelation.

"Mystery is one of the greatest lures of romance and intimacy. The magnetism draws us, woos us, even propels us to find what we have yet to experience, to find what our heart knows is there," wrote John Paul Jackson in *7 Days Behind the Veil*. "We can sense it. Our logic argues against it, but the mystery becomes so much our desire that in the end, we pursue it with everything we have, unmindful of the cost."

PRAYER

Father, in the name of Jesus, would You give me a revelation that I am seated in heavenly places in Christ—behind the veil. Help me see through the eyes of my spirit what's hidden behind the veil.

NOVEMBER 30

MULTIPLIED VISIONS

...and have multiplied visions; I have given symbols through the witness of the prophets.

Hosea 12:10

Many seers experience the reality of multiplied visions but don't have language for it. When I speak of multiplied visions, I am pointing to what *The Seer's Dictionary* describes as, "a season of increase in visions; numerous visions; a strong increase in visions." In other words, the visions seem to multiply. It's a season of heavy revelation.

I heard the Lord say:

I am pouring out multiplied visions upon the seers and the prophets. The eyes of the prophets will be opened at a new level. Multiplied visions. Multiplied visions. Multiplied visions. I will show you things to come, even things in the latter years and in the end times. I will show you things through multiplied visions. You will have one after another after another as you begin to gaze upon My beauty.

For I hold the key and I will unlock the mysteries and I will show you things you could never even imagine, and you will know that it is Me because you couldn't even imagine it. As wild as your imagine may be, the visions I will show you will be much wilder. I will show you visions unto the likeness of what Ezekiel saw and what John saw and what Zechariah saw.

I will show you these things as you pursue Me and as you cleanse your eyes, wiping away the tears and wiping away the distractions and wiping away the negativity and wiping away those things that burned you, that hurt you. Look upon Me because I am not only the Author of visions but multiplied visions in this season for the seers and the prophets.

Visions are mentioned in the Bible far more than dreams, yet we have largely focused on dreams for the past several decades. God is giving seers great visions, many visions and numerous visions, and exceedingly increased visions. You might wonder why. One reason is because of the times we are in. Times of acceleration demand more rapid revelation.

PRAYER

Father, in the name of Jesus, You gave multiplied visions in Hosea's day, how much more in this time when Your seers are filled with Your Spirit. Help me to position myself for multiplied visions and to steward them well.

DECEMBER

Then, being divinely warned in a dream that they should not return to Herod, they departed for their own country another way.

Matthew 2:12

DECEMBER 1

SEEING FROM HEAVENLY PLACES

Even when we were dead in trespasses, made us alive together with Christ (by grace you have been saved), and raised us up together, and made us sit together in the heavenly places in Christ Jesus.

Ephesians 2:5-6

In Christ, we are seated in heavenly places. That is our legal position. If we understand this, we can build our faith to discern from God's viewpoint. Seeing from heavenly places brings a completely different perspective and another level of discernment.

Remember what God told Isaiah, "For my thoughts are not your thoughts, neither are your ways my ways.... As the heavens are higher than the earth, so are my ways higher than your ways and my thoughts than your thoughts" (Isaiah 55:8-9).

The Lord's discernment is also higher than your natural discernment. You need a Heaven-down perspective.

Seeing from Heaven down requires practice. First, it requires waiting on the Lord before you make a judgment between what is good or what is bad. Isaiah 40:31 tells us, "But those who wait on the Lord shall renew their strength; they shall mount up with wings like eagles...." An eagle soars higher than any other bird. When we wait on the Lord, we soar like an eagle above the distractions of life—and above the enemy. That's a Heaven-down perspective.

Ask the Lord what He sees. Waiting isn't a passive state. Usually you have to seek while you wait and then wait until He speaks. While you are waiting, ask the Lord what and how He sees something, then wait on His perspective. Seeing from Heaven down is how you get the Lord's heart on the matters at hand. Sometimes natural discernment doesn't wait and it doesn't ask. Discerning of spirits can be accurate in knowing but poor in application. God's perspective is flawless.

Developing Heaven-down discernment demands humility. Pride assumes and presumes. Pride thinks it knows what the Lord wants to do. A humble seer is a discerning seer. Romans 12:3 (NLT) says, "Don't think you are better than you really are." And walk in love. Love-based discernment builds the Church—and builds people rather than tearing them down. Love-based discernment is life-giving, even where correction has to be made. Love-based discernment has the heart of the Father.

PRAYER

Father, in the name of Jesus, would You teach me to wait on You and Your perspective instead of getting into my head on what I see? I want to see from Your viewpoint. I want to see from Heaven down.

DECEMBER 2

RELEASING VISUAL WORDS OF KNOWLEDGE

For to one is given the word of wisdom through the Spirit, to another the word of knowledge through the same Spirit.

1 Corinthians 12:8

When I was in Europe ministering at a supernatural conference, I was pacing across the stage praying when I suddenly saw a popsicle in the spirit. I know! I thought it was strange also! So I turned the other way and I saw it again. Then I turned and walked back in the other direction and saw it a third time.

I finally discerned the Holy Spirit was giving me a visual word of knowledge. I asked, "Does popsicle mean anything to anyone?" A woman started screaming. I said, "Does this mean something to you?" She was shaking, and cried out, "My husband! My husband!" I asked, "Where is your husband?" She went out to the lobby to get him.

When he came in, bewildered, I asked him, "Sir, does a popsicle mean anything to you?" The man of God told me he was seeking confirmation on opening a popsicle business. The visual word of knowledge was his confirmation. I prayed over his business and he was deeply touched.

That's the power of a visual word of knowledge, which is a word of knowledge that you can see, according to *The Seer's Dictionary*. A word of knowledge is revelation with information related to the past or present. God reveals a word or "fragment" of information related to people, places, or things. It's one of the nine gifts of the Spirit.

Put another way, a word of knowledge is a supernatural revelation of information received through the Holy Spirit. It is knowledge received without natural analysis or human means. If you can know it in the natural, it's not a supernatural revelation. The word of knowledge has to do with God giving divine knowledge and insight into certain situations.

The purpose of the Word of knowledge is to build faith for someone to receive something, healing, instruction, etc. A visual word of knowledge is powerful because it builds faith in the one to whom it relates. Another purpose of a visual word of knowledge is for intercession.

In Acts 9:11-12 (NIV), a prophet received a word of knowledge in a vision: "The Lord told him, 'Go to the house of Judas on Straight Street and ask for a man from Tarsus named Saul, for he is praying. In a vision he has seen a man named Ananias come and place his hands on him to restore his sight.'"

Pay attention to visual words of knowledge. They can change lives.

PRAYER

Father, in the name of Jesus, I am intrigued by visual words of knowledge. Help me to discern them and to be willing to release them, even if it seems foolish to do so.

DECEMBER 3

SHARING VISUAL WORDS OF WISDOM

For to one is given the word of wisdom through the Spirit....
1 Corinthians 12:8

When the Holy Spirit wills, you can receive a visual word of wisdom. A visual word of wisdom is a word of wisdom expressed visually, according to *The Seer's Dictionary*. You see something in the spirit that brings wisdom to a situation.

A word of wisdom is characterized by purity, peace, gentleness, reason, mercy, good fruits, impartiality and righteousness. A word of wisdom has to do with the present or future.

We don't talk much about the word of wisdom in the Church today. Most are more concerned with the word of knowledge or the gift of prophecy or the working of miracles. But we need the word of wisdom today perhaps more than ever before.

Kenneth E. Hagin defined it this way: "[The gift of a word of wisdom] is a supernatural revelation by the Spirit of God concerning the divine purpose in the mind and will of God. It is revelation concerning the plan and purpose in the mind of God, speaking of the future."

You can't choose to operate in a visual word of wisdom. As one of the nine gifts of the Holy Spirit, He allows you to see a visual word of knowledge according to His will. But we can pray for this gift and be sensitive to the Holy Spirit working to express this gift through us. I believe sometimes we just miss this!

Much the same as with prophecy or a word of knowledge, you could have a visual impression of what is right without any head knowledge that what you are sensing is accurate. You can also get a word of wisdom in a dream, a vision, or a trance. In Acts 10:1-6, Peter received a word of wisdom during a trance that instructed him to go with some men who were coming to introduce him to Cornelius.

Wisdom is greatly needed in times of change. It produces conviction, unanimity, progress, success, open hearts, open doors, justice, perspective, peace, and much more. How do you judge a visual word of wisdom? James 3:17-18 tells us, "But the wisdom that is from above is first pure, then peaceable, gentle, open to reason, full of mercy and good fruits, without partiality, and without hypocrisy. And the fruit of righteousness is sown in peace by those who make peace."

PRAYER

Father, in the name of Jesus, help me understand the dynamics of visual words of wisdom—and help me discern this gift expression in my visions. Teach me to receive and release visual words of wisdom.

DECEMBER 4

THE PLANK THAT BLOCKS YOUR VISION

Therefore you are inexcusable, O man, whoever you are who judge, for in whatever you judge another you condemn yourself; for you who judge practice the same things.

Romans 2:1

I hate the "something in my eye" feeling. There have been times when I gazed in the mirror trying to find what was irritating my eye only to find nothing, but at least I looked. The more dangerous scenario would be not noticing something is in my eye causing damage to my vision.

Many people have more than sand in their eyes. They have a pole in their eye and are blind to it. It's hard to see with a pole in your eye. There are many types of "poles" we can have in our eyes, from anger to bitterness and resentment to grief and trauma and beyond. But Jesus pointed specifically to a pole called judgment.

In Matthew 7:1-5 ESV, Jesus said, "Judge not, that you be not judged. For with the judgment you pronounce you will be judged, and with the measure you use it will be measured to you. Why do you see the speck that is in your brother's eye, but do not notice the log that is in your own eye? Or how can you say to your brother, 'Let me take the speck out of your eye,' when there is the log in your own eye? You hypocrite, first take the log out of your own eye, and then you will see clearly to take the speck out of your brother's eye."

How can you see clearly with a pole in your eyes? As seers and seeing people, we need to keep our vision clear. That means periodically asking the Lord to, as I say, cleanse your lens. I wear glasses. I have to clean my glasses every day because particles of dust gather on the lens. Sometimes water splashes on the lens or there's a smudge from my fingers. I can't see accurately when my lens is not clear. Neither can you.

Judgment is not the only pole that will cloud your seer eyes, but it is an especially dangerous one. If we want to see through God's eyes—if we want to see what He is showing us accurately—we need to avoid the temptation to look at the world through our carnal eyes. Ask God to cleanse your lens.

PRAYER

Father, in the name of Jesus, help me to notice if there is a pole in my eye. Better yet, would You help me not to take on attitudes and emotions that allow specks in my eyes that cause me to not see accurately?

DECEMBER 5

UNDERSTANDING X-RAY VISION

I, the Lord, search the heart, I test the mind, even to give every man according to his ways, according to the fruit of his doings.

Jeremiah 17:10

When I heard the Lord say He was going to give X-ray vision to the seers—certain seers—it caught my attention. I have never heard of such a thing, except in science fiction movies. Of course, God is a God who supersedes science and nothing about Him is fiction.

What is X-ray vision? It's the ability to see inside something or someone. An X-ray sees what we can't see with our human eyes or our natural vision. In part, God is speaking of a greater level of discernment to judge motives and intentions, to see demons inspiring the activities of people, and to discern the war in the heavens so that we can take our authority.

We know God Himself has X-ray vision in the sense that He sees in us and through us. God looks at the heart (1 Samuel 16:7). God sees our motives. God sees our thoughts. God sees the desires of our hearts. God sees whether there is truth in our inward parts (Psalm 51:6). God also sees right through the enemy—and his plots and plans.

Hebrews 4:13 reveals, "There is no creature hidden from His sight, but all things are naked and open to the eyes of Him to whom we must give account." God sees everything—and through everything and into everything—all the time.

Just as X-rays will allow medical doctors to see inside the human body—showing fractures, infections, decay, cancer, enlarged hearts, blocked blood vessels, swallowed items and digestive tract problems—X-ray vision will allow seers to look deeper into things to see the enemy's hidden work.

I started experiencing X-ray vision some years ago. In my hotel room, I started seeing people walking down hallways. I would head to the door and open it to find they were just a few steps away or, at times, with their hand up about to knock. When this happens, it always startles people. They ask, "How did you know I was here?" I can't explain it, other than X-ray vision.

PRAYER

Father, in the name of Jesus, I would love to experience X-ray vision but only if it serves Your purposes. I refuse to strive in the seer dimensions, but I am open to any form of revelation You offer me.

DECEMBER 6

THE ZADOK ANOINTING

The king also said to Zadok the priest, "Are you not a seer? Return to the city in peace, and your two sons with you, Ahimaaz your son, and Jonathan the son of Abiathar."

2 Samuel 15:27

Most seers don't pay much attention to Zadok. He didn't have any recorded visions of a wheel within a wheel like Ezekiel. He didn't see the future Second Coming of our King and the apocalypse like the apostle John. He didn't have an out-of-body experience like Paul or a vision of the four beasts like Daniel.

While Zadok may have had such encounters, the Holy Spirit chose not to highlight them in Scripture. In fact, in the realm of seers, Zadok was more like John the Baptist in the sense that he wasn't flashy. Most seers don't think much about Zadok or his anointing. But God does. So should you.

Zadok was a Levite and a high priest during King David's reign. And 2 Samuel 15:27 marks him as a seer. David asks Zadok in 2 Samuel 15:27-29, "The king also said to Zadok the priest, 'Are you not a seer? Return to the city in peace, and your two sons with you, Ahimaaz your son, and Jonathan the son of Abiathar. See, I will wait in the plains of the wilderness until word comes from you to inform me.' Therefore Zadok and Abiathar carried the ark of God back to Jerusalem. And they remained there."

David was demonstrating his trust for the seer in two realms. First, to watch over the ark. Remember, the ark of the covenant was a symbol of God's presence and glory. Zadok was entrusted to steward the glory. That's a big deal! David also trusted Zadok and relied on him to go back to Jerusalem in the midst of Absalom's insurrection attempts to be an informant. He trusted him to be loyal to the crown.

The name Zadok means righteous and just. He goes down in Bible history as loyal to David. Proverbs 17:17, "A friend loves at all times, and a brother is born for adversity." That speaks of loyalty.

The Zadok anointing is a seer anointing to steward the presence and glory of God and to be loyal to God's leaders. Ask the Lord for the Zadok anointing when you need to steward what you see in the glory realm.

PRAYER

Father, in the name of Jesus, impart to me the Zadok seer anointing. Make me a seer of Your presence, discerning enough to guard the anointing and Your purposes in the earth. Help me to see and steward the glory realm.

DECEMBER 7

LEARNING TO WAIT ON THE LORD

The Lord is good to those who wait for Him, to the soul who seeks Him.

Lamentations 3:25

Many of us rush through our days. Starting from the moment we wake up, we're in a hurry. Some of you feel like you are always running late. We can't take that attitude into the seer dimensions. We must learn to wait on the Lord.

What does it mean to wait on the Lord? Let me compare and contrast to drive home the point. It's not a passive exercise. It's an active pursuit. It's not about striving. It's about stilling your soul, cutting out the clutter, and being mindful of His presence. Waiting on the Lord implies a seeking—and He is a rewarder of those who diligently seek Him (Hebrews 11:6). When you seek, You will see.

Waiting on the Lord is part of prayer. We ask, He answers in the still small voice—or with visual revelation that comes suddenly in response to our heartfelt petition. Waiting on the Lord is an expectation that He will show up and open your eyes or speak to your heart.

We grow in faith to see in the spirit when we wait on the Lord. We develop our spiritual ears to hear Him more clearly when we wait on the Lord. We receive the grace we need to succeed in our seer ministries when we wait on the Lord. We learn of His ways when we wait on the Lord. We gain the wisdom we need to interpret and apply our visual revelation when we wait on the Lord. We become more like Him as we spend that time with Him.

Isaiah 40:30-31 (AMPC) tells us, "Even youths shall faint and be weary, and [selected] young men shall feebly stumble and fall exhausted; but those who wait for the Lord [who expect, look for, and hope in Him] shall change and renew their strength and power; they shall lift their wings and mount up [close to God] as eagles [mount up to the sun]; they shall run and not be weary, they shall walk and not faint or become tired."

PRAYER

Father, in the name of Jesus, help me to slow down and wait on You. Help me learn the art of waiting on You. Help me to still my soul so I can hear and see what You want to share with me today.

DECEMBER 8

SEEING WITH SURROUND SOUND

And when he brings out his own sheep, he goes before them; and the sheep follow him, for they know his voice. Yet they will by no means follow a stranger, but will flee from him, for they do not know the voice of strangers.

John 10:4-5

Visions often come with an audio element. Indeed, they are often in more than "stereo" sound as we know it. It's more like surround sound! In other words, it can feel to your spiritual ears like you are immersed in the sounds you hear in the spirit. It's as if the sound is coming from all directions at once.

Ezekiel put it this way: "And behold, the glory of the God of Israel came from the way of the east. His voice was like the sound of many waters; and the earth shone with His glory" (Ezekiel 43:2). And John echoed this experience in Revelation 1:15, "His feet were like fine brass, as if refined in a furnace, and His voice as the sound of many waters."

The sounds we hear in a vision can be unlike anything we have ever experienced on earth. That's because you are hearing into another dimension. Daniel described God's voice "like the voice of a multitude" (Daniel 10:6). Ezekiel also described God's voice as "a tumult like the noise of an army" (Ezekiel 1:24).

Yes, sometimes we just see pictures without a corresponding sound. Those are quick flashes or visual revelation. But as the Holy Spirit leads us deeper into the seer dimensions we may also hear spectacular sounds, including the sound of God's voice.

In Psalm 29, David spends nearly a whole chapter talking about the voice of the Lord. Every seer should read this chapter. He says, "The voice of the Lord is powerful; the voice of the Lord is full of majesty. The voice of the Lord breaks the cedars.... The voice of the Lord shakes the wilderness."

When you see a thing, start to listen closely. You never know when God may choose to speak, even if He doesn't appear. Sometimes, if we're not careful, we can be so overtaken by what we see that we don't capture the audio message. Ask God to make all your spiritual senses more sensitive so you can catch everything you are supposed to see, hear, and feel.

PRAYER

Father, in the name of Jesus, help me learn to tune my spiritual ears to what you are saying in the seer dimensions. Help me listen not only for the dramatic or audible voice, but also the still small voice.

DECEMBER 9

TOUCHING IN THE SPIRIT

Then again, the one having the likeness of a man touched me and strengthened me.

Daniel 10:18

Seers often find themselves doing more than seeing—even more than feeling or knowing or tasting. They may enter the dimension of spiritual touch.

Touching is an active. You receive a feeling. You reach out and touch—or are touched. Touching is the only two-way sense. You can touch something and feel something touching you. Touch can be positive or negative. It can feel good or cause pain. We can understand physical touch this way: a baby's skin is soft, a cactus is prickly.

You can see, smell, or hear a person from a distance, but to touch someone or something, you need to be up close. Touch is more intimate. In the spirit, we can be touched by God, an angel, or demons.

When Jacob wrestled with God, God touched His hip. And in Jeremiah 1:8-9 we read, "'Do not be afraid of their faces, for I am with you to deliver you,' says the Lord. Then the Lord put forth His hand and touched my mouth, and the Lord said to me: 'Behold, I have put My words in your mouth.'" God touched his mouth.

Daniel experienced this sort of spiritual touch on a few occasions. In Daniel 8:18 we read about an angel touching him: "Now, as he was speaking with me, I was in a deep sleep with my face to the ground; but he touched me, and stood me upright." Again in Daniel 10:10 we read, "Suddenly, a hand touched me, which made me tremble on my knees and on the palms of my hands." And in Daniel 10:16, we see, "And suddenly, one having the likeness of the sons of men touched my lips; then I opened my mouth and spoke...."

John also experienced spiritual touch from the glorified Jesus in Revelation 1:17: "And when I saw Him, I fell at His feet as dead. But He laid His right hand on me, saying to me, 'Do not be afraid; I am the First and the Last.'"

Pretty wild, isn't it? This isn't something you ask for or invite. This is the will of the Lord (or an instruction from the demonic realm) and is relatively rare, but seers need to understand the reality of touching in the spirit so you know what you are dealing with, whether demonic or divine.

PRAYER

Father, in the name of Jesus, help me to understand the dimension of spiritual touch. I see it in the pages of Scripture. Give me a deeper revelation of Your purposes for spiritual touch.

DECEMBER 10

PRAYING THROUGH YOUR DREAMS

It is the glory of God to conceal a thing: but the honour of kings is to search out a matter.

Proverbs 25:2 KJV

Prayer is part and parcel of searching out the layers of meaning in your dreams. Once you've judged the dream to be accurate, it's time to exercise good stewardship by praying about the various aspects of what you experienced. Right now you may be asking, "How do I pray through a dream?"

First, sit quietly before the Lord and still your soul. Shut out all distractions and give yourself enough time to explore with the Lord in prayer. Take out your journal in which you wrote down the dream and read the dream slowly.

Although you may have interpreted large parts of your dream, as you read and pray it's possible to get more revelation on what the Lord said, what it means, or how to apply it. As you pray, you may see things you never saw before or even remember parts of the dream you forgot. This exercise could unlock new spiritual insights and strategies that are vital to understanding or applying the dream.

After you read the dream, drill down and pray more specifically. Ask the Lord to give you the full understanding of every element, symbol, number, name, or creature in the dream so that you can pray according to His will through every part of it.

Remember, there are layers of revelation in your dream. Some of it may apply for now, but there may be other parts that apply to the future. Wait on the Lord. Praying through a dream is the primary way of unlocking deeper meanings. Second Timothy 2:7 (ESV) tells us, "Think over what I say, for the Lord will give you understanding in everything."

After all this, spend a little more time praying about specific parts of the dream that you don't understand. Be careful trying to figure it out on your own. Proverbs 3:5: "Trust in the Lord with all your heart, and do not lean on your own understanding." You don't want your interpretation or application. You want God's interpretation and application. Check out my course Dream Keepers at www.schoolofthespirit.tv for more teaching on this.

PRAYER

Father, in the name of Jesus, help me not to neglect praying through my dreams. I know prayer unlocks revelation and I don't want to miss or misinterpret anything You are showing me.

DECEMBER 11

THE NAZARITE SEER

...When either a man or woman consecrates an offering to take the vow of a Nazirite, to separate himself to the Lord.

Numbers 6:2

The Delilah spirit has worked to blind the eyes of seers for thousands of years. In fact, you might say Delilah has been to seers what Jezebel has been to prophets. Although these two wicked spirits share many of the same characteristics, the major difference is Delilah works to blind the seer's eyes. Jezebel works to cut off the prophet's voice.

First, what is the Delilah spirit, specifically? We name this spirit after the woman Delijah in Judges 16. She seduced and nagged Samson until he finally shared the secret of his anointing. Like Jezebel, Delilah uses manipulation and control. But Deliah also operates in betrayal and robs seers of their spiritual strength.

God is raising up Nazarite seers in this era who will wage war against the Delilah spirit, gaining retribution for the blinding attacks on seer eyes in past generations.

What is a Nazarite? A Nazarite is one who takes the Numbers 6:1-21 vow. It's too long to rehash here, but I would invite you to read it. I will give you the gist of it. As you will see, it's beyond the normal Christian consecration.

Not every seer will commit to this vow—and every part of this Old Testament vow does not apply to a New Testament believer—but we will see consecrated companies of seers around the world that we'll call Nazarites. Again, this is beyond the traditional consecration. You might call it radical consecration.

In essence, the seer who takes a Nazarite vow separates themselves unto the Lord. It means no drinking. It means a lifestyle of repentance. It means offering your life as a drink offering to the Lord. It means making sacrifices in obedience to God. It means being a sold-out seer.

On January 14, 2024, for example, I decided not to look at anything that wasn't motivational, educational, or inspirational. I don't watch movies or TV or doom scroll on social media. Consecrating my eyes to that level and putting my nose in the Word, so to speak, led to deeper and more frequent encounters with the Lord in the seer dimensions.

PRAYER

Father, in the name of Jesus, may my consecration be an act of war. Help me to go deeper in the things of the Spirit and shun the things of the world so I have no open doors for Delilah.

DECEMBER 12

WATCH OUT FOR MONITORING SPIRITS

So they watched Him, and sent spies who pretended to be righteous, that they might seize on His words, in order to deliver Him to the power and the authority of the governor.

Luke 20:20

When I was in London in June 2018, I was expecting a radical encounter with the Lord. The Holy Spirit had told me in January I would be healed of some serious health issues when I went to London six months later. But I wasn't expecting what happened next.

We were sitting on the top level of a double decker tour bus riding around London when bees suddenly started swarming around us. When I looked around, these bees were not bothering the other 75 people on top of the bus. But the bees buzzed around our heads, flew away, and then came back again. This happened repeatedly.

Suddenly, it dawned on me. These were monitoring spirits spying on us and reporting back to a demonic network. I firmly believe their assignment was ultimately to thwart my encounter with a prophet who broke the curse that was making me sick.

Monitoring spirits are a device of the devil. Paul the apostle said these words about the enemy in 2 Corinthians 2:11, "for we are not ignorant of his devices." Operating under satan's hierarchy, the purpose of a monitoring spirit is to observe, report, and ultimately sabotage you.

Monitoring spirits are lower-level demons, but they serve higher-ranking powers by gathering data on your spiritual life, relationships, and weaknesses. Think of these demons as demonic surveillance agents, constantly seeking intel to pass along to demonic networks.

These spirits are dispatched to observe your behaviors, track your emotions, and discern your strengths and vulnerabilities. They're listening to your conversations, watching your interactions, and gathering details to form demonic strategies against you.

Monitoring spirits are more dangerous than most people realize. These are not random spiritual entities. They are highly strategic and intentional in their actions. They are very focused on their assignment.

Monitoring spirits don't want to be seen. They don't want to be discerned because once you discern them, you can defeat them. Seers are a threat to monitoring spirits because, well, you can see them watching you and other people. I have an entire course titled Blinding Monitoring Spirits at School of the Spirit.

PRAYER

Father, in the name of Jesus, would You help me discern these demonic watchers—these monitoring spirits that try to set up God's people for targeted attacks? Help me discern this demonic device.

DECEMBER 13

DIVIDING BETWEEN SOUL AND SPIRIT

For the word of God is living and powerful, and sharper than any two-edged sword, piercing even to the division of soul and spirit....
Hebrews 4:12

Visual revelation can come from any one of three sources: your soul, your God, or your adversary the devil. Your job—your responsibility—is to divide between the soulish realm and the spirit realm. The living Word of God helps you do that with razor-sharp precision.

And we need that precision because sometimes there is a mixture. It's part you and part God or part you and part the enemy or part the enemy and part God. Your imagination, which is part of your soul, can get carried away and go beyond the bounds of what God is showing you. Likewise, the enemy can also subtly intrude on your visual revelation and you can end up with a mixture.

But the Word of God will cut out what doesn't belong to Him. The AMPC version of the Bible puts it this way: "...it is sharper than any two-edged sword, penetrating to the dividing line of the breath of life (soul) and [the immortal] spirit, and of joints and marrow [of the deepest parts of our nature], exposing and sifting and analyzing and judging the very thoughts and purposes of the heart."

The Word doesn't just help you divide, it penetrates the mixture. The Word doesn't just help you judge. It is the judge. It's the exposer, the sifter, the analyzer. It judges the source of the visual revelation because modern-day revelation will never contradict the ancient texts. It sifts through what is God and what is not with pinpoint accuracy. It exposes the enemy's intrusion.

Paul the apostle, who operated in the seer dimensions and also saw plenty of false operators, put it this way, "...taking his stand on visions [he claims] he has seen, vainly puffed up by his sensuous notions and inflated by his unspiritual thoughts and fleshly conceit, and not holding fast to the Head, from Whom the entire body, supplied and knit together by means of its joints and ligaments, grows with a growth that is from God" (Colossians 2:18-19 AMPC).

Notice how they are not connected to the Head. They are not connected to Jesus. They are not connected to the Word. That's scary! Let the Word sift, analyze, judge, and expose. Your visual revelation will be more accurate for it.

PRAYER

Father, in the name of Jesus, help me lean on the Word to help me sift, analyze, judge, and expose the source of my visual revelation. I want to stay connected to the Head, from whom true revelation flows.

DECEMBER 14

THE REVELATION KEY MANY OVERLOOK

There remains therefore a rest for the people of God.

Hebrews 4:9

Many years ago I was on a broadcast with James Goll. He prophesied over me. He said, "Jennifer, I declare Romans 16:20 over you. That soon you will crush satan even under your feet. No, that's not what it says. And soon the *God of peace will crush satan* even under your feet. I declare over you, Jennifer, that there is coming a new place of the shalom of God. There is coming another manifestation of warfare that the level we rest is the level that we war. God is going to give you divine insight as resting as a method of warring."

At the time he prophesied that to me, I was in the midst of a massive battle. What I learned through that prophetic word is that the enemy brings warfare against seers—some of it is in the spirit realm and some of it through people—that can weary our eyes. We have to learn to rest in Him. There's rest in the anointing.

Isaiah 40:31 reminds us, "But those who wait on the Lord shall renew their strength; they shall mount up with wings like eagles, they shall run and not be weary, and they shall walk and not faint."

I received a confirmation of James' prophecy through a word from Chuck Pierce sometime later. He gave me Isaiah 28:12, "To whom He said, 'This is the rest with which you may cause the weary to rest,' And, 'This is the refreshing'; yet they would not hear."

I had to learn to rest in the warfare, rest in the drama—rest in Him. Without setting time aside to rest, seers risk burn out. That burnout can cause us to miss opportunities to see what God (or the enemy) is doing in the seer dimensions. Think about it for a minute. If Jesus had to rest—and suggested His disciples do the same—so do we.

In Mark 6:31, Jesus said to them, "'Come aside by yourselves to a deserted place and rest a while.' For there were many coming and going, and they did not even have time to eat." Of course, resting is not just about sleep. It's sitting in His presence and letting Him bring rest to your soul.

PRAYER

Father, in the name of Jesus, would You teach me how to rest in You? There is so much to do and so little time. I don't want to grow weary and burn out. Teach me how to tap into the supernatural rest You offer me.

DECEMBER 15

CHECKING YOUR MOTIVES FOR SHARING SEER REVELATION

> *All the ways of a man are pure in his own eyes, but the Lord weighs the spirits.*
>
> Proverbs 16:2

What are your motives for sharing that revelation, really? Did God tell you to share it—or to share on social media how accurate you were after your visual revelation came to pass?

When we put on a show for people, we have our reward in full. That reward is called the recognition and admiration of others. I don't know about you, but I'd rather receive God's slight nod over someone's standing ovation. And you get more than God's slight nod when His Kingdom purposes motivate your heart.

In Matthew 6:1-4, Jesus said:

> Take heed that you do not do your charitable deeds before men, to be seen by them. Otherwise you have no reward from your Father in heaven. Therefore, when you do a charitable deed, do not sound a trumpet before you as the hypocrites do in the synagogues and in the streets, that they may have glory from men. Assuredly, I say to you, they have their reward. But when you do a charitable deed, do not let your left hand know what your right hand is doing, that your charitable deed may be in secret; and your Father who sees in secret will Himself reward you openly.

Can you imagine? The religious leaders of the day—Jesus called them hypocrites—actually sounded a trumpet to draw attention to their good deeds. Their motive was clearly to look like the hotshots of Israel. And despite how deeply they dug into their pockets, the only reward they would ever get was the people's attention. God wants no part in that pretense.

This relates to our seer ministry because some people have a need for people's attention. So before you share your seer success, ask yourself, *Am I doing this to the glory of God or to show people how accurate I am? Am I tooting my own horn? What is my motive, really?* The purity of your seer gifts demands pure-heart motives.

PRAYER

Father, in the name of Jesus, search me, and know my heart; try me, and know my anxieties; see if there is any wicked way in me, and lead me in the way everlasting.

DECEMBER 16

WHEN YOUR DREAM CONFIRMS YOUR VISION

...By the mouth of two or three witnesses every word shall be established.
2 Corinthians 13:1

Sometimes a prophetic word can be a confirmation of what the Lord has already said to you. But have you ever thought about a dream confirming a vision, or a vision confirming a dream? In the seer dimensions, God can use one visual revelation to confirm another visual revelation. It's just like that.

In our community, Awakening House of Prayer in Fort Lauderdale, we were going through an intense attack through people operating in evil spirits. One of our elders had a dream about three snakes slithering in the hallway behind the wall of the sanctuary. One snake was green, the second one was black, and the third one was brown. He crushed the black snake, which was the biggest, underfoot. But the other snakes got away. Separately, an intercessor had a dream of a big fat green iguana in the church.

What does this mean? The common denominator was reptiles. South Florida is no stranger to green iguanas, with their spiny tails. They are considered an invasive species. Catch that. They are an invasive species. Notice also both dreams had a green reptile. Green can symbolize health on the positive side and envy on the negative side. Brown can symbolize the flesh and black can symbolize death.

The intercessor's dream confirmed the elder's dream and we gained unmistakable prophetic intelligence that was helpful in completely eradicating the attack against the church. Part of the attack was that the church would be shut down in two months. The elder killed the black snake, which represented a death curse against the church.

From this dream, though, we also saw clearly that jealousy was growing. What started out as a small green reptile in one dream ended up as a large green reptile a few days later. We needed to bind up word curses coming from jealous people who wanted to see us fail.

This is one reason why it's important to develop a seer culture in your church. Visual revelations from multiple people can bring confirmation and paint a broader picture of what the enemy—or what God—is doing. In the same way, God can give you a dream to confirm your own vision. Look for visual confirmations.

PRAYER

Father, in the name of Jesus, I am fascinated by visual revelation confirming visual revelation. Help me to see when my dreams and visions are confirming what You already showed me or someone else.

DECEMBER 17

PAY ATTENTION TO YOUR PERIPHERAL VISION

Your ears shall hear a word behind you, saying, "This is the way, walk in it," whenever you turn to the right hand or whenever you turn to the left.

Isaiah 30:21

Shortly after the Holy Spirit spoke to me about a seer upgrade, I stepped into a clear visual enhancement: I started seeing in the spirit peripherally. Call it a supernatural extended peripheral vision. I saw people coming from my right or left moments before they arrived. I lifted my eyes just seconds before they entered my natural view. I felt them coming.

Also called side vision, peripheral vision is the ability to see what is to either side of you while you're looking straight ahead, according to *The Seer's Dictionary*. While our natural vision is strongest looking forward, God can open the periphery to the eyes of our heart. Put another way, He can allow our spiritual eyes to see at angles our natural eyes could never reach.

Seers who cultivate and consecrate their supernatural sight will see with strong peripheral vision. During my School of the Prophets & Seers in London, I heard the Lord say:

I am giving my seers and seeing people peripheral vision. I am removing the blinders that religion has put on one side and the other. And you will begin to see even in 360-degree vision. You see what is going on behind you—those who have come with knives to stick in your back—and you will turn and confront them in My name. For I am giving My seers peripheral vision. You will see to the left and you will see to the right. You will see even from behind with a 360-degree view. When you look up at Me, that is what you will see.

In the prophetic word, God said He is removing blinders. What are these blinders? When you were saved, satan's blinders were removed from your eyes—but there are activities that will pollute, dim, or even blind your seer eyes. If you've stopped seeing in the spirit like you once did, it's possible that your eyes have been partially blinded through a spirit of religion. I write at length about this in my book, *Power Seers*.

PRAYER

Father, in the name of Jesus, would You give me peripheral vision in the seer dimensions? I don't only want to miss anything going on around me. Help me develop this aspect of my spiritual sight.

DECEMBER 18

THE OVERAMBITIOUS SEER

Let nothing be done through selfish ambition or conceit, but in lowliness of mind let each esteem others better than himself.

Philippians 2:3

The enemy sets a snare for overambitious seers, and overambitious seers often walk right into it. The problem is that most overambitious seers don't realize they are overambitious. They are blind to their own ambition.

Paul's ambition was to preach the gospel (Romans 15:20), not to have out-of-body experiences, fall into trances, or have visions. His ambition was to run and finish his race, to complete his assignment. Because his ambition was godly, God opened his eyes in ways that many people on earth today rarely, if ever, experience.

One of Paul's key messages was, "I die daily" (1 Corinthians 15:31). Paul spoke of crucifying, even mortifying the flesh. Anything of "self" needs to be crucified. Likewise, John the Baptist did not have ambitions to be the greatest prophet ever born of a woman (Luke 7:28). His ambition was to prepare the way of the Lord. He sought to decrease so Christ's ministry would increase and he goes down in biblical history.

We should seek to see Christ's ministry increase in our lives. We should seek to build Christ's Kingdom. While marketing and promotion are necessary elements of getting the Word out about books and events, the spirit in which you promote yourself matters. There are boundaries to godly promotion. The way you pursue revelation matters. If you are overambitious, you could find yourself in divination.

Ambition in and of itself is not wrong. There are godly ambitions, but the line is thinner than some people realize. The overambitious seer wants to be noticed, wants to be promoted, wants to be applauded. This can turn into a self-seeking attitude. And it's dangerous.

James, the apostle of practical faith, asserted: "But if you have bitter envy and self-seeking in your hearts, do not boast and lie against the truth. This wisdom does not descend from above, but is earthly, sensual, demonic. For where envy and self-seeking exist, confusion and every evil thing are there" (James 3:14-16).

PRAYER

Father, in the name of Jesus, would you root out of me any self-ambition. I don't want to be a self-seeking seer. I want to be a God-seeking seer. Help me not to cross the line but to stay in line with Your Word.

DECEMBER 19

BEWARE JEZEBEL'S SEERS

Nevertheless I have a few things against you, because you allow that woman Jezebel, who calls herself a prophetess, to teach and seduce My servants to commit sexual immorality and eat things sacrificed to idols.

Revelation 2:20

Just as Jezebel posed a deadly threat to the prophetic ministry in the Old Testament, this nefarious spirit poses a credibility threat to seer ministry today. Jezebel is aiming to infiltrate and discredit the seer ministry with false visual revelation that seduces the saints.

Jezebel loves to prophesy and share visual revelation both publicly and privately. If she can't share from a platform, she'll share with people in the parking lot. Remember, Jezebel called herself a prophetess (Revelation 2:20). She wasn't ordained. She wasn't Christ-given. She was not part of the legitimate fivefold ministry. But that didn't stop her.

Jezebel's seers often start out with, "Let me pray for you." But sooner or later they begin to share visions or dreams. Hurt and wounded souls who are desperate for direction begin to lean on them instead of cultivating their own relationship with the Holy Spirit, which is dangerous on many levels.

What many don't discern is Jezebel's seers are not operating in Holy Spirit-inspired visual revelation but are operating in seer witchcraft. In my book *Discerning Prophetic Witchcraft,* I go in-depth into discerning this practice. In case you haven't read that book (and you should), it's helpful to understand what prophetic witchcraft is.

Let me assure you, as one who has walked on the front lines of the prophetic and intercessory prayer movements for decades, Jezebel's seers are emerging rapidly with manipulative cunning.

Jezebel's seers appear to the undiscerning eye as genuine, but they are seeking to devour. They seem sincere, but they are sincerely wrong in their motives. It's important to exercise discernment, to examine the fruit rather than being enamored with a spiritual gift or charisma.

The spirit of prophecy, which includes visual revelation, is the testimony of Jesus (Revelation 19:10). Jezebel's seers are usually not sharing the testimony of Jesus. Instead, they share visual revelation that seeks to flatter, manipulate, or control you into freely giving your time, money, or loyalty. Jezebel's seers also operate in a spirit of divination, essentially a message straight from the enemy's camp. The message may sound like God, but that doesn't mean God said it.

PRAYER

Father, in the name of Jesus, would You help me discern Jezebel's seers? Would You help me model true seer ministry so that people can better discern the counterfeit Jezebel offers?

DECEMBER 20

RAISING UP SEER KIDS

> *Train up a child in the way he should go, and when he is old he will not depart from it.*
>
> Proverbs 22:6

During a Facebook Live broadcast, the Lord spoke to me suddenly about prophetic children. I saw the eyes of children opening. I exhorted parents with children to begin to teach them the principles of seeing in the spirit through the door of Jesus. I declared children are going to begin to prophesy through dreams and visions.

I heard the Lord say:

> *Don't be concerned when some of your children start falling into trances. Don't take them to the doctor because it's Me, and they will come out of that trance and they will have prophetic insight, wisdom, and knowledge of things to come because I'm showing them things that eye has not seen nor ear heard.*
>
> *Encourage the young ones. Encourage the children. Encourage them. Don't push them away. Don't tell them, "Later on, I'll talk to you," but take the time even now because in this season I'm pouring out My Spirit on all flesh. But I have a special eye on the young ones who have not yet been corrupted and polluted by the ways of the world. And I want to use them as pure voices and pure visionaries in their generation.*
>
> *So encourage them. Teach them. Show them the way. I am the Way and you will see and know that I will activate even the very young ones in these gifts and the gifts of My Spirit, and they will see with clarity and know and understand even be able to articulate things that their human capacity could not possibly comprehend.*

Let's take this seriously. In Joel 2:28 God assures us: "And it shall come to pass afterward that I will pour out My Spirit on all flesh; your sons and your daughters shall prophesy, your old men shall dream dreams, your young men shall see visions." When Joel prophesied those words, God wasn't leaving out the children.

I launched a Seer Activations for Kids course at my School of the Spirit. But you also need to do your part. Teach them about Jesus and the Holy Spirit. Encourage them to express what they are seeing in the spirit with scriptural guardrails. Help them judge what they see in the spirit. Teach them to obey the Lord.

PRAYER

Father, in the name of Jesus, help me be a good role model to the children in my life. Give me discernment with regard to how to teach them to navigate the seer dimensions when You open their eyes.

DECEMBER 21

YOUR SEER RANKING

For I also am a man under authority, having soldiers under me. And I say to this one, "Go," and he goes; and to another, "Come," and he comes; and to my servant, "Do this," and he does it.

Matthew 8:9

I sit on the Apostolic Council of Prophetic Elders, which was formed by C. Peter Wagner many years ago to help steward the prophetic movement. The ACPE is a company of prophets who come together to share what the Lord is saying and issue reports to the Body of Christ on the consensus.

At that council, there are people with different measures of prophetic authority and rank. Cindy Jacobs is the head of the council and facilitates the meetings. Right next to her is Bishop Bill Hamon, the father of the modern-day prophetic movement, who brings tremendous wisdom to help steer the group.

Bishop Bill Hamon has the highest rank in that room. Cindy Jacobs, though, is the leader of that council. Others like Dr. Sharon Stone carry a high ranking in the spirit.

Why am I telling you all this? When you operate in the prophetic, you need to understand ranks so you can submit to the greater authority. Rank in the spirit is someone's position or degree of authority in the spirit realm, according to *The Seer's Dictionary*.

Everyone recognized Samuel's seer rank. First Samuel 3:19-20, "So Samuel grew, and the Lord was with him and let none of his words fall to the ground. And all Israel from Dan to Beersheba knew that Samuel had been established as a prophet of the Lord." When Israel sinned, Samuel was the one they called on to intercede for them.

Why do you need to discern rank in the spirit? You don't want to be out of order. When you walk into any ministry or meeting, you need to discern the highest ranking authority there and defer to them, serve them, and learn from them. If you don't discern their ranking in the spirit, you may overstep your bounds or miss out on an opportunity for impartation. Check out my course on Ranks & Authority in the Spirit at www.schoolofthespirit.tv.

PRAYER

Father, in the name of Jesus, would You help me to recognize ranks in the spirit? There are demonic ranks, angelic ranks, and ranks among Your servants. I want to carry myself rightly.

DECEMBER 22

BEWARE OF AN INDEPENDENT SPIRIT

He who willfully separates and estranges himself [from God and man] seeks his own desire and pretext to break out against all wise and sound judgment.

Proverbs 18:1 AMPC

Seers should be part of a company—an association, fellowship, or network of seers who understand the gift and appreciate accountability. Some can't find anywhere to connect, and others left their company hurt or wounded because they joined the wrong company and were misunderstood.

Others walk with a company for a season until pride puffs them up and they break rank. These are the ones who wind up operating in what I call an independent spirit. An independent spirit is marked by a Rambo-like attitude.

Someone with an independent spirit is self-willed, refuses to submit to authority, and rejects the status quo because they think more highly of themselves as they ought, an attitude which violates Scripture (Romans 12:3). When a seer moves in an independent spirit they isolate themselves. This is a subtle deception that's rising in the Body of Christ—and it's dangerous.

First Corinthians 12:28 (KJV) says: "And God hath set some in the church, first apostles, secondarily prophets, thirdly teachers, after that miracles, then gifts of healings, helps, governments, diversities of tongues."

Where did God set prophets? In the Church. True prophets understand that they shouldn't be free from the influence, guidance, and input from others. Why would you want to be? There is wisdom and protection in the counsel of many.

Ephesians 5:21 tells us to submit to one another out of reverence for Christ. And Philippians 2:3-4 tells us, "Let nothing be done through selfish ambition or conceit, but in lowliness of mind let each esteem others better than himself. Let each of you look out not only for his own interests, but also for the interests of others."

You won't go far and you won't last long in the seer ministry if you have a Rambo got-to-do-it-my-way spirit. Seers need to work with other ministry gifts and we all need to be submitted to the King of kings and to our leaders. Someone has to be able to tell you "no."

Hebrews 13:17 tells us, "Obey them that have the rule over you, and submit yourselves: for they watch for your souls, as they that must give account, that they may do it with joy, and not with grief: for that is unprofitable for you."

PRAYER

Father, in the name of Jesus, would You help me never to think more highly of myself than I ought? I am part of a Body and I know I need people around me who can see what I can't see.

DECEMBER 23

EXPERIENCING EPIC DREAMS

After this I looked, and there was another, like a leopard, which had on its back four wings of a bird. The beast also had four heads, and dominion was given to it.

Daniel 7:6

Nebuchadnezzar had an epic dream that outlined both world history that was yet to happen and divine sovereignty. In Daniel 2, the king's epic dream is outlined in great detail. Specifically, Nebuchadnezzar saw a gigantic statue made with four different materials.

Consider the details: The head of the statue was made of pure gold. The chest and arms were made of silver. The belly and thighs were made of bronze. The legs were made of iron, and the feet were made of partly clay and partly iron. Suddenly, a stone "not cut by human hands" struck the statue's feet and the image crumbled and was blown away like chaff. Meanwhile, the stone became a humongous mountain that filled the earth. Nebuchadnezzar had no idea what this epic dream meant, but God gave Daniel the interpretation.

Epic dreams are a unique and powerful dimension of prophetic dreaming. Unlike typical dreams, which may contain fragmented imagery or brief moments of clarity, epic dreams are extended in length, filled with vivid details, and often unfold like a captivating story with a beginning, middle, and end, according to *The Seer's Dictionary*. These dreams are packed with meaning and purpose, often carrying a weight of revelation that demands our full attention and discernment.

Epic dreams can be overwhelming because of the weightiness of the visual encounter. Be sure to record every detail of the dream immediately. Use your phone or some other audio device to record yourself recounting the dream, or write down the details—even the minute details—because epic dreams often have layers of meaning. Small details can shift the interpretation. Speaking of which, pray for the interpretation, knowing some parts of the dream may be literal and some may be symbolic.

Since epic dreams can reveal short-term warnings or long-term assignments, wait on the Lord for what to do next. Let Him confirm to you how to apply the dream through further watching, praying, and advice from mature seers. Since the fullness of epic dreams can unfold over months or years, revisit the dream when you are led. There may be more revelation waiting.

PRAYER

Father, in the name of Jesus, if You can give a pagan king an epic dream, I know I am in line for this type of visual revelation as it suits Your purposes. Help me not to miss a single detail of what You are revealing.

DECEMBER 24

THE INQUISITIVE SEER

So I say to you, ask, and it will be given to you; seek, and you will find; knock, and it will be opened to you.

Luke 11:9

As a journalist-turned-fivefold-minister, I never lost my curiosity. I never forgot the journalist's mandate to ask who, what, where, how, when, and why. As a seer, that comes in handy, and you should adopt this line of questioning during and after your visual encounters.

Zechariah had this mindset. He was perhaps the most inquisitive prophet we see in the pages of Scripture. I can easily count 10 times when he asked questions in the midst of an encounter. Let's look at them, and may it inspire you to ask the right questions.

In Zechariah 1:9, he asks, "Then I said, 'My lord, what are these?' So the angel who talked with me said to me, 'I will show you what they are." In Zechariah 1:19, he asked, "I said to the angel who talked with me, 'What are these?' So he answered me, 'These are the horns that have scattered Judah, Israel and Jerusalem.'"

In Zechariah 1:21 (NIV) he asked, "'What are these coming to do?' He answered, 'These are the horns that scattered Judah so that no one could raise their head, but the craftsmen have come to terrify them and throw down these horns of the nations who lifted up their horns against the land of Judah to scatter its people.'" In Zechariah 2:2, "I asked, 'Where are you going?' He answered me, 'To measure Jerusalem, to see how wide and how long it is.'"

In Zechariah 4:4-5, he asked, "So I answered and spoke to the angel who talked with me, saying, 'What are these, my lord?' Then the angel who talked with me answered and said to me, 'Do you not know what these are?' And I said, 'No, my lord.'"

In Zechariah 4:11-13 (NIV): "Then I asked the angel, 'What are these two olive trees on the right and the left of the lampstand?' Again I asked him, 'What are these two olive branches beside the two gold pipes that pour out golden oil?' He replied, 'Do you not know what these are?'"

I'll stop there, but notice how inquisitive he was. And notice how he got answers. This is truly an example of why so many people walk away from encounters without answers: They ask not. Ask!

PRAYER

Father, in the name of Jesus, would You inspire spiritual curiosity in me? Help me to ask the right questions at the right time so I can get the right answers. Help me to be inquisitive.

DECEMBER 25

I SAW JESUS

As he journeyed he came near Damascus, and suddenly a light shone around him from heaven. Then he fell to the ground, and heard a voice saying to him, "Saul, Saul, why are you persecuting Me?"

Acts 9:3-4

I was sitting in my prayer chair meditating on the Word of God when suddenly I saw an imposing figure cloaked in glory. It was an overwhelming sight, in a good way. At first, I thought it was an angel coming to bring me a message. But when I looked closer I saw plainly that it was the glorified Jesus.

As I kept on looking, I saw both His arms stretched out toward me. In one hand, He had a sword that was radiating glory. His other hand was completely empty. I did not hear any words, but I knew in my heart that He was giving me a choice. I could choose the sword or I could choose His hand.

I didn't have to think about it long. I didn't waste any time. I immediately chose His hand. And when I did, I heard Him say, "Because you chose My hand, I will also give you My sword." That was an open vision and it changed my life.

Open visions appear to you like a movie or imagery acting out before your very eyes, according to *The Seer's Dictionary*. Your eyes are open and you are immune to what is going on around you. It's like the world around you stops. Ezekiel also had an open vision in Ezekiel 1:4-9. Paul had an open vision in the night when he received the Macedonian call (Acts 16:9) and on the road to Damascus in Acts 9:3-5:

> As he journeyed he came near Damascus, and suddenly a light shone around him from heaven. Then he fell to the ground, and heard a voice saying to him, "Saul, Saul, why are you persecuting Me?" And he said, "Who are You, Lord?" Then the Lord said, "I am Jesus, whom you are persecuting. It is hard for you to kick against the goads."

You can't force an open vision, but you'll know one when you see one. This are some of the most dramatic visions seers have.

PRAYER

Father, in the name of Jesus, I know open visions are more rare than inner visions and You have a purpose in all things. If it suits Your plans, would You show me open visions like You did with Ezekiel and John?

DECEMBER 26

DON'T EXALT EXTRA-BIBLICAL REVELATION

For prophecy never came by the will of man, but holy men of God spoke as they were moved by the Holy Spirit.

2 Peter 1:21

The Word of God should be the final authority in every believer's life—and the seer is no exception. Scripture is like an anchor that tethers the seer to truth.

Although seers can experience many encounters and visual revelations that are not found in the Bible (no one, for example, ever experienced what Ezekiel saw until Ezekiel saw it) our revelations must be in line with Scripture. In other words, the Holy Spirit will not lead you into an encounter that violates the principles of His Word.

One of the pitfalls I've seen in seer ministry is exalting extra-biblical revelation above the Word of God. What is extra-biblical revelation? A revelation that is outside the 66 books of the Bible. Extra-biblical revelation can be absolutely true, but it must never take precedence over the written Word of God, which is infallible. Extra-biblical revelation can contain errors. But, "The words of the Lord are pure words, like silver tried in a furnace of earth, purified seven times" (Psalm 12:6).

What am I saying? Let me put it another way. No vision, no dream, no encounter can supersede the authority of Scripture. Paul tells us in 2 Timothy 3:16-17, "All Scripture is given by inspiration of God, and is profitable for doctrine, for reproof, for correction, for instruction in righteousness, that the man of God may be complete, thoroughly equipped for every good work."

Always "plumb line" your revelation with the Word. If you are a student of the Word, you should be able to find parallels between your extra-biblical revelation and the Scripture. If your revelation contradicts the Bible, your revelation is not just extra-biblical—it's false. The Word acts as a filter by which to sift your extra-biblical revelations. When you are tethered to the Word, you avoid deception and elevating personal experiences above God's truth.

I've seen too many seers puffed up with pride, convinced that what they saw or experienced in the spirit carries more weight than the Word. That's a dangerous attitude. The truth of Scripture is the seer's anchor and safety net. Stick with the Word and judge every experience.

PRAYER

Father, in the name of Jesus, help me to embrace the visual revelation You give me, but to never exalt it above what the Bible teaches. Help me not make a doctrine out of my visions, dreams, and encounters.

DECEMBER 27

THE WATCHMAN SEER ANOINTING

Now a watchman stood on the tower in Jezreel, and he saw the company of Jehu as he came, and said, "I see a company of men...."
2 Kings 9:17

Not all watchmen are seers, but all seers have a watchman function. Watching and praying may not be the exclusive emphasis of your seer anointing, but God will call you to step into watchman operations as it serves His purpose.

So what is a watchman seer anointing? As I write in my book, *The Making of a Watchman*, there are four categories of watchman, and, of course, these categories overlap. Just as there are different types of singers or different types of preachers, there are unique expressions of the watchman anointing.

One Hebrew word for *watchman* is *tsaphah,* which means "to look out or about, spy, keep watch, observe, or watch," according to the *KJV Old Testament Hebrew Lexicon*. When watchmen stood at the tower in Jezreel spying out Jehu as he came in the glory of God in 2 Kings 9:17, this was *tsaphah*.

Another Hebrew expression of *watchman* is *natsar*. This is a type of watchman that includes a stronger thrust to guard. According to the *KJV Old Testament Hebrew Lexicon*, *natsar* means "to guard, watch, watch over, keep" and "to preserve, guard from dangers, to keep, observe, guard with fidelity, to keep secret, to be kept close, be blockaded." Jeremiah 31:6 (NLT) reads, "The day will come when watchmen will shout from the hill country of Ephraim, 'Come, let us go up to Jerusalem to worship the Lord our God.'"

Shamar has become a popular expression of the watchman with some modern-day teachers. The Hebrew word *shamar* speaks of a watchman who is "to keep, guard, observe, give heed, have charge of, save life, wait for, retain, treasure up (in memory), to keep (within bounds), restrain, celebrate, keep (sabbath or covenant), to be on one's guard, take heed, take care, beware, abstain."

This may not be your main function, but remember this: Jesus told all believers to watch and pray. That's one way we stay ahead of what the enemy is doing and cooperate with what the Lord wants to do.

PRAYER

Father, in the name of Jesus, I am willing to watch if You want me to. Help me to understand the watchman anointing so I can function effectively in that role. Make me a seer watchman according to Your will.

DECEMBER 28

THE KENNETH HAGIN SEER ANOINTING

All Scripture is given by inspiration of God, and is profitable for doctrine, for reproof, for correction, for instruction in righteousness.
2 Timothy 3:16

When you think of Kenneth E. Hagin, you probably think of the Word of Faith movement that God birthed through him. But Hagin was also a man of profound encounters.

In his book, *I Believe in Visions*, Hagin describes six major visions of Jesus Christ in great detail. In one, he writes, "I heard footsteps coming down the corridor toward my [hospital] room. I looked toward the door to see who it was, because it was only 6:30 am, too early for visitors. Someone dressed in white came through the door and at first I supposed it was a nurse. As I looked closer, I saw it was Jesus! It seemed as if my hair stood on end. Cold chill bumps popped out all over my body, and I couldn't say a word. Jesus approached my bed and sat down on a chair. He was robed in white and had some sort of sandals on." That encounter lasted an hour and a half.

Hagin was often caught up in the spirit, where Jesus would speak to him about the state of the Church, the healing ministry, or specific instructions for his own life. He recounts his visions—and the revelations he received during them—with great detail. When he shared them, those who heard him could feel the weight and authority.

Known as a prophet, Hagin's seer anointing blended well with his teaching mantle. His ability to break down the Word of God and offer real-life practical examples helped make the supernatural more accessible to the average believer. Together with his teachings on faith, healing, and the authority of the believer, upon which his legacy was built, his equipping in the supernatural realms opened the eyes of many.

Hagin also served as a model for rooting his visual revelation in the Word of God. He "plumb lined" every visual revelation through the infallible written words of God—the Scripture. He also taught that prophetic revelation should never contradict the Scripture. This is a standard for today's seer.

PRAYER

Father, in the name of Jesus, thank You for sending Kenneth E. Hagin to demonstrate the supernatural rooted in the Word—and for helping generations beyond him operate in the seer dimensions by faith.

DECEMBER 29

THE ZECHARIAH 4:10 PRINCIPLE

Though your beginning was small, yet your latter end would increase abundantly.

Job 8:7

I remember when God planted a seed in my heart to pray for the nations. I had a large multicolored map on my wall and I was in awe of the massive opportunities for prophetic intercession.

Suddenly, the Lord illuminated a tiny speck of an island on this map, one of the smallest islands in the Caribbean. This was my prayer assignment. I was somewhat disappointed. I wanted to storm the heavens of pivotal nations in the earth, but the Lord gave me a small beginning.

It was a lesson in "He who is faithful in what is least is faithful also in much..." (Luke 16:10). I prayed faithfully for that tiny nation, its people, its safety, and that the gospel would break in there and bring salvation. God would later wake me up at midnight to share His heart about the state of the United States of America and the coming Great Awakening. Today, God has allowed me to have a prayer movement, Awakening Prayer Hubs, in almost every nation of the world.

"Do not despise these small beginnings, for the Lord rejoices to see the work begin..." (Zechariah 4:10 NLT). All promotion comes from God.

I also remember when God planted a seed in my heart to impact the nations through the written word. I had the best computer I could afford and plenty of ideas, but no platform. Suddenly, God gave me an opportunity to edit books for other Christian ministers. I did my best to add value to their work, hoping one day to write my own Christian books and materials.

When I started seeing in the spirit, it was the same way. I wanted to have epic visions like John the Revelator but I would only see a flash or an inner vision. Just like most prophets don't start out prophesying over nations, most seers don't start out with epic visions.

In fact, in my experience most seers start out dreaming before they see major visions. And when visions come, it often starts out as a picture or a faint impression. In other words, the gift doesn't come fully grown and we shouldn't be surprised by that. Our gifts and callings flourish as we spend time in the Word and exercise those gifts—and steward the revelation we receive.

PRAYER

Father, in the name of Jesus, would You help me not to get impatient as I grow into my seer anointing? Help me not to blow off inner visions or pictures. I appreciate anything You show me. Help me steward it.

DECEMBER 30

WHEN JESUS SPEAKS TO YOU IN A DREAM

And it shall come to pass afterward that I will pour out My Spirit on all flesh; your sons and your daughters shall prophesy, your old men shall dream dreams, your young men shall see visions.

Joel 2:28

You don't have to be a seer to receive divine revelation in your dreams. In fact, you don't even have to be a believer. God spoke to unbelievers, such as King Nebuchadnezzar and King Abimelech, in prophetic dreams.

That said, seers tend to have what I call next-level dreams, which may even include encounters with the Lord while they are fast asleep. While 80 to 90 percent of the average person's dreams will concern their own life or circumstances, seers also tend to have dreams that shed revelatory light on issues in the world or the Church.

The Holy Spirit shines a light on this facet of the seer's ministry that we need to pay close attention to. Numbers 12:5-6 reads:

> Then the Lord came down in the pillar of cloud and stood in the door of the tabernacle, and called Aaron and Miriam. And they both went forward. Then He said, "Hear now My words: If there is a prophet among you, I, the Lord, make Myself known to him in a vision; I speak to him in a dream."

The International Standard Version offers this verse as a question: "Won't I speak with him in a dream?" The Voice puts it this way, "Listen to Me. When there are prophets in your midst, I, the Eternal One, will show Myself to them in visions, and will sound My voice in their dreams." I like that.

Matthew Poole's Commentary expounds on this: "By a vision God represents things to the mind of a prophet when he is awake, as Genesis 15:1 46:2 Daniel 8:18 10:8. By a dream God manifests his mind to them when asleep, as Genesis 20:3 28:12."

We see God speaking to people in dreams throughout the pages of Scripture. There are twenty-one dreams in the Bible—fifteen in the Old Testament and six in the New Testament. Seers should expect to encounter God's truth in dreams.

PRAYER

Father, in the name of Jesus, help me prepare my heart to receive the revelations You want to transmit in the dream dimension. Speak to me about Your plans and purposes in my dreams so I can steward Your will.

DECEMBER 31

SEE YOURSELF

Examine yourselves as to whether you are in the faith. Test yourselves. Do you not know yourselves, that Jesus Christ is in you?—unless indeed you are disqualified.

2 Corinthians 13:5

At the end of every year, I reflect. I'm not talking about reflecting on the visual revelations I received, though it's wise to do that. I am talking about reflecting on my own spiritual growth.

Did I grow in the grace and knowledge of my Lord and Savior Jesus Christ? (See 2 Peter 3:18.) Did I walk in a manner worthy of the Lord, fully pleasing to Him and bearing fruit in every good work? (See Colossians 1:9-10.) Did I display the fruit of the Spirit? (See Galatians 5:22-23.) Did I make every effort to supplement my faith with virtue, knowledge, self-control, steadfastness, godliness, brotherly affection and love? (See 2 Peter 1:5-8.)

Did I present my body as a living sacrifice? (See Romans 12:1-2.) Did I walk in love? Did I abide in Him? Did I stir up my spiritual gifts? Did I store up His Word in my heart so my mind could be transformed? Did I put off the old self and put on Christ? What are my biases and blind spots?

Notice that I didn't mention my seer gift in any of those questions. My first priority is becoming more Christlike. Usually, I find that I've grown in many areas, and still have room to grow. I don't beat myself up. Rather, I focus on how far I've come. After all, I can't change myself. I can only yield to the hand of the Potter. And I am confident of this very thing, that He who began a good work in me will complete it until the day of Jesus Christ (Philippians 1:6).

Our primary focus should be to know Him and make Him known, to seek first the Kingdom of God and His righteousness, to be ambassadors of Christ and ministers of reconciliation. If we get too wrapped up in our gift, we can lose sight of the gift Giver.

Apart from Him, we are nothing. Apart from Him, we can't see in the spirit (legally). But as we press into becoming more like Him, greater visual revelation is the by-product. We will see more without even trying.

PRAYER

Father, in the name of Jesus, would You help me examine myself in the light of Your Word? More than anything, I want to know You. I want to yield to You. I want to please You. You are my everything.

ABOUT JENNIFER LECLAIRE

Jennifer LeClaire's passion is to see the lost come to Christ and equip believers to understand the will and ways of God. She carries a reforming voice that seeks to turn hearts to the Lord and edify the Body of Christ.

Jennifer is the founder of Jennifer LeClaire Ministries, former senior editor of *Charisma* magazine. She has written many books, including *Jezebel's Puppets* and *The Making of a Prophet*. Some of her materials have been archived at the Flower Pentecostal Heritage Museum and translated into Spanish, Korean, Chinese, Dutch, Malagasy, Tamil, Urdu, and Portuguese. She is also the founder of SchooloftheSpirit.tv, an online training platform that equips the saints for the work of the ministry in prayer, prophecy, spiritual warfare, healing and many other topics.

Jennifer LeClaire is senior leader of Awakening House of Prayer in Fort Lauderdale, Florida, founder of the Ignite Accelerator and founder of the Awakening Prayer Hubs prayer movement in nearly every nation of the earth, as well as the Awakening House Church Movement. She is a prolific author of more than 60 books.

You can find Jennifer online at www.jenniferleclaire.org.